PREPARING FRS 101 ACCOUNTS

PREPARING FRS 101 ACCOUNTS

Helen Lloyd FCA

© 2016 Wolters Kluwer (UK) Ltd

Wolters Kluwer (UK) Limited
145 London Road
Kingston upon Thames
KT2 6SR
Tel: 0844 561 8166
Fax: 0208 547 2638
E-mail: cch@wolterskluwer.co.uk
www.cch.co.uk

© Financial Reporting Council (FRC). Financial Reporting Council material is adapted and reproduced with the kind permission of the Financial Reporting Council. All rights reserved. For further information, please visit www.frc.org.uk or call +44 (0)20 7492 2300.

ISBN 978-1-78540-338-5

British Library Cataloguing-in-Publication Data

A catalogue record for this book is available from the British Library.

Typeset by Innodata Inc., India.
Printed by Gutenberg Press Ltd, Malta.

Abbreviations

AAC	Audit and Assurance Council (part of the FRC)
APB	Auditing Practices Board (disbanded in July 2012, replaced by the FRC's Audit and Assurance Council)
ARC	Accounting Regulatory Committee
ASB	Accounting Standards Board (disbanded in July 2012, replaced by the FRC's Accounting Council)
BIS	Department for Business, Innovation and Skills
C(AICE) 2004	*Companies (Audit, Investigations and Community Enterprise) Act* 2004
CA 2006	*Companies Act* 2006
CCAB	Consultative Committee of Accountancy Bodies
EC	European Commission
EEA	European Economic Area
EFRAG	European Financial Reporting Advisory Group
ESOP	Employee share ownership plan
EU	European Union
EU Micros Directive	Directive 2012/06/EU of the European Parliament and of the Council (dated 14 March 2012)
EU Regulation	Regulation (EC) No. 1606/2002 of the European Parliament (dated 19 July 2002) on the application of international accounting standards
FA	Finance Act
FASB	US Financial Accounting Standards Board
FRC	Financial Reporting Council
FRED	Financial Reporting Exposure Draft
FRRP	Financial Reporting Review Panel (disbanded in July 2012, replaced by the FRC Monitoring Committee)
FRS	Financial Reporting Standard
FRSSE	Financial Reporting Standard for Smaller Entities (being the 'FRSSE (effective April 2008)' unless otherwise indicated or as the circumstances dictate)
FSMA	*Financial Services and Markets Act* 2000
GAAP	Generally accepted accounting practice (or principles) (see also 'UK GAAP')
HMRC	Her Majesty's Revenue and Customs
IAASB	International Auditing and Assurance Standards Board
IAS	International accounting standards issued or adopted by IASB
IAS Regulation	Regulation (EC) No. 1606/2002 of the European Parliament (dated 19 July 2002) on the application of international accounting standards

IASB	International Accounting Standards Board
ICTA	*Income and Corporation Taxes Act* 1988
IFRIC	International Financial Reporting Interpretations Committee (an IASB committee)
IFRS	International Financial Reporting Standards (including IAS and interpretations adopted by IASB)
IFRS for SMEs	International Financial Reporting Standard for Small and Medium-sized Entities
ISA	International Standard on Auditing ('ISA (UK and Ireland)': an ISA applicable within the UK and Ireland)
KPIs	Key Performance Indicators
LLP	Limited Liability Partnership
NIC	National Insurance contribution
MiFID	MiFID investment firm – an investment firm within the meaning of Directive 2004/39/EC, art. 4.1.1 of the European Parliament and of the Council of 21 April 2004 on markets in financial instruments (but see CA 2006, s. 474)
OFR	Operating and Financial Review
OPSI	Office of Public Sector Information
P & L account	Profit and loss account
PAYE	Pay as you earn
PN	APB Practice Note
POB	Professional Oversight Board (part of the FRC) (disbanded in July 2012, replaced by the FRC Conduct Committee)
Reg.	Regulation (for example, SI 2008/409 reg. 4(2) means regulation 4(2) of SI 2008/409)
s.	section (unless otherwise stated, section references refer to CA 2006, as amended or inserted from time to time)
Sch.	Schedule (for example: 'CA 2006, Sch. 7.7(2)' means Companies Act 2006, Schedule 7, paragraph 7(2); or for SI 2008/409, 'SI 2008/409, Sch. 4.5(2)' or simply 'Sch. 4.5(2)' means Schedule 4, paragraph 5(2))
SI	Statutory instrument
SIC	Standing Interpretation Committee of IASB (or an interpretation of SIC e.g. 'SIC-1')
SME	Small or medium-sized entity (or enterprise)
SORP	Statement of Recommended Practice
SSAP	Statement of Standard Accounting Practice
SSRA	Statement of Standards for Reporting Accountants
STRGL	Statement of total recognised gains and losses
UCITS	Undertaking for Collective Investment in Transferable Securities (see CA 2006, s. 471(1))

UITF	Urgent Issues Task Force (part of FRC since July 2012, previously part of the ASB)
UK GAAP	Financial reporting requirements (as specified by the FRC) in the United Kingdom and the Republic of Ireland (see 'GAAP')
VAT	Value added tax

Statutory instruments

SI 2015/980	*Companies, Partnerships and Groups (Accounts and Reports) Regulations* 2015 (this amends SI 2008/410)
SI 2013/3008	*Small Companies (Micro-Entities' Accounts) Regulations* 2013
SI 2013/1970	*Companies Act 2006 (Strategic Report and Directors' Report) Regulations* 2013
SI 2012/2301	*Companies and Limited Liability Partnerships (Accounts and Audit Exemptions and Change of Accounting Framework) Regulations* 2012
SI 2012/952	*Companies Act 2006 (Amendment of Part 23) (Investment Companies) Regulations* 2012
SI 2011/2198	*Companies (Disclosure of Auditor Remuneration and Liability Limitation Agreements) (Amendment) Regulations* 2011
SI 2009/1802	*Companies Act 2006 (Part 35) (Consequential Amendments, Transitional Provisions and Savings) Order* 2009
SI 2009/1581	*Companies Act 2006 (Accounts, Reports and Audit) Regulations* 2009
SI 2008/2860	*Companies Act 2006 (Commencement No. 8, Transitional Provisions and Savings) Order* 2008
SI 2008/489	*Companies (Disclosure of Auditor Remuneration and Liability Limitation Agreements) Regulations* 2008
SI 2008/410	*Large and Medium-sized Companies and Groups (Accounts and Reports) Regulations* 2008 (as amended by SI 2015/980). Included in full in Appendix 2.
SI 2008/409	*Small Companies and Groups (Accounts and Directors' Report) Regulations* 2008
SI 2008/393	*Companies Act 2006 (Amendment) (Accounts and Reports) Regulations* 2008
SI 2008/374	*Companies (Summary Financial Statement) Regulations* 2008
SI 2007/3495	*Companies Act 2006 (Commencement No. 5, Transitional Provisions and Savings) Order* 2007

EC Regulations and Directives

EC 1004/2008	Adoption of certain IASs in accordance with regulation EC 1606/2002 (amending regulation EC 1725/2003) (15 October 2008)
EC 707/2004	Adoption of certain IASs in accordance with regulation EC 1606/2002 (amending regulation EC 1725/2003) (6 April 2004)
EC 1606/2002	Requirement for use of IASs by listed companies (by 2005) (19 September 2002)
2003/51/EC	The 'Modernisation Directive' amending earlier Directives on annual and consolidated accounts (18 June 2003)
2001/65/EC	The 'Fair Value Directive' on valuation rules for annual and consolidated accounts of certain companies (21 September 2001)

Contents

		Page
Abbreviations		*v*
PART I GENERAL		1
1	**Introduction**	3
2	**The UK Financial Reporting Framework**	5
	2.1 Introduction	5
	2.2 Accounting standards in the new framework	5
	2.3 Which entities can use which standards?	10
3	**Choosing FRS 101**	11
	3.1 Eligibility for FRS 101 – the basics	11
	3.2 Shareholder notification	11
	3.3 The concept of equivalence	12
	3.4 A note on disclosures	15
	3.5 Reasons to choose FRS 101	15
PART II THE LAW		17
4	**Company accounts, FRS 101, and the law**	19
	4.1 The legal status of FRS 101 accounts	19
	4.2 Accounting adjustments	21
	4.3 Adapting accounts formats	21
	4.4 Special considerations for financial instruments	23
	4.5 Realised profits	25
5	**FRS 101 for LLPs**	27
	5.1 LLP eligibility to apply FRS 101	27
	5.2 Specifics within the standard	27
	5.3 A note on challenging areas	28
6	**FRS 101 and the law in the Republic of Ireland**	31
	6.1 Introduction	31
	6.2 Irish legislation	31
	6.3 Small companies under Irish law	32
	6.4 Financial instruments	32
PART III DETAILS		33
7	**How FRS 101 works**	35
	7.1 Accounting for transactions and year end balances – using IFRS	35
	7.2 Disclosures – overlaying the FRS 101 exemptions	36
	7.3 Keeping up with change	37
	7.4 Transition to FRS 101	37
8	**The special cases of financial institutions and investment entities**	41
	8.1 Definition of a financial institution	41
	8.2 Special provisions for financial institutions	42
	8.3 Definition of an investment entity	42
	8.4 Special provisions for investment entities	43

Contents

9 General points and financial statement presentation 45
   9.1   Primary statements 45
   9.2   Discontinued operations and disposal groups 47
   9.3   Transition to FRS 101 50

10 Assets and liabilities 53
   10.1 Groups and business combinations 53
   10.2 Tangible and intangible assets and impairment 58
   10.3 Borrowing costs 66
   10.4 Investment property 66
   10.5 Inventories 69
   10.6 Financial instruments 70
   10.7 Leasing 71
   10.8 Provisions and contingencies 74

11 Income and Expenses 77
   11.1 Revenue including grant income 77
   11.2 Income taxes 81
   11.3 Foreign currency issues 84
   11.4 Employee benefits and share-based payments 86
   11.5 Other expenses 92

12 Other accounting and disclosures 93
   12.1 Post balance sheet events 93
   12.2 Related parties 94
   12.3 Other disclosures 98

PART IV OTHER INFORMATION 105

13 Other documents with the accounts 107
   13.1 Strategic report 107
   13.2 Directors' report 109
   13.3 Auditor's report 111
   13.4 Other information 115

APPENDICES 117

Appendix 1   FRS 101 Limited 119
Appendix 2   SI 2008/410 – Large and Medium-sized Companies and Groups (Accounts and Reports) Regulations 2008 149

INDEX 331

Part I General

Chapter 1   Introduction

While the withdrawal of old UK GAAP will be significant for all preparers, those planning to apply FRS 101 might be the most affected. As a standard, it has escaped the bulk of commentary, overshadowed by its more glamorous cousin, FRS 102. Even small entities are having their moment in the sun, with many pages devoted to the question of whether to apply the FRSSE 2015 or the small entities regime in FRS 102, and how exactly they will be affected.

This publication seeks to redress that balance by focusing in on issues specific to FRS 101 preparers.

Structure of the publication

In **Part I**, we look at the structure of options available to UK preparers in their financial statements from 2015 onwards. This runs through from a general review of the new UK financial reporting framework in chapter 2, which includes non-corporate entities, and then chapter 3 moves on to reasons to choose FRS 101, with a close examination of the scope and eligibility criteria.

In Part II, we focus on the law, looking in **Chapter 4** at FRS 101's interaction with UK company law, and the various application difficulties that have been anticipated and mapped out by the FRC. **Chapter 5** then looks specifically at Limited Liability Partnerships and how FRS 101 can apply to them, and finally in this section **Chapter 6** sets out the situation for preparers in the Republic of Ireland.

Part III contains the detailed meat of the standard. **Chapters 7** and **8** serve as an introduction to this part, first setting out how the different parts of FRS 101 interact with each other and with IFRS, and then noting two special cases, financial institutions and investment entities. The remainder of the Part works through all the main financial reporting topics, setting out for each area:

- the relevant IFRS standards and interpretations;
- the main accounting differences between old UK GAAP and IFRS-based FRS 101;
- amendments that FRS 101 makes to the relevant IFRS standards;
- disclosure exemptions allowed by FRS 101; and
- a list of the disclosure requirements that remain.

This document is best used not as a disclosure checklist, but as a thematic summary of key disclosure requirements.

Finally, **Part IV** contains one chapter looking at other documents issued with the financial statements.

Appendix 1 shows a set of example accounts prepared under FRS 101. To illustrate the volume savings that can be achieved by using FRS 101, these accounts have been based on the model accounts in our companion volume *Preparing IFRS Accounts*. They do not therefore contain every possible permutation of disclosures, but give a good indication of how a set of FRS 101 accounts might look. **Appendix 2** reproduces the *Large and Medium-sized Companies and Groups (Accounts and Reports) Regulations* 2008, since these are referred to throughout the publication and it is highly useful to have an up to date version for reference.

Areas not covered within this publication

Although as we saw above for each accounting topic we include a brief overview of accounting differences from old UK GAAP, this is by no means a comprehensive review of the accounting. Readers are recommended to read this in parallel with a reliable information source on IFRS, using the standard themselves and a companion such as CCH's *International Accounting/Financial Reporting Standards Guide* or *Preparing IFRS accounts*. For an accessible overview, we also recommend *CCH New UK GAAP: An at a glance comparison between new and old UK GAAP and IFRS*.

A moving target

This publication was written based on standards in issue as at the beginning of December 2015. As discussed in **Chapter 7** below, the issue with a standard that relies heavily on another framework is that it will always struggle to keep pace with that other framework, and to illustrate that the FRC has already proposed changes to FRS 101. These were issued in an Exposure Draft in December 2015, which proposes exemptions relating to the IASB's new revenue standard, IFRS 15. This will not affect UK preparers yet, since IFRS 15 is not effective until 2018, and since it is not yet endorsed for use in the EU, it cannot be early adopted. It is worth being mindful, though, of the potential for continuing changes to the standard.

Chapter 2   The UK Financial Reporting Framework

2.1   Introduction

For many years, financial reporting in the UK has been based on a patchwork of accounting standards, interwoven with company law and with a thick overlay of built up accepted practice. This led to a status quo where most private companies applied nominally the same GAAP as each other but often with quite a range of outcomes, and where new standards became increasingly hard to reconcile with the body of existing guidance because of the wide range of sources and insufficiently coherent underlying framework.

Recognising this, the UK's Financial Reporting Council (FRC), then in its old sub-body, the Accounting Standards Board, set out to reform UK GAAP. Already the top slice of companies had been sectioned off with the requirement for listed companies to use EU-adopted IFRS in their group accounts, but the bold proposal was to replace all existing standards for the remaining companies with a single new standard, originally planned to be based on the IASB's *IFRS for SMEs*. This would have applied to any entity not meeting the definition of 'publicly accountable' which included listed entities and those with fiduciary duties over the assets of others.

After some years of consultation, and many discussion papers and exposure drafts, the basic model has stuck, in that there is one core standard now, FRS 102, for most entities that do not apply IFRS. The simple version of the new framework was issued in 2012 and 2013, with FRSs 100, 101 and 102.

The idea originally was that small entities would, for a certain limited time, continue to apply the FRSSE, though the FRC also promised an update of this for consistency with FRS 102 – this update is known as the FRSSE 2015. No more drastic overhauls were put in place at this original stage relating to small companies because there was some uncertainty with what would happen with EU (and hence UK) law with respect to accounts of small and micro-entities. It was also expected that the limits to qualify as small would be significantly raised, and to some extent the precise details of the desired accounting for small companies depends on how wide a bracket this is. The changes in size limits are discussed further in the section below on FRS 102.

The new standards were issued with an effective date of periods beginning on or after 1 January 2015, and early adoption was permitted. Potential early adopters, and those engaged in advanced planning, were warned, though, that the FRC was intending to make changes to FRS 102 before the effective date, particularly with regard to financial instruments. This was on pragmatic grounds. The IASB had been working for some years on a new financial instruments standard and the FRC was keen to ensure its new standard contained provisions consistent with IFRS 9. It would have been unreasonable, though, to delay the issue of FRS 102 while waiting for the IASB, whose timetable was still unclear. As expected, IFRS 9 was eventually issued in full, so in July 2014 (after due process) the FRC issued its amendments to FRS 102 in respect of hedge accounting and some detail on the definition of basic financial instruments.

2.2   Accounting standards in the new framework

There was a good deal of progress in the period following the issue of the first version of new UK GAAP.

The new framework as it stands at the time of writing (late 2015) now includes six standards:

- FRS 100 *Application of Financial Reporting Requirements*;
- FRS 101 *Reduced Disclosure Framework*;

- FRS 102 *The Financial Reporting Standard applicable in the UK and Republic of Ireland*;
- FRS 103 *Insurance Contracts*;
- FRS 104 *Interim Financial Reporting*;
- FRS 105 *The Financial Reporting Standard applicable to the Micro-entities Regime.*

FRS 100 Application of Financial Reporting Requirements

FRS 100 underpins the whole new GAAP by setting out which entities are required or permitted to apply each standard. It applies to financial statements within its scope that are not required by the IAS Regulation or other legislation to be prepared in accordance with EU-adopted IFRS, and states simply that:

- entities eligible to apply FRS 105 may use FRS 105;
- all other entities in scope must use FRS 102, EU-adopted IFRS or, if eligible, FRS 101.

FRS 100 also addresses the use of SORPs, which are industry-specific additional guidance. They do not replace accounting standards, but give more detail on the application of the rules for niche areas that are not covered in the standards. The implementation of new UK GAAP included a review of the SORPs, with decisions on which would be retained, which would be withdrawn, and which would be rewritten to reflect the newer standards.

SORPs are not written or issued by the FRC, but by the relevant SORP-making body in each case. The FRC (or previously the ASB) then issues a statement confirming that the SORP 'does not appear to contain any fundamental points of principle that are unacceptable in the context of current accounting practice or to conflict with an accounting standard'.

At the time of writing, the SORPs in existence were as follows:

Industry/sector	Date of issue	Notes
Authorised funds	May 2014	
Charities	July 2014	Two versions – one for charities applying the FRSSE, and one for charities applying FRS 102
Further and Higher Education	March 2014	
Investment Trust Companies and Venture Capital Trusts	November 2014	
Limited Liability Partnerships (LLPs)	July 2014	
Pension Schemes	November 2014	
Registered Providers of Social Housing	September 2014	

The insurance SORP was withdrawn from 2015.

FRS 100 addresses a few other areas, some of which are slightly incongruous: for instance, it sets out how to deal with transition to the FRS 101 reduced disclosure framework (a subject addressed in more detail in **7.4** below). It also includes some critical guidance on the interpretation of the word 'equivalent' as used in FRS 101 and FRS 102. This is a crucial concept for determining exactly which disclosure exemptions are available to entities applying these standards, and presumably appears in FRS 100 to save needing to duplicate the guidance within the other two standards. It is discussed in detail in **3.3** below.

FRS 101 Reduced Disclosure Framework

This is the subject of this publication. It gives the detail of the option for qualifying entities to apply EU-adopted IFRS in their individual accounts, setting out a list of disclosure exemptions. The structure of the standard, and then its detail, are covered in **Part III** of this publication. The legal consequences, and the complex interplay between accounting standards and the law, including the legal status of FRS 101 accounts, are discussed in **Part II**.

FRS 102 The Financial Reporting Standard applicable in the UK and Republic of Ireland

FRS 102 contains the bulk of the new accounting requirements in new UK GAAP. Most entities with a choice will be comparing their options with FRS 102 acting as the baseline for these comparisons.

Originally based on the IFRS for SMEs, it has moved on some way from its early drafts, mainly to incorporate accounting options that UK preparers were unwilling to relinquish. It also needed to be amended for consistency with UK law, and in some cases was tweaked to ensure there was no 'gold plating'.

FRS 102 was issued for the first time in March 2013 and several sets of amendments have already been made to it. The most significant were probably the first, relating to financial instruments and hedge accounting. These tidied up the definitions of a basic instrument to ensure this category had as broad a scope as had been planned, and rewrote the original hedge accounting model so that it is now essentially consistent with that set out in (the then newly issued) IFRS 9. Subsequent amendments have cleared up pension scheme accounting and made editorial corrections, and then in July 2015 the other significant change took place, introducing the small entities regime. The new small entities regime applies to entities meeting the definition of a small company in the Companies Act, and not excluded by the Act, or an LLP qualifying as small, or any other entity that would have met these criteria had it been an incorporated company. So the definition is dynamic and can change as company law changes, and we have already seen this happen, with the changes to the small company limits effective from 2016. These changes, which are available for early adoption, make many more companies eligible for the small entities regime, meaning that using section 1A of the standard becomes a genuine option for a larger group.

The new and old limits are as follows:

	Old limit	New limit
Turnover	£6.5m	£10.2m
Balance sheet total	£3.26m	£5.1m
Number of employees	50	50

This new regime, set out in the new section 1A of FRS 102, ties in with changes to company law since the original standard was issued. One effect of the changes was to limit what governments (and hence standard-setters) are permitted to require small entities to include in their accounts. Small entities cannot legally be required to prepare accounts that comply in full with FRS 102 because this would involve requiring too many disclosures of them. So the FRC's response was to write section 1A which exempts small entities using FRS 102 from most of the disclosures set out in the standard, and instead sets out a minimum list of items to be disclosed.

Unfortunately for small preparers, this is something of a mixed blessing. The legal changes, and consequent new section 1A, do not remove the requirement for accounts to give a true and fair view. Now, accounts that comply with the requirements of accounting standards – formerly those in old UK GAAP, and now FRS 102 – can be assumed to give a true and fair view, in other words complying with every requirement in FRS 102 should mean that directors can assume they have met their duty to ensure the accounts are true and fair. But if this is the case, then preparing FRS 102 accounts without most of the disclosures cannot reasonably be expected also to give a true and fair view. Because of this, there is an awkward additional requirement. Small entities using the small entities regime are advised in paragraph 1A.17 that:

> '... because [FRS 102] disclosures are usually considered relevant to giving a true and fair view, a small entity is encouraged to consider and provide any of those disclosures that are relevant to material transactions, other events or conditions of the small entity in order to meet the requirement [for the accounts to give a true and fair view].'

In other words, they will still need to review all of the disclosure requirements throughout the standard and will find themselves giving more information than might have appeared necessary on a first casual reading of section 1A.

Almost all of the detailed amendments to FRS 102 made since its issue affect the 'first version' in that an entity applying the standard for the first time in its 2015 accounts will apply the version after these amendments. The only exceptions are the small companies exemptions, which are mandatory from 2016 but can be early-adopted, and minor changes to the detail of accounting for share-based payments with cash alternatives, which are also effective from 2016 but with early adoption available. In practice, the mandatory date for the small entities regime is not particularly meaningful since no entity has to take advantage of any or all of the disclosure exemptions.

Aside from the small companies regime, FRS 102 also gives certain disclosure exemptions to a wider range of 'qualifying entities'. This category includes any subsidiary entity that is not a financial institution, providing that its results are included in consolidated financial statements that are publicly available and are intended to give a true and fair view of the group's assets, liabilities, financial position and profit or loss. The exemptions are only available in individual, not group, accounts, and also may only be taken where shareholders have been notified and do not, in the main, object. The exemptions are not particularly far-reaching; they cover only:

- certain share capital disclosures;
- the requirement to present a cash flow statement;
- some financial instrument disclosures;
- some share based payment disclosures when the arrangement relates to equity instruments of another group entity or, in the case of a parent, where it relates to its own instruments but the disclosures are also in the consolidated accounts; and
- some related party disclosures.

They also in some cases require equivalent disclosures to be made elsewhere.

The definition of a qualifying entity for the purposes of FRS 102 and its slightly different definition in FRS 101 are discussed and compared in **3.1** below. The concept of equivalence is addressed in **3.3**.

FRS 103 Insurance Contracts

FRS 103 is something of a stopgap standard. Accounting for insurance contracts is an area that has never been quite satisfactorily resolved, and the old UK GAAP had FRS 27 in place which essentially told insurers to keep doing whatever they were doing. FRS 103, which is to be applied by any entity issuing insurance contracts, runs alongside FRS 102 and again allows continuity of accounting policies from their policies pre-transition.

It also requires disclosure that, in the standard's own words:

'(i) identifies and explains the amounts in an insurer's financial statements arising from the insurance contracts (including reinsurance contracts) it issues and reinsurance contracts that it holds;

(ii) relate to the financial strength of entities carrying on long-term insurance business; and

(iii) helps users of those financial statements understand the amount, timing and uncertainty of future cash flows from those insurance contracts.'

The expectation is that FRS 103 will be reviewed and amended as necessary once the IASB has completed its own project to review insurance accounting. This is the main driver for its being such a non-demanding standard in the sense of allowing insurers to continue their current practice: it might have been seen as unreasonable to require them to implement accounting changes when it was already known that there was change on the horizon.

FRS 104 Interim Financial Reporting

FRS 104 is a little different from the other standards in the suite because it has no mandatory application, except for entities claiming to apply it. It also does not relate to annual accounts, instead being focused on interim financial reports which are any set of financial statements that cover an interim period rather than an annual one.

Groups headed by listed companies are required by law to use EU-adopted IFRS in their annual accounts and IAS 34 in their interim accounts; those headed by AIM companies are required by the AIM rules to use EU-adopted IFRS. Interestingly the AIM rules, while they do require interim accounts, do not specify that they must be compliant with IAS 34; however, AIM companies are in the scope of the Disclosure and Transparency Rules which have the effect of requiring that their interims are prepared in accordance with either IAS 34 or any relevant standard issued by the FRC, which would previously have been the ASB statement on half-yearly reports and is now FRS 104.

Not many other entities choose to prepare interims, and FRS 104 does not require them to, though in the relatively unusual case of a listed company with no subsidiaries preparing individual company UK GAAP accounts (i.e., now, FRS 102 accounts), there will be a DTR requirement to prepare interims, and these will need to be under FRS 104, since it would be inappropriate to use IAS 34 when the annual accounts do not use IFRS.

The standard itself sets out the minimum contents of an interim report, being as follows:

- a condensed statement of financial position;
- a single condensed statement of comprehensive income or a separate condensed income statement and a separate condensed statement of comprehensive income;
- a condensed statement of changes in equity;
- a condensed statement of cash flows; and
- selected explanatory notes.

It then gives brief additional guidance such as what constitutes a significant event or transaction that would be required to be disclosed, and how to deal with issues such as seasonal revenues.

Preparers are instructed on the core interim periods to be presented, though as with any set of accounts additional information can be presented if this is chosen.

FRS 105 The Financial Reporting Standard applicable to the Micro-entities Regime

This is the newest standard in the suite, only having been issued in July 2015.

It sets out requirements for a very simple set of financial statements, with absolutely minimal disclosures. This restriction was brought about by the law – once the EU Micros Directive was in place, regulators could not legally require more than these very brief accounts.

Because of the brevity of a set of micro accounts prepared in accordance with FRS 105, its scope is highly limited. A micro entity must meet two of the following size conditions:

- Annual turnover – less than £632,000.
- Balance sheet total – less than £316,000.
- Average number of employees – fewer than 10.

As with applying the other size conditions, there is a year of grace available in that once a company is classified as a micro entity it would need to breach the size conditions for two years in a row before it was reclassified as small. If a company is also a parent, it can only be a micro entity if the group it heads qualifies as a small group. (The micro entity provisions, and hence FRS 105 cannot be applied in group accounts, but groups qualifying as small would usually take the exemption from preparing these accounts anyway.)

The other conditions are that a micro entity must be a company; that it must not be excluded from the small entities regime; and that it is not on a list of prohibited types of company including investment undertakings, financial holding undertakings, credit institutions, insurance undertakings, and charities.

The content of FRS 105 is based on FRS 102, and follows most of its section and paragraph numbering, but it allows virtually no accounting policy choices, and also omits guidance on what are considered to be irrelevant areas for such small entities, for instance earnings per share.

2.3   Which entities can use which standards?

We have seen that the only inescapable category is listed groups, or others subject to their own regulations, which are required to apply EU-adopted IFRS. For all other types of entity, there is some degree of choice. This is illustrated in the table below, which shows an expected default for each entity chosen, but also shows the other options. Note this table does not include all entity types. It is also important to bear in mind that, in general, it is not possible to mix frameworks within a group, in other words a group cannot have some of its subsidiaries using IFRS and some using UK GAAP (although it is acceptable for the parent to use IFRS while all the subsidiaries use UK GAAP). Since 'UK GAAP' is now quite a broad umbrella, it would be permissible for some group companies to use FRS 102 while others used FRS 101, if the directors considered this to be most appropriate.

Entity type	FRS 105	FRSSE 2015	FRS 102 with small entities regime	FRS 102	FRS 101	EU-adopted IFRS
Micro entity (company)	Default	Option in 2015 only	Option	Option	Option	Option
Small company		Option in 2015 only	Default	Option	Option	Option
Small LLP		Option in 2015 only	Default – with LLP SORP	Option – with LLP SORP	Option – but LLP SORP does not apply	Option – but LLP SORP does not apply
Medium or large private company				Default	Option	Option
Medium or large LLP				Default – with LLP SORP	Option – but LLP SORP does not apply	Option – but LLP SORP does not apply
Small charity		Default – with FRSSE-specific Charities SORP		Option – with FRS 102-specific Charities SORP		
Medium or large charity				Default – with FRS 102-specific Charities SORP		
Subsidiary in private group				Default – with some disclosure exemptions	Option	Option
Subsidiary in listed group				Option	Default	Option
Listed group						Default

This provides a good visual demonstration of how the options close down as an entity becomes more complex and larger. In **Chapter 3**, we will be exploring in more detail how an entity will make the choice to apply FRS 101 rather than any of its other options, and the precise eligibility conditions.

Chapter 3 Choosing FRS 101

3.1 Eligibility for FRS 101 – the basics

The scope of FRS 101 is set out in paragraphs 2 and 3, though these do not give the core definition. Paragraph 2 states that:

'This FRS may be applied to the individual financial statements of a qualifying entity, as defined in the glossary, that are intended to give a true and fair view of the assets, liabilities, financial position and profit or loss for a period.'

The definition of a qualifying entity, which appears in the glossary, does not on the face of it appear to be complex, stating that a qualifying entity is:

'A member of a group where the parent of that group prepares publicly available consolidated financial statements which are intended to give a true and fair view (of the assets, liabilities, financial position and profit or loss) and that member is included in the consolidation. A charity may not be a qualifying entity.'

So it is not only subsidiaries that can use FRS 101 – a parent can, too – but a standalone company is not eligible, and nor are associates or joint ventures.

The only other immediate restriction is that FRS 101 may not be applied in consolidated accounts, whether these are prepared because the entity is required to or is doing so voluntarily. This is because so many of the exemptions rely on users being able to access the relevant information – albeit in a more aggregated form – elsewhere, namely somewhere higher up in a group. If it were applied in group accounts themselves then there would be a risk of information being obscured entirely.

Meeting the basic definition of a qualifying entity, though, is only the first part of the battle. To be able to apply FRS 101, preparers also need to notify their shareholders of the disclosure exemptions they are taking, and must provide disclosures relating to their use of the standard. There is also, at the beginning of the standard, some clear signposting on how to use EU-adopted IFRS.

3.2 Shareholder notification

FRS 101 essentially allows preparers to take a set of accounting standards designed to give a true and fair view (or the IFRS equivalent, a fair presentation: the FRC obtained a counsel's opinion stating that these amount to the same thing) and then disclose less information than those standards envisaged. It is clear that this could be theoretically problematic to shareholders, who might reasonably enough argue that their information needs trump any hope of management to be allowed to prepare simpler and less voluminous accounts.

To protect the interests of shareholders, paragraph 5.5(a) places the following condition on using the standard:

'[the company's] shareholders have been notified in writing about, and do not object to, the use of the disclosure exemptions. Objections to the use of the disclosure exemptions may be served on the qualifying entity, in accordance with reasonable specified timeframes and format requirements, by a shareholder that is the immediate parent of the entity, or by a shareholder or shareholders holding in aggregate 5% or more of the total allotted shares in the entity or more than half of the allotted shares in the entity that are not held by the immediate parent.'

This is a passive sort of permission. A company needs only to write to its members telling them of its intentions, and if objections are not received then it can continue.

It does seem open to a certain amount of interpretation, though. There is no ruling as to when a company should notify its shareholders of its intentions, and nor is there anything about how diligent it needs to be in ensuring they have received its communication.

The standard specifies that there must be 'reasonable specified timeframes and format requirements', presumably to avoid preposterous situations where an entity writes to its shareholders two weeks before the accounts are due to be filed, specifying that they must respond within 48 hours by telegram if they object. It might have been helpful, though, if it had been more precise, even to the extent of specifying whether the communication should be before the relevant year end. We might compare this to the small companies' audit exemption, where shareholders can require an audit by giving written notice but have to do so within a set window, and newly for each financial year.

There is also silence on whether this communication needs to be repeated each year. We can probably assume that this is necessary, since each year a new set of accounts is prepared so FRS 101 will be applied afresh, and shareholders may change, but it is not made explicit. An entity might argue that a one-off communication to shareholders saying 'we intend to use FRS 101 in our forthcoming accounts and for the foreseeable future' and stating the disclosure exemptions taken meets the letter of the standard.

To be clear on the thresholds, these are some examples of shareholder objections that would be sufficient to prevent the use of FRS 101:

- a subsidiary's parent objects, whether it owns 100% or 51%, and even if one other investor owns the balance and is very enthusiastic;
- an entity is owned by 100 holders of one share each, and five of these write to object;
- an entity is 95% owned by its parent with the other 5% owned by one other investor, who writes to object;
- an entity is 96% owned by its parent and an investor in a further 3% writes to object (this is sufficient prevention because the 3% is more than half of the 4% not owned by the parent).

So it can be seen that in some cases a holder of a tiny proportion of shares, which could be less than 5%, can still block the preparation of FRS 101 accounts. This possibility caused some discomfort during the various discussions and consultations as the standard was drafted, but the value of protecting shareholders won out over the competing aim of some expedience for directors. It may serve as a useful prompt for directors to ensure their investor relations are as strong as possible so that their plans are not blocked. Fortunately the requirement was not flipped to be more onerous: an alternative would have been to require positive written consent, if not from all holders, at least from a majority, or a majority of non-parent owners. This would have been a far greater administrative burden and could have led to the unproductive situation where an entity was prevented from preparing accounts using the most appropriate standard simple because it could not track down one or two individual shareholders, or could not elicit a timely response.

3.3   The concept of equivalence

Background

We can see from the definition of a qualifying entity above, and the further conditions in paragraph 5, that an entity can be in the scope of FRS 101 if its parent prepares publicly available consolidated accounts designed to give a true and fair view. This is an echo of the provisions of the Companies Act, where an intermediate parent company could take an exemption from preparing group accounts if its results were consolidated into those of a higher group, with that group's accounts publicly available and prepared on a basis equivalent to the provisions of the Seventh Directive. (Since the Accounting Directive was issued, this reference has been updated.)

In practice, this meant that the group accounts exemption could be claimed if the ultimate parent was preparing UK GAAP or EU-IFRS accounts, but some interpretation difficulties arose when it came to GAAPs such as US GAAP or Japanese GAAP, where there were known differences. Preparers questioned whether they were 'sufficiently equivalent' to allow the exemption. So the ASB, as it was then, issued UITF Abstract 43 *The interpretation of equivalence for the purposes of section 228A of the Companies Act 1985.*

The UITF emphasised that equivalence does not require every point of detail to be identical to the Seventh Directive, and recommends a qualitative approach, 'i.e. with a focus on compliance with the basic requirements of the Directive and in particular the requirement to give a true and fair view'. It gave some examples, and discussed GAAPs that were based on IFRS but more restrictive, which would usually qualify as equivalent. It also addressed frameworks like US GAAP, and pointed out that although there are areas of substantive difference, these will not automatically disqualify an entity with a US parent from taking the exemption, since it may be that these areas of difference are not relevant to the parent's accounts.

When the FRC issued drafts of the new standards comprising new UK GAAP, it proposed withdrawing all extant SSAPs, FRSs and UITF Abstracts apart from Abstract 43. This is because although equivalence is used differently in this standard, and differently again in FRS 102, some of the core principles from UITF 43 can still be helpful. However the final conclusion was that UITF 43 should be withdrawn too, to avoid confusion.

Equivalence in FRS 102

Before we turn to the detail within FRS 101, our main topic of interest, we can look at how equivalence is relevant to FRS 102. As we saw in **2.1** above, entities using FRS 102 in their accounts can claim some limited exemptions if they are qualifying entities, based on the FRS 102 definition not the FRS 101 definition. These qualifying entities can claim some exemptions regardless, and others (relating to financial instruments) if 'the equivalent disclosures required by this FRS are included in the consolidated financial statements of the group in which the entity is consolidated'. Preparers are then directed to the Application Guidance in FRS 100.

Equivalence in FRS 101

Most, but not all, of the disclosure exemptions in FRS 101 are predicated in the same way on the existence of equivalent disclosures in the parent's consolidated accounts. The main exceptions relate to presentation of comparative information in areas such as fixed asset movements, and areas such as details of accounting policies, where there is no directly equivalent information in a parent's accounts. It can be assumed that the parent will make reasonable disclosure of their accounting policies and any changes to them, and also that the results of the subsidiary included in the consolidation have been adjusted appropriately so that the same policies are applied across the group – so in that sense the subsidiary's policies in its own accounts are entirely detached from the policies of its parent in the group accounts.

Application guidance to FRS 100

Because both FRS 101 and FRS 102 rely on the concept of equivalent disclosures, the relevant guidance is included in FRS 100 so that it is easily accessed by both.

Parent's accounts using an equivalent GAAP

The Application Guidance covers the two different uses of equivalence: first in the Companies Act sense, where the parent's accounts as a whole need to be prepared on a basis equivalent to the Accounting Directive for a consolidation exemption to be taken, and then on the detailed level that allows individual disclosure exemptions to be taken through FRS 101 or FRS 102. Note that the references to the Act have been updated: UITF 43 referred to the *Companies Act* 1985, s. 228A, but this has now been replaced the *Companies Act* 2006, s. 401, and the EU Fourth and Seventh

Directives have been replaced with the Accounting Directive. In both cases much of the application detail remained the same but it is helpful to have the terminology updated. The exemption from consolidation is actually somewhat broader than it was in the old Act, now allowing an intermediate parent to choose not to prepare group accounts if its results are included in consolidated accounts that are drawn up:

(a) in accordance with, or in a manner that is equivalent to, the Accounting Directive;

(b) in accordance with EU-adopted IFRS; or

(c) in accordance with accounting standards which are equivalent to EU-adopted IFRS, as determined in accordance with the EU mechanism.

It is interesting to see how things have been made explicit here. In general, IFRS standards are not adopted for use in the EU unless they are also consistent with the Accounting Directive, but this wording effectively allows for some discrepancy between the two (if it did not, then point (b) would not need to exist separately from point (a)).

The exemption from preparing group accounts will not be discussed in more detail here since it is not directly relevant to FRS 101; instead we will focus on the second sense of equivalence.

Equivalent disclosures in the financial statements of the group

Interestingly, one of the first things that the FRS 100 Application Guidance says about this sense of equivalence is that it is intended to be aligned to that which is used for the purposes of s. 401 of the Act. On the face of it, individual disclosures are quite different from a full set of accounts. They are (obviously) not a matter of recognition and measurement, where this is surely a key element of equivalence on a macro level between two GAAPs. And by their very nature, there is a good deal of detail present: it would be reasonable to think that where a subsidiary is to successfully claim an exemption from some share based payment disclosures, there would need to be reasonably similar disclosures in the group accounts.

The Application Guidance then peters out somewhat disappointingly, with only one paragraph about equivalent disclosures. AG10 (in full) states that:

'Disclosure exemptions for subsidiaries are permitted where the relevant disclosure requirements are met in the consolidated financial statements, even where the disclosures are made in aggregate or in an abbreviated form, or in relation to intra-group balances, those intra-group balances have been eliminated on consolidation. If, however, no disclosure is made in the consolidated financial statements on the grounds of materiality, the relevant disclosures should be made at the subsidiary level if material in those financial statements.'

In **Part III** of this publication, we will look at all the disclosures in detail, and this will include investigation of what might constitute sufficient disclosures in a parent's accounts. The permission for the information to be included in an aggregated form seems to be a statement of common sense: if, for instance, a parent P has subsidiaries A, B and C then its financial instruments note is highly unlikely to distinguish between instruments held by these three subsidiaries separately, so will aggregate the three to reach totals. And because a group will usually have a higher reporting materiality than individual subsidiaries, it is likely that some detail will be lost as part of this aggregation, since a line of disclosure necessary to give a true and fair view in a set of individual accounts could easily be immaterial or even trivial in a large set of group accounts, so it will not be just aggregated but actually lost completely.

The paragraph quoted above seems at first glance to mitigate this issue somewhat by requiring that disclosures are excluded in the consolidated accounts on the grounds of materiality, they must be included in the subsidiary: so effectively saying that that particular exemption is no longer available. But it is not quite clear what this means. It may refer to the situation discussed above where one individual disclosure disappears through being aggregated with others to give materiality-appropriate size buckets. But it seems more likely to be referring to a whole substantive disclosure requirement. As a slightly far-fetched example, if a subsidiary offered cash-settled share-based payments to its employees but the norm in the group was equity-settled payments, then the group might find that to apply the disclosure requirements of IFRS 2 it would give a lot of detail about the equity settled scheme and minimal to no information on the cash-settled scheme, simply because the charge was of such low value in the group accounts. In this case its subsidiary with the cash-settled scheme would be unable to take advantage of this particular exemption given by FRS 101, unless the parent changed its own disclosures. This is a useful reminder that FRS 101 is not an 'all or nothing' standard – a qualifying entity may not be able, or wish, to take advantage of every one of its disclosure exemptions.

This type of loss of information, through the combination of aggregation and the application of materiality, would happen even where the relevant consolidated accounts were prepared using EU-adopted IFRS, and therefore were theoretically giving exactly the disclosures omitted in the FRS 101 accounts of the subsidiary. But another level of loss will occur if the parent's accounts are based on a different GAAP which does not even ask for all of the disclosures. It does not seem that this would give an automatic disqualification from applying a particular exemption, since the relevant note in the group accounts might be argued to give an 'abbreviated' version of the equivalent disclosures, but again there is no steer as to how abbreviated is too abbreviated.

3.4   A note on disclosures

An entity choosing to apply FRS 101 must, to comply fully, make a clear disclosure including the following information (from para. 5(c)):

(i)   a brief narrative summary of the disclosure exemptions adopted; and
(ii) the name of the parent of the group in whose consolidated financial statements its financial statements are consolidated, and from where those financial statements may be obtained.

The reference to the parent here means the parent whose existence, and preparation of group accounts, allows the entity to be a qualifying entity in the first place.

As can be seen in the example accounts included in **Appendix 1** to this publication, the brief narrative summary truly can be brief: it seems sufficient to outline the types of information not provided, without going into further detail.

3.5   Reasons to choose FRS 101

We have explored, here, the precise eligibility conditions first to be in the scope of FRS 101 and then to be able actually to apply it and take any of its disclosure exemptions. It only remains to explore why an entity would choose to use this standard rather than defaulting to FRS 102 or upgrading to full EU-adopted IFRS.

Subsidiaries of listed parents

It was relatively rare, under old UK GAAP, to see subsidiaries of a listed parent using anything other than UK GAAP in their accounts, even though their parent had made the move to EU-adopted IFRS in its group accounts when it was required to in 2005. This was probably caused by a mix of two factors: an aversion to the apparent complexity of IFRS, and a certain inertia. It was possible to continue with old GAAP, so this is what happened, and the cost of calculating IFRS adjustments to go into the group reporting pack still seemed less than the cost of making an actual move to IFRS.

Now, of course, there is no option to continue with the status quo and subsidiaries in listed groups need to jump one way or another. Converting to FRS 102 is not a straightforward process even where it turns out that few accounting changes are needed, since it is necessary to perform a full and detailed review first to be sure this is the case. And a new accounts template will be needed since the primary statements required are not the same as under old GAAP, and the detail of note disclosures differs too. Equally, a move to full EU-adopted IFRS might have some efficiencies if the subsidiary is already used to preparing IFRS-adjusted group reporting, but there would still be considerable effort involved in preparing IFRS accounts for the first time.

So neither of the two alternatives to FRS 101 is effortless, and FRS 101 might seem to give the best balance of costs and benefits. The recognition and measurement, for a subsidiary that is already at least somewhat familiar with IFRS requirements through previous years of being included in group accounts, should not be too much of a culture shock. Then the disclosures are, arguably, the best of both worlds: the FRS 101 accounts will be slimmer and more concise than they would have been under IFRS, and the basic accounting is already familiar.

Put this way, it is hard to see why an entity in this position would *not* use FRS 101. Perhaps the biggest deterrent is its difficult structure though in practice there may also be issues around tax and determination and use of distributable profits. We explore this in more detail in **Part II** below, but effectively there are several places to look:

- to the 'big book' of EU-adopted IFRS, for all recognition and measurement requirements and for a starting point for disclosures;
- to the body of FRS 101 for the main exemptions from disclosures, which are set out by paragraph number and therefore require continual reference back to full IFRS to determine what they relate to;
- to the Application Guidance in FRS 100 in respect of what constitutes an equivalent disclosure;
- to Appendix II of FRS 101, which needs to be read and understood to ensure legal requirements are met; and
- to the Application Guidance of FRS 101 which sets out adjustments to the accounting in full IFRS to make it compatible with UK law.

There are very good reasons for the existence of each of these sections of guidance, but they mean that applying the new standard will take a lot of effort in the first year. Of course, the aim of this publication is to simplify this as much as possible, both by setting out the scope and pre-conditions clearly, and then by cutting through the disclosures and amendments to give a final definitive list, also showing examples of how the final requirements may be satisfied, as well as what to look for in the parent's group accounts. It is still possible that a preparer will look at the sheer volume of disclosures still remaining and conclude that the exemptions are not sufficiently generous to justify stepping into the unknown while also perhaps being seen as 'opting out' of taking the more significant leap to full EU-adopted IFRS.

Part II   The Law

Chapter 4   Company accounts, FRS 101, and the law

4.1   The legal status of FRS 101 accounts

Company accounts prepared under FRS 101 are in an unusual position, because their outward form does not necessarily match their legal status.

The Companies Act requires that entities in its scope prepare either 'Companies Act accounts' or 'IAS accounts' and the critical point is that accounts prepared under FRS 101 are 'Companies Act accounts' even though they have the principles – as well as some of the cosmetic appearance – of IFRS accounts. FRS 101 modifies IFRS in order to ensure that those applying the standard do not thereby breach any legal requirements, most notably in terms of accounts formats, realised profits and financial instruments disclosures.

Following through the legal requirements:

- CA 2006, s. 395(1) states that a company's individual accounts may be prepared in accordance with s. 396 ('Companies Act individual accounts') or in accordance with international accounting standards ('IAS individual accounts');
- the overriding objective of Companies Act accounts is that the accounts give a true and fair view (CA 2006, s. 393), and BIS have confirmed that 'in the vast majority of cases, compliance with accounting standards will give a true and fair view';
- IAS accounts technically require a 'fair presentation' rather than a 'true and fair view' but the FRC has obtained a counsel's opinion confirming that the two terms are equivalent;
- charitable companies must prepare Companies Act individual accounts (note that a charity is not permitted to use FRS 101 so its options for 'Companies Act accounts' are more limited);
- after IAS individual accounts have been prepared in one year, a company must keep on preparing IAS individual accounts unless there is a 'relevant change in circumstance'. This includes the company becoming a subsidiary or ceasing to be a subsidiary, or the company or its parent ceasing to be listed (more precisely, ceasing to be 'an undertaking with securities admitted to trading on a regulated market in an EEA state');
- companies may also revert from preparing IAS accounts to Companies Act accounts without a relevant change of circumstances if it has been at least five years since the last change to Companies Act accounts for a reason other than a relevant change of circumstance; and
- CA 2006, s. 396 sets out the basic requirements of Companies Act accounts. These are discussed in more detail below but the most important point is that s. 396 points to the Regulations, for large and medium or small companies as appropriate. Looking at this from the opposite direction, Companies Act accounts need to comply with the Regulations whereas IAS accounts do not (but they do still need to comply with the accounting and disclosure requirements in Pt. 15 of the Act itself).

Clearly, there is a splitting off here that sets out quite distinct requirements for Companies Act accounts and IAS accounts. When the idea of a reduced disclosure framework was first discussed, issues were raised about how to treat accounts that used the recognition and measurement principles of IFRS, since on the face of it they appear to be like IFRS accounts. If a set of IFRS accounts is agreed to 'fairly present' an entity's position and performance, it can be assumed that this fair presentation involves applying all of the recognition and measurement principles and meeting all of the disclosure requirements. Here, though, the FRC has set out an alternative approach which uses the accounting rules but cuts down the disclosure requirements thus seeming, on the face of it, to make it impossible that the accounts give a fair presentation of position and performance, because insufficient information is provided.

The FRC, as a standard-setter, is empowered to set out financial reporting standards such that, when an entity's accounts comply with them in full, they are assumed to give a true and fair view. This is what has taken place with FRS 101 – the FRC performed a very detailed review of all the disclosure requirements in IFRS and reached conclusions, on a line by line basis, about which were necessary. This is what makes FRS 101 'belong' to the FRC, so that it has become a UK standard. And once it is clear that this is a UK accounting standard, it also becomes clear that compliance with it will not give 'IAS accounts' and so must instead give 'Companies Act accounts'.

Requirements in UK law concerning accounts

Returning to s. 396 of the Act, the requirements for Companies Act individual accounts are set out with a broad brush:

'(1) Companies Act individual accounts must comprise –
  (a) A balance sheet as at the last day of the financial year, and
  (b) A profit and loss account
(2) The accounts must –
  (a) In the case of the balance sheet, give a true and fair view of the state of affairs of the company as at the end of the financial year, and
  (b) In the case of the profit and loss accounts, give a true and fair view of the profit or loss of the company for the financial year.
(3) The accounts must comply with provision made by the Secretary of State by regulations as to –
  (a) The form and content of the balance sheet and profit and loss account, and
  (b) Additional information to be provided by way of notes to the accounts.
(4) If compliance with the regulations, and any other provision made by or under this Act as to the matters to be included in a company's individual accounts or in notes to those accounts, would not be sufficient to give a true and fair view, the necessary additional information must be given in the accounts or in a note to them.
(5) If in special circumstances compliance with any of those provisions is inconsistent with the requirement to give a true and fair view, the directors must depart from that provision to the extent necessary to give a true and fair view. Particulars of any such departure, the reasons for it and its effect must be given in a note to the accounts.'

The regulations referred to above are the *Large and Medium-sized Companies and Groups (Accounts and Reports) Regulations* 2008 (SI 2008/410) or, where relevant, the *Small Companies and Groups (Accounts and Directors' Report) Regulations* 2008 (SI 2008/409).

Accounting standards are drafted within the context of the law, and a key consideration for the FRC is ensuring their standards fit within that framework, so that there are no accounting treatments that are permissible under the standards but not legal. This has not always been the case: in particular, the non-depreciation of investment properties under SSAP 19 conflicted with the requirement in company law to write properties off over their useful lives, and so entities that used this policy in their accounts had to disclose the so-called 'true and fair override'. The judgment at the time was that the SSAP 19 treatment gave the best representation of the situation and was therefore necessary to give a true and fair view. In general, it would be hoped that the law, in its generalities and particulars, would facilitate rather than obstruct this. Occasionally, there was an apparent clash in the opposite direction, where the law allowed an accounting treatment that was then prohibited by standards, for instance the use of the LIFO method in stock valuation, which was permitted in the Act but not in SSAP 9. This is not in itself an issue, though, since it is legitimate for accounting standards to restrict the options that the law makes available, so long as they do not introduce options that the law prohibits.

We will see below some areas where there is some apparent initial conflict between the law and the requirements of FRS 101, all of which arise because of the way that FRS 101 uses IFRS recognition and measurement, and IFRS standards were not drafted with UK law in mind. The issue of accounts formats is dealt with by complex references to using or adapting the formats in the Regulations; the issues around financial instruments disclosures are discussed in depth within the standard, and set out below; and the issues with realised profits are addressed by showing where exceptions are made in the law, and pointing out the critical difference between amounts reported in profit and amounts that are, ultimately, distributable. Some accounting issues simply cannot be reconciled, though, and this is where the FRC was forced to provide a list of changes to IFRS. It is not in the FRC's power to change IFRS standards themselves, but FRS 101's instruction to apply IFRS is actually read as 'apply IFRS with these accounting modifications'. These are discussed further in **4.2** below.

The need to cut and alter IFRS standards to fit into the UK legal framework was a significant challenge in the process of devising and issuing new UK GAAP. The idea of a simple approach of picking up the big book and deleting some disclosures was a pleasing one, but the legal complications only became fully apparent during the drafting process. They had never arisen before because companies preparing IAS accounts do not need to comply with the Regulations, where most of the law's accounting requirements, including the primary statement formats, are contained.

4.2   Accounting adjustments

In a few areas, the accounting requirements of full IFRS are not compatible with UK law. This might be slightly surprising, given that most IFRSs to date have been endorsed for use in the EU, and UK law is necessarily derived from EU law, but individual jurisdictions do still have some discretion over the detail of how they enact the law locally, so differences can arise. In particular, there are areas where local jurisdictions are permitted to narrow down accounting options from those included in EU law. So a standard might 'pass' for consistency with EU law but fail at the UK level because it offers or mandates an accounting option that UK law has chosen not to offer. Moreover, the status of being endorsed in the EU does not come with a guarantee of full compliance with the Accounting Directive (previously the Fourth and Seventh Directives), rather, it reassures on general consistency instead of points of detail.

As described above, UK accounting standards cannot prescribe treatment which is illegal. So in the cases where applying IFRS would clash with UK law, the FRC has issued a series of modifications to IFRS – in other words, FRS 101 preparers do not apply unadulterated EU-adopted IFRS with reduced disclosures, but rather slightly amended EU-adopted IFRS with reduced disclosures (note again that a similar problem does not arise for preparers using full IFRS since they are preparing 'IAS accounts' and thus do not need to comply with the Regulations but only with the body of the Act itself).

The accounting areas that need to be adjusted for legal purposes are set out in the Application Guidance to the standard, titled *Amendments to International Financial Reporting Standards as Adopted in the European Union for Compliance with the Act and the Regulations.* They are discussed within the detailed chapters of **Part III** of this publication, and cover the following main areas:

- first time adoption;
- business combinations;
- non-current assets held for sale and discontinued operations;
- property, plant and equipment;
- government grants; and
- provisions.

4.3   Adapting accounts formats

As we can see above, the Act itself barely puts any structure in place regarding accounts formats, requiring only that an entity provides a profit and loss account and a balance sheet.

If this were all there is to it, then there would be no issue with simply using the prescribed formats in IAS 1 for the income statement and statement of financial position, using the permission in IAS 1 para. 10 to use alternative names for the primary statements. Unfortunately though, Sch. 1 of the Regulations sets out two permissible formats for the profit and loss account and two for the balance sheet, with a fairly rigid set of rules (these can be seen in the parts of the Regulations reproduced in **Appendix 2** of this volume).

In general, the Regulations state that the line items in the prescribed formats must be shown in the order and under the headings and sub-headings given, but (from Sch. 1, para. 1(3)):

(a) the notes to the formats may permit alternative positions for any particular items; and
(b) the heading or sub-heading for any item does not have to be distinguished by any letter or number assigned to that item in the format used.

Point (b) above refers to the Roman and Arabic numerals and the letters used to distinguish line items in the formats, and states for the avoidance of doubt that a balance sheet does not have to include a line titled 'B Fixed assets'.

This would on the face of it appear to be very constricting, and would seem to make it virtually impossible to produce primary statements that comply with both IAS 1 and the law.

Fortunately, a change came into the Regulations through the *Companies, Partnerships and Groups (Accounts and Reports) Regulations* 2015 (SI 2015/980), effective for periods beginning on or after 1 January 2016 but available for periods beginning on or after 1 January 2015. Because the new paragraph 1A is so critical, it is worth quoting in full:

'(1) The company's directors may adapt one of the balance sheet formats in Section B so to distinguish between current and non-current items in a different way, provided that –
    (a) The information given is at least equivalent to that which would have been required by the use of such format had it not been thus adapted, and
    (b) The presentation of those items is in accordance with generally accepted accounting principles or practice.
(2) The company's directors may adapt one of the profit and loss account formats in Section B, provided that –
    (a) The information given is at least equivalent to that which would have been required by the use of such format had it not been thus adapted, and
    (b) The presentation is in accordance with generally accepted accounting principles or practice.
(3) So far as is practicable, the following provisions of Section 1A of this Part of this Schedule apply to the balance sheet or profit and loss account of a company notwithstanding any such adaptation pursuant to this paragraph.'

The adaptation allowed for the balance sheet is much more restrictive than that for the profit and loss account, with the balance sheet only permitted adaptation for a current/non-current asset distinction, but no boundaries placed on the profit and loss account.

Nonetheless, this is enough to open the door for IAS compliance. The FRC picked this up in their 2015 amendments to FRS 101, which are in this respect effective from the same dates as the changes to the Regulations. The new paragraph 81C states that:

'A qualifying entity choosing to apply paragraph 1A(2) of Schedule 1 to the Regulations and adapt one of the profit and loss account formats shall apply the relevant presentation requirements of IAS 1 *Presentation of Financial Statements*, and in addition shall disclose 'profit or loss before taxation'. A qualifying entity not permitted or not choosing to apply paragraph 1A(2) of Schedule 1 to the Regulations shall present the components of profit or loss in the statement of comprehensive income (in either the single statement or the two statement approach) in accordance with the profit and loss format requirements of the Act instead of paragraphs 82 and 85 to 86 of IAS 1.'

In other words, there are two options for FRS 101 preparers:

• take the permission from the Regulations to adapt the P&L formats but ONLY in a way that results in a fully IAS 1-compliant format by adding more information, where necessary, and also including everything required by IAS 1; or
• ignore the income statement formats in IAS 1 completely and instead use those set out in the Regulations.

There is no third way – it does not appear to be acceptable to elect to use the accounts formats from company law while also modifying them based on para. 1A.

The same approach applies to the modification of the balance sheet formats – the only situation in which it is acceptable for FRS 101 preparers to take the permission in para. 1A to adapt the balance sheet formats is when they are doing this to allow them to apply the IAS 1 formats in full. Otherwise, they must use one of the Regulations formats, unadapted.

As with so many aspects of the law, there is one further exception, and it is not entirely clear how FRS 101 views this. Although paragraph 1A was inserted only very recently, para. 4(1) has been there much longer, has not been removed, and states that:

'Where the special nature of the company's business requires it, the company's directors must adapt the arrangement, headings and sub-headings otherwise required in respect of items given an Arabic number in the balance sheet or profit and loss account format used.'

This paragraph forms part of the legal requirements for the profit and loss account and balance sheet so it does appear to continue to be acceptable for an FRS 101 preparer to make this level of adaptation in their accounts even if they are not performing the more wholesale adaptation in para. 1A. Perhaps, this is more clear through illustration – to illustrate this, the assets part of the format 1 balance sheet in the Regulations includes the following headings and sub-headings with letters and Roman numerals, which are not in the scope of the universal 'special nature' option to adapt in para. 4:

A   Called up share capital not paid

B   Fixed assets

    I   Intangible assets
    II   Tangible assets
    III   Investments

C   Current assets

    I   Stocks
    II   Debtors
    III   Investments
    IV   Cash at bank and in hand

D   Prepayments and accrued income

So these headings are immutable (ignoring the new para. 1A) – it is only the lower level subheadings (e.g. the tangible fixed assets breakdown between land and buildings, plant and machinery, fixtures, fittings, tools and equipment, and payments on account and assets in the course of construction) that can be rearranged using para. 4.

4.4 Special considerations for financial instruments

Disclosures about financial instruments caused some of the most persistent difficulties in drafting the new UK standards. The problems have come about because EU law introduced an option to hold certain financial instruments at fair value, and this was – as it had to be – picked up in UK law too. This was regardless of whether the entity choosing this option was applying FRS 26, the UK version of IAS 39 *Financial instruments: recognition and measurement*.

The fair value option on its own was not a particularly momentous introduction for most entities, since those with significant financial instruments would often be either scoped into IFRS anyway or voluntarily applying FRS 26 (and therefore getting the option that way, albeit with some limitations).

However it needed to come with suitable disclosures, and instead of making any specification in this regard, Sch. 1, para. 36(4) to the Regulations simply stated that:

'Financial instruments which under international accounting standards may be included in accounts at fair value may be so included, provided that the disclosures required by such accounting standards are made.'

Although on the face of it this seems like a simple paragraph, it is fraught with difficulties. In particular, it does not make it clear which version of international accounting standards is referred to in respect of either the permission to measure at fair value or the disclosures. It also sends even a 'normal' UK preparer off to a completely distinct framework (i.e. IFRS) to prepare their otherwise unblemished UK GAAP accounts.

The wording before the most recent amendments was somewhat more helpful in that it referred to financial instruments that may be included in accounts at fair value 'under international accounting standards adopted by the European Commission on or before 5 September 2006', so it was possible to look at the version of IAS 39 in force at that point. Now that this modifier has been removed, though, it seems the most reasonable assumption is that the clause refers to a moving target – at the point of accounts preparation, an entity should look to the IFRS applicable for that period as endorsed for use in the EU (this is what UK company law always means when it refers to 'international accounting standards').

Since FRS 101 involves applying the recognition and measurement rules of IFRS, an FRS 101 preparer will have available all the options to hold instruments at fair value that are set out in IAS 39 until it is withdrawn, with the alternative of early-adopting IFRS 9 now that it has been EU-endorsed. Appendix II to the standard points this out, quoting para. 36 of the Regulations then stating in para. A2.7 that:

'A qualifying entity that has financial instruments measured at fair value in accordance with the requirements of paragraph 36(4) of Schedule 1 to the Regulations (or equivalent) is legally required to provide the relevant disclosures set out in international accounting standards adopted by the European Commission. Such disclosures should be based on extant standards.'

This matters because in the main body of the standard, para. 8(d) gives an exemption from the requirements of IFRS 7. But an FRS 101 preparer holding financial instruments at fair value is then guided by a footnote back to the requirement to provide 'relevant disclosures' notwithstanding this exemption.

Here, there is an interesting point of interpretation. A similar issue arose in FRS 102, where the accounting requirements included some optional and some mandatory occasions when financial instruments would be measured at fair value. In FRS 102, though, the FRC has reproduced the relevant disclosures from IFRS 7 but states that these disclosures are needed 'only for financial instruments measured at fair value through profit or loss in accordance with Sch. 1, para. 36(4) to the Regulations. This does not include financial liabilities held as part of a trading portfolio or derivatives'. Effectively this means the 'extra' disclosures are only needed under FRS 102 in situations where the entity has elected to use fair value, rather than those where it is simply required to by the standard.

To square this circle, we look back to the Regulations, and note that para. 36(1) states that 'subject to sub-paragraphs (2) to (5), financial instruments (including derivatives) may be included at fair value'. Sub-paragraph (2) then limits this drastically in the case of liabilities, saying that there are only three types of liability that may – under the Regulations – be held at fair value:

(a) those held as part of a trading portfolio;
(b) derivatives; and
(c) financial instruments falling within sub-paragraph 4 [i.e. those which international financial reporting standards require to be held at fair value].

Para. 36(3) then scopes out more instruments from the 36(1) option to hold at fair value:

(a) financial instruments (other than derivatives) held to maturity;
(b) loans and receivables originated by the company and not held for trading purposes;
(c) interests in subsidiary undertakings, associated undertakings and joint ventures;
(d) equity instruments issued by the company;
(e) contracts for contingent consideration in a business combination; or
(f) other financial instruments with such special characteristics that the instruments, according to generally accepted accounting principles or practice, should be accounted for differently from other financial instruments.

So, the Regulations allow many financial assets, and a few financial liabilities, to be held at fair value. Where an FRS 101 preparer only has financial asset and liabilities that are held at amortised cost or that fit into one of the Regulation permitted categories to be held at fair value, then it can safely apply the exemption in the body of the standard and not provide any disclosures. It is only where financial assets or liabilities are held at fair value because IFRS (over and above the company law permissions) requires it, or because the preparer has chosen it as an accounting option, and they are an asset or liability not on the lists above, that the entity is considered to be holding them at fair value by virtue of para. 36(4), thus needing to provide the relevant disclosures.

The detail of 'relevant disclosures' in this case is discussed in greater detail in **10.6.5** below, but it will seem reasonable to base it at least on the disclosures already identified in FRS 102, since these are attempting to achieve the same end, of compliance with UK law as it relates to financial instrument disclosures.

4.5   Realised profits

One of the criticisms sometimes levelled at IFRS is about the way it appears to allow some items to appear in the income statements that do not represent realised profits. Some argue that this makes the income statement unhelpful, since profits are only of interest to shareholders if they are available for distribution. Again, this has not been such a pressing issue when it comes just to IFRS accounts, which are covered separately in law, but needed to be resolved by a clear statement from the FRC when they issued FRS 101 which allowed IFRS measurement in accounts that must also comply with UK law. A recent report from the FRC's Financial Reporting Lab, in November 2015, discusses disclosures around dividends, both amounts actually paid but also policies and strategy surrounding dividends. This shows it is an area of interest for stakeholders at the moment, and users might quite reasonably ask searching questions about how distributable profits are determined even before decisions are taken on whether to pay dividends and at what level.

Appendix II para. A2.12–A2.20 summarise the legal position, pointing out that Sch. 1, para. 13(a) to the Regulations requires that only profits realised at the balance sheet date are included in the profit and loss account. This is the UK version of the reference to profits 'made' at the balance sheet which was included in the Fourth Directive. A later paragraph in the Regulations then effectively overrides para. 13(a) by allowing, in para. 39, investment properties and living animals and plants to be held at fair value, with para. 40 following up by requiring movements in the value of financial instruments, stocks, investment properties or living animals or plants to be recognised in the profit and loss account.

This effective exception from the general restriction on recognising unrealised profits in the profit and loss account does not affect the question of whether profits are distributable. So para. A2.15 states that 'entities may transfer [fair value movements on investment properties, living animals or plants, or financial instruments at fair value] to a separate non-distributable reserve instead of carrying them forward in retained earnings but are not required to do so', going on to note that 'presenting fair value movements that are not distributable profits in a separate reserve may assist with the identification of profits available for that purpose'. Preparers are then guided to the ICAEW and ICAS's joint publication Tech 02/10 *Guidance on Realised and Distributable Profits under the Companies Act 2006*. Some preparers will find their distributable profits change as a result of transition to FRS 101, but for others the effect will just be of needing more vigilance and extra record-keeping to ensure that distributable profits are properly tracked, since amounts included in the income statement may include both distributable and undistributable elements.

Chapter 5   FRS 101 for LLPs

5.1   LLP eligibility to apply FRS 101

Limited Liability Partnerships occupy a peculiar position in accounting standards and law. Legally, they are distinct from companies, with the main accounting requirements in law set out in three statutory instruments known collectively as the LLP Regulations: the *Limited Liability Partnerships (Accounts and Audit) (Application of Companies Act 2006) Regulations* 2008 (SI 2008/1911), the *Small Limited Liability Partnerships (Accounts) Regulations* 2008 (SI 2008/1912) or the *Large and Medium-sized Limited Liability Partnerships (Accounts) Regulations* 2008 (SI 2008/1913). In accounting terms, though, LLPs have always been subject to the same standards as companies, though they have also had the LLP SORP available for additional guidance on LLP-specific areas.

Moving into new UK GAAP, matters are complicated for LLPs by certain delays in legislation. At present, an LLP cannot apply the micro-entities regime.

LLPs can, however, be qualifying entities for the purposes of being in the scope of FRS 101. This will only arise for LLPs with a corporate member, because of the need to have a parent that prepares consolidated financial statements, so is not relevant to, for instance, professional services firms where the partners are all individuals.

Unfortunately, for the small subset of LLPs which might consider applying FRS 101, there is no direct help available from the LLP SORP. This document, which was last updated in 2014, states explicitly that it only applies to LLPs reporting under FRS 102 or the 2015 FRSSE, and that it does not apply to LLPs complying with IFRS or FRS 101. This is a highly reasonable position for the CCAB, who issued the SORP, to take: extending it to cover accounting under IFRS standards as well as FRS 102 would be a substantial project with only limited beneficiaries, since many LLPs do not have a corporate member, so are ruled out from being qualifying entities. But it means that LLP preparers using FRS 101 are somewhat out on a limb. The hierarchy in IAS 8 does not make any allowance for local guidance such as SORPs, so there is no obvious scope for an LLP to cite the SORP as an authority for any interpreting it needs to do of IFRS standards. Having said this, though, the SORP is carefully written with detailed reference made to the accounting standards it complements. So a preparer seeking guidance on an LLP-specific issue which is not addressed within IFRS may well still be able to develop an accounting policy using the arguments of the SORP, in situations where the IFRS requirements are comparable to those in FRS 102, such that a new argument can be constructed simply by replacing the references to FRS 102 with references to the equivalent passages in IFRS.

5.2   Specifics within the standard

The early part of FRS 101, setting out the status of FRS 101 accounts, does not make direct references, however, the general point about preparing 'Companies Act accounts' rather than 'individual accounts' still holds. So as it says in para. 4A, 'a qualifying entity must ensure it complies with any legal requirements applicable to it', and although the standard goes on to give examples for a company, exactly the same principle holds for an LLP – it must comply with the LLP Act, FRS 101, and the relevant LLP Regulations, whether these are for large and medium-sized or small LLPs.

When it comes to a discussion of accounts formats, in the Application Guidance to the standard, the distinct formats in the LLP Regulations are explicitly acknowledged. But the most significant point on LLPs is in para. A2.21 in Appendix II *Note on legal requirements*. This paragraph was added by the 2015 amendments, and is reproduced here in full:

'Limited Liability Partnerships (LLPs) applying FRS 101 will be doing so in conjunction with the LLP Regulations. In many cases these Regulations are similar to the [comparable company] Regulations, limiting the situations in which legal matters relevant to the financial statements of LLPs are not addressed in this Appendix. However, amendments made to the Regulations by *The Companies, Partnerships and Groups (Accounts and Reports) Regulations 2015* (SI 2015/980) have not been reflected in the LLP Regulations. This gives rise to some differences for LLPs. Areas where this may have an impact include:

(a) the flexibility available in relation to the format of the balance sheet and of the profit and loss account;
(b) the scope of financial instruments that can be measured at fair value;
(c) the reversal of impairment losses in relation to goodwill; and
(d) the application of merger accounting.

If following the requirements of FRS 101 would lead to a conflict with applicable legislation, an LLP shall instead apply its own legal requirements and consider whether disclosure of a departure from FRS 101 is required.'

As can be seen, there are some fairly significant areas here where the FRS 101 requirement is in conflict with current legislation as it applies to LLPs. It seems clear that in these circumstances and through applying the passage above that it would be necessary to depart from FRS 101, not from the law, so disclosure of this would be needed. FRS 101 gives no further guidance on how this would be disclosed or in what level of detail, but we could look to the comparable guidance in FRS 102, where para. 3.4 requires that in the case of a departure from FRS 102 or from relevant legislation, the following disclosures are made:

(a) that management has concluded that the financial statements present fairly the entity's financial position, financial performance and cash flows;
(b) that it has complied with this FRS or applicable legislation, except that it has departed from a particular requirement of this FRS or applicable legislation to achieve a fair presentation; and
(c) the nature of the departure, including the treatment that this FRS or applicable legislation would require, the reason why that treatment would be so misleading in the circumstances that it would conflict with the objective of financial statements set out in s. 2, and the treatment adopted.

There is technically no requirement on FRS 101 preparers to make exactly these disclosures, but they seem to be a reasonable framework.

Example

X LLP records an impairment loss in its 2015 FRS 101 accounts but in 2016 the reasons for the impairment no longer exist and it is reversed. X might make the following disclosure:

The income statement for 2016 includes a £250,000 credit relating to the reversal of an impairment charge in the previous year [plus normal reversal disclosures per IAS 36] which includes £60,000 relating to goodwill. The LLP Regulations require that impairment losses are reversed when the reasons for the impairment cease to apply, regardless of the nature of the asset was impaired, but IAS 36, and hence FRS 101, prohibits the reversal of impairment losses relating to goodwill. In order to comply with UK law, the impairment loss has been reversed despite the prohibition in FRS 101.

5.3   A note on challenging areas

Although most LLP transactions are comparable with those undertaken by companies, there are a few areas of difficulty that LLPs will need to be aware of if they choose to move from old UK GAAP to an IFRS-based framework.

Members' capital and loans

The accounting for members' capital and loans will need careful inspection, in the first instance in determining whether these amounts represent financial liabilities or equity. The basic test to determine this distinction is the same in IAS 32 as in FRS 25, so it is to be hoped that the classification will not change on transition from old UK GAAP to FRS 101 but for balances classified as liabilities some work may well be needed. IFRS 9, the new financial instruments standard, is available for early adoption in the EU, but will not be mandatory for some years; alternatively LLPs applying FRS 101 for the first time can choose to use IAS 39 for recognition and measurement. Either way, financial liabilities will need to be reviewed to ensure that the amortised cost basis, which was almost certainly used for measurement under old UK GAAP, continues to be appropriate.

Members' remuneration

The treatment of remuneration to members as an expense or as drawings, effectively payments to equity holders, is closely linked to their classification as loans or capital. This is always a challenging area for LLPs, and the transition to any new accounting standard is a good opportunity for revisiting accounting policies and ensuring they are robust.

Pension promises

LLPs often have obligations in respect of members' pensions even after those members have retired. This is more complex than typical post-employment benefits because the members are not employees, so the arrangements would not usually be in the scope of IAS 19. Instead, the SORP tells FRS 102 preparers to assess whether these obligations fall under the scope of one of the following areas:

– FRS 103 *Insurance contracts*;
– FRS 102 section 11 *Basic Financial Instruments*;
– FRS 102 section 12 *Other financial instruments issues*;
– FRS 102 section 21 *Provisions and Contingencies*.

LLPs using FRS 101 need to perform a comparable exercise looking to the equivalent IFRS standards, namely IFRS 4 *Insurance contracts*, IAS 39 *Financial instruments: recognition and measurement* and IAS 37 *Provisions, contingent liabilities and contingent assets*. The scope sections in particular will need careful review, as the biggest challenge in this area is identifying the right set of requirements in the first place.

Merger accounting and group reconstructions

The SORP addresses issues arising where an LLP expands its membership in such a way that it constitutes a group reconstruction, as well as other more general issues on business combinations. It also looks at the original transition, by an existing undertaking, to being an LLP, stating that where a single-entity LLP is formed for the purpose of the transfer of existing undertakings or partnerships, this should be accounted for using merger accounting, providing the group reconstruction conditions are met. This cannot be applied by FRS 101 preparers because of the SORP's specific exclusion, and moreover the framework under IFRS is somewhat different from FRS 102 in this regard. Under IFRS, acquisition accounting must be used for all group reconstructions, so the outcome for an LLP using FRS 101 and undergoing this type of transaction could look very different from the outcome for a comparable LLP under FRS 102.

Chapter 6 FRS 101 and the law in the Republic of Ireland

6.1 Introduction

Although casual language often refers to 'new UK GAAP', the FRC's new framework actually has broader applicability, in that it applies not just to entities in the UK but also to those in the Republic of Ireland.

This chapter very briefly sets out considerations particular to RoI entities, since they operate under a different jurisdiction from the UK. In all other respects, the remainder of the publication is as relevant to RoI entities as it is to UK entities.

6.2 Irish legislation

Under UK law, the two pieces of legislation that are directly relevant to large and medium-sized company accounts are the *Companies Act* 2006 and the *Large and Medium-sized Companies and Groups (Accounts and Reports) Regulations* 2008. In Irish law, the number of pieces of legislation is much higher, including:

- the *Companies Act* 1963;
- the *Companies (Amendment) Act* 1986;
- the *Companies Act* 1990;
- the *Companies (Amendment) (No. 2) Act* 1999;
- the *European Communities (Companies: Group Accounts) Regulations* 1992 (SI 1992/201);
- the *European Communities (Credit Institutions: Accounts) Regulations* 1992 (SI 1992/294);
- the *European Communities (Insurance Undertakings: Accounts) Regulations* 1996 (SI 1996/23).

There is a blanket provision in place, mentioned in Appendix IV to FRS 101, stating that whenever general references are made within the standard to pieces of UK legislation such as the Act and the Regulations, readers looking for an Irish context should refer to the corresponding section in relevant Irish legislation. A detailed table is provided in the Appendix showing the relevant reference for each individual reference within the standard. The July 2015 amendments to FRS 101 delete Appendix IV with effect from 1 January 2016. This does not mean that there will no longer be any references to Irish law, merely that this law is expected to change soon in order to reflect the EU Accounting Directive (as UK law has already changed). So the FRC expects to issue a new version of Appendix IV in due course, and the old version still applies for 2015 year ends.

Even the terminology differs slightly, in that Irish parent companies are required by law to prepare either 'Companies Act accounts' or 'IFRS accounts' – in this case 'IFRS accounts' has the same meaning as 'IAS accounts' in UK law, so it is still the case that an Irish company using FRS 101 is not preparing IFRS accounts, but rather Companies Act accounts (in this case, referring to the Irish Acts).

To add another complication, not all companies in the Republic of Ireland are restricted to using FRC standards for their Companies Act accounts. Some parent companies are allowed to prepare their Companies Act individual accounts or group accounts in accordance with US GAAP, modified for consistency with Irish company law. Also, some investment companies can use 'an alternative body of accounting standards', being the GAAP of the United States, Canada or Japan.

So Irish companies need to look carefully to their own law before making a choice of financial reporting framework.

6.3   Small companies under Irish law

The small companies regime in UK law has no equivalent in Irish law. Small companies are defined in the *Companies (Amendment) Act* 1986, s. 8 but the exemptions granted for these companies are only in relation to the accounts they file with the Registrar, not to those they prepare for members.

This would make the small companies regime under FRS 102 effectively unavailable for Irish companies, as applying section 1A would not be sufficient to meet their relevant legal obligations.

6.4   Financial instruments

Section **4.4** above discusses the particular problems for UK companies in reconciling the measurement requirements of IFRS as they relate to financial instruments with the disclosures requirements of UK law. The key paragraph in UK law – Sch. 1, para. 36(4) to the Regulations – has its closest equivalents in para. 22AA of Part IIIA of the Schedule to the 1986 Act, and para. 46A(4A) and 46A(4B) of Part I of the Schedule. These paragraphs have broadly the same effect as those in UK law, though they still refer to international standards adopted as at 5 September 2006, so they are 'frozen' in time. This means that an Irish company using FRS 101 would have problems early-adopting IFRS 9 if this required any of its financial instruments to be held at fair value where this would not have been required under IAS 39.

Part III   Details

Chapter 7 How FRS 101 works

7.1 Accounting for transactions and year end balances – using IFRS

7.1.1 Overview

As discussed briefly in **2.2** above, FRS 101 requires preparers to base their accounts on EU-adopted IFRS. They are instructed to apply all the recognition, measurement and disclosure requirements of EU-adopted IFRS, with the following exceptions:

- amendments to certain aspects of some standards are needed to ensure compliance with UK law. These amendments are set out in the Application Guidance, and they apply to all qualifying entities using FRS 101, not just those that are companies. This principle of adjustment for legal compliance is discussed in much more detail in **Chapter 4** above, and the individual amendments are set out in the relevant chapters below;
- some detailed disclosures are not required. These are set out with precise reference to the paragraphs in IFRS that do not apply, in paragraphs 7A to 9 of the standard (some of these exemptions apply to all entities, and some only to those where equivalent disclosures are made in the group accounts); and
- there are exceptions to the exceptions, in that there are some cases where financial instruments disclosures are needed despite the general exemption from the requirements of IFRS 7.

7.1.2 Which version of IFRS?

Those familiar with the IFRS landscape will know that it is constantly shifting, with new standards being issued on a conveyor belt, and regular amendments to other standards throughout the year. Matters are further complicated by the sometimes very lengthy EU endorsement process. Before a standard counts as EU-adopted, it must first be issued by the IASB. The European Financial Reporting Advisory Group (EFRAG), then consider it, and issue endorsement advice which is then passed on to ARC, the Accounting Regulatory Committee, who will cause the advice to be approved and published in the Official Journal.

Some small amendments to IFRS standards are uncontroversial and pass through the EU endorsement process fairly rapidly, certainly before their effective dates. In other cases, however, there can be considerable debate and disagreement, which can delay the process. This might have one of several outcomes.

- The standard in question may be EU endorsed, but with the process taking so long that the 'EU effective date' is later than the IASB effective date in the original standard. This happened with the bundle of standards on consolidated accounts (IFRS 10, IFRS 11, IFRS 12 and the updated versions of IAS 27 and 28) which had IASB effective dates of 2013 but EU effective dates of 2014, because they were not officially adopted until the very end of 2012, so mandatory application from 1 January 2013 would have been unreasonable.
- The standard may be adopted, but with modifications for the EU. This is a rare outcome, with the famous example of the 'EU carve out' from IAS 39, which removed certain fair value options and meant there were two distinct versions of the standard, that applicable within the EU and that applicable everywhere else (this difference no longer exists).
- In theory, a standard could be never adopted. Some commentators believed that this would apply to IFRS 9, the IASB's relatively new financial instruments standard. There was considerable disquiet over some of the standard's contents, particularly when it came to impairments, and

the use of the 'expected loss' model. But this was eventually resolved and in September 2015 EFRAG issued positive endorsement advice; at the time of writing, formal EU endorsement is expected in early 2016.

Standards that are EU endorsed but not yet effective

Most IFRS standards allow early adoption, and once they have been EU endorsed this becomes a legitimate option for EU preparers, including those using FRS 101.

Standards that are not yet EU endorsed but have been issued by the IASB

In general, new standards in IFRS are re-addressing issues that were previously covered in a different standard, and as part of their issue the previous standard is withdrawn. One example is the new revenue standard, IFRS 15, which is effective from 2018 (and expected to be EU endorsed shortly) but replaces IAS 18 and IAS 11. Although IFRS 15 allows early adoption and will give very similar outcomes to the old standards for many entities, it would still not be acceptable for a preparer in the EU, including those using FRS 101, to adopt it early before it has been EU endorsed. This is because it gives rise to accounting changes that are not officially recognised as acceptable and that contradict or are inconsistent with requirements within standards that are still current.

Other guidance

IFRIC Interpretations provide guidance on points of detail that are not covered by IFRS standards, and have the same status, in that they must be complied with to claim overall IFRS compliance. And as with the full standards, each Interpretation needs to be endorsed, and can take some time.

It will often be easier, though, to early adopt an IFRIC Interpretation. This is because they tend to provide additional guidance on an area where there is no clear standard already in the guidance, and where the most appropriate accounting policy is not obvious from applying the hierarchy in IAS 8. Where this is the case, a preparer might find they apply the guidance in the Interpretation but stop short of claiming compliance with it, until it has been EU endorsed. This is because, again, a standard or an interpretation is not officially available for use by EU preparers until it has been endorsed. But there will usually be nothing within the content that would contradict anything in already-published material.

7.2   Disclosures – overlaying the FRS 101 exemptions

Once a preparer has generated its primary statements measured in accordance with EU-adopted IFRS subject to the FRS 101 adjustments, it next ensures that those primary statements are presented in one of the ways permitted within the standard – through a somewhat convoluted pathway set out in **4.3** above, this will involve using either the Companies Act formats or those set out in IAS 1.

After this, all that remains is to provide all the relevant disclosures. FRS 101 does not give a list of disclosure requirements, but rather a list of exemptions, so a preparer might be best to begin by assuming that all IFRS disclosures are required, then reviewing the detail in FRS 101 carefully to look for exemptions. In **Chapters 9 to 12** we look at each balance sheet and income statement area in detail and review the full IFRS disclosures, any accounting adjustments, any disclosure exemptions, and what the resulting note might look like.

The exercise of preparing an accounts template to comply with FRS 101 may be onerous in the first instance. Preparers determined to embark on this framework but lacking time in the year of transition could, of course, elect to risk over-disclosure, by producing a set of accounts which have all the IFRS disclosures in. It is unlikely that these would be viewed as in breach of FRS 101, since almost by definition they would include all of the disclosures it requires with more. Having said this, though, there is a risk of falling foul of the requirement to present only relevant information – the non-required disclosures might be viewed as clutter, damaging the user's ability to form a clear view of the reporting entity's position and performance.

To illustrate this point, we can look at an area such as financial instruments. IFRS 7 requires voluminous disclosures, none of which are required of FRS 101 preparers (except in limited circumstances to do with holding certain financial instruments at fair value, as discussed in **4.4** above). A preparer ignoring the exemption and giving some or all of the IFRS 7 disclosures might be filling pages with clutter, but might just as well be giving information that some view as critical. There is a set of commenters that disapprove strongly of any kind of fair value accounting, and even of amortised cost accounting in situations where this means a liability value on the balance sheet is less than the amount that will eventually be repaid. Without financial instruments notes, it can indeed be hard for a user to understand the full situation, but an IFRS 7 liquidity analysis that groups actual future cash flows into time buckets is much more readily comprehensible, and allows an at-a-glance view of the entity's immediate cash position, since financial assets are also required to be analysed in a note based on when the cash is to be realised.

It would be reasonable for an auditor to provide a gentle but firm challenge to an FRS 101 preparer who provides the full suite of IFRS 7 notes for a set of vanilla financial instruments. But it would be well within management's rights to argue the need for at least certain elements of these notes.

7.3   Keeping up with change

The FRC, in issuing a standard that gives precisely referenced disclosure exemptions, is facing something of a moving target, given the constantly shifting body of standards. Even in between the issue of FRED 47 – the Exposure Draft of the reduced disclosure framework – and the issue of the first version of the standard, the IASB issued *Annual Improvements to IFRS 2009-2011 cycle* which made various amendments to a range of standards. The FRC was able to respond to this by updating some disclosure exemptions, and the Accounting Council's Advice to the FRC includes a recommendation 'to update FRS 101 at regular intervals, to ensure the disclosure framework maintains consistency with EU-adopted IFRS'.

There will inevitably be time lags, though, where an FRS 101 preparer will have a new or amended standard available, or even mandatory, and although this new standard or amendment comes with extra disclosure requirements, the FRC has not yet issued any exemptions. Unfortunately, there is no way round this, so even if the new disclosures are onerous, they must be provided. This serves as a reminder that FRS 101 is a subtracting standard not an adding one – the default is to apply everything in IFRS, unless there is explicit written permission in FRS 101 not to do this. It may provide a good reason to delay adoption of new standards for as long as possible to give the FRC time to update FRS 101 in respect of them.

7.4   Transition to FRS 101

Since FRS 101 preparers are basing their recognition and measurement on EU-adopted IFRS, transition to the standard is dealt with through IFRS 1. There are very few modifications that FRS 101 preparers need to make, so in general they will follow the instructions of IFRS 1 set out below.

Interestingly, FRS 101 exempts preparers from paragraphs 6 to 21 of IFRS 1, which require the preparation and presentation respectively of an opening statement of financial position as at the date of transition. The presentation exemption is useful but the preparation one has less value, since FRS 101 preparers will still need to perform all the relevant work to ensure their opening (and hence subsequent) assets and liabilities are measured correctly. So the list below still includes this requirement because it is a necessary starting point.

- Prepare an opening IFRS statement of financial position at the date of transition (the beginning of the earliest period presented), using IFRS accounting policies that are based on the standards effective at the end of the first reporting period (so, for an entity preparing its first IFRS accounts to December 2015, the standards used for all periods reported would be those effective for 2015 year ends, and the transition balance sheet would be prepared at 1 January 2014).

- In the opening statement of financial position:
  - recognise all assets and liabilities whose recognition is required by IFRSs;
  - not recognise items as assets or liabilities if IFRSs do not permit such recognition;
  - reclassify items that were recognised in accordance with previous GAAP as one type of asset, liability or component of equity, but are a different type of asset, liability or component of equity in accordance with IFRSs; and
  - apply IFRSs in measuring all recognised assets and liabilities [IFRS 1.10].
- Apply certain compulsory exceptions (i.e. areas where IFRS 1 prohibits retrospective application of some aspects of other standards). These relate to:
  - estimates;
  - de-recognition of financial assets and financial liabilities;
  - hedge accounting;
  - non-controlling interests;
  - classification and measurement of financial assets;
  - embedded derivatives; and
  - government loans.
- Choose any number of the voluntary exemptions from Appendices C to E of IFRS 1. These cover a wide range of areas:
  - business combinations;
  - share-based payments;
  - insurance contracts;
  - deemed cost;
  - leases;
  - cumulative translation differences;
  - investments in subsidiaries, jointly controlled entities and associates;
  - assets and liabilities of subsidiaries, associates and joint ventures;
  - compound financial instruments;
  - designation of previously recognised financial instruments;
  - fair value measurement of financial assets or financial liabilities at initial recognition;
  - decommissioning liabilities included in the cost of property, plant and equipment;
  - financial assets or intangible assets accounted for in accordance with IFRIC 12;
  - borrowing costs;
  - transfers of assets from customers;
  - extinguishing financial liabilities with equity instruments;
  - severe hyperinflation;
  - joint arrangements; and
  - stripping costs in the production phase of a surface mine.
- Provide an explanation of transition to IFRSs, through a reconciliation of previously reported equity to equity reported in accordance with IFRS for both the transition date and the last balance sheet reported under old GAAP. There must also be a reconciliation of total comprehensive income last reported under old GAAP and the amount now shown as a comparative under IFRS.

The only amendments that FRS 101 makes to the basic procedures and the exemptions in IFRS 1, other than the 'third balance sheet' exemption above, relate to when a subsidiary becomes a first-time adopter later than its parent, or a parent later than its subsidiary. Even then, the changes are not significant. They clarify that:

- when a subsidiary adopts later than its parent, the subsidiary measures its assets and liabilities at either the carrying amounts that would be included in the parent's group accounts based on the parent's transition date, or at the carrying amounts required by IFRS 1, based on the subsidiary's own transition date. Either way, the amendment says, measurement must be in accordance with FRS 101 (in other words, the accounting adjustments from the rest of the Application Guidance must also be taken account of); and

- when a parent adopts later than its subsidiary, the parent's first consolidated accounts measure the subsidiary's assets and liabilities at the same amounts as in the subsidiary's financial statements (so the subsidiary does not have the parent's transition date imposed on them and IFRS 1 're-applied'). Again, AG1 to FRS 101 adds the condition that 'a qualifying entity that applies this provision must ensure that its assets and liabilities are measured in compliance with FRS 101'.

Chapter 8 The special cases of financial institutions and investment entities

8.1 Definition of a financial institution

Although most types of entity are treated entirely equally under FRS 101, we have seen some modifications for LLPs, and financial institutions need special provisions too. This is so that users can have access to disclosures and accounting treatments that reflect the risks in such entities around managing financial instruments.

A financial institution is defined in the glossary as:

'Any of the following:

(a) A bank which is:
    (i) A firm with a Part IV permission which includes accepting deposits and:
        (a) Which is a credit institution; or
        (b) Whose Part IV permission includes a requirement that it complies with the rules in the General Prudential sourcebook and the Prudential sourcebook for Banks, Building Societies and Investment Firms relating to banks, but which is not a building society, a friendly society or a credit union;
    (ii) An EEA bank which is a full credit institution;
(b) A building society which is defined in section 119(1) of the Building Societies Act 1986 as a building society incorporated (or deemed to be incorporated) under that act;
(c) A credit union, being a body corporate registered under the Industrial and Provident Societies Act 1965 as a credit union in accordance with the Credit Unions Act 1979, which is an authorised person;
(d) Custodian bank, broker-dealer or stockbroker;
(e) An entity that undertakes the business of effecting or carrying out insurance contracts, including general and life assurance entities;
(f) An incorporated friendly society incorporated under the Friendly Societies Act 1992 or a registered friendly society registered under section 7(1)(a) of the Friendly Societies Act 1974 or any enactment which it replaced, including any registered branches;
(g) An investment trust, Irish Investment Company, venture capital trust, mutual fund, exchange traded fund, unit trust, open-ended investment company (OEIC);
(h) A retirement benefit plan; or
(i) Any other entity whose principal activity is to generate wealth or manage risk through financial instruments. This is intended to cover entities that have business activities similar to those listed above but are not specifically included in the list above.

A parent entity whose sole activity is to hold investments in other group entities is not a financial institution.'

As we can see from this list, the definition captures quite a range of entities, but the broad common theme is that they have responsibility for the funds of others. There is a considerable overlap between this definition and that used in the IFRS for SMEs when it refers to entities that hold assets 'in a fiduciary capacity for a broad group of outsiders' (and prohibits them from using the standard). Looking briefly at the history of new UK GAAP, the FRC worked hard on the thorny issue of what to do with this kind of entity. Originally, the proposal was just to exclude them from using the main new standard (now FRS 102) which would have left them with no choice but to apply full IFRS. While some argued this was reasonable given the heightened risk of their activities, others argued it was disproportionate since some entities in this position are very small and local in their activities.

This last point was particularly relevant for the many small credit unions and some small building societies, that had great concern about having to produce massive, detailed financial statements despite having very modest activities.

To be clear, most large banks and other financial institutions are also listed, so will need to apply full IFRS in their group accounts. Other financial institutions as per this definition (which is the same as that used in FRS 102) have two options: they can use FRS 102 or FRS 101 (assuming, of course, that the other conditions are met too). In either case, though, they will need to use full financial instruments accounting (e.g. holding derivatives at fair value, recognising financial asset impairments based on objective evidence, and so on) and will not be able to take most financial instruments disclosure exemptions. In FRS 102, a financial institution which is also a subsidiary or parent (and hence a 'qualifying entity' for that standard) can take the disclosure exemptions available in there, except it must still provide full section 11 and 12 disclosures. If this mixed approach is not appealing, its alternative is to choose to apply the provisions of IAS 39 or IFRS 9, with IFRS 7 disclosures.

The definition of a financial institution is broad, and will capture entities that may not previously have needed any special treatment. Despite the lengthy definition, though, and the catch-all clause in sub-para (i), the definition is still not entirely objective. There is a grey area, for instance, around the treatment of treasury companies that might work within a group to be the borrower and lender for the whole group. If they have an active management role in the choice of financing inwards and the determination of terms of intragroup loans then they would seem to meet the financial institution definition, but they might have an entirely passive role, with finance just passing through. In this latter case there would be an interesting discussion to have in order to assess whether this intermediate company is truly generating wealth or managing risk through financial instruments.

8.2   Special provisions for financial institutions

FRS 101 has a similar approach to FRS 102, in that financial institutions are allowed to apply the standard and use reduced disclosures, apart from when it comes to financial instruments.

So para. 7 states that a qualifying entity which is a financial institution may take all of the disclosure exemptions except:

- it must provide all of the disclosures required by IFRS 7 *Financial Instruments: Disclosures*;
- it must provide all of the disclosures required by IFRS 13 *Fair Value Measurement* insofar as they relate to financial instruments; and
- it must provide the disclosures from paras. 134 to 136 of IAS 1 *Presentation of Financial Statements*. These relate to the entity's objectives, policies and processes for managing capital and include both qualitative and quantitative disclosures.

In practice, of course this means that smaller financial institutions will still face a more onerous disclosure burden than they previously would have suffered under UK GAAP, along with more rigorous accounting requirements. But taking the option to apply FRS 101 rather than going into full EU-adopted IFRS does mean that the remainder of the disclosures can be more proportional to the entity's size, and that the accounts preparation effort can be focused on the risk areas, which are the financial assets held and liabilities owed.

8.3   Definition of an investment entity

Investment entities are another slightly distinct type of entity that need slightly different treatment, although this does not manifest in different disclosures, but rather in a slight restriction on accounting options.

An investment entity is defined in IFRS 10 as:

'An entity that:

(a) Obtains funds from one or more investors for the purpose of providing those investor(s) with investment management services;

(b) Commits to its investor(s) that its business purpose is to invest funds solely for returns from capital appreciation, investment income, or both; and

(c) Measures and evaluates the performance of substantially all of its investments on a fair value basis.'

The definition is reasonably self-explanatory and most entities will already know whether they meet it, or will be able to discern this readily from reading the definition.

8.4 Special provisions for investment entities

Paragraph A2.17 of Appendix II on legal requirements points out that FRS 101 does not apply to consolidated financial statements. But if an entity meets the definition of an investment entity, then para. 31 of IFRS 10 requires it to measure its investments in subsidiaries at fair value through profit or loss in its group accounts, and then para. 11A of IAS 27 requires this treatment to be carried through into the separate financial statements.

The Appendix then goes on to state that the Regulations normally permit a choice of three measurement bases for investments in subsidiaries: historical cost, fair value with movements in reserves (based on the 'alternative accounting rules') or fair value with movements in profit or loss (based on the fair value accounting rules). So the special requirement for investment entities just limits their choices so they are not permitted to choose either of the first two options.

The sting in the tail is that when an investment entity follows this IAS 27 rule and measures its investments in subsidiaries at fair value in its individual Companies Act accounts, it is able to do this only because of Sch. 1, para. 36(4) to the Regulations. So, as discussed in **4.4** above, this means it will have to provide a number of disclosures from IFRS 7 relating to financial instruments held at fair value.

Chapter 9 General points and financial statement presentation

9.1 Primary statements

As discussed in **4.3** above, FRS 101 preparers are in an interesting position when it comes to the primary statements in their accounts.

The key components of IFRS financial statements are set out in IAS 1 para. 10:

(a) a statement of financial position as at the end of the period;
(b) a statement of profit or loss and other comprehensive income for the period;
(c) a statement of changes in equity for the period;
(d) a statement of cash flows for the period;
(e) notes, comprising a summary of significant accounting policies and other explanatory information;
(ea) comparative information in respect of the preceding period as specified in paragraphs 38 and 38A; and
(f) a statement of financial position as at the beginning of the preceding period when an entity applies an accounting policy retrospectively or makes a retrospective restatement of items in itsfinancial statements, or when it reclassifies items in its financial statements in accordance with paragraphs 40A–40D.

Other titles may be used.

Through the convoluted interaction between UK law and IFRS, in practice FRS 101 preparers have two basic options for their statement of financial position format and that of the statement of profit or loss and other comprehensive income – and it may choose to call these the balance sheet and the profit and loss account, though this latter name could be misleading if other comprehensive income is also included. They can either use the IAS 1 formats or the formats from the Regulations. This is discussed in depth in **4.3**, and preparers anticipating choosing the formats from the Regulations can see these in **Appendix 2**.

Either way, FRS 101 preparers are also exempt from presenting a cash flow statement (paragraph 10(d)) and from paragraph 10(f), and in some cases are excused from presenting comparatives too, so the revised list of required contents is as follows:

- a statement of financial position, or balance sheet, using IAS 1 formats or Regulations formats;
- a statement of profit or loss and other comprehensive income, using IAS 1 formats or Regulations formats;
- a statement of changes in equity;
- notes, comprising a summary of significant accounting policies and other explanatory information; and
- comparative information in respect of the preceding period, with exceptions for property, plant and equipment, intangible assets, investment property, and agricultural produce and biological assets.

The 'third balance sheet' exemption does not just apply when an entity transitions to FRS 101 (discussed in **7.4** above) but more broadly. IAS 1 requires IFRS preparers to present a third balance sheet in most situations where comparatives have been restated (for instance relating to a change in accounting policy) but FRS 101 preparers are always exempt from this.

The IAS 1 formats for the three remaining primary statements are reproduced below. It is worth noting that the line between presentation and disclosure is particularly blurred when it comes to IAS 1, so preparers should review the standard carefully to ensure that any recognition, measurement or presentation requirements are also assessed for their effects on disclosures.

Statement of financial position – minimum line items (IAS 1 para. 54)

(a)   property, plant and equipment;
(b)   investment property;
(c)   intangible assets;
(d)   financial assets (excluding amounts shown under (e), (h) and (i));
(e)   investments accounted for using the equity method;
(f)   biological assets;
(g)   inventories;
(h)   trade and other receivables;
(i)   cash and cash equivalents;
(j)   the total of assets classified as held for sale and assets included in disposal groups classified as held for sale in accordance with **IFRS 5 *Non-current Assets Held for Sale and Discontinued Operations***;
(k)   trade and other payables;
(l)   provisions;
(m)   financial liabilities (excluding amounts shown under (k) and (l));
(n)   liabilities and assets for current tax, as defined in IAS 12 *Income Taxes*;
(o)   deferred tax liabilities and deferred tax assets, as defined in IAS 12;
(p)   liabilities included in disposal groups classified as held for sale in accordance with IFRS 5;
(q)   non-controlling interests, presented within equity; and
(r)   issued capital and reserves attributable to owners of the parent.

Minimum line items in the statement of profit or loss and other comprehensive income

Preparers have a choice between presenting one statement that combines profit or loss and other comprehensive income, or splitting these into two statements. The required line items do not change between the two.

Profit or loss items (IAS 1 para. 82)

(a)   revenue;
(b)   finance costs;
(c)   share of the profit or loss of associates and joint ventures accounted for using the equity method;
(d)   tax expense; and
(ea) a single amount for the total of discontinued operations (see IFRS 5). [This is also discussed in **9.2** below, as it presents issues for 'Companies Act accounts'.]

Other comprehensive income items (IAS 1 para. 81A and 82)

(a)   profit or loss;
(b)   total other comprehensive income; and
(c)   comprehensive income for the period, being the total of profit or loss and other comprehensive income.

If an entity presents a separate statement of profit or loss, it does not present the profit or loss section in the statement presenting comprehensive income.

The other comprehensive income section shall present line items for amounts of other comprehensive income in the period, classified by nature (including share of the other comprehensive income of associates and joint ventures accounted for using the equity method) and grouped into those that, in accordance with other IFRSs:

(i)   will not be reclassified subsequently to profit or loss; and
(ii) will be reclassified subsequently to profit or loss when specific conditions are met.

Allocation of profit or loss and other comprehensive income (IAS 1 para. 81B)

An entity shall present the following items, in addition to the profit or loss and other comprehensive income sections, as allocation of profit or loss and other comprehensive income for the period:

(a) profit or loss for the period attributable to:
     (i)   non-controlling interests;
     (ii) owners of the parent;
(b) comprehensive income for the period attributable to:
     (i)   non-controlling interests;
     (ii) owners of the parent.

If an entity presents profit or loss in a separate statement it shall present (a) in that statement.

Statement of changes in equity (IAS 1 para. 106, 106A, 107)

An entity shall present a statement of changes in equity as required by paragraph 10. The statement of changes in equity includes the following information showing in the statement:

(a) total comprehensive income for the period, showing separately the total amounts attributable to owners of the parent and to non-controlling interests [note this latter part is not relevant for FRS 101 preparers since non-controlling interests appear only in consolidated accounts];
(b) for each component of equity, the effects of retrospective application or retrospective restatement recognised in accordance with IAS 8; and
(c) [deleted]
(d) for each component of equity, a reconciliation between the carrying amount at the beginning and the end of the period, separately disclosing changes resulting from:
     (i)   profit or loss;
     (ii)   other comprehensive income; and
     (iii) transactions with owners in their capacity as owners, showing separately contributions by and distributions to owners and changes in ownership interests in subsidiaries that do not result in a loss of control.

For each component of equity an entity shall present, either in the statement of changes in equity or in the notes, an analysis of other comprehensive income by item (see para. 106(d)(ii)).

An entity shall present, either in the statement of changes in equity or in the notes, the amount of dividends recognised as distributions to owners during the period, and the related amount of dividends per share.

9.2   Discontinued operations and disposal groups

IFRS 5 *Non-current assets held for sale and discontinued operations* presents some new challenges to those familiar with old UK GAAP. It starts with the concept of non-current assets and disposal groups held for sale, which applies when their carrying amount is expected to be 'recovered principally through a sale transaction rather than through continuing use'. The relevant assets or groups of assets are measured at the lower of their previous carrying amount and their fair value less costs to sell, when the classification is first triggered. The aggregate values of the assets and liabilities are then each shown as a line item in the statement of financial position.

The definition of discontinued operations follows from this: a discontinued operation is a component of an entity that has either been disposed of or is classified as held for sale (with limits placed on how a component is defined and how significant it needs to be). Though this is similar to the FRS 3 discontinued operation, it is broader in scope since FRS 3 requires a disposal to be completed within three months of the year end for a component to be treated as discontinued, whereas under IFRS (and hence FRS 101) the conditions are wider:

- the asset or disposal group must be available for immediate sale in its present condition subject only to usual terms; and
- the sale must be highly probable, meaning the appropriate level of management are committed to a plan to sell it, and there must be in place an active programme to locate a buyer and complete the plan. The asset or disposal group must also be actively marketed for sale.

Assuming those conditions are met, FRS 101 preparers must comply with most of the disclosure requirements in IFRS 5. The only exception is for the requirement in para. 33(c) to disclose separately net cash flows from discontinuing operations – this is reasonable since FRS 101 preparers need not present a cash flow statement at all.

There is also a complication arising from the interaction between the standard and the law. Schedule 1 of the Regulations requires in para. 6 that 'every profit and loss account must show the amount of a company's profit or loss on ordinary activities before taxation'. The IAS 1 income statement format, which is one of the available options for FRS 101 preparers as we saw in **Chapter 4** above, has discontinued operations presented separately a long way down the income statement, with a single line item required on the face of the income statement and a more detailed analysis which may be included in the notes or on the face of the income statement. This presentation would not give a total for profit before tax for the year, since the line for continuing operations is drawn before the single discontinued items 'post-tax profit' line. After much reflection, the FRC concluded that the best way to deal with this was through a columnar format, so para. AG1(g) amends IFRS 5 para. 33 so that the choice to present split analysis in the notes is removed, with a statement that:

> 'The analysis shall be presented in the statement of comprehensive income in a column identified as relating to discontinued operations, i.e. separately from continuing operations; a total column shall also be presented.'

This presentation is illustrated in the example accounts included as **Appendix 1** to this publication.

The other disclosure requirements are reproduced below.

An entity shall disclose:

(a) a single amount in the statement of comprehensive income comprising the total of:
  (i) the post-tax profit or loss of discontinued operations; and
  (ii) the post-tax gain or loss recognised on the measurement to fair value less costs to sell or on the disposal of the assets or disposal group(s) constituting the discontinued operation;
(b) an analysis of the single amount in (a) into:
  (i) the revenue, expenses and pre-tax profit or loss of discontinued operations;
  (ii) the related income tax expense as required by paragraph 81(h) of IAS 12;
  (iii) the gain or loss recognised on the measurement to fair value less costs to sell or on the disposal of the assets or disposal group(s) constituting the discontinued operation; and
  (iv) the related income tax expense as required by paragraph 81(h) of IAS 12.

The analysis may be presented in the notes or in the statement of comprehensive income. If it is presented in the statement of comprehensive income it shall be presented in a section identified as relating to discontinued operations, i.e. separately from continuing operations. The analysis is not required for disposal groups that are newly acquired subsidiaries that meet the criteria to be classified as held for sale on acquisition (see paragraph 11).

(d) the amount of income from continuing operations and from discontinued operations attributable to owners of the parent. These disclosures may be presented either in the notes or in the statement of comprehensive income.

[IFRS 5 para. 33, with 33(c) removed]

If an entity presents the items of profit or loss in a separate statement as described in paragraph 10A of IAS 1 (as amended in 2011), a section identified as relating to discontinued operations is presented in that statement.

[IFRS 5 para. 33A, unamended]

An entity shall re-present the disclosures in paragraph 33 for prior periods presented in the financial statements so that the disclosures relate to all operations that have been discontinued by the end of the reporting period for the latest period presented.

[IFRS 5 para. 34, unamended]

Adjustments in the current period to amounts previously presented in discontinued operations that are directly related to the disposal of a discontinued operation in a prior period shall be classified separately in discontinued operations. The nature and amount of such adjustments shall be disclosed. Examples of circumstances in which these adjustments may arise include the following:

(a) the resolution of uncertainties that arise from the terms of the disposal transaction, such as the resolution of purchase price adjustments and indemnification issues with the purchaser;
(b) the resolution of uncertainties that arise from and are directly related to the operations of the component before its disposal, such as environmental and product warranty obligations retained by the seller; and
(c) the settlement of employee benefit plan obligations, provided that the settlement is directly related to the disposal transaction.

[IFRS 5 para. 35, unamended]

If an entity ceases to classify a component of an entity as held for sale, the results of operations of the component previously presented in discontinued operations in accordance with paragraphs 33–35 shall be reclassified and included in income from continuing operations for all periods presented. The amounts for prior periods shall be described as having been re-presented.

[IFRS 5 para. 36, unamended]

An entity that is committed to a sale plan involving loss of control of a subsidiary shall disclose the information required in para. 33–36 when the subsidiary is a disposal group that meets the definition of a discontinued operation in accordance with paragraph 32.

[IFRS 5 para. 36A, unamended – note this will not apply to FRS 101 preparers since FRS 101 cannot be applied in consolidated accounts]

An entity shall disclose the following information in the notes in the period in which a non-current asset (or disposal group) has been either classified as held for sale or sold:

(a) a description of the non-current asset (or disposal group);
(b) a description of the facts and circumstances of the sale, or leading to the expected disposal, and the expected manner and timing of that disposal;
(c) the gain or loss recognised in accordance with para. 20–22 and, if not separately presented in the statement of comprehensive income, the caption in the statement of comprehensive income that includes that gain or loss; and
(d) if applicable, the reportable segment in which the non-current asset (or disposal group) is presented in accordance with IFRS 8 *Operating Segments*.

[IFRS 5 para. 41, unamended]

If either para. 26 or 29 applies, an entity shall disclose, in the period of the decision to change the plan to sell the non-current asset (or disposal group), a description of the facts and circumstances leading to the decision and the effect of the decision on the results of operations for the period and any prior periods presented.

[IFRS 5 para. 42, unamended]

9.3   Transition to FRS 101

The accounting requirements in respect of transition to FRS 101, which is mostly in accordance with IFRS 1, are discussed in **7.4** above, as are the exemptions relating to entities within groups. The key points are that an opening (transition date) balance sheet needs to be prepared, but need not be included in the accounts, and that reconciliations from old GAAP to FRS 101 are needed for equity at the last balance sheet date and the opening balance sheet date, and for the last period's profit. For completeness, the required disclosures are reproduced here.

An entity shall explain how the transition from previous GAAP to IFRSs affected its reported financial position, financial performance and cash flows.

[IFRS 1 para. 23, unamended – note it is reasonable to assume that in this and following paragraphs references to 'IFRS' should be read for these purposes as references to 'FRS 101'.]

An entity that has applied IFRSs in a previous period, as described in paragraph 4A, shall disclose:

(a)   the reason it stopped applying IFRSs; and
(b)   the reason it is resuming the application of IFRSs.

[IFRS 1 para. 23A, unamended]

23B When an entity, in accordance with paragraph 4A, does not elect to apply IFRS 1, the entity shall explain the reasons for electing to apply IFRSs as if it had never stopped applying IFRSs.

[IFRS 1 para. 23B, unamended]

Reconciliations

To comply with para. 23, an entity's first IFRS financial statements shall include:

(a)   reconciliations of its equity reported in accordance with previous GAAP to its equity in accordance with IFRSs for both of the following dates:
    (i)   the date of transition to IFRSs; and
    (ii)   the end of the latest period presented in the entity's most recent annual financial statements in accordance with previous GAAP;
(b)   a reconciliation to its total comprehensive income in accordance with IFRSs for the latest period in the entity's most recent annual financial statements. The starting point for that reconciliation shall be total comprehensive income in accordance with previous GAAP for the same period or, if an entity did not report such a total, profit or loss under previous GAAP; and
(c)   if the entity recognised or reversed any impairment losses for the first time in preparing its opening IFRS statement of financial position, the disclosures that IAS 36 Impairment of Assets would have required if the entity had recognised those impairment losses or reversals in the period beginning with the date of transition to IFRSs.

[IFRS 1 para. 24, unamended]

The reconciliations required by para. 24(a) and (b) shall give sufficient detail to enable users to understand the material adjustments to the statement of financial position and statement of comprehensive income. If an entity presented a statement of cash flows under its previous GAAP, it shall also explain the material adjustments to the statement of cash flows.

[IFRS 1 para. 25, unamended]

If an entity becomes aware of errors made under previous GAAP, the reconciliations required by para. 24(a) and (b) shall distinguish the correction of those errors from changes in accounting policies.

[IFRS 1 para. 26, unamended]

IAS 8 does not apply to the changes in accounting policies an entity makes when it adopts IFRSs or to changes in those policies until after it presents its first IFRS financial statements. Therefore, IAS 8's requirements for disclosures about changes in accounting policies do not apply in an entity's first IFRS financial statements.

[IFRS 1 para. 27, unamended]

If during the period covered by its first IFRS financial statements an entity changes its accounting policies or its use of the exemptions contained in this IFRS, it shall explain the changes between its first IFRS interim financial report and its first IFRS financial statements, in accordance with paragraph 23, and it shall update the reconciliations required by para. 24(a) and (b).

[IFRS 1 para. 27A, unamended]

If an entity did not present financial statements for previous periods, its first IFRS financial statements shall disclose that fact.

[IFRS 1 para. 28, unamended]

Designation of financial assets or financial liabilities

An entity is permitted to designate a previously recognised financial asset or financial liability as a financial asset or financial liability at fair value through profit or loss or a financial asset as available for sale in accordance with paragraph D19. The entity shall disclose the fair value of financial assets or financial liabilities designated into each category at the date of designation and their classification and carrying amount in the previous financial statements.

[IFRS 1 para. 29, unamended]

Use of fair value as deemed cost

If an entity uses fair value in its opening IFRS statement of financial position as deemed cost for an item of property, plant and equipment, an investment property or an intangible asset (see para. D5 and D7), the entity's first IFRS financial statements shall disclose, for each line item in the opening IFRS statement of financial position:

(a) the aggregate of those fair values; and
(b) the aggregate adjustment to the carrying amounts reported under previous GAAP.

[IFRS 1 para. 30, unamended]

Use of deemed cost for investments in subsidiaries, jointly controlled entities and associates

31 Similarly, if an entity uses a deemed cost in its opening IFRS statement of financial position for an investment in a subsidiary, jointly controlled entity or associate in its separate financial statements (see para. D15), the entity's first IFRS separate financial statements shall disclose:

(a) the aggregate deemed cost of those investments for which deemed cost is their previous GAAP carrying amount;

(b) the aggregate deemed cost of those investments for which deemed cost is fair value; and

(c) the aggregate adjustment to the carrying amounts reported under previous GAAP.

[IFRS 1 para. 31, unamended]

Use of deemed cost for oil and gas assets

If an entity uses the exemption in para. D8A(b) for oil and gas assets, it shall disclose that fact and the basis on which carrying amounts determined under previous GAAP were allocated.

[IFRS 1 para. 31A, unamended]

Use of deemed cost for operations subject to rate regulation

If an entity uses the exemption in para. D8B for operations subject to rate regulation, it shall disclose that fact and the basis on which carrying amounts were determined under previous GAAP.

[IFRS 1 para. 31B, unamended]

Use of deemed cost after severe hyperinflation

If an entity elects to measure assets and liabilities at fair value and to use that fair value as the deemed cost in its opening IFRS statement of financial position because of severe hyperinflation (see para. D26–D30), the entity's first IFRS financial statements shall disclose an explanation of how, and why, the entity had, and then ceased to have, a functional currency that has both of the following characteristics:

(a) a reliable general price index is not available to all entities with transactions and balances in the currency; and

(b) exchangeability between the currency and a relatively stable foreign currency does not exist.

[IFRS 1 para. 31C, unamended]

Chapter 10   Assets and liabilities

10.1   Groups and business combinations

10.1.1   Relevant standards under IFRS

The relevant standards and interpretations under IFRS are:

- IAS 27 *Separate Financial Statements*;
- IAS 28 *Investments in Associates and Joint Ventures*;
- IFRS 3 *Business Combinations*;
- IFRS 10 *Consolidated Financial Statements*;
- IFRS 11 *Joint Arrangements*;
- IFRS 12 *Disclosures of interests in other entities*.

10.1.2   Overview of accounting differences between IFRS-based FRS 101 and old UK GAAP

The list of relevant standards above is included only for completeness. FRS 101 cannot be applied in group accounts, so the required steps for preparing consolidated accounts will never be relevant here, and the accounting for business combinations will be uncommon. Most business combinations involve separate legal entities, so they result in one owner that prepares consolidated accounts, which is where purchased goodwill, non-controlling interests, etc. would be recognised. However, for an entity acquiring a business in the form of trade and assets, IFRS 3 accounting and disclosures will still, in the main, and subject to the exemptions discussed below, be relevant.

For most FRS 101 accounts, the relevant accounting and disclosure requirements are those relating to the recording of investments in subsidiaries, associates and joint ventures in separate or individual financial statements. IFRS 3 also includes some requirements in relation to business combinations even in a parent's company-only accounts, so these are relevant too.

10.1.3   Exemptions given by FRS 101

FRS 101 para. 8(b) exempts qualifying entities from the requirements of IFRS 3 para. 62, B64(d), B64(e), B64(g), B64(h), B64(j) to (m), B64(n)(ii), B64(o)(ii), B64(p), B64(q)(ii), B66 and B67 of IFRS 3, providing that equivalent disclosures are included in the consolidated financial statements of the group in which the entity is consolidated.

This is a slightly odd set of exemptions in that it removes some of the detail required to be given about a business combination, but leaves other details in. So an FRS 101 preparer must still give the name and description of the acquiree, the acquisition date and percentage of voting equity interests acquired, but need not disclose the reasons for the business combination or any qualitative comments with respect to goodwill (presumably because this would only appear in group accounts). It must comply with B64(f) specifying the acquisition date fair value of the total consideration, sorted by major class of consideration, but needs make no disclosures about contingent consideration disclosures. For assets and liabilities acquired, the exemptions cover much of the detail that IFRS 3 requires, for instance on acquired receivables, goodwill expected to be deductible for tax purposes, and transactions recognised separately from the business combination: all that really remains is the requirement in B64(i) to disclose 'the amounts recognised as of the acquisition date for each major class of assets acquired and liabilities assumed'.

Where a gain is recognised from a bargain purchase (more familiar to UK preparers as negative goodwill), FRS 101 preparers still need to disclose the gain but need not give a description of why the transaction resulted in a gain. When the acquisition is of less than 100% of an acquiree, again basic information is needed about the non-controlling interest, but valuation techniques and significant inputs need not be specified.

There is a blanket exemption from the requirements with respect to business combinations achieved in stages.

While the requirement from B64(q)(i) remains, to disclose the amounts of revenue and profit or loss of the acquiree since the acquisition date included in the consolidated statement of comprehensive income, the second part of that para is subject to the exemption, so it is not necessary to disclose the revenue and profit or loss of the combined entity as though the acquisition date had been as at the beginning of the period. This is an odd pair of decisions, since as already noted FRS 101 cannot be applied in consolidated accounts, so it is not at all clear what information could be given to satisfy B64(q)(i).

Finally, the exemptions from B66 and B67 cover all the IFRS 3 disclosures in relation to business combinations that took place after the balance sheet date but before the financial statements were authorised and in relation to details of incomplete initial accounting for business combinations and subsequent accounting for contingent consideration assets or liabilities.

There are no exemptions from the disclosure requirements relating to investments in associates and joint ventures.

The outcome here may be surprising in that even though swathes of disclosures have been removed, there are still a good number of disclosures needed even in FRS 101 individual accounts. So an FRS 101 preparer that is an intermediate parent cannot leave the details to its own parent if it acquires a business in the year, as it still needs to disclose considerable amounts itself. Moreover, it could be the case that from the perspective of the parent preparing group accounts, the business combination is not material, so details would not be disclosed. In this case, equivalent disclosures are not in the group accounts so the FRS 101 exemption would not be available.

The biggest difference from a set of full IFRS consolidated accounts is that FRS 101 preparers are, by definition, presenting only separate financial statements rather than consolidated financial statements. This means that they are subject to the modest disclosure requirements of IAS 27 rather than the highly detailed voluminous requirements of IFRS 12. The only entities that will still need to look to IFRS 12 are investment entities, which need to look to para. 9A and 9B as well as 19A–19G.

10.1.4   *Accounting amendments arising from the law*

There is one relevant accounting amendment identified in the Application Guidance to FRS 101: para. AG1(f) states that:

> 'Without amending paragraph B63(a) of IFRS 3 *Business Combinations*, its requirement shall be read in conjunction with paragraph A2.8 of this standard.'

To make sense of this, the relevant paragraph of IFRS 3 refers to the guidance in IAS 38 for accounting for identifiable intangible assets acquired in a business combination and the guidance in IAS 36 relating to impairment.

Paragraph A2.8 of FRS 101, in the appendix on legal requirements, observes that while IFRS 3 requires that goodwill is not amortised (and is therefore reviewed for impairment each year instead), this is in conflict with para. 22 of Sch. 1 to the Regulations. So an FRS 101 preparer complying with IFRS 3 and leaving its goodwill unamortised will also have to disclose a departure from the requirements of the Regulations in order to give a true and fair view. This is the other side of the 'true and fair override' discussed in **Chapter 2**.

It can be seen that this is not, in truth, an accounting amendment, rather a signpost to an uncommon situation and a highlighting of a clash between IFRS and UK law.

It is also worth noting that it is not likely to be a common issue for IFRS preparers since in most cases a business combination involves the combining of two legal entities and so will result in consolidated accounts, where goodwill will be recognised. Purchased goodwill will appear on the acquiring entity's individual balance sheet where the business combination has been through a trade and assets acquisition, which is more rare.

10.1.5 Resulting disclosures

The remaining disclosure requirements, assuming the equivalence test is met, come from a number of standards. Each paragraph is either referenced as quoted in full, or it is noted that it has been amended by FRS 101.

Separate financial statements

An entity shall apply all applicable IFRSs when providing disclosures in its separate financial statements, including the requirements in para. 16–17.

[IAS 27 para. 15, unamended]

When a parent, in accordance with paragraph 4(a) of IFRS 10, elects not to prepare consolidated financial statements and instead prepares separate financial statements, it shall disclose in those separate financial statements:

(a) the fact that the financial statements are separate financial statements; that the exemption from consolidation has been used; the name and principal place of business (and country of incorporation, if different) of the entity whose consolidated financial statements that comply with International Financial Reporting Standards have been produced for public use; and the address where those consolidated financial statements are obtainable.
(b) a list of significant investments in subsidiaries, joint ventures and associates, including:
    (i) the name of those investees;
    (ii) the principal place of business (and country of incorporation, if different) of those investees;
    (iii) its proportion of the ownership interest (and its proportion of the voting rights, if different) held in those investees;
(c) a description of the method used to account for the investments listed under (b).

[IAS 27 para. 16, unamended]

When an investment entity that is a parent (other than a parent covered by paragraph 16) prepares, in accordance with paragraph 8A, separate financial statements as its only financial statements, it shall disclose that fact. The investment entity shall also present the disclosures relating to investment entities required by IFRS 12 *Disclosure of Interests in Other Entities*.

[IAS 27 para. 16A, unamended – note investment entities are also discussed in **Chapter 8**]

When a parent (other than a parent covered by paragraph 16–16A) or an investor with joint control of, or significant influence over, an investee prepares separate financial statements, the parent or investor shall identify the financial statements prepared in accordance with IFRS 10, IFRS 11 or IAS 28 (as amended in 2011) to which they relate. The parent or investor shall also disclose in its separate financial statements:

(a) the fact that the statements are separate financial statements and the reasons why those statements are prepared if not required by law;
(b) a list of significant investments in subsidiaries, joint ventures and associates, including:
    (i) the name of those investees;
    (ii) the principal place of business (and country of incorporation, if different) of those investees;
    (iii) its proportion of the ownership interest (and its proportion of the voting rights, if different) held in those investees;
(c) a description of the method used to account for the investments listed under (b).

[IAS 27 para. 17, unamended]

Business combinations

The acquirer shall disclose information that enables users of its financial statements to evaluate the nature and financial effect of a business combination that occurs either:

(a)   during the current reporting period; or

(b)   after the end of the reporting period but before the financial statements are authorised for issue.

[IFRS 3 para. 59, unamended]

To meet the objective in paragraph 59, the acquirer shall disclose the information specified in paragraphs B64–B66.

[IFRS 3 para. 60, unamended]

The acquirer shall disclose information that enables users of its financial statements to evaluate the financial effects of adjustments recognised in the current reporting period that relate to business combinations that occurred in the period or previous reporting periods.

[IFRS 3 para. 61, unamended]

If the specific disclosures required by this and other IFRSs do not meet the objectives set out in paragraphs 59 and 61, the acquirer shall disclose whatever additional information is necessary to meet those objectives.

[IFRS 3 para. 63, unamended]

To meet the objective in paragraph 59, the acquirer shall disclose the following information for each business combination that occurs during the reporting period:

(a)   the name and a description of the acquiree;

(b)   the acquisition date;

(c)   the percentage of voting equity interests acquired;

(f)   the acquisition-date fair value of the total consideration transferred and the acquisition-date fair value of each major class of consideration, such as:

(i)   cash;

(ii)   other tangible or intangible assets, including a business or subsidiary of the acquirer;

(iii) liabilities incurred, for example, a liability for contingent consideration; and

(iv)   equity interests of the acquirer, including the number of instruments or interests issued or issuable and the method of measuring the fair value of those instruments or interests.

(i)   the amounts recognised as of the acquisition date for each major class of assets acquired and liabilities assumed.

(n)   in a bargain purchase (see paragraphs 34–36):

(i)   the amount of any gain recognised in accordance with paragraph 34 and the line item in the statement of comprehensive income in which the gain is recognised; and

(o)   for each business combination in which the acquirer holds less than 100% of the equity interests in the acquiree at the acquisition date:

(i)   the amount of the non-controlling interest in the acquiree recognised at the acquisition date and the measurement basis for that amount; and

(q)   the following information:

(i)   the amounts of revenue and profit or loss of the acquiree since the acquisition date included in the consolidated statement of comprehensive income for the reporting period; and

If disclosure of any of the information required by this subparagraph is impracticable, the acquirer shall disclose that fact and explain why the disclosure is impracticable. This IFRS uses the term 'impracticable' with the same meaning as in IAS 8 Accounting Policies, Changes in Accounting Estimates and Errors.

[IFRS 3 para. B64, with multiple paragraphs and sub-paragraphs removed (hence non-sequential numbering]

For individually immaterial business combinations occurring during the reporting period that are material collectively, the acquirer shall disclose in aggregate the information required by paragraph B64(e)–(q).

[IFRS 3 para. B65, unamended]

Interests in other entities (IFRS 12, with the only relevant parts being for investment entities)

Investment entity status

When a parent determines that it is an investment entity in accordance with paragraph 27 of IFRS 10, the investment entity shall disclose information about significant judgements and assumptions it has made in determining that it is an investment entity. If the investment entity does not have one or more of the typical characteristics of an investment entity (see paragraph 28 of IFRS 10), it shall disclose its reasons for concluding that it is nevertheless an investment entity.

[IFRS 12 para. 9A, unamended]

When an entity becomes, or ceases to be, an investment entity, it shall disclose the change of investment entity status and the reasons for the change. In addition, an entity that becomes an investment entity shall disclose the effect of the change of status on the financial statements for the period presented, including:

(a) the total fair value, as of the date of change of status, of the subsidiaries that cease to be consolidated;
(b) the total gain or loss, if any, calculated in accordance with paragraph B101 of IFRS 10; and
(c) the line item(s) in profit or loss in which the gain or loss is recognised (if not presented separately).

[IFRS 12 para. 9B, unamended]

Interests in unconsolidated subsidiaries (investment entities)

An investment entity that, in accordance with IFRS 10, is required to apply the exception to consolidation and instead account for its investment in a subsidiary at fair value through profit or loss shall disclose that fact.

[IFRS 12 para. 19A, unamended]

For each unconsolidated subsidiary, an investment entity shall disclose:

(a) the subsidiary's name;
(b) the principal place of business (and country of incorporation if different from the principal place of business) of the subsidiary; and
(c) the proportion of ownership interest held by the investment entity and, if different, the proportion of voting rights held.

[IFRS 12 para. 19B, unamended]

If an investment entity is the parent of another investment entity, the parent shall also provide the disclosures in 19B(a)–(c) for investments that are controlled by its investment entity subsidiary. The disclosure may be provided by including, in the financial statements of the parent, the financial statements of the subsidiary (or subsidiaries) that contain the above information.

[IFRS 12 para. 19C, unamended]

An investment entity shall disclose:

(a)   the nature and extent of any significant restrictions (e.g. resulting from borrowing arrangements, regulatory requirements or contractual arrangements) on the ability of an unconsolidated subsidiary to transfer funds to the investment entity in the form of cash dividends or to repay loans or advances made to the unconsolidated subsidiary by the investment entity; and

(b)   any current commitments or intentions to provide financial or other support to an unconsolidated subsidiary, including commitments or intentions to assist the subsidiary in obtaining financial support.

[IFRS 12 para. 19D, unamended]

If, during the reporting period, an investment entity or any of its subsidiaries has, without having a contractual obligation to do so, provided financial or other support to an unconsolidated subsidiary (egg purchasing assets of, or instruments issued by, the subsidiary or assisting the subsidiary in obtaining financial support), the entity shall disclose:

(a)   the type and amount of support provided to each unconsolidated subsidiary; and
(b)   the reasons for providing the support.

[IFRS 12 para. 19E, unamended]

An investment entity shall disclose the terms of any contractual arrangements that could require the entity or its unconsolidated subsidiaries to provide financial support to an unconsolidated, controlled, structured entity, including events or circumstances that could expose the reporting entity to a loss (e.g. liquidity arrangements or credit rating triggers associated with obligations to purchase assets of the structured entity or to provide financial support).

[IFRS 12 para 19F, unamended]

If during the reporting period an investment entity or any of its unconsolidated subsidiaries has, without having a contractual obligation to do so, provided financial or other support to an unconsolidated, structured entity that the investment entity did not control, and if that provision of support resulted in the investment entity controlling the structured entity, the investment entity shall disclose an explanation of the relevant factors in reaching the decision to provide that support.

[IFRS 12 para. 19G, unamended]

10.2   Tangible and intangible assets and impairment

10.2.1   Relevant standards under IFRS

The relevant standards and interpretations under IFRS are:

- IAS 16 *Property, Plant and Equipment*;
- IAS 36 *Impairment of Assets*;
- IAS 38 *Intangible Assets;*
- SIC-32 *Intangible Assets – Web Site Costs.*

10.2.2 Overview of accounting differences between IFRS-based FRS 101 and old UK GAAP

Much of the accounting for tangible and intangible assets is similar between old UK GAAP and IFRS. There are though, as ever, differences in detail – for example, when it comes to borrowing costs old UK GAAP gave the choice of whether they were included in the costs of constructing an asset, but IFRS requires that where the conditions are met, they are capitalised.

For property revaluations, the complex categories of FRS 15 (specialised properties/non-specialised properties/properties surplus to requirements) do not appear in IAS 16, which has one approach for all assets, with the general requirement that revaluations are to fair value. Fair value itself is not defined in IAS 16, since IFRS 13 covers fair value measurement across standards, and requires relevant disclosures too. However, FRS 101 preparers are exempt from the disclosure requirements of IFRS 13 if equivalent disclosures are provided in the group accounts. The treatment of revaluation losses also differs slightly: FRS 15 distinguished between those caused by a clear consumption of economic benefits and those that were not, whereas IAS 16 simply takes all revaluation losses to other comprehensive income to the extent that they reverse previously recognised gains, and then to profit.

With intangible assets, perhaps the key difference is that under IFRS development costs meeting certain conditions (very similar to those in SSAP 13) must be capitalised, unlike under old UK GAAP where there was an accounting policy choice. There is a general expectation that more intangible assets might fall to be recognised under IFRS. And amortisation is different: while old UK GAAP set a default useful life of twenty years or less, IFRS gives no presumed period, which generally will create slightly more work for preparers who have to come up with a concrete figure rather than using this cap by default.

Finally looking at impairment, many of the differences are in terminology (e.g. 'cash-generating unit' vs 'income generating unit' and some precise detail of application – under IFRS, where an income generating unit is impaired the loss is allocated first to goodwill then pro rata across the other assets in the unit, whereas FRS 11 included an intermediate step of next allocating to intangible assets. The treatment of the reversal of impairment losses is the same between old GAAP and IFRS except in respect of goodwill: under IAS 36, impairment losses on goodwill are not reversed, whereas under FRS 11 they would be reversed if the effects of the event that originally caused the loss had been demonstrably reversed in a way that had not been anticipated.

10.2.3 Exemptions given by FRS 101

Most of the disclosures for property, plant and equipment from IAS 16 are retained for FRS 101 preparers. Interestingly, the only exemption is from IAS 16 para. 73(e), which requires a comparative table to be presented for the reconciliation of movements in PPE, showing additions, impairments, disposals, etc. separately.

Similarly, for intangible assets the only exemption from IAS 38 is the parallel paragraph, para. 118(e) which again would require comparatives for the movements table.

When it comes to impairments, preparers will be pleased to see the exemptions are slightly more wide-reaching: the disclosures in IAS 36 are widely known to be challenging to comply with, both in terms of time burden and disclosing commercially sensitive information. So FRS 101 preparers with a parent that provides equivalent information in the consolidated accounts need not give such details on the value in use calculation as a list of key assumptions, discount rates, etc., and nor do they need to specify the valuation technique used if recoverable amounts are based on fair value less costs of disposal. Perhaps most fortunately for preparers, they are not required to perform the 134(f) exercise of looking at reasonably possible changes in key assumptions that would take the recoverable amount below the carrying amount. This exercise – effectively a sensitivity test – has caused headaches for many and represents real additional work in the financial statements preparation exercise, so the exemption should give a definite time saving for entities with impaired assets. The relief is not complete, though, in that IAS 1 still applies. Paragraph 125 requires disclosure of sources of estimation uncertainty, including (in para. 129) sensitivity analyses in some cases. There is less detail prescribed, and management judgment will be needed on a case by case basis to establish how much information is needed in relation to impairments even after the exemption from the IAS 36 disclosures is taken.

There is also some relief when it comes to disclosing details around goodwill allocated across multiple cash-generating units, again mainly relating to narrative disclosures and to performing (and disclosing the results of) sensitivity analysis.

FRS 101 para. 8(e) also exempts preparers from all of the disclosure requirements of IFRS 13 in respect of fair values if equivalent disclosures are provided in the group accounts.

10.2.4 Accounting amendments arising from the law

FRS 101 preparers need only make one amendment to the standards in this area in order to ensure their IFRS-based accounts are still compliant with UK law. Paragraph AG1(l) requires that IAS 16 para. 28 is deleted. This is the paragraph that allows the proceeds of government grants to be offset against the carrying value of the related assets, which is a practice explicitly prohibited by UK law. With this option removed, FRS 101 preparers must recognise grant proceeds as deferred income until they are recognised in income.

10.2.5 Resulting disclosure requirements

Property, plant and equipment

The financial statements shall disclose, for each class of property, plant and equipment:

(a) the measurement bases used for determining the gross carrying amount;
(b) the depreciation methods used;
(c) the useful lives or the depreciation rates used;
(d) the gross carrying amount and the accumulated depreciation (aggregated with accumulated impairment losses) at the beginning and end of the period.

[IAS 16 para. 73, with sub-paragraph (e) removed]

The financial statements shall also disclose:

(a) the existence and amounts of restrictions on title, and property, plant and equipment pledged as security for liabilities;
(b) the amount of expenditures recognised in the carrying amount of an item of property, plant and equipment in the course of its construction;
(c) the amount of contractual commitments for the acquisition of property, plant and equipment; and
(d) if it is not disclosed separately in the statement of comprehensive income, the amount of compensation from third parties for items of property, plant and equipment that were impaired, lost or given up that is included in profit or loss.

[IAS 16 para. 74, unamended]

Selection of the depreciation method and estimation of the useful life of assets are matters of judgment. Therefore, disclosure of the methods adopted and the estimated useful lives or depreciation rates provides users of financial statements with information that allows them to review the policies selected by management and enables comparisons to be made with other entities. For similar reasons, it is necessary to disclose:

(a) depreciation, whether recognised in profit or loss or as a part of the cost of other assets, during a period; and
(b) accumulated depreciation at the end of the period.

[IAS 16 para. 75, unamended]

In accordance with IAS 8 an entity discloses the nature and effect of a change in an accounting estimate that has an effect in the current period or is expected to have an effect in subsequent periods. For property, plant and equipment, such disclosure may arise from changes in estimates with respect to:

(a) residual values;
(b) the estimated costs of dismantling, removing or restoring items of property, plant and equipment;
(c) useful lives; and
(d) depreciation methods.

[IAS 16 para. 76, unamended]

If items of property, plant and equipment are stated at revalued amounts, the following shall be disclosed in addition to the disclosures required by IFRS 13:

(a) the effective date of the revaluation;
(b) whether an independent valuer was involved;
(c) [deleted]
(d) [deleted]
(e) for each revalued class of property, plant and equipment, the carrying amount that would have been recognised had the assets been carried under the cost model; and
(f) the revaluation surplus, indicating the change for the period and any restrictions on the distribution of the balance to shareholders.

[IAS 16 para. 77, unamended] [note that the IFRS 13 disclosures are not required if equivalent disclosures are included in the group accounts, so are not reproduced here]

In accordance with IAS 36 an entity discloses information on impaired property, plant and equipment in addition to the information required by paragraph 73(e)(iv)–(vi).

[IAS 16 para. 78, unamended]

Users of financial statements may also find the following information relevant to their needs:

(a) the carrying amount of temporarily idle property, plant and equipment;
(b) the gross carrying amount of any fully depreciated property, plant and equipment that is still in use;
(c) the carrying amount of property, plant and equipment retired from active use and not classified as held for sale in accordance with IFRS 5; and
(d) when the cost model is used, the fair value of property, plant and equipment when this is materially different from the carrying amount.

Therefore, entities are encouraged to disclose these amounts.

[IAS 16 para. 79, unamended]

Intangible assets

An entity shall disclose the following for each class of intangible assets, distinguishing between internally generated intangible assets and other intangible assets:

(a) whether the useful lives are indefinite or finite and, if finite, the useful lives or the amortisation rates used;
(b) the amortisation methods used for intangible assets with finite useful lives;
(c) the gross carrying amount and any accumulated amortisation (aggregated with accumulated impairment losses) at the beginning and end of the period;

(d)   the line item(s) of the statement of comprehensive income in which any amortisation of intangible assets is included.

[IAS 38 para. 118, with sub-paragraph (e) excluded]

A class of intangible assets is a grouping of assets of a similar nature and use in an entity's operations. Examples of separate classes may include:

(a)   brand names;
(b)   mastheads and publishing titles;
(c)   computer software;
(d)   licences and franchises;
(e)   copyrights, patents and other industrial property rights, service and operating rights;
(f)   recipes, formulae, models, designs and prototypes; and
(g)   intangible assets under development.

The classes mentioned above are disaggregated (aggregated) into smaller (larger) classes if this results in more relevant information for the users of the financial statements.

[IAS 38 para. 119, unamended]

An entity discloses information on impaired intangible assets in accordance with IAS 36 in addition to the information required by paragraph 118(e)(iii)–(v).

[IAS 38 para. 120, unamended]

IAS 8 requires an entity to disclose the nature and amount of a change in an accounting estimate that has a material effect in the current period or is expected to have a material effect in subsequent periods. Such disclosure may arise from changes in:

(a)   the assessment of an intangible asset's useful life;
(b)   the amortisation method; or
(c)   residual values.

[IAS 38 para. 121, unamended]

An entity shall also disclose:

(a)   for an intangible asset assessed as having an indefinite useful life, the carrying amount of that asset and the reasons supporting the assessment of an indefinite useful life. In giving these reasons, the entity shall describe the factor(s) that played a significant role in determining that the asset has an indefinite useful life;
(b)   a description, the carrying amount and remaining amortisation period of any individual intangible asset that is material to the entity's financial statements;
(c)   for intangible assets acquired by way of a government grant and initially recognised at fair value (see paragraph 44):
   (i)   the fair value initially recognised for these assets;
   (ii)   their carrying amount; and
   (iii) whether they are measured after recognition under the cost model or the revaluation model.
(d)   the existence and carrying amounts of intangible assets whose title is restricted and the carrying amounts of intangible assets pledged as security for liabilities;
(e)   the amount of contractual commitments for the acquisition of intangible assets.

[IAS 38 para. 122, unamended]

When an entity describes the factor(s) that played a significant role in determining that the useful life of an intangible asset is indefinite, the entity considers the list of factors in paragraph 90.

[IAS 38 para. 123, unamended]

Intangible assets measured after recognition using the revaluation model

If intangible assets are accounted for at revalued amounts, an entity shall disclose the following:

(a) by class of intangible assets:
    (i) the effective date of the revaluation;
    (ii) the carrying amount of revalued intangible assets; and
    (iii) the carrying amount that would have been recognised had the revalued class of intangible assets been measured after recognition using the cost model in paragraph 74; and
(b) the amount of the revaluation surplus that relates to intangible assets at the beginning and end of the period, indicating the changes during the period and any restrictions on the distribution of the balance to shareholders.
(c) [deleted]

[IAS 38 para. 124, unamended]

It may be necessary to aggregate the classes of revalued assets into larger classes for disclosure purposes. However, classes are not aggregated if this would result in the combination of a class of intangible assets that includes amounts measured under both the cost and revaluation models.

[IAS 38 para. 125, unamended]

Research and development expenditure

An entity shall disclose the aggregate amount of research and development expenditure recognised as an expense during the period.

[IAS 38 para. 126, unamended]

Other information

An entity is encouraged, but not required, to disclose the following information:

(a) a description of any fully amortised intangible asset that is still in use; and
(b) a brief description of significant intangible assets controlled by the entity but not recognised as assets because they did not meet the recognition criteria in this Standard or because they were acquired or generated before the version of IAS 38 Intangible Assets issued in 1998 was effective.

[IAS 38 para. 128, unamended]

Impairment

An entity shall disclose the following for each class of assets:

(a) the amount of impairment losses recognised in profit or loss during the period and the line item(s) of the statement of comprehensive income in which those impairment losses are included;
(b) the amount of reversals of impairment losses recognised in profit or loss during the period and the line item(s) of the statement of comprehensive income in which those impairment losses are reversed;
(c) the amount of impairment losses on revalued assets recognised in other comprehensive income during the period;
(d) the amount of reversals of impairment losses on revalued assets recognised in other comprehensive income during the period;

[IAS 36 para. 126, unamended]

A class of assets is a grouping of assets of similar nature and use in an entity's operations.

[IAS 36 para. 127, unamended]

The information required in paragraph 126 may be presented with other information disclosed for the class of assets. For example, this information may be included in a reconciliation of the carrying amount of property, plant and equipment, at the beginning and end of the period, as required by IAS 16.

[IAS 36 para. 128, unamended]

An entity that reports segment information in accordance with IFRS 8 shall disclose the following for each reportable segment:

(a)   the amount of impairment losses recognised in profit or loss and in other comprehensive income during the period;
(b)   the amount of reversals of impairment losses recognised in profit or loss and in other comprehensive income during the period;

[IAS 36 para. 129, unamended]

An entity shall disclose the following for an individual asset (including goodwill) or a cash-generating unit, for which an impairment loss has been recognised or reversed during the period:

(a)   the events and circumstances that led to the recognition or reversal of the impairment loss;
(b)   the amount of the impairment loss recognised or reversed;
(c)   for an individual asset:
    (i)   the nature of the asset; and
    (ii)   if the entity reports segment information in accordance with IFRS 8, the reportable segment to which the asset belongs;
(d)   for a cash-generating unit:
    (i)   a description of the cash-generating unit (such as whether it is a product line, a plant, a business operation, a geographical area, or a reportable segment as defined in IFRS 8);
    (ii)   the amount of the impairment loss recognised or reversed by class of assets and, if the entity reports segment information in accordance with IFRS 8, by reportable segment; and
    (iii) if the aggregation of assets for identifying the cash-generating unit has changed since the previous estimate of the cash-generating unit's recoverable amount (if any), a description of the current and former way of aggregating assets and the reasons for changing the way the cash-generating unit is identified;
(e)   the recoverable amount of the asset (cash-generating unit) and whether the recoverable amount of the asset (cash-generating unit) is its fair value less costs of disposal or its value in use.
(f)   if the recoverable amount is fair value less costs of disposal, the entity shall disclose the following information:
    (i)   the level of the fair value hierarchy (see IFRS 13) within which the fair value measurement of the asset (cash-generating unit) is categorised in its entirety (without taking into account whether the 'costs of disposal' are observable);
(g)   if recoverable amount is value in use, the discount rate(s) used in the current estimate and previous estimate (if any) of value in use.

[IAS 36 para. 130, with paras (f)(ii) and (f)(iii) removed]

An entity shall disclose the following information for the aggregate impairment losses and the aggregate reversals of impairment losses recognised during the period for which no information is disclosed in accordance with paragraph 130:

(a)   the main classes of assets affected by impairment losses and the main classes of assets affected by reversals of impairment losses;

(b)   the main events and circumstances that led to the recognition of these impairment losses and reversals of impairment losses.

[IAS 36 para. 131, unamended]

An entity is encouraged to disclose assumptions used to determine the recoverable amount of assets (cash-generating units) during the period. However, paragraph 134 requires an entity to disclose information about the estimates used to measure the recoverable amount of a cash-generating unit when goodwill or an intangible asset with an indefinite useful life is included in the carrying amount of that unit.

[IAS 36 para. 132, unamended]

If, in accordance with paragraph 84, any portion of the goodwill acquired in a business combination during the period has not been allocated to a cash-generating unit (group of units) at the end of the reporting period, the amount of the unallocated goodwill shall be disclosed together with the reasons why that amount remains unallocated.

[IAS 36 para 133, unamended]

Estimates used to measure recoverable amounts of cash-generating units containing goodwill or intangible assets with indefinite useful lives

An entity shall disclose the information required by (a)–(f) for each cash-generating unit (group of units) for which the carrying amount of goodwill or intangible assets with indefinite useful lives allocated to that unit (group of units) is significant in comparison with the entity's total carrying amount of goodwill or intangible assets with indefinite useful lives:

(a)   the carrying amount of goodwill allocated to the unit (group of units);

(b)   the carrying amount of intangible assets with indefinite useful lives allocated to the unit (group of units);

(c)   the basis on which the unit's (group of units') recoverable amount has been determined (ie value in use or fair value less costs of disposal).

[IAS 36 para. 134, with sub-paragraphs 134(d) to 134(f) removed]

If some or all of the carrying amount of goodwill or intangible assets with indefinite useful lives is allocated across multiple cash-generating units (groups of units), and the amount so allocated to each unit (group of units) is not significant in comparison with the entity's total carrying amount of goodwill or intangible assets with indefinite useful lives, that fact shall be disclosed, together with the aggregate carrying amount of goodwill or intangible assets with indefinite useful lives allocated to those units (groups of units). In addition, if the recoverable amounts of any of those units (groups of units) are based on the same key assumption(s) and the aggregate carrying amount of goodwill or intangible assets with indefinite useful lives allocated to them is significant in comparison with the entity's total carrying amount of goodwill or intangible assets with indefinite useful lives, an entity shall disclose that fact, together with:

(a)   the aggregate carrying amount of goodwill allocated to those units (groups of units);

(b)   the aggregate carrying amount of intangible assets with indefinite useful lives allocated to those units (groups of units).

[IAS 36 para. 135, with sub-paragraphs 135(c) to 135(e) removed]

The most recent detailed calculation made in a preceding period of the recoverable amount of a cash-generating unit (group of units) may, in accordance with paragraph 24 or 99, be carried forward and used in the impairment test for that unit (group of units) in the current period provided specified criteria are met. When this is the case, the information for that unit (group of units) that is incorporated into the disclosures required by paragraphs 134 and 135 relate to the carried forward calculation of recoverable amount.

[IAS 36 para. 136, unamended]

10.3   Borrowing costs

10.3.1   Relevant standards under IFRS

The relevant standard under IFRS is IAS 23 *Borrowing Costs,* although it also has effects on other standards.

10.3.2   Overview of accounting differences between IFRS-based FRS 101 and old UK GAAP

Old UK GAAP did not include a specific standard on borrowing costs, although there was some guidance within FRS 15 on the capitalisation of finance costs relating to constructing a qualifying asset. These could be capitalised as a matter of accounting policy choice; under IAS 23 costs meeting the conditions relating to assets meeting the conditions must be capitalised, and this relates to both tangible and intangible assets.

10.3.3   Exemptions given by FRS 101

FRS 101 does not grant any exemptions from the disclosure requirements of IAS 23.

10.3.4   Accounting amendments arising from the law

There are no amendments to IAS 23 arising from the law.

10.3.5   Resulting disclosure requirements

An entity shall disclose:

(a)   the amount of borrowing costs capitalised during the period; and
(b)   the capitalisation rate used to determine the amount of borrowing costs eligible for capitalisation.

[IAS 23 para. 26, unamended]

10.4   Investment property

10.4.1   Relevant standards under IFRS

The relevant standard under IFRS is IAS 40 *Investment Property.*

10.4.2   Overview of accounting differences between IFRS-based FRS 101 and old UK GAAP

The most significant difference between old UK GAAP and IFRS with respect to investment properties is that changes in fair value are recognised in the STRGL under SSAP 19, but in profit under IAS 40. IAS 40 also offers the cost model, whereby an investment property is treated like a normal piece of property, plant and equipment and held at depreciated cost. There are also definitional differences, in that properties let to other group companies were excluded from the scope of SSAP 19, but are treated as investment properties under IFRS (and hence under FRS 101). And preparers need to be careful in assessing whether the fair value of investment properties is a source of estimation uncertainty, since as discussed in **10.2** this can mean that IAS 1 requires disclosures including sensitivity analyses showing where the uncertainty is.

10.4.3 Exemptions given by FRS 101

FRS 101 does not give any exemptions from the disclosure requirements of IAS 40.

10.4.4 Accounting amendments arising from the law

There are no amendments to IAS 40 arising from the law.

10.4.5 Resulting disclosure requirements

The disclosures below apply in addition to those in IAS 17 (which are reproduced in **10.7.5**). In accordance with IAS 17, the owner of an investment property provides lessors' disclosures about leases into which it has entered. An entity that holds an investment property under a finance or operating lease provides lessees' disclosures for finance leases and lessors' disclosures for any operating leases into which it has entered.

[IAS 40 para. 74, unamended]

An entity shall disclose:

(a) whether it applies the fair value model or the cost model;
(b) if it applies the fair value model, whether, and in what circumstances, property interests held under operating leases are classified and accounted for as investment property;
(c) when classification is difficult (see paragraph 14), the criteria it uses to distinguish investment property from owner-occupied property and from property held for sale in the ordinary course of business;
(d) [deleted]
(e) the extent to which the fair value of investment property (as measured or disclosed in the financial statements) is based on a valuation by an independent valuer who holds a recognised and relevant professional qualification and has recent experience in the location and category of the investment property being valued. If there has been no such valuation, that fact shall be disclosed;
(f) the amounts recognised in profit or loss for:
    (i) rental income from investment property;
    (ii) direct operating expenses (including repairs and maintenance) arising from investment property that generated rental income during the period;
    (iii) direct operating expenses (including repairs and maintenance) arising from investment property that did not generate rental income during the period; and
    (iv) the cumulative change in fair value recognised in profit or loss on a sale of investment property from a pool of assets in which the cost model is used into a pool in which the fair value model is used (see paragraph 32C);
(g) the existence and amounts of restrictions on the realisability of investment property or the remittance of income and proceeds of disposal;
(h) contractual obligations to purchase, construct or develop investment property or for repairs, maintenance or enhancements.

[IAS 40 para. 75, unamended]

Fair value model

In addition to the disclosures required by paragraph 75, an entity that applies the fair value model in paragraphs 33–55 shall disclose a reconciliation between the carrying amounts of investment property at the beginning and end of the period, showing the following:

(a) additions, disclosing separately those additions resulting from acquisitions and those resulting from subsequent expenditure recognised in the carrying amount of an asset;
(b) additions resulting from acquisitions through business combinations;
(c) assets classified as held for sale or included in a disposal group classified as held for sale in accordance with IFRS 5 and other disposals;
(d) net gains or losses from fair value adjustments;
(e) the net exchange differences arising on the translation of the financial statements into a different presentation currency, and on translation of a foreign operation into the presentation currency of the reporting entity;
(f) transfers to and from inventories and owner-occupied property; and
(g) other changes.

[IAS 40 para. 76, unamended]

When a valuation obtained for investment property is adjusted significantly for the purpose of the financial statements, for example to avoid double-counting of assets or liabilities that are recognised as separate assets and liabilities as described in paragraph 50, the entity shall disclose a reconciliation between the valuation obtained and the adjusted valuation included in the financial statements, showing separately the aggregate amount of any recognised lease obligations that have been added back, and any other significant adjustments.

[IAS 40 para. 77, unamended]

In the exceptional cases referred to in paragraph 53, when an entity measures investment property using the cost model in IAS 16, the reconciliation required by paragraph 76 shall disclose amounts relating to that investment property separately from amounts relating to other investment property. In addition, an entity shall disclose:

(a) a description of the investment property;
(b) an explanation of why fair value cannot be measured reliably;
(c) if possible, the range of estimates within which fair value is highly likely to lie; and
(d) on disposal of investment property not carried at fair value:
    (i) the fact that the entity has disposed of investment property not carried at fair value;
    (ii) the carrying amount of that investment property at the time of sale; and
    (iii) the amount of gain or loss recognised.

[IAS 40 para. 78, unamended]

Cost model

In addition to the disclosures required by paragraph 75, an entity that applies the cost model in paragraph 56 shall disclose:

(a) the depreciation methods used;
(b) the useful lives or the depreciation rates used;
(c) the gross carrying amount and the accumulated depreciation (aggregated with accumulated impairment losses) at the beginning and end of the period;
(d) a reconciliation of the carrying amount of investment property at the beginning and end of the period, showing the following:
    (i) additions, disclosing separately those additions resulting from acquisitions and those resulting from subsequent expenditure recognised as an asset;
    (ii) additions resulting from acquisitions through business combinations;

(iii) assets classified as held for sale or included in a disposal group classified as held for sale in accordance with IFRS 5 and other disposals;

(iv) depreciation;

(v) the amount of impairment losses recognised, and the amount of impairment losses reversed, during the period in accordance with IAS 36;

(vi) the net exchange differences arising on the translation of the financial statements into a different presentation currency, and on translation of a foreign operation into the presentation currency of the reporting entity;

(vii) transfers to and from inventories and owner-occupied property; and

(viii) other changes;

(e) the fair value of investment property. In the exceptional cases described in paragraph 53, when an entity cannot measure the fair value of the investment property reliably, it shall disclose:

(i) a description of the investment property;

(ii) an explanation of why fair value cannot be measured reliably; and

(iii) if possible, the range of estimates within which fair value is highly likely to lie.

[IAS 40 para. 79, unamended]

10.5 Inventories

10.5.1 Relevant standards under IFRS

The main relevant standard under IFRS is IAS 2 *Inventories.*

10.5.2 Overview of accounting differences between IFRS-based FRS 101 and old UK GAAP

There are no significant accounting differences relating to inventory between old UK GAAP and IFRS.

10.5.3 Exemptions given by FRS 101

FRS 101 gives no exemptions from the disclosure requirements of IAS 2.

10.5.4 Accounting amendments arising from the law

The Application Guidance to FRS 101 makes no amendments to IAS 2 for compliance with UK law.

10.5.5 Resulting disclosure requirements

The financial statements shall disclose:

(a) the accounting policies adopted in measuring inventories, including the cost formula used;

(b) the total carrying amount of inventories and the carrying amount in classifications appropriate to the entity;

(c) the carrying amount of inventories carried at fair value less costs to sell;

(d) the amount of inventories recognised as an expense during the period;

(e) the amount of any write-down of inventories recognised as an expense in the period in accordance with paragraph 34;

(f) the amount of any reversal of any write-down that is recognised as a reduction in the amount of inventories recognised as expense in the period in accordance with paragraph 34;

(g) the circumstances or events that led to the reversal of a write-down of inventories in accordance with paragraph 34; and

(h) the carrying amount of inventories pledged as security for liabilities.

[IAS 2 para. 36, unamended]

Information about the carrying amounts held in different classifications of inventories and the extent of the changes in these assets is useful to financial statement users. Common classifications of inventories are merchandise, production supplies, materials, work in progress and finished goods. The inventories of a service provider may be described as work in progress.

[IAS 2 para. 37, unamended]

The amount of inventories recognised as an expense during the period, which is often referred to as cost of sales, consists of those costs previously included in the measurement of inventory that has now been sold and unallocated production overheads and abnormal amounts of production costs of inventories. The circumstances of the entity may also warrant the inclusion of other amounts, such as distribution costs.

[IAS 2 para. 38, unamended]

Some entities adopt a format for profit or loss that results in amounts being disclosed other than the cost of inventories recognised as an expense during the period. Under this format, an entity presents an analysis of expenses using a classification based on the nature of expenses. In this case, the entity discloses the costs recognised as an expense for raw materials and consumables, labour costs and other costs together with the amount of the net change in inventories for the period.

[IAS 2 para. 39, unamended]

10.6   Financial instruments

10.6.1   Relevant standards under IFRS

The standard under IFRS that covers this area is IFRS 7 *Financial Instruments: Disclosures.*

10.6.2   Overview of accounting differences between IFRS-based FRS 101 and old UK GAAP

IFRS has a very different approach to financial instruments from that in old UK GAAP, and the differences cannot be briefly summarised. FRS 101 preparers coming freshly to IFRS will find the distinction between liabilities and equity to be familiar, since this was already present for them in FRS 25, but the IFRS landscape of multiple categories of financial assets and liabilities (in IAS 39) or the distinction between basic and other instruments (in IFRS 9) will all be new.

Those applying FRS 101 – or indeed, full IFRS – for the first time are strongly advised to read fully into this area.

10.6.3   Exemptions given by FRS 101

For most FRS 101 preparers, FRS 101 para. 8(d) gives a full exemption from applying the requirements of IFRS 7.

There are two groups to whom this does not apply, though. Financial institutions need to give all IFRS 7 disclosures, as discussed in **8.2** above – these are not reproduced here as the entire standard runs to many pages and is of niche interest.

However as discussed in **4.4** above, preparers holding certain financial instruments at fair value are required by para. 36(4) of Sch. 1 to the Regulations to give the relevant disclosures from IFRS. It has been clarified that this relates to the version of IFRS that is current for the relevant accounting period.

In this publication, we have taken the approach of assuming that relevant disclosures are the same in this case for FRS 101 preparers and FRS 102 preparers, who are subject to the same piece of UK law. In the latest version of FRS 102, issued in 2015, preparers are helpfully given paragraph 11.48A. This is directed at the goal of meeting the legal requirement, so it seems reasonable to assume that compliance with this paragraph will be suitable for FRS 101 preparers too. It is reproduced in full in **10.6.5** below.

10.6.4 Accounting amendments arising from the law

There are no amendments to IAS 39 or IFRS 9 arising from the law.

10.6.5 Resulting disclosure requirements

As described above, financial instruments are a special case in that most preparers are exempt from the requirements of IFRS 7 but then have to comply with UK law. It appears that compliance with FRS 102 para. 11.48A will achieve this:

An entity, including an entity that is not a company, shall providethe following disclosures for financial instruments measured at fair value through profit or loss in accordance with para. 36(4) of Sch. 1 to the Regulations. This does not include financial liabilities held as part of a trading portfolio nor derivatives. The required disclosures are:

(a) the amount of change, during the period and cumulatively, in the fair value of the financial instrument that is attributable to changes in the credit risk of that instrument, determined either:
  (i) as the amount of change in its fair value that is not attributable to changes in market conditions that give rise to **market risk**; or
  (ii) using an alternative method the entity believes more faithfully represents the amount of change in its fair value that is attributable to changes in the credit risk of the instrument;
(b) the method used to establish the amount of change attributable to changes in own credit risk, or, if the change cannot be measured reliably or is not **material**, that fact;
(c) for a financial liability, the difference between the financial liability's carrying amount and the amount the entity would be contractually required to pay at maturity to the holder of the obligation;
(d) if an instrument contains both a liability and an equity feature, and the instrument has multiple features that substantially modify the cash flows and the values of those features are interdependent (such as a callable convertible debt instrument), the existence of those features;
(e) if there is a difference between the fair value of a financial instrument at initial recognition and the amount determined at that date using a valuation technique, the aggregate difference yet to be recognised in profit or loss at the beginning and end of the period and a reconciliation of the changes in the balance of this difference;
(f) information that enables users of the entity's financial statements to evaluate the nature and extent of relevant risks arising from financial instruments to which the entity is exposed at the end of the reporting period. These risks typically include, but are not limited to, credit risk, **liquidity risk** and market risk. The disclosure should include both the entity's exposure to each type of risk and how it manages those risks.

10.7 Leasing

10.7.1 Relevant standards under IFRS

The relevant standards and interpretations under IFRS are:

- IAS 17 *Leasing;*
- IFRIC Interpretation 4 *Determining whether an arrangement contains a lease;*
- SIC-15 *Operating Leases – Incentives;*
- SIC-27 *Evaluating the substance of transactions involving the legal form of a lease.*

10.7.2   Overview of accounting differences between IFRS-based FRS 101 and old UK GAAP

The accounting for leases is similar in many ways between old UK GAAP and IFRS. It is one of the areas where only the detailed application is likely to give issues, and even then these will only be relevant to a small group of preparers. Note this discussion is all in terms of the current leasing standard, IAS 17. A new standard, IFRS 16, was issued in January 2016 with an effective date of 2019, so its disclosures will replace these in due course, and the FRC will consider whether to grant any exemptions from them for FRS 101 purposes. Because the new standard is not yet endorsed in the EU, it is not available for early adoption by UK preparers at the time of writing.

IFRS places less focus on a 'bright-line' test to establish whether a lease is a finance lease or an operating lease, looking instead at a range of indicators.

There are also some definitional differences, for instance regarding the 'lease term', that can affect the period over which lease incentives are written off.

Preparers applying FRS 101 for the first time will need to review the classification of all of their leases and check for treatment of incentives and inflationary increases.

10.7.3   Exemptions given by FRS 101

FRS 101 does not give any disclosure exemptions relating to leases, so all of the requirements of full EU-adopted IFRS apply, as set out in **10.7.5** below.

10.7.4   Accounting amendments arising from the law

There are no amendments to the IFRS requirements needed for compliance with UK law.

10.7.5   Resulting disclosure requirements

Most of the disclosure requirements below are copied directly from IAS 17, with the exception of one small additional disclosure from IFRIC 4 for lessees under operating leases. For brevity, disclosures from IFRS 7 and other standards referred to by IAS 17 are not reproduced again here. As stated above, FRS 101 does not give any exemptions from the IFRS disclosures.

Lessees – finance leases

Lessees shall, in addition to meeting the requirements of IFRS 7 *Financial Instruments: Disclosures*, make the following disclosures for finance leases:

(a)   for each class of asset, the net carrying amount at the end of the reporting period;
(b)   a reconciliation between the total of future minimum lease payments at the end of the reporting period, and their present value. In addition, an entity shall disclose the total of future minimum lease payments at the end of the reporting period, and their present value, for each of the following periods:
    (i)   not later than one year;
    (ii)   later than one year and not later than five years;
    (iii) later than five years;
(c)   contingent rents recognised as an expense in the period;
(d)   the total of future minimum sublease payments expected to be received under non-cancellable subleases at the end of the reporting period;
(e)   a general description of the lessee's material leasing arrangements including, but not limited to, the following:
    (i)   the basis on which contingent rent payable is determined;
    (ii)   the existence and terms of renewal or purchase options and escalation clauses; and
    (iii) restrictions imposed by lease arrangements, such as those concerning dividends, additional debt, and further leasing.

[IAS 17 para. 31, unamended]

In addition, the requirements for disclosure in accordance with IAS 16, IAS 36, IAS 38, IAS 40 and IAS 41 apply to lessees for assets leased under finance leases.

[IAS 17 para. 32, unamended]

Lessees – operating leases

Lessees shall, in addition to meeting the requirements of IFRS 7, make the following disclosures for operating leases:

(a) the total of future minimum lease payments under non-cancellable operating leases for each of the following periods:
    (i) not later than one year;
    (ii) later than one year and not later than five years;
    (iii) later than five years;
(b) the total of future minimum sublease payments expected to be received under non-cancellable subleases at the end of the reporting period;
(c) lease and sublease payments recognised as an expense in the period, with separate amounts for minimum lease payments, contingent rents, and sublease payments;
(d) a general description of the lessee's significant leasing arrangements including, but not limited to, the following:
    (i) the basis on which contingent rent payable is determined;
    (ii) the existence and terms of renewal or purchase options and escalation clauses; and
    (iii) restrictions imposed by lease arrangements, such as those concerning dividends, additional debt and further leasing.

[IAS 17 para. 35, unamended]

If a purchaser concludes that it is impracticable to separate the payments reliably:

For arrangements containing a lease, if the purchaser concludes that it is impracticable to separate the payments reliably, all payments under the arrangement are treated as lease payments for the purposes of complying with the disclosure requirements of IAS 17, but:

(i) disclose those payments separately from minimum lease payments of other arrangements that do not include payments for non-lease elements; and
(ii) state that the disclosed payments also include payments for non-lease elements in the arrangement.

[IFRIC 4 para. 15, unamended]

Lessors – finance leases

Lessors shall, in addition to meeting the requirements in IFRS 7, disclose the following for finance leases:

(a) a reconciliation between the gross investment in the lease at the end of the reporting period, and the present value of minimum lease payments receivable at the end of the reporting period. In addition, an entity shall disclose the gross investment in the lease and the present value of minimum lease payments receivable at the end of the reporting period, for each of the following periods:
    (i) not later than one year;
    (ii) later than one year and not later than five years;
    (iii) later than five years;
(b) unearned finance income;
(c) the unguaranteed residual values accruing to the benefit of the lessor;

(d)   the accumulated allowance for uncollectible minimum lease payments receivable;
(e)   contingent rents recognised as income in the period;
(f)   a general description of the lessor's material leasing arrangements.

[IAS 17 para. 47, unamended]

As an indicator of growth it is often useful also to disclose the gross investment less unearned income in new business added during the period, after deducting the relevant amounts for cancelled leases.

[IAS 17 para. 48, unamended]

Lessors – operating leases

Lessors shall, in addition to meeting the requirements of IFRS 7, disclose the following for operating leases:

(a)   the future minimum lease payments under non-cancellable operating leases in the aggregate and for each of the following periods:
    (i)   not later than one year;
    (ii)   later than one year and not later than five years;
    (iii)   later than five years;
(b)   total contingent rents recognised as income in the period;
(c)   a general description of the lessor's leasing arrangements.

[IAS 17 para. 56, unamended]

In addition, the disclosure requirements in IAS 16, IAS 36, IAS 38, IAS 40 and IAS 41 apply to lessors for assets provided under operating leases.

[IAS 17 para. 57, unamended]

10.8   Provisions and contingencies

10.8.1   Relevant standards under IFRS

The relevant standard under IFRS is IAS 37 *Provisions, Contingent Liabilities and Contingent Assets.*

10.8.2   Overview of accounting differences between IFRS-based FRS 101 and old UK GAAP

There are no accounting differences between FRS 12 and IAS 37.

10.8.3   Exemptions given by FRS 101

FRS 101 does not give any direct exemptions from the disclosure requirements of IAS 37.

10.8.4   Accounting amendments arising from the law

There is an unusual amendment made in respect of provisions, added by a set of changes to FRS 101 after it was released.

Changes in UK law meant the old 'seriously prejudicial' exemption is now much more restricted in its use. So where para. 92 of IAS 37 still allows a very general refraining from disclosure of sensitive information, the amendments in para AG1(s) of FRS 101 now set out a list of information that must be included instead. This is included in **10.8.5** as an amended version of IAS 37 para. 92.

10.8.5   *Resulting disclosure requirements*

For each class of provision, an entity shall disclose:

(a)   the carrying amount at the beginning and end of the period;
(b)   additional provisions made in the period, including increases to existing provisions;
(c)   amounts used (i.e. incurred and charged against the provision) during the period;
(d)   unused amounts reversed during the period; and
(e)   the increase during the period in the discounted amount arising from the passage of time and the effect of any change in the discount rate.

Comparative information is not required.

[IAS 37 para. 84, unamended]

An entity shall disclose the following for each class of provision:

(a)   a brief description of the nature of the obligation and the expected timing of any resulting outflows of economic benefits;
(b)   an indication of the uncertainties about the amount or timing of those outflows. Where necessary to provide adequate information, an entity shall disclose the major assumptions made concerning future events, as addressed in paragraph 48; and
(c)   the amount of any expected reimbursement, stating the amount of any asset that has been recognised for that expected reimbursement.

[IAS 37 para. 85, unamended]

Unless the possibility of any outflow in settlement is remote, an entity shall disclose for each class of contingent liability at the end of the reporting period a brief description of the nature of the contingent liability and, where practicable:

(a)   an estimate of its financial effect, measured under paragraphs 36–52;
(b)   an indication of the uncertainties relating to the amount or timing of any outflow; and
(c)   the possibility of any reimbursement.

[IAS 37 para. 86, unamended]

In determining which provisions or contingent liabilities may be aggregated to form a class, it is necessary to consider whether the nature of the items is sufficiently similar for a single statement about them to fulfil the requirements of paragraphs 85(a) and (b) and 86(a) and (b). Thus, it may be appropriate to treat as a single class of provision amounts relating to warranties of different products, but it would not be appropriate to treat as a single class amounts relating to normal warranties and amounts that are subject to legal proceedings.

[IAS 37 para. 87, unamended]

Where a provision and a contingent liability arise from the same set of circumstances, an entity makes the disclosures required by paragraphs 84–86 in a way that shows the link between the provision and the contingent liability.

[IAS 37 para. 88, unamended]

Where an inflow of economic benefits is probable, an entity shall disclose a brief description of the nature of the contingent assets at the end of the reporting period, and, where practicable, an estimate of their financial effect, measured using the principles set out for provisions in paragraphs 36–52.

[IAS 37 para. 89, unamended]

It is important that disclosures for contingent assets avoid giving misleading indications of the likelihood of income arising.

[IAS 37 para. 90, unamended]

Where any of the information required by paragraphs 86 and 89 is not disclosed because it is not practicable to do so, that fact shall be stated.

[IAS 37 para. 91, unamended]

In extremely rare cases, disclosure of some or all of the information required by paragraphs 84–89 can be expected to prejudice seriously the position of the entity in a dispute with other parties on the subject matter of the provision, contingent liability or contingent asset. In such cases, an entity need not disclose all of the information required by those paragraphs insofar as it relates to the dispute, but shall disclose at least the following.

In relation to provisions, the following information shall be given:

(a)   a table showing the reconciliation required by paragraph 84 in aggregate, including the source and application of any amounts transferred to or from provisions during the reporting period;
(b)   particulars of each provision in any case where the amount of the provision is material; and
(c)   the fact that, and reason why, the information required by paragraphs 84 and 85 has not been disclosed.

In relation to contingent liabilities, the following information shall be given:

(a)   particulars and the total amount of any contingent liabilities (excluding those which arise out of insurance contracts) that are not included in the statement of financial position;
(b)   the total amount of contingent liabilities which are undertaken on behalf of or for the benefit of:
    (i)   any parent or fellow subsidiary of the entity;
    (ii)   any subsidiary of the entity; or
    (iii) any entity in which the reporting entity has a participating interest, shall each be stated separately; and
(c)   the fact that, and reason why, the information required by paragraph 86 has not been disclosed.

In relation to contingent assets, the entity shall disclose the general nature of the dispute, together with the fact that, and reason why, the information required by paragraph 89 has not been disclosed.

[IAS 37 para. 92, heavily amended as set out in para. AG1(s) of FRS 101]

Chapter 11   Income and Expenses

11.1   Revenue including grant income

11.1.1   Relevant standards under IFRS, and summary of disclosure requirements

At present, there are a number of relevant standards and interpretations under IFRS:

- IAS 11 *Construction contracts*;
- IAS 18 *Revenue*;
- IAS 20 *Accounting for government grants and disclosure of government assistance*;
- SIC-29 *Disclosure – service concession arrangements*;
- SIC-31 *Revenue – barter transactions involving advertising services*;
- IFRIC 12 *Service concession arrangements*;
- IFRIC 13 *Customer loyalty programmes*;
- IFRIC 15 *Agreements for the construction of real estate*.

When the new revenue standard, IFRS 15, becomes effective in 2018 it will replace most of these, but in this chapter it is the old suite that we discuss since they are currently relevant. At the time of writing, the FRC had just issued an Exposure Draft proposing exemptions for FRS 101 preparers from the IFRS 15 disclosures, but this is still at an early stage.

11.1.2   Overview of accounting differences between IFRS-based FRS 101 and old UK GAAP

Revenue

IFRS has a more structured approach to revenue accounting than in old UK GAAP, where there was no revenue standard but instead a series of appendices to FRS 5 and miscellaneous other guidance. In many cases, the point of revenue recognition and the values recognised will be identical between the two GAAPs, although it will be a change for FRS 101 preparers to need to look at something slightly more nuanced than the simple point when the seller obtains the right to consideration in exchange for performance.

Construction contracts

Again, IFRS has a specific standard for construction contracts, where old UK GAAP covered them only fairly briefly within SSAP 9.

Service concession arrangements

Service concession arrangements are where infrastructure assets are developed (or upgraded), operated and maintained by a private operator, under a contract granted by a public sector body or public benefit entity. Under IFRS, IFRIC 12 addresses the accounting, which is driven for operators by a split model where the operator will have an intangible asset (based on the right or licence to charge users) or a financial asset (an unconditional contractual right to receive cash), or both. The guidance on this within old UK GAAP was contained in FRS 5 Application Note F and has many similarities but a different scope, in that an arrangement where the infrastructure asset remains the operator's property is scoped into Application Note F but out of IFRIC 12. Preparers for whom this is a relevant topic will need to review the guidance carefully.

Government grants

Interestingly, IFRS is very similar to old UK GAAP in its accounting for government grants, even though FRS 102 has widened the field somewhat by introducing an option to use the 'performance model' as well as the more familiar 'accrual model'.

The only significant difference is that IAS 20 permits grants to be deducted from the carrying values of the relevant assets, and we have already seen above that FRS 101 overlays UK law on the standard at this point and restricts FRS 101 preparers so that they can only use the other option, of showing unrecognised amounts in deferred income (and as a credit in the income statement, not deducted from the relevant expenses).

11.1.3 Exemptions given by FRS 101

There are no disclosure exemptions given by FRS 101 for any aspect of revenue or government grant income.

11.1.4 Accounting amendments arising from the law

For normal revenue and that arising from construction contracts and service concession arrangements, FRS 101 does not make any accounting amendments to IFRS to ensure legal compliance.

But in relation to government grants, there is one key issue: IAS 20 allows entities with grant proceeds received before they are recognised to have an accounting policy choice between showing these in deferred income or deducting them from the related asset. UK law forbids this latter option, so FRS 101 places a limit on preparers, only allowing them to use the other option (which is the same balance sheet accounting as will have been familiar from old UK GAAP). There are a number of changes to the standard to effect this, with paras. 25 and 27 deleted and paras. 24, 26, 28 and 29 amended. The change to para 29. removes the parallel income statement option to deduct grants received from the related expenses, leaving only the option of showing grant income either separately or under a general heading such as 'other income'.

11.1.5 Resulting disclosures

Revenue

An entity shall disclose:

(a) the accounting policies adopted for the recognition of revenue, including the methods adopted to determine the stage of completion of transactions involving the rendering of services;
(b) the amount of each significant category of revenue recognised during the period, including revenue arising from:
    (i)   the sale of goods;
    (ii) the rendering of services;
    (iii) interest;
    (iv) royalties;
    (v) dividends; and
(c) the amount of revenue arising from exchanges of goods or services included in each significant category of revenue.

[IAS 18 para. 35, unamended]

An entity discloses any contingent liabilities and contingent assets in accordance with IAS 37 *Provisions, Contingent Liabilities and Contingent Assets*. Contingent liabilities and contingent assets may arise from items such as warranty costs, claims, penalties or possible losses.

[IAS 18 para. 36, unamended]

Construction contracts

An entity shall disclose:

(a)   the amount of contract revenue recognised as revenue in the period;
(b)   the methods used to determine the contract revenue recognised in the period; and
(c)   the methods used to determine the stage of completion of contracts in progress.

[IAS 11 para. 39, unamended]

An entity shall disclose each of the following for contracts in progress at the end of the reporting period:

(a)   the aggregate amount of costs incurred and recognised profits (less recognised losses) to date;
(b)   the amount of advances received; and
(c)   the amount of retentions.

[IAS 11 para. 40, unamended]

Retentions are amounts of progress billings that are not paid until the satisfaction of conditions specified in the contract for the payment of such amounts or until defects have been rectified. Progress billings are amounts billed for work performed on a contract whether or not they have been paid by the customer. Advances are amounts received by the contractor before the related work is performed.

[IAS 11 para. 41, unamended]

An entity shall present:

(a)   the gross amount due from customers for contract work as an asset; and
(b)   the gross amount due to customers for contract work as a liability.

[IAS 11 para. 42, unamended]

The gross amount due from customers for contract work is the net amount of:

(a)   costs incurred plus recognised profits; less
(b)   the sum of recognised losses and progress billings

for all contracts in progress for which costs incurred plus recognised profits (less recognised losses) exceeds progress billings.

[IAS 11 para. 43, unamended]

The gross amount due to customers for contract work is the net amount of:

(a)   costs incurred plus recognised profits; less
(b)   the sum of recognised losses and progress billings

for all contracts in progress for which progress billings exceed costs incurred plus recognised profits (less recognised losses).

[IAS 11 para. 44, unamended]

An entity discloses any contingent liabilities and contingent assets in accordance with IAS 37 *Provisions, Contingent Liabilities and Contingent Assets*. Contingent liabilities and contingent assets may arise from such items as warranty costs, claims, penalties or possible losses.

[IAS 11 para. 45, unamended]

When an entity recognises revenue using the percentage of completion method for agreements that meet all the criteria in paragraph 14 of IAS 18 continuously as construction progresses (see paragraph 17 of the Interpretation), it shall disclose:

(a) how it determines which agreements meet all the criteria in paragraph 14 of IAS 18 continuously as construction progresses;
(b) the amount of revenue arising from such agreements in the period; and
(c) the methods used to determine the stage of completion of agreements in progress.

[IFRIC 15 para. 20, unamended]

For the agreements described in paragraph 20 that are in progress at the reporting date, the entity shall also disclose:

(a) the aggregate amount of costs incurred and recognised profits (less recognised losses) to date; and
(b) the amount of advances received.

[IFRIC 15 para. 21, unamended]

Service concession arrangements

All aspects of a service concession arrangement shall be considered in determining the appropriate disclosures in the notes. An operator and a grantor shall disclose the following in each period:

(a) a description of the arrangement;
(b) significant terms of the arrangement that may affect the amount, timing and certainty of future cash flows (e.g. the period of the concession, re-pricing dates and the basis upon which re-pricing or re-negotiation is determined);
(c) the nature and extent (e.g. quantity, time period or amount as appropriate) of:
    (i) rights to use specified assets;
    (ii) obligations to provide or rights to expect provision of services;
    (iii) obligations to acquire or build items of property, plant and equipment;
    (iv) obligations to deliver or rights to receive specified assets at the end of the concession period;
    (v) renewal and termination options; and
    (vi) other rights and obligations (e.g. major overhauls);
(d) changes in the arrangement occurring during the period; and
(e) how the service arrangement has been classified.

[SIC-29 para. 6, unamended]

An operator shall disclose the amount of revenue and profits or losses recognised in the period on exchanging construction services for a financial asset or an intangible asset.

[SIC-29 para. 6A, unamended]

The disclosures required in accordance with paragraph 6 of this Interpretation shall be provided individually for each service concession arrangement or in aggregate for each class of service concession arrangements. A class is a grouping of service concession arrangements involving services of a similar nature (e.g. toll collections, telecommunications and water treatment services).

[SIC-29 para. 7, unamended]

Government grants

The following matters shall be disclosed:

(a) the accounting policy adopted for government grants, including the methods of presentation adopted in the financial statements;

(b) the nature and extent of government grants recognised in the financial statements and an indication of other forms of government assistance from which the entity has directly benefited; and

(c) unfulfilled conditions and other contingencies attaching to government assistance that has been recognised.

[IAS 20 para. 39, unamended]

11.2 Income taxes

11.2.1 Relevant standards under IFRS, and summary of disclosure requirements

The relevant standards and interpretations under IFRS are:

- IAS 12 *Income taxes*;
- SIC-25 *Income taxes – changes in the tax status of an enterprise or its shareholders*.

11.2.2 Overview of accounting differences between IFRS-based FRS 101 and old UK GAAP

Although the accounting for current tax is straightforwardly similar between IFRS and old UK GAAP, things are more challenging when it comes to deferred tax. IFRS takes a very different perspective: instead of a profit-focused 'timing differences' approach, it looks at 'temporary differences' which are driven by the carrying values of assets and liabilities compared to their deductible or taxable amounts. It will sometimes be the case that this leads to the same deferred tax position, albeit via a different route. However, there will be some differences in outcome, most notably in relation to revaluation of fixed assets (this will give a taxable temporary difference, hence a deferred tax liability, under IFRS but under UK GAAP would usually not give rise to any deferred tax unless the entity had made a binding commitment to sell); the discounting of deferred tax assets and liabilities (not permitted under IFRS) and the conditions for recognising deferred tax assets in respect of carried forward losses and unremitted earnings of subsidiaries.

11.2.3 Exemptions given by FRS 101

FRS 101 does not give any disclosure exemptions in respect of current or deferred tax.

11.2.4 Accounting amendments arising from the law

There are no accounting amendments made to IAS 12 for compliance with UK law.

11.2.5 Resulting disclosures

The major components of tax expense (income) shall be disclosed separately.

[IAS 12 para. 79, unamended]

Components of tax expense (income) may include:

(a)   current tax expense (income);
(b)   any adjustments recognised in the period for current tax of prior periods;
(c)   the amount of deferred tax expense (income) relating to the origination and reversal of temporary differences;
(d)   the amount of deferred tax expense (income) relating to changes in tax rates or the imposition of new taxes;
(e)   the amount of the benefit arising from a previously unrecognised tax loss, tax credit or temporary difference of a prior period that is used to reduce current tax expense;
(f)   the amount of the benefit from a previously unrecognised tax loss, tax credit or temporary difference of a prior period that is used to reduce deferred tax expense;
(g)   deferred tax expense arising from the write-down, or reversal of a previous write-down, of a deferred tax asset in accordance with paragraph 56; and
(h)   the amount of tax expense (income) relating to those changes in accounting policies and errors that are included in profit or loss in accordance with IAS 8, because they cannot be accounted for retrospectively.

[IAS 12 para. 80, unamended]

The following shall also be disclosed separately:

(a)   the aggregate current and deferred tax relating to items that are charged or credited directly to equity (see paragraph 62A);
(ab) the amount of income tax relating to each component of other comprehensive income (see paragraph 62 and IAS 1 (as revised in 2007));
(b)   [deleted];
(c)   an explanation of the relationship between tax expense (income) and accounting profit in either or both of the following forms:
      (i)   a numerical reconciliation between tax expense (income) and the product of accounting profit multiplied by the applicable tax rate(s), disclosing also the basis on which the applicable tax rate(s) is (are) computed; or
      (ii) a numerical reconciliation between the average effective tax rate and the applicable tax rate, disclosing also the basis on which the applicable tax rate is computed;
(d)   an explanation of changes in the applicable tax rate(s) compared to the previous accounting period;
(e)   the amount (and expiry date, if any) of deductible temporary differences, unused tax losses, and unused tax credits for which no deferred tax asset is recognised in the statement of financial position;
(f)   the aggregate amount of temporary differences associated with investments in subsidiaries, branches and associates and interests in joint ventures, for which deferred tax liabilities have not been recognised (see paragraph 39);
(g)   in respect of each type of temporary difference, and in respect of each type of unused tax losses and unused tax credits:
      (i)   the amount of the deferred tax assets and liabilities recognised in the statement of financial position for each period presented;
      (ii) the amount of the deferred tax income or expense recognised in profit or loss, if this is not apparent from the changes in the amounts recognised in the statement of financial position;
(h)   in respect of discontinued operations, the tax expense relating to:
      (i)   the gain or loss on discontinuance; and
      (ii) the profit or loss from the ordinary activities of the discontinued operation for the period, together with the corresponding amounts for each prior period presented;
(i)   the amount of income tax consequences of dividends to shareholders of the entity that were proposed or declared before the financial statements were authorised for issue, but are not recognised as a liability in the financial statements;
(j)   if a business combination in which the entity is the acquirer causes a change in the amount recognised for its pre-acquisition deferred tax asset (see paragraph 67), the amount of that change; and

(k)   if the deferred tax benefits acquired in a business combination are not recognised at the acquisition date but are recognised after the acquisition date (see paragraph 68), a description of the event or change in circumstances that caused the deferred tax benefits to be recognised.

[IAS 12 para. 81, unamended]

An entity shall disclose the amount of a deferred tax asset and the nature of the evidence supporting its recognition, when:

(a)   the utilisation of the deferred tax asset is dependent on future taxable profits in excess of the profits arising from the reversal of existing taxable temporary differences; and
(b)   the entity has suffered a loss in either the current or preceding period in the tax jurisdiction to which the deferred tax asset relates.

[IAS 12 para. 82, unamended]

In the circumstances described in paragraph 52A, an entity shall disclose the nature of the potential income tax consequences that would result from the payment of dividends to its shareholders. In addition, the entity shall disclose the amounts of the potential income tax consequences practicably determinable and whether there are any potential income tax consequences not practicably determinable.

[IAS 12 para. 82A, unamended]

The disclosures required by paragraph 81(c) enable users of financial statements to understand whether the relationship between tax expense (income) and accounting profit is unusual and to understand the significant factors that could affect that relationship in the future. The relationship between tax expense (income) and accounting profit may be affected by such factors as revenue that is exempt from taxation, expenses that are not deductible in determining taxable profit (tax loss), the effect of tax losses and the effect of foreign tax rates.

[IAS 12 para. 84, unamended – note IAS 12 no longer has an active para. 83]

In explaining the relationship between tax expense (income) and accounting profit, an entity uses an applicable tax rate that provides the most meaningful information to the users of its financial statements. Often, the most meaningful rate is the domestic rate of tax in the country in which the entity is domiciled, aggregating the tax rate applied for national taxes with the rates applied for any local taxes which are computed on a substantially similar level of taxable profit (tax loss). However, for an entity operating in several jurisdictions, it may be more meaningful to aggregate separate reconciliations prepared using the domestic rate in each individual jurisdiction. The following example illustrates how the selection of the applicable tax rate affects the presentation of the numerical reconciliation.

[IAS 12 para. 85, unamended]

The average effective tax rate is the tax expense (income) divided by the accounting profit.

[IAS 12 para. 86, unamended]

It would often be impracticable to compute the amount of unrecognised deferred tax liabilities arising from investments in subsidiaries, branches and associates and interests in joint ventures (see paragraph 39). Therefore, this Standard requires an entity to disclose the aggregate amount of the underlying temporary differences but does not require disclosure of the deferred tax liabilities. Nevertheless, where practicable, entities are encouraged to disclose the amounts of the unrecognised deferred tax liabilities because financial statement users may find such information useful.

[IAS 12 para. 87, unamended]

Paragraph 82A requires an entity to disclose the nature of the potential income tax consequences that would result from the payment of dividends to its shareholders. An entity discloses the important features of the income tax systems and the factors that will affect the amount of the potential income tax consequences of dividends.

[IAS 12 para. 87A, unamended]

It would sometimes not be practicable to compute the total amount of the potential income tax consequences that would result from the payment of dividends to shareholders. This may be the case, for example, where an entity has a large number of foreign subsidiaries. However, even in such circumstances, some portions of the total amount may be easily determinable. For example, in a consolidated group, a parent and some of its subsidiaries may have paid income taxes at a higher rate on undistributed profits and be aware of the amount that would be refunded on the payment of future dividends to shareholders from consolidated retained earnings. In this case, that refundable amount is disclosed. If applicable, the entity also discloses that there are additional potential income tax consequences not practicably determinable. In the parent's separate financial statements, if any, the disclosure of the potential income tax consequences relates to the parent's retained earnings.

[IAS 12 para. 87B, unamended]

An entity required to provide the disclosures in paragraph 82A may also be required to provide disclosures related to temporary differences associated with investments in subsidiaries, branches and associates or interests in joint ventures. In such cases, an entity considers this in determining the information to be disclosed under paragraph 82A. For example, an entity may be required to disclose the aggregate amount of temporary differences associated with investments in subsidiaries for which no deferred tax liabilities have been recognised (see paragraph 81(f)). If it is impracticable to compute the amounts of unrecognised deferred tax liabilities (see paragraph 87) there may be amounts of potential income tax consequences of dividends not practicably determinable related to these subsidiaries.

[IAS 12 para. 87C, unamended]

An entity discloses any tax-related contingent liabilities and contingent assets in accordance with IAS 37 Provisions, Contingent Liabilities and Contingent Assets. Contingent liabilities and contingent assets may arise, for example, from unresolved disputes with the taxation authorities. Similarly, where changes in tax rates or tax laws are enacted or announced after the reporting period, an entity discloses any significant effect of those changes on its current and deferred tax assets and liabilities (see IAS 10 Events after the Reporting Period).

[IAS 12 para. 88, unamended]

11.3   Foreign currency issues

11.3.1   *Relevant standards under IFRS, and summary of disclosure requirements*

The relevant standards and interpretations under IFRS are:

- IAS 21 *The effects of changes in foreign exchange rates*;
- IAS 29 *Financial reporting in hyperinflationary economies*;
- IFRIC 7 *Applying the restatement approach under IAS 29.*

11.3.2   *Overview of accounting differences between IFRS-based FRS 101 and old UK GAAP*

For entities that have adopted FRS 26 and therefore use FRS 23, old UK GAAP and IFRS are the same. But for entities applying SSAP 20, there is a conceptual difference at the outset between IFRS and old UK GAAP, in that IFRS has separate concepts of functional and presentation currency.

The functional currency is a matter of fact, and the presentation currency a matter of choice; SSAP 20 only describes a 'local currency' which is effectively equivalent to the functional currency.

Beyond this, most day to day transactions and balances will be translated in the same way in both GAAPs. IFRS does not allow the SSAP 20 shortcut hedge accounting, where future transactions can be recorded at a forward rate if they are matched by a forward currency contract – an entity wishing to demonstrate this kind of matching in its financial reporting would need to engage in proper hedge accounting and look to IAS 39. And there is a difference in the accounting treatment of long term loans to an investee – in old UK GAAP, the investor/lender could treat this as part of the investment if it was 'as permanent as equity' and this would mean it was not retranslated from the historic exchange rate in the investor's individual balance sheet. In IFRS, though, even where the loan is treated as part of the investment in the group accounts, the individual company accounts would still retranslate the asset each balance sheet date, with gains or losses in profit.

11.3.3 Exemptions given by FRS 101

There are no disclosure exemptions for FRS 101 preparers relating to foreign currency transactions or hyperinflation.

11.3.4 Accounting amendments arising from the law

There are no accounting amendments to IAS 21 or IAS 29 for compliance with UK law.

11.3.5 Resulting disclosures

Foreign exchange

In paragraphs 53 and 55–57 references to 'functional currency' apply, in the case of a group, to the functional currency of the parent.

[IAS 21 para. 51, unamended]

An entity shall disclose:

(a) the amount of exchange differences recognised in profit or loss except for those arising on financial instruments measured at fair value through profit or loss in accordance with IAS 39; and
(b) net exchange differences recognised in other comprehensive income and accumulated in a separate component of equity, and a reconciliation of the amount of such exchange differences at the beginning and end of the period.

[IAS 21 para. 52, unamended]

When the presentation currency is different from the functional currency, that fact shall be stated, together with disclosure of the functional currency and the reason for using a different presentation currency.

[IAS 21 para. 53, unamended]

When there is a change in the functional currency of either the reporting entity or a significant foreign operation, that fact and the reason for the change in functional currency shall be disclosed.

[IAS 21 para. 54, unamended]

When an entity presents its financial statements in a currency that is different from its functional currency, it shall describe the financial statements as complying with IFRSs only if they comply with all the requirements of IFRSs including the translation method set out in paragraphs 39 and 42.

[IAS 21 para. 55, unamended]

An entity sometimes presents its financial statements or other financial information in a currency that is not its functional currency without meeting the requirements of paragraph 55. For example, an entity may convert into another currency only selected items from its financial statements. Or, an entity whose functional currency is not the currency of a hyperinflationary economy may convert the financial statements into another currency by translating all items at the most recent closing rate. Such conversions are not in accordance with IFRSs and the disclosures set out in paragraph 57 are required.

[IAS 21 para. 56, unamended]

When an entity displays its financial statements or other financial information in a currency that is different from either its functional currency or its presentation currency and the requirements of paragraph 55 are not met, it shall:

(a)   clearly identify the information as supplementary information to distinguish it from the information that complies with IFRSs;

(b)   disclose the currency in which the supplementary information is displayed; and

(c)   disclose the entity's functional currency and the method of translation used to determine the supplementary information.

[IAS 21 para. 57, unamended]

Hyperinflation

The following disclosures shall be made:

(a)   the fact that the financial statements and the corresponding figures for previous periods have been restated for the changes in the general purchasing power of the functional currency and, as a result, are stated in terms of the measuring unit current at the end of the reporting period;

(b)   whether the financial statements are based on a historical cost approach or a current cost approach; and

(c)   the identity and level of the price index at the end of the reporting period and the movement in the index during the current and the previous reporting period.

[IAS 29 para. 39, unamended]

The disclosures required by this Standard are needed to make clear the basis of dealing with the effects of inflation in the financial statements. They are also intended to provide other information necessary to understand that basis and the resulting amounts.

[IAS 29 para. 40, unamended]

11.4   Employee benefits and share-based payments

11.4.1   *Relevant standards under IFRS, and summary of disclosure requirements*

The relevant standards and interpretations under IFRS are:

- IAS 19 *Employee benefits*;
- IFRS 2 *Share-based payment*;
- IFRIC 14 *IAS 19 – The limit on a defined benefit asset, minimum funding requirements and their interaction.*

11.4.2 Overview of accounting differences between IFRS-based FRS 101 and old UK GAAP

The basic distinction between defined benefit and defined contribution schemes is the same in IFRS as in old UK GAAP, as is the accounting principle of reflecting net pension obligations for defined benefit schemes on the balance sheet. Some of the detail differs, though, both in the precise way of measuring the components of the net pension obligation (or surplus) and in the way that movements are accounted for. Under old UK GAAP, actuarial gains and losses are recognised in the STRGL, and all other movements in the net obligation in profit; under IFRS both actuarial gains and losses and other remeasurement effects are recognised immediately in other comprehensive income (note that the 'corridor approach' previously included in IAS 19 is no longer permissible).

Unlike FRS 17, IAS 19 draws a distinction – and gives different accounting – between group plans and other multi-employer plans. Perhaps the most noticeable effect is that where there is a group plan, at least one of the participants will need to apply defined benefit accounting and recognise the relevant position (whether a liability or a surplus) on the balance sheet. This is in contrast with other multi-employer plans where in theory all participants could use quasi defined contribution accounting so the liability is not reported anywhere.

Share-based payment accounting is almost identical between the two GAAPs, which is unsurprising as FRS 20 was originally a copy of IFRS 2.

11.4.3 Exemptions given by FRS 101

FRS 101 does not give any exemptions in respect of disclosures for employee benefits.

For share-based payments, on the other hand, FRS 101 preparers are exempted from virtually all of the requirements of IFRS 2, with only one very general requirement remaining (in para. 44 expanded by part of para. 45), to disclose information enabling the users of the accounts to understand the nature and extent of share-based payments during the period. This reflects the fact that in most cases, where a subsidiary has a share-based payment incentive to employees, this involves the parent's shares, and thus will be reflected (and suitably disclosed) in the group accounts. The exemption comes with the caveat that equivalent information must be included in the relevant group accounts, so users will be able to find it.

11.4.4 Accounting amendments arising from the law

There are no amendments to IAS 19 or IFRS 2 arising from the law.

11.4.5 Resulting disclosures

Defined contribution plans

An entity shall disclose the amount recognised as an expense for defined contribution plans.

[IAS 19 para. 53, unamended]

Where required by IAS 24 an entity discloses information about contributions to defined contribution plans for key management personnel.

[IAS 19 para. 54, unamended]

Defined benefit plans

An entity shall disclose information that:

(a) explains the characteristics of its defined benefit plans and risks associated with them (see paragraph 139);
(b) identifies and explains the amounts in its financial statements arising from its defined benefit plans (see paragraphs 140 to144); and
(c) describes how its defined benefit plans may affect the amount, timing and uncertainty of the entity's future cash flows (see paragraphs 145 to147).

[IAS 19 para. 135, unamended]

To meet the objectives in paragraph 135, an entity shall consider all the following:

(a) the level of detail necessary to satisfy the disclosure requirements;
(b) how much emphasis to place on each of the various requirements;
(c) how much aggregation or disaggregation to undertake; and
(d) whether users of financial statements need additional information to evaluate the quantitative information disclosed.

[IAS 19 para. 136, unamended]

If the disclosures provided in accordance with the requirements in this Standard and other IFRSs are insufficient to meet the objectives in paragraph 135, an entity shall disclose additional information necessary to meet those objectives. For example, an entity may present an analysis of the present value of the defined benefit obligation that distinguishes the nature, characteristics and risks of the obligation. Such a disclosure could distinguish:

(a) between amounts owing to active members, deferred members, and pensioners;
(b) between vested benefits and accrued but not vested benefits; and
(c) between conditional benefits, amounts attributable to future salary increases and other benefits.

[IAS 19 para. 137, unamended]

An entity shall assess whether all or some disclosures should be disaggregated to distinguish plans or groups of plans with materially different risks. For example, an entity may disaggregate disclosure about plans showing one or more of the following features:

(a) different geographical locations;
(b) different characteristics such as flat salary pension plans, final salary pension plans or post-employment medical plans;
(c) different regulatory environments;
(d) different reporting segments; and
(e) different funding arrangements (e.g. wholly unfunded, wholly or partly funded).

[IAS 19 para. 138, unamended]

Characteristics of defined benefit plans and risks associated with them

An entity shall disclose:

(a) information about the characteristics of its defined benefit plans, including:
    (i) the nature of the benefits provided by the plan (e.g. final salary defined benefit plan or contribution-based plan with guarantee);
    (ii) a description of the regulatory framework in which the plan operates, for example the level of any minimum funding requirements, and any effect of the regulatory framework on the plan, such as the asset ceiling (see paragraph 64); and
    (iii) a description of any other entity's responsibilities for the governance of the plan, for example responsibilities of trustees or of board members of the plan.

(b) a description of the risks to which the plan exposes the entity, focused on any unusual, entity-specific or plan-specific risks, and of any significant concentrations of risk. For example, if plan assets are invested primarily in one class of investments, eg property, the plan may expose the entity to a concentration of property market risk; and

(c) a description of any plan amendments, curtailments and settlements.

[IAS 19 para. 139, unamended]

Explanation of amounts in the financial statements

An entity shall provide a reconciliation from the opening balance to the closing balance for each of the following, if applicable:

(a) the net defined benefit liability (asset), showing separate reconciliations for:
    (i) plan assets;
    (ii) the present value of the defined benefit obligation;
    (iii) the effect of the asset ceiling;
(b) any reimbursement rights.

An entity shall also describe the relationship between any reimbursement right and the related obligation.

[IAS 19 para. 140, unamended]

Each reconciliation listed in paragraph 140 shall show each of the following, if applicable:

(a) current service cost;
(b) interest income or expense;
(c) remeasurements of the net defined benefit liability (asset), showing separately:
    (i) the return on plan assets, excluding amounts included in interest in (b);
    (ii) actuarial gains and losses arising from changes in demographic assumptions (see paragraph 76(a));
    (iii) actuarial gains and losses arising from changes in financial assumptions (see paragraph 76(b)); and
    (iv) changes in the effect of limiting a net defined benefit asset to the asset ceiling, excluding amounts included in interest in (b). An entity shall also disclose how it determined the maximum economic benefit available, i.e., whether those benefits would be in the form of refunds, reductions in future contributions or a combination of both.
(d) past service cost and gains and losses arising from settlements;
    As permitted by paragraph 100, past service cost and gains and losses arising from settlements need not be distinguished if they occur together.
(e) the effect of changes in foreign exchange rates;
(f) contributions to the plan, showing separately those by the employer and by plan participants;
(g) payments from the plan, showing separately the amount paid in respect of any settlements; and
(h) the effects of business combinations and disposals.

[IAS 19 para. 141, unamended]

An entity shall disaggregate the fair value of the plan assets into classes that distinguish the nature and risks of those assets, subdividing each class of plan asset into those that have a quoted market price in an active market (as defined in IFRS 13 *Fair Value Measurement**) and those that do not. For example, and considering the level of disclosure discussed in paragraph 136, an entity could distinguish between:

(a) cash and cash equivalents;
(b) equity instruments (segregated by industry type, company size, geography, etc.);
(c) debt instruments (segregated by type of issuer, credit quality, geography, etc.);
(d) real estate (segregated by geography, etc.);

(e) derivatives (segregated by type of underlying risk in the contract, for example, interest rate contracts, foreign exchange contracts, equity contracts, credit contracts, longevity swaps, etc.);

(f) investment funds (segregated by type of fund);

(g) asset-backed securities; and

(h) structured debt.

[IAS 19 para. 142, unamended]

An entity shall disclose the fair value of the entity's own transferable financial instruments held as plan assets, and the fair value of plan assets that are property occupied by, or other assets used by, the entity.

[IAS 19 para. 143, unamended]

An entity shall disclose the significant actuarial assumptions used to determine the present value of the defined benefit obligation (see paragraph 76). Such disclosure shall be in absolute terms (e.g. as an absolute percentage, and not just as a margin between different percentages and other variables). When an entity provides disclosures in total for a grouping of plans, it shall provide such disclosures in the form of weighted averages or relatively narrow ranges.

[IAS 19 para. 144, unamended]

Amount, timing and uncertainty of future cash flows

An entity shall disclose:

(a) a sensitivity analysis for each significant actuarial assumption (as disclosed under paragraph 144) as of the end of the reporting period, showing how the defined benefit obligation would have been affected by changes in the relevant actuarial assumption that were reasonably possible at that date;

(b) the methods and assumptions used in preparing the sensitivity analyses required by (a) and the limitations of those methods; and

(c) changes from the previous period in the methods and assumptions used in preparing the sensitivity analyses, and the reasons for such changes.

[IAS 19 para. 145, unamended]

An entity shall disclose a description of any asset-liability matching strategies used by the plan or the entity, including the use of annuities and other techniques, such as longevity swaps, to manage risk.

[IAS 19 para. 146, unamended]

To provide an indication of the effect of the defined benefit plan on the entity's future cash flows, an entity shall disclose:

(a) a description of any funding arrangements and funding policy that affect future contributions;

(b) the expected contributions to the plan for the next annual reporting period; and

(c) information about the maturity profile of the defined benefit obligation. This will include the weighted average duration of the defined benefit obligation and may include other information about the distribution of the timing of benefit payments, such as a maturity analysis of the benefit payments.

[IAS 19 para. 147, unamended]

Multi-employer plans

If an entity participates in a multi-employer defined benefit plan, it shall disclose:

(a) a description of the funding arrangements, including the method used to determine the entity's rate of contributions and any minimum funding requirements;

(b) a description of the extent to which the entity can be liable to the plan for other entities' obligations under the terms and conditions of the multi-employer plan;

(c) a description of any agreed allocation of a deficit or surplus on:
   (i) wind-up of the plan; or
   (ii) the entity's withdrawal from the plan.

(d) if the entity accounts for that plan as if it were a defined contribution plan in accordance with paragraph 34, it shall disclose the following, in addition to the information required by (a)-(c) and instead of the information required by paragraphs 139–147:
   (i) the fact that the plan is a defined benefit plan;
   (ii) the reason why sufficient information is not available to enable the entity to account for the plan as a defined benefit plan;
   (iii) the expected contributions to the plan for the next annual reporting period;
   (iv) information about any deficit or surplus in the plan that may affect the amount of future contributions, including the basis used to determine that deficit or surplus and the implications, if any, for the entity; and
   (v) an indication of the level of participation of the entity in the plan compared with other participating entities. Examples of measures that might provide such an indication include the entity's proportion of the total contributions to the plan or the entity's proportion of the total number of active members, retired members, and former members entitled to benefits, if that information is available.

[IAS 19 para. 148, unamended]

Defined benefit plans that share risks between entities under common control

If an entity participates in a defined benefit plan that shares risks between entities under common control, it shall disclose:

(a) the contractual agreement or stated policy for charging the net defined benefit cost or the fact that there is no such policy;

(b) the policy for determining the contribution to be paid by the entity;

(c) if the entity accounts for an allocation of the net defined benefit cost as noted in paragraph 41, all the information about the plan as a whole required by paragraphs 135–147; and

(d) if the entity accounts for the contribution payable for the period as noted in paragraph 41, the information about the plan as a whole required by paragraphs 135–137, 139, 142–144 and 147(a) and (b).

[IAS 19 para 149, unamended]

The information required by paragraph 149(c) and (d) can be disclosed by cross-reference to disclosures in another group entity's financial statements if:

(a) that group entity's financial statements separately identify and disclose the information required about the plan; and

(b) that group entity's financial statements are available to users of the financial statements on the same terms as the financial statements of the entity and at the same time as, or earlier than, the financial statements of the entity.

[IAS 19 para. 150, unamended]

Share-based payments

An entity shall disclose information that enables users of the financial statements to understand the nature and extent of share-based payment arrangements that existed during the period.

[IFRS 2 para. 44, unamended]

To give effect to the principle in paragraph 44, the entity shall disclose at least the following:

(a) a description of each type of share-based payment arrangement that existed at any time during the period, including the general terms and conditions of each arrangement, such as vesting requirements, the maximum term of options granted, and the method of settlement (e.g. whether in cash or equity). An entity with substantially similar types of share-based payment arrangements may aggregate this information, unless separate disclosure of each arrangement is necessary to satisfy the principle in paragraph 44.

[IFRS 2 para. 45, sub-paragraph (b) removed]

(c) for share options exercised during the period, the weighted average share price at the date of exercise. If options were exercised on a regular basis throughout the period, the entity may instead disclose the weighted average share price during the period.

(d) for share options outstanding at the end of the period, the range of exercise prices and weighted average remaining contractual life. If the range of exercise prices is wide, the outstanding options shall be divided into ranges that are meaningful for assessing the number and timing of additional shares that may be issued and the cash that may be received upon the exercise of those options.

11.5   Other expenses

Although there are no other explicit requirements included in IFRS in relation to expenses, there are some general points to note about principles of expense recognition.

The Statement of Principles in UK GAAP defines losses (which include expenses) as 'decreases in ownership interest not resulting from contributions from owners'. FRS 3 para 27 goes on to make it clear that gains and losses attributable to owners are not recognised in profit, but rather in the statement of total recognised gains and losses. The Conceptual Framework in IFRS comes from a slightly different angle, stating that 'expenses are recognised in the income statement when a decrease in future economic benefits related to a decrease in an asset or an increase of a liability has arisen that can be measured reliably'.

There are no general disclosure requirements, though, in relation to expenses in IFRS. Specific requirements are covered in the sections in this chapter (or, in the case of borrowing costs, in **Chapter 10**).

Chapter 12   Other accounting and disclosures

12.1   Post balance sheet events

12.1.1   Relevant standards under IFRS

The relevant standard under IFRS is IAS 10 *Events after the reporting period.*

12.1.2   Overview of accounting differences between IFRS-based FRS 101 and old UK GAAP

There are no differences of substance between IFRS and old UK GAAP in this area because FRS 21 mirrors IAS 10.

12.1.3   Exemptions given by FRS 101

FRS 101 gives no exemptions from the disclosure requirements of IAS 10.

12.1.4   Accounting amendments arising from the law

There are no accounting amendments to be made to IAS 10 for compliance with UK law.

12.1.5   Resulting disclosures

Date of authorisation for issue

An entity shall disclose the date when the financial statements were authorised for issue and who gave that authorisation. If the entity's owners or others have the power to amend the financial statements after issue, the entity shall disclose that fact.

[IAS 10 para. 17, unamended]

It is important for users to know when the financial statements were authorised for issue, because the financial statements do not reflect events after this date.

[IAS 10 para. 18, unamended]

Updating disclosure about conditions at the end of the reporting period

If an entity receives information after the reporting period about conditions that existed at the end of the reporting period, it shall update disclosures that relate to those conditions, in the light of the new information.

[IAS 10 para. 19, unamended]

In some cases, an entity needs to update the disclosures in its financial statements to reflect information received after the reporting period, even when the information does not affect the amounts that it recognises in its financial statements. One example of the need to update disclosures is when evidence becomes available after the reporting period about a contingent liability that existed at the end of the reporting period. In addition to considering whether it should recognise or change a provision under IAS 37, an entity updates its disclosures about the contingent liability in the light of that evidence.

[IAS 10 para. 20, unamended]

Non-adjusting events after the reporting period

If non-adjusting events after the reporting period are material, non-disclosure could influence the economic decisions that users make on the basis of the financial statements. Accordingly, an entity shall disclose the following for each material category of non-adjusting event after the reporting period:

(a) the nature of the event; and
(b) an estimate of its financial effect, or a statement that such an estimate cannot be made.

[IAS 10 para. 21, unamended]

The following are examples of non-adjusting events after the reporting period that would generally result in disclosure:

(a) a major business combination after the reporting period (IFRS 3 *Business Combinations* requires specific disclosures in such cases) or disposing of a major subsidiary;
(b) announcing a plan to discontinue an operation;
(c) major purchases of assets, classification of assets as held for sale in accordance with IFRS 5 *Non-current Assets Held for Sale and Discontinued Operations*, other disposals of assets, or expropriation of major assets by government;
(d) the destruction of a major production plant by a fire after the reporting period;
(e) announcing, or commencing the implementation of, a major restructuring (see IAS 37);
(f) major ordinary share transactions and potential ordinary share transactions after the reporting period (IAS 33 *Earnings per Share* requires an entity to disclose a description of such transactions, other than when such transactions involve capitalisation or bonus issues, share splits or reverse share splits all of which are required to be adjusted under IAS 33);
(g) abnormally large changes after the reporting period in asset prices or foreign exchange rates;
(h) changes in tax rates or tax laws enacted or announced after the reporting period that have a significant effect on current and deferred tax assets and liabilities (see IAS 12 *Income Taxes*);
(i) entering into significant commitments or contingent liabilities, for example, by issuing significant guarantees; and
(j) commencing major litigation arising solely out of events that occurred after the reporting period.

[IAS 10 para. 22, unamended]

12.2   Related parties

12.2.1   *Relevant standards under IFRS, and summary of disclosure requirements*

The relevant standard under IFRS is IAS 24 *Related party disclosures.*

12.2.2   *Overview of accounting differences between IFRS-based FRS 101 and old UK GAAP*

IAS 24 is a disclosure-only standard so there are no accounting differences as such. Some of the detailed disclosures and ways in which transactions and balances can be aggregated do differ slightly, so the best approach will be to work through the IAS 24 disclosures in detail.

12.2.3 Exemptions given by FRS 101

FRS 101 gives no exemptions from the disclosure requirements of IAS 24.

12.2.4 Accounting amendments arising from the law

There are no amendments needed to IAS 24 to ensure compliance with UK law.

12.2.5 Resulting disclosures

All entities

Relationships between a parent and its subsidiaries shall be disclosed irrespective of whether there have been transactions between them. An entity shall disclose the name of its parent and, if different, the ultimate controlling party. If neither the entity's parent nor the ultimate controlling party produces consolidated financial statements available for public use, the name of the next most senior parent that does so shall also be disclosed.

[IAS 24 para. 13, unamended]

To enable users of financial statements to form a view about the effects of related party relationships on an entity, it is appropriate to disclose the related party relationship when control exists, irrespective of whether there have been transactions between the related parties.

[IAS 24 para. 14, unamended]

The requirement to disclose related party relationships between a parent and its subsidiaries is in addition to the disclosure requirements in IAS 27 and IFRS 12 *Disclosure of Interests in Other Entities*.

[IAS 24 para. 15, unamended]

Paragraph 13 refers to the next most senior parent. This is the first parent in the group above the immediate parent that produces consolidated financial statements available for public use.

[IAS 24 para. 16, unamended]

An entity shall disclose key management personnel compensation in total and for each of the following categories:

(a) short-term employee benefits;
(b) post-employment benefits;
(c) other long-term benefits;
(d) termination benefits; and
(e) share-based payment.

[IAS 24 para. 17, unamended]

If an entity obtains key management personnel services from another entity (the 'management entity'), the entity is not required to apply the requirements in paragraph 17 to the compensation paid or payable by the management entity to the management entity's employees or directors.

[IAS 24 para. 17A, unamended]

If an entity has had related party transactions during the periods covered by the financial statements, it shall disclose the nature of the related party relationship as well as information about those transactions and outstanding balances, including commitments, necessary for users to understand the potential effect of the relationship on the financial statements. These disclosure requirements are in addition to those in paragraph 17. At a minimum, disclosures shall include:

(a)   the amount of the transactions;
(b)   the amount of outstanding balances, including commitments, and:
    (i)   their terms and conditions, including whether they are secured, and the nature of the consideration to be provided in settlement; and
    (ii)   details of any guarantees given or received;
(c)   provisions for doubtful debts related to the amount of outstanding balances; and
(d)   the expense recognised during the period in respect of bad or doubtful debts due from related parties.

[IAS 24 para. 18, unamended]

Amounts incurred by the entity for the provision of key management personnel services that are provided by a separate management entity shall be disclosed.

[IAS 24 para. 18A, unamended]

The disclosures required by paragraph 18 shall be made separately for each of the following categories:

(a)   the parent;
(b)   entities with joint control of, or significant influence over, the entity;
(c)   subsidiaries;
(d)   associates;
(e)   joint ventures in which the entity is a venturer;
(f)   key management personnel of the entity or its parent; and
(g)   other related parties.

[IAS 24 para. 19, unamended]

The classification of amounts payable to, and receivable from, related parties in the different categories as required in paragraph 19 is an extension of the disclosure requirement in IAS 1 *Presentation of Financial Statements* for information to be presented either in the statement of financial position or in the notes. The categories are extended to provide a more comprehensive analysis of related party balances and apply to related party transactions.

[IAS 24 para. 20, unamended]

The following are examples of transactions that are disclosed if they are with a related party:

(a)   purchases or sales of goods (finished or unfinished);
(b)   purchases or sales of property and other assets;
(c)   rendering or receiving of services;
(d)   leases;
(e)   transfers of research and development;
(f)   transfers under licence agreements;
(g)   transfers under finance arrangements (including loans and equity contributions in cash or in kind);
(h)   provision of guarantees or collateral;
(i)   commitments to do something if a particular event occurs or does not occur in the future, including executory contracts* (recognised and unrecognised); and
(j)   settlement of liabilities on behalf of the entity or by the entity on behalf of that related party.

[IAS 24 para. 21, unamended]

Participation by a parent or subsidiary in a defined benefit plan that shares risks between group entities is a transaction between related parties (see paragraph 42 of IAS 19 (as amended in 2011)).

[IAS 24 para. 22, unamended]

Disclosures that related party transactions were made on terms equivalent to those that prevail in arm's length transactions are made only if such terms can be substantiated.

[IAS 24 para. 23, unamended]

Items of a similar nature may be disclosed in aggregate except when separate disclosure is necessary for an understanding of the effects of related party transactions on the financial statements of the entity.

[IAS 24 para. 24, unamended]

Government-related entities

A reporting entity is exempt from the disclosure requirements of paragraph 18 in relation to related party transactions and outstanding balances, including commitments, with:

(a) a government that has control, or joint control or significant influence over the reporting entity; and
(b) another entity that is a related party because the same government has control, or joint control of, or significant influence over, both the reporting entity and the other entity.

[IAS 24 para. 25, unamended]

If a reporting entity applies the exemption in paragraph 25, it shall disclose the following about the transactions and related outstanding balances referred to in paragraph 25:

(a) the name of the government and the nature of its relationship with the reporting entity (ie control, joint control or significant influence);
(b) the following information in sufficient detail to enable users of the entity's financial statements to understand the effect of related party transactions on its financial statements:
    (i) the nature and amount of each individually significant transaction; and
    (ii) for other transactions that are collectively, but not individually, significant, a qualitative or quantitative indication of their extent. Types of transactions include those listed in paragraph 21.

[IAS 24 para. 26, unamended]

In using its judgement to determine the level of detail to be disclosed in accordance with the requirements in paragraph 26(b), the reporting entity shall consider the closeness of the related party relationship and other factors relevant in establishing the level of significance of the transaction such as whether it is:

(a) significant in terms of size;
(b) carried out on non-market terms;
(c) outside normal day-to-day business operations, such as the purchase and sale of businesses;
(d) disclosed to regulatory or supervisory authorities;
(e) reported to senior management;
(f) subject to shareholder approval.

[IAS 24 para. 14, unamended]

12.3   Other disclosures

12.3.1   Relevant standards under IFRS, and summary of disclosure requirements

Most of the key standards under IFRS have been covered in one of the sections in **Chapters 9**, **10** or **11**. The only standards not yet discussed are:

- IAS 33 *Earnings per share;*
- IAS 41 *Agriculture;*
- IFRS 4 *Insurance contracts;*
- IFRS 6 *Exploration for and evaluation of mineral resources.*

Earnings per share are not discussed here since the only entities required to provide this information will also be required to present IFRS accounts, either by virtue of their listed status or through the rules of their own exchange.

12.3.2   Overview of accounting differences between IFRS-based FRS 101 and old UK GAAP

There is no old UK GAAP standard explicitly addressing agriculture, so the concepts of biological assets and agricultural produce are new, as is the idea of measuring such assets at fair value in certain cases.

IFRS 4 and IFRS 6 are both effectively temporary standards, allowing entities to continue with their previous accounting policies for insurance and exploration activity respectively. As such it would not be expected that there would be automatic GAAP differences on a transition, though as with any transition this might serve as an opportunity for a preparer to revisit and adjust their accounting policies.

12.3.3   Exemptions given by FRS 101

FRS 101 gives no exemptions from IAS 41, IFRS 4 or IFRS 6.

12.3.4   Accounting amendments arising from the law

There are no accounting amendments to IAS 41, IFRS 4 or IFRS 6 for compliance with UK law. Revaluation gains on biological assets will, under IAS 41, be recognised in income even though they are not realised profits and losses, as discussed in **4.5** above, but this is not a clash with the law, as the Appendix clarified.

12.3.5   Resulting disclosures

Agriculture

General

An entity shall disclose the aggregate gain or loss arising during the current period on initial recognition of biological assets and agricultural produce and from the change in fair value less costs to sell of biological assets.

[IAS 40 para. 40, unamended]

An entity shall provide a description of each group of biological assets.

[IAS 41 para. 41, unamended]

The disclosure required by paragraph 41 may take the form of a narrative or quantified description.

[IAS 41 para. 42, unamended]

An entity is encouraged to provide a quantified description of each group of biological assets, distinguishing between consumable and bearer biological assets or between mature and immature biological assets, as appropriate. For example, an entity may disclose the carrying amounts of consumable biological assets and bearer biological assets by group. An entity may further divide those carrying amounts between mature and immature assets. These distinctions provide information that may be helpful in assessing the timing of future cash flows. An entity discloses the basis for making any such distinctions.

[IAS 41 para. 43, unamended]

Biological assets may be classified either as mature biological assets or immature biological assets. Mature biological assets are those that have attained harvestable specifications (for consumable biological assets) or are able to sustain regular harvests (for bearer biological assets).

[IAS 41 para. 45, unamended – note para. 44 contains definitions rather than any distinct disclosure requirements so is not included here]

If not disclosed elsewhere in information published with the financial statements, an entity shall describe:

(a)   the nature of its activities involving each group of biological assets; and
(b)   non-financial measures or estimates of the physical quantities of:
    (i)   each group of the entity's biological assets at the end of the period; and
    (ii)   output of agricultural produce during the period.

[IAS 41 para. 46, unamended]

An entity shall disclose:

(a)   the existence and carrying amounts of biological assets whose title is restricted, and the carrying amounts of biological assets pledged as security for liabilities;
(b)   the amount of commitments for the development or acquisition of biological assets; and
(c)   financial risk management strategies related to agricultural activity.

[IAS 41 para. 49, unamended – note para. 47 and 48 are not used in the standard]

An entity shall present a reconciliation of changes in the carrying amount of biological assets between the beginning and the end of the current period. The reconciliation shall include:

(a)   the gain or loss arising from changes in fair value less costs to sell;
(b)   increases due to purchases;
(c)   decreases attributable to sales and biological assets classified as held for sale (or included in a disposal group that is classified as held for sale) in accordance with IFRS 5;
(d)   decreases due to harvest;
(e)   increases resulting from business combinations;
(f)   net exchange differences arising on the translation of financial statements into a different presentation currency, and on the translation of a foreign operation into the presentation currency of the reporting entity; and
(g)   other changes.

[IAS 41 para. 50, unamended]

The fair value less costs to sell of a biological asset can change due to both physical changes and price changes in the market. Separate disclosure of physical and price changes is useful in appraising current period performance and future prospects, particularly when there is a production cycle of more than one year. In such cases, an entity is encouraged to disclose, by group or otherwise, the amount of change in fair value less costs to sell included in profit or loss due to physical changes and due to price changes. This information is generally less useful when the production cycle is less than one year (for example, when raising chickens or growing cereal crops).

[IAS 41 para. 51, unamended – note para. 51 expands on the concept of physical change rather than introducing new disclosure requirements, so is not included here]

Agricultural activity is often exposed to climatic, disease and other natural risks. If an event occurs that gives rise to a material item of income or expense, the nature and amount of that item are disclosed in accordance with IAS 1 *Presentation of Financial Statements*. Examples of such an event include an outbreak of a virulent disease, a flood, a severe drought or frost, and a plague of insects.

[IAS 41 para. 53, unamended]

Additional disclosures for biological assets where fair value cannot be measured reliably

If an entity measures biological assets at their cost less any accumulated depreciation and any accumulated impairment losses (see paragraph 30) at the end of the period, the entity shall disclose for such biological assets:

(a)   a description of the biological assets;
(b)   an explanation of why fair value cannot be measured reliably;
(c)   if possible, the range of estimates within which fair value is highly likely to lie;
(d)   the depreciation method used;
(e)   the useful lives or the depreciation rates used; and
(f)   the gross carrying amount and the accumulated depreciation (aggregated with accumulated impairment losses) at the beginning and end of the period.

[IAS 41 para. 54, unamended]

If, during the current period, an entity measures biological assets at their cost less any accumulated depreciation and any accumulated impairment losses (see paragraph 30), an entity shall disclose any gain or loss recognised on disposal of such biological assets and the reconciliation required by paragraph 50 shall disclose amounts related to such biological assets separately. In addition, the reconciliation shall include the following amounts included in profit or loss related to those biological assets:

(a)   impairment losses;
(b)   reversals of impairment losses; and
(c)   depreciation.

[IAS 41 para. 55, unamended]

If the fair value of biological assets previously measured at their cost less any accumulated depreciation and any accumulated impairment losses becomes reliably measurable during the current period, an entity shall disclose for those biological assets:

(a)   a description of the biological assets;
(b)   an explanation of why fair value has become reliably measurable; and
(c)   the effect of the change.

[IAS 41 para. 56, unamended]

Government grants

An entity shall disclose the following related to agricultural activity covered by this Standard:

(a)   the nature and extent of government grants recognised in the financial statements;
(b)   unfulfilled conditions and other contingencies attaching to government grants; and
(c)   significant decreases expected in the level of government grants.

[IAS 41 para. 57, unamended]

Insurance contracts

Explanation of recognised amounts

An insurer shall disclose information that identifies and explains the amounts in its financial statements arising from insurance contracts.

[IFRS 4 para. 36, unamended]

To comply with paragraph 36, an insurer shall disclose:

(a)   its accounting policies for insurance contracts and related assets, liabilities, income and expense;
(b)   the recognised assets, liabilities, income and expense (and, if it presents its statement of cash flows using the direct method, cash flows) arising from insurance contracts. Furthermore, if the insurer is a cedant, it shall disclose:
     (i)   gains and losses recognised in profit or loss on buying reinsurance; and
     (ii) if the cedant defers and amortises gains and losses arising on buying reinsurance, the amortisation for the period and the amounts remaining unamortised at the beginning and end of the period;
(c)   the process used to determine the assumptions that have the greatest effect on the measurement of the recognised amounts described in (b). When practicable, an insurer shall also give quantified disclosure of those assumptions;
(d)   the effect of changes in assumptions used to measure insurance assets and insurance liabilities, showing separately the effect of each change that has a material effect on the financial statements;
(e)   reconciliations of changes in insurance liabilities, reinsurance assets and, if any, related deferred acquisition costs.

[IFRS 4 para. 37, unamended]

Nature and extent of risks arising from insurance contracts

An insurer shall disclose information that enables users of its financial statements to evaluate the nature and extent of risks arising from insurance contracts.

[IFRS 4 para. 38, unamended]

To comply with paragraph 38, an insurer shall disclose:

(a)   its objectives, policies and processes for managing risks arising from insurance contracts and the methods used to manage those risks;
(b)   [deleted]
(c)   information about *insurance risk* (both before and after risk mitigation by reinsurance), including information about:
     (i)   sensitivity to insurance risk (see paragraph 39A);

(ii)   concentrations of insurance risk, including a description of how management determines concentrations and a description of the shared characteristic that identifies each concentration (eg type of insured event, geographical area, or currency);

(iii)   actual claims compared with previous estimates (i.e. claims development). The disclosure about claims development shall go back to the period when the earliest material claim arose for which there is still uncertainty about the amount and timing of the claims payments, but need not go back more than ten years. An insurer need not disclose this information for claims for which uncertainty about the amount and timing of claims payments is typically resolved within one year;

(d)   information about credit risk, liquidity risk and market risk that paragraphs 31–42 of IFRS 7 would require if the insurance contracts were within the scope of IFRS 7. However:

(i)   an insurer need not provide the maturity analyses required by paragraph 39(a) and (b) of IFRS 7 if it discloses information about the estimated timing of the net cash outflows resulting from recognised insurance liabilities instead. This may take the form of an analysis, by estimated timing, of the amounts recognised in the statement of financial position;

(ii)   if an insurer uses an alternative method to manage sensitivity to market conditions, such as an embedded value analysis, it may use that sensitivity analysis to meet the requirement in paragraph 40(a) of IFRS 7. Such an insurer shall also provide the disclosures required by paragraph 41 of IFRS 7;

(e)   information about exposures to market risk arising from embedded derivatives contained in a host insurance contract if the insurer is not required to, and does not, measure the embedded derivatives at fair value.

[IFRS 4 para. 39, unamended]

To comply with paragraph 39(c)(i), an insurer shall disclose either (a) or (b) as follows:

(a)   a sensitivity analysis that shows how profit or loss and equity would have been affected if changes in the relevant risk variable that were reasonably possible at the end of the reporting period had occurred; the methods and assumptions used in preparing the sensitivity analysis; and any changes from the previous period in the methods and assumptions used. However, if an insurer uses an alternative method to manage sensitivity to market conditions, such as an embedded value analysis, it may meet this requirement by disclosing that alternative sensitivity analysis and the disclosures required by paragraph 41 of IFRS 7;

(b)   qualitative information about sensitivity, and information about those terms and conditions of insurance contracts that have a material effect on the amount, timing and uncertainty of the insurer's future cash flows.

[IFRS 4 para. 39A, unamended]

Exploration for and evaluation of mineral resources

An entity shall disclose information that identifies and explains the amounts recognised in its financial statements arising from the exploration for and evaluation of mineral resources.

[IFRS 6 para. 23, unamended]

To comply with paragraph 23, an entity shall disclose:

(a)   its accounting policies for exploration and evaluation expenditures including the recognition of exploration and evaluation assets;

(b)   the amounts of assets, liabilities, income and expense and operating and investing cash flows arising from the exploration for and evaluation of mineral resources.

[IFRS 6 para. 24, unamended]

An entity shall treat exploration and evaluation assets as a separate class of assets and make the disclosures required by either IAS 16 or IAS 38 consistent with how the assets are classified.

[IFRS 6 para 25, unamended]

Part IV   Other information

Chapter 13 Other documents with the accounts

13.1 Strategic report

All companies except those qualifying as small must provide a strategic report as part of their financial statements, according to CA 2006, s. 414–419A.

This requirement was put in place comparatively recently, but there was an equivalent in place before, in the shape of the old s. 417 requirement for the directors' report to contain an enhanced business review.

Because FRS 101 does not apply to entities preparing consolidated accounts, the requirement to prepare a consolidated strategic report with group accounts is not relevant here.

The small companies exemption from preparing a strategic report is actually marginally more subtle than just applying to small companies that meet all of the conditions to apply the small companies regime – it also applies to those that would meet the conditions but are disqualified for being part of an ineligible group.

Section 414C sets out the purpose and required contents of the strategic report:

'(1) The purpose of the strategic report is to inform members of the company and help them assess how the directors have performed their duty under section 172 (duty to promote the success of the company).

(2) The strategic report must contain—
   (a) a fair review of the company's business, and
   (b) a description of the principal risks and uncertainties facing the company.

(3) The review required is a balanced and comprehensive analysis of—
   (a) the development and performance of the company's business during the financial year, and
   (b) the position of the company's business at the end of that year,

   consistent with the size and complexity of the business.

(4) The review must, to the extent necessary for an understanding of the development, performance or position of the company's business, include—
   (a) analysis using financial key performance indicators, and
   (b) where appropriate, analysis using other key performance indicators, including information relating to environmental matters and employee matters.

(5) In subsection (4), "key performance indicators" means factors by reference to which the development, performance or position of the company's business can be measured effectively.

(6) Where a company qualifies as medium-sized in relation to a financial year (see sections 465 to 467), the review for the year need not comply with the requirements of subsection (4) so far as they relate to non-financial information.

(7) In the case of a quoted company the strategic report must, to the extent necessary for an understanding of the development, performance or position of the company's business, include—
   (a) the main trends and factors likely to affect the future development, performance and position of the company's business, and

   (b) information about—
      (i) environmental matters (including the impact of the company's business on the environment),
      (ii) the company's employees, and
      (iii) social, community and human rights issues,

including information about any policies of the company in relation to those matters and the effectiveness of those policies.

If the report does not contain information of each kind mentioned in paragraphs (b)(i), (ii) and (iii), it must state which of those kinds of information it does not contain.

(8) In the case of a quoted company the strategic report must include—
   (a) a description of the company's strategy,
   (b) a description of the company's business model,
   (c) a breakdown showing at the end of the financial year—
      (i) the number of persons of each sex who were directors of the company;
      (ii) the number of persons of each sex who were senior managers of the company (other than persons falling within sub-paragraph (i)); and
      (iii) the number of persons of each sex who were employees of the company.

(9) In subsection (8), "senior manager" means a person who—
   (a) has responsibility for planning, directing or controlling the activities of the company, or a strategically significant part of the company, and
   (b) is an employee of the company.

(10) In relation to a group strategic report—
   (a) the reference to the company in subsection (8)(c)(i) is to the parent company; and
   (b) the breakdown required by subsection (8)(c)(ii) must include the number of persons of each sex who were the directors of the undertakings included in the consolidation.

(11) The strategic report may also contain such of the matters otherwise required by regulations made under section 416(4) to be disclosed in the directors' report as the directors consider are of strategic importance to the company.

(12) The report must, where appropriate, include references to, and additional explanations of, amounts included in the company's annual accounts.

(13) Subject to paragraph (10), in relation to a group strategic report this section has effect as if the references to the company were references to the undertakings included in the consolidation.

(14) Nothing in this section requires the disclosure of information about impending developments or matters in the course of negotiation if the disclosure would, in the opinion of the directors, be seriously prejudicial to the interests of the company.'

There are many points of interest within this list of requirements. It should be borne in mind that for FRS 101 preparers, users of the accounts have a very significant change to deal with, because the shift from old, familiar UK GAAP to a new IFRS-based framework involves a new language, new presentation and, in many cases, accounting adjustments. A good informative narrative, consistent with the reported figures and adding context, explanation, and information about how the results fit in with and reflect the business, is a priceless complement to a carefully prepared set of primary statements and notes. The strategic report should not, then, be seen as a box-ticking exercise; rather it might give some structure, and shows areas that need to be covered, but really acts as a starting point for a meaningful communication to users. Some readers might attempt to argue that this is unnecessary since FRS 101 preparers are subsidiaries anyway, so their shareholder (i.e. the parent company) does not need to see further information – but this misses the point about how wide the range of users of accounts is. Customers, suppliers, local government, employees, and current and potential future providers of finance may all need to understand the business and want to obtain, read and understand the accounts.

The wording in the earlier subsections sets out the general tone of the requirements: the report needs to include a 'fair review' with a 'balanced and comprehensive analysis'. It is unsurprising that this is included: the strategic report is not meant to be an advertising piece, and should not ignore difficult areas. This resonates with the 2012 updates to the UK Corporate Governance Code, where Boards are asked to confirm that the annual report and accounts taken as a whole are 'fair, balanced and understandable'. It shows the FRC's interest in this area, and in making narrative reporting much more than a box-ticking exercise.

The requirement to identify and include key performance indicators was problematic for many when it was first introduced in s. 417 (now withdrawn), with a surprising number of preparers arguing that there were no relevant non-financial KPIs. So many companies simply reproduced some headline figures from their primary statements, arguing that these were the most informative financial KPIs and that non-financial KPIs were not necessary for an understanding of the business. This is still available as an argument, but preparers taking this line should be aware that this may lead some users to ask challenging questions of management, and should ask themselves carefully whether it really is the case that the only markers of whether the business is going to plan are a small number of lines from the published accounts.

Medium-sized companies are exempt from the requirement to provide non-financial KPIs, so this is only an issue for large companies.

Sub-paragraphs (7) to (9) are not relevant to FRS 101 preparers in that they only apply to quoted companies, but this does not mean they cannot be read to give additional ideas on areas that users might find useful or interesting.

Sub-paragraphs (10) and (13) only apply to consolidated strategic business reports, so again is not relevant to an FRS 101 preparer.

Sub-paragraph (12) is interesting because of the powerful requirements included in a very brief piece of wording: 'The report must, where appropriate, include references to, and additional explanations of, amounts included in the company's annual accounts'. This is not an optional requirement – the report **must** include references to amounts in the accounts, and give additional explanations where appropriate. In other words it cannot exist as a detached piece of narrative, which adds weight to the point above that these reports are meant to be read in conjunction with a close reading of the accounts, each adding both clarity and weight to the other. It is unlikely that simply reproducing a few key lines from the primary statements as key performance indicators would be enough to satisfy this requirement, though here as with the others there is considerable judgement involved.

Finally, there is another line that needs careful application, in (14), where there is an exemption from providing information about impending developments or matters in the course of negotiation if the directors believe this would be seriously prejudicial to the business. It is not possible for users to make this judgement, since they can only see the information that does reach the strategic report, but it is not an exemption to be taken lightly. There is a careful balance to be struck because information about future possibilities is very relevant to decision-making, and in some cases can make a very real difference to the way a company's position seems. It might, for instance, be in a poor net asset position with cash outflows and minimal reserves, but at the year end be in advanced negotiations for a contract that would transform its results – in this case users would benefit significantly from knowing at least some information about the possibility. The same applies for potential bad news, though companies will not wish to expose their weaknesses in a way that could make this weakness too apparent and undermine them with their existing customers, suppliers and investors. Where a decision is taken to omit key information based on 'seriously prejudicial' grounds, the directors should ensure that this decision is well documented, along with its justification.

13.2   Directors' report

Basic information requirements

The directors' report used to be required to contain a broad spectrum of information, from the highly factual to the more commercial and narrative, when the business review from s. 417 was part of it.

Now, with the strategic report replacing the business review, there is much less information required in the directors' report. The requirements are, however, split between two sources: the Act itself and the Regulations.

In the Act, the initial information requirements are:

(a) the names of the persons who, at any time during the financial year, were directors of the company; and

(b) the amount (if any) that the directors recommend should be paid by way of dividend. [Both from s. 416, para. (c) not required for small companies.]

The other requirements appear in Sch. 7 of the Regulations, and cover a number of areas:

(1) Asset values – disclosure where the market value of fixed assets differs substantially from their carrying value.

(2) Political donations and expenditure – companies that are not wholly owned subsidiaries must make a number of disclosures if their political donations or expenditure exceeded £2,000 in the year.

(3) Charitable donations – companies that are not wholly owned subsidiaries must detail charitable donations if the total given in aggregate exceeded £2,000.

(4) Financial instruments – the directors' report must contain an indication of the company's financial risk management objectives and policies, the company's exposure to price risk, credit risk, liquidity risk and cash flow risk.

(5) Particulars of any important events affecting the company which have occurred since the end of the financial year.

(6) An indication of likely future developments in the business of the company.

(7) An indication of the activities (if any) of the company in the field of research and development.

(8) (Unless the company is an unlimited company) an indication of the existence of branches (as defined in s. 1046(3) of the 2006 Act) of the company outside the United Kingdom.

Whereas we noted above that the strategic report is best not written with a checklist mentality, the list of information requirements for the directors' report can be fulfilled more mechanically. The full detail of the requirements in Sch. 7 of the Regulations is reproduced in **Appendix 2**. It should be noted that where the Directors' Report refers to financial reporting, it is incorrect to refer to the accounts as using IFRS. FRS 101 is, as discussed in **4.1**, one form of UK GAAP and this is a distinction that should be kept clear.

Statement about disclosure of information to auditors

Section 418 goes on to require a statement in respect of disclosure of information to auditors:

'(2) The directors' report must contain a statement to the effect that, in the case of each of the persons who are directors at the time the report is approved—

(a) so far as the director is aware, there is no relevant audit information of which the company's auditor is unaware, and

(b) he has taken all the steps that he ought to have taken as a director in order to make himself aware of any relevant audit information and to establish that the company's auditor is aware of that information.

(3) 'Relevant audit information' means information needed by the company's auditor in connection with preparing his report.

(4) A director is regarded as having taken all the steps that he ought to have taken as a director in order to do the things mentioned in subsection (2)(b) if he has—

(a) made such enquiries of his fellow directors and of the company's auditors for that purpose, and

(b) taken such other steps (if any) for that purpose,

as are required by his duty as a director of the company to exercise reasonable care, skill and diligence.'

Statement of directors' responsibilities

The statement of directors' responsibilities is not a requirement of law, but rather of auditing standards. This is driven by ISA (UK and Ireland) 700 *The auditor's report on financial statements* which states that the auditor's report must contain 'a statement that those charged with governance are responsible for the preparation of the financial statements and a statement that the responsibility of the auditor is to audit and express an opinion on the financial statements in accordance with applicable legal requirements and International Standards on Auditing (UK and Ireland)'. The relevant APB Bulletin, Bulletin 2010/2 *Compendium of illustrative auditor's reports on United Kingdom private sector financial statements for periods ended on or after 15 December 2010 (revised)* approaches this by expecting entities to include a separate directors' responsibilities statement, to which the audit report can then refer. It gives an example of this statement, reproduced here from Appendix 17 example 47:

'DIRECTORS' RESPONSIBILITIES STATEMENT

The directors are responsible for preparing the Directors' Report and the financial statements in accordance with applicable law and regulations.

Company law requires the directors to prepare financial statements for each financial year. Under that law the directors have elected to prepare the financial statements in accordance with United Kingdom Generally Accepted Accounting Practice (United Kingdom Accounting Standards and applicable law). Under company law the directors must not approve the financial statements unless they are satisfied that they give a true and fair view of the state of affairs of the company and the profit or loss of the company for that period.

In preparing these financial statements, the directors are required to:

- select suitable accounting policies and then apply them consistently;
- make judgments and accounting estimates that are reasonable and prudent;
- state whether applicable UK Accounting Standards have been followed, subject to any material departures disclosed and explained in the financial statements;
- prepare the financial statements on the going concern basis unless it is inappropriate to presume that the company will continue in business.

The directors are responsible for keeping adequate accounting records that are sufficient to show and explain the company's transactions and disclose with reasonable accuracy at any time the financial position of the company and enable them to ensure that the financial statements comply with the Companies Act 2006. They are also responsible for safeguarding the assets of the company and hence for taking reasonable steps for the prevention and detection of fraud and other irregularities.'

FRS 101 preparers would not be inaccurate in stating that their accounts are prepared under UK GAAP, being UK accounting standards and applicable law, since FRS 101 is a UK accounting standard even though it effectively acts as an envelope for IFRS accounting. The legal status of FRS 101 accounts, and their treatment as 'Companies Act accounts' rather than 'IAS accounts' is discussed at length in **Chapter 4**.

13.3 Auditor's report

This section is included mainly for completeness, and is of necessity an overview, since the detail of the requirements needs considerable volume to do it justice. Readers are recommended to look to the publications *The CCH Audit Reports Handbook 2015–16* and *Implementing GAAS 2015–16* available from www.cch.co.uk/books. Auditing standards are changing significantly in 2016 and the publications will be updated accordingly.

More than one source of regulation exists in respect of auditor's reports. First there is UK law, which sets out minimum elements of an audit report and also defines which entities are required to undergo an audit and which are exempt. Then auditing standards (ISAs (UK and Ireland)) apply too, giving detail on the required form and content of an audit report.

Because this publication is primarily aimed at preparers of FRS 101 accounts, rather than their auditors, this section is an overview, serving to help preparers with an understanding of what their auditors need to be able to say about their accounts.

13.3.1   The requirements of the law

There is extensive documentation within CA 2006 on the requirements for audited accounts and what needs to be included in an audit report.

Requirements for audited accounts

The basic requirement for a company to have audited accounts appears in CA 2006, s. 475, which states that all companies require an audit unless they qualify for an exemption by virtue of being small (s. 477), a subsidiary (s. 479A), dormant (s. 480) or a non-profit making company subject to public sector audit (s. 482).

In any case, the audit exemption is only valid if:

- the balance sheet contains a statement by the directors to the effect that the exemption is being taken;
- the statement by directors confirms that the members have not required the directors to obtain an audit; and
- the statement acknowledges the directors' responsibilities for complying with the requirements of the Act in respect of maintaining records and preparing accounts.

Note that the influence of members requires more engagement from those members than is needed for the preparation of FRS 101 accounts. For FRS 101 accounts, the company must contact the members and receive no more than a set proportion of disagreements; for the audit exemptions, however, there is no obligation on the company to contact members and tell them of their intentions. Members of a company qualifying for an audit exemption must actively contact the company and notify it that they require an audit (and still meet a minimum percentage) (s. 476).

The subsidiary exemption is only for those with a parent in an EEA state. To take this exemption, the requirements in respect of members are also tightened further, in that the following conditions also apply [s. 479A (2)]:

'(a) all members of the company must agree to the exemption in respect of the financial year in question,

(b) the parent undertaking must give a guarantee under section 479C in respect of that year,

(c) the company must be included in the consolidated accounts drawn up for that year or to an earlier date in that year by the parent undertaking in accordance with—
  (i)   the provisions of the Seventh Directive (83/349/EEC), or
  (ii) international accounting standards,

(d) the parent undertaking must disclose in the notes to the consolidated accounts that the company is exempt from the requirements of this Act relating to the audit of individual accounts by virtue of this section, and

(e) the directors of the company must deliver to the registrar on or before the date that they file the accounts for that year—
  (i)   a written notice of the agreement referred to in subsection (2)(a),
  (ii) the statement referred to in section 479C(1),
  (iii) a copy of the consolidated accounts referred to in subsection (2)(c),
  (iv) a copy of the auditor's report on those accounts, and
  (v)   a copy of the consolidated annual report drawn up by the parent undertaking.'

Contents of an audit report

Section 495(2) states the two required components of an audit report that are not the opinion:

'(a) an introduction identifying the annual accounts that are the subject of the audit and the financial reporting framework that has been applied in their preparation, and

(b) a description of the scope of the audit identifying the auditing standards in accordance with which the audit was conducted.'

And then s. 495(3) gives conditions for the audit opinion:

'The report must state clearly whether, in the auditor's opinion, the annual accounts—

(a) give a true and fair view—
   (i) in the case of an individual balance sheet, of the state of affairs of the company as at the end of the financial year,
   (ii) in the case of an individual profit and loss account, of the profit or loss of the company for the financial year,
   (iii) in the case of group accounts, of the state of affairs as at the end of the financial year and of the profit or loss for the financial year of the undertakings included in the consolidation as a whole, so far as concerns members of the company;
(b) have been properly prepared in accordance with the relevant financial reporting framework; and
(c) have been prepared in accordance with the requirements of this Act (and, where applicable, Article 4 of the IAS Regulation).'

Auditors also have to report on the strategic report and directors' report, though they do not have to be audited as such. Rather, the auditor must confirm that in his opinion the information included in the directors' report and strategic report is consistent with the accounts. The full text of s. 496 reads as follows:

'In his report on the company's annual accounts, the auditor must—

(a) state whether, in his opinion, based on the work undertaken in the course of the audit—
   (i) the information given in the strategic report (if any) and the directors' report for the financial year for which the accounts are prepared is consistent with those accounts, and
   (ii) any such strategic report and the directors' report have been prepared in accordance with applicable legal requirements,
(b) state whether, in the light of the knowledge and understanding of the company and its environment obtained in the course of the audit, he has identified material misstatements in the strategic report (if any) and the directors' report, and
(c) if applicable, give an indication of the nature of each of the misstatements referred to in paragraph (b)'

13.3.2 *The requirements of auditing standards*

The relevant auditing standard is ISA (UK and Ireland) 700, *The Independent Auditor's Report on Financial Statements.* The ISA prescribes the minimum content of an auditor's report, but generally steers clear of giving example wording, with the exception of the requirement to describe the scope of the audit, where auditors are given the option of cross referring to the FRC website or elsewhere in the annual report, or reproducing the following paragraph verbatim:

'An audit involves obtaining evidence about the amounts and disclosures in the financial statements sufficient to give reasonable assurance that the financial statements are free from material misstatement, whether caused by fraud or error. This includes an assessment of: whether the accounting policies are appropriate to the [describe nature of entity] circumstances and have been consistently applied and adequately disclosed; the reasonableness of significant accounting estimates made by [describe those charged with governance]; and the overall presentation of the financial statements. In addition, we read all the financial and non-financial information in the [describe the annual report] to identify material inconsistencies with the audited financial statements and to identify any information that is apparently materially incorrect based on, or materially inconsistent with, the knowledge acquired by us in the course of performing the audit. If we become aware of any apparent material misstatements or inconsistencies we consider the implications for our report.'

Beyond this, though, auditors will usually look to the most recent APB Bulletin, at present APB Bulletin 2010/02 (Revised), *Compendium of Illustrative Auditor's Reports on United Kingdom Private Sector Financial Statements for periods ended on or after 15 December 2010.*

In this chapter, we provide one example audit report, for a large or medium-sized company, since this is the most likely group of constituents for applying FRS 101. It is an unqualified report with no emphasis of matter and assumes that the company is not quoted, does not prepare group accounts, and either does not qualify as small or does qualify but has chosen not to use the FRSSE or other small companies provisions. It is modified from Example 2 in Appendix 1 to Bulletin 2010/02, both to update primary statement names as appropriate and to eliminate options so the report reads as a continuous document. The second paragraph, clarifying that the report is made solely to members, is not in the example wording from Bulletin 2010/2, but is recommended for inclusion by the ICAEW in their document Audit 1/03 *The Audit Report and the Auditor's Duty of Care to Third Parties).*

INDEPENDENT AUDITOR'S REPORT TO THE MEMBERS OF FRS 101 LIMITED

We have audited the financial statements of FRS 101 Limited for the year ended 31 December 2015 which comprise the Statement of Comprehensive Income, Statement of Financial Position, Statement of Cash Flows and the related notes. The financial reporting framework that has been applied in their preparation is applicable law and United Kingdom Accounting Standards (United Kingdom Generally Accepted Accounting Practice).

This report is made solely to the company's members, as a body, in accordance with the *Companies Act* 2006, Pt. 16, Ch. 3. Our audit work has been undertaken so that we might state to the company's members those matters that we are required to state to them in an auditor's report and for no other purpose. To the fullest extent permitted by law, we do not accept or assume responsibility to anyone other than the company and the company's members as a body, for our audit work, for this report, or for the opinions we have formed.

Respective responsibilities of directors and auditor

As explained more fully in the Directors' Responsibilities Statement set out on page xx, the directors are responsible for the preparation of the financial statements and for being satisfied that they give a true and fair view. Our responsibility is to audit and express an opinion on the financial statements in accordance with applicable law and International Standards on Auditing (UK and Ireland). Those standards require us to comply with the Financial Reporting Council's [FRC's] Ethical Standards for Auditors.

Scope of the audit of the financial statements

A description of the scope of an audit of financial statements is provided on the APB's website at www.frc.org.uk/apb/scope/private.cfm

Opinion on financial statements

In our opinion the financial statements:

- give a true and fair view of the state of the company's affairs as at and of its profit [loss] for the year then ended;
- have been properly prepared in accordance with United Kingdom Generally Accepted Accounting Practice; and
- have been prepared in accordance with the requirements of the *Companies Act* 2006.

Opinion on other matter prescribed by the Companies Act 2006

In our opinion the information given in the Strategic Report and the Directors' Report for the financial year for which the financial statements are prepared is consistent with the financial statements.

Matters on which we are required to report by exception

We have nothing to report in respect of the following matters where the *Companies Act* 2006 requires us to report to you if, in our opinion:

- adequate accounting records have not been kept, or returns adequate for our audit have not been received from branches not visited by us;
- the financial statements are not in agreement with the accounting records and returns;
- certain disclosures of directors' remuneration specified by law are not made; or
- we have not received all the information and explanations we require for our audit.

[Signature]   *Address*

John Smith (Senior statutory auditor)   *Date*

for and on behalf of ABC LLP, Statutory Auditor

13.4   Other information

The latest amendments to company law have also introduced another disclosure requirement, without specifying where it needs to appear.

Accounts authorised after 1 July 2015 need to include a full listing of subsidiaries, rather than just listing principal subsidiaries and including a full list with the annual return. For periods beginning on or after 1 January 2016 (rather than accounts authorised after this date) the list will also need to show the registered office of each subsidiary. For ultimate or intermediate parents in large groups, preparing this list could be onerous.

Appendices

Appendix 1   FRS 101 Limited

Financial statements for the year ended 31 December 2015

Contents	Page
Statement of comprehensive income	121
Statement of financial position	122
Statement of changes in equity	124
Notes to the consolidated financial statements	124

Note on scope

These example accounts are based on a full set of IFRS accounts, with disclosures removed where permitted by FRS 101. They contain only the primary statements and notes, therefore there is no directors' report, strategic review or auditor's report. A cash flow statement is not included as this is not a requirement of FRS 101.

A full set of FRS 101 accounts would be more tailored to a company's individual situation, so the very general accounting policies included here would need to be tailored and made more entity-specific. 'Boilerplate' accounting policies are frowned upon by the FRC.

*The income statement uses a format based on IAS 1, which is permissible as discussed in **4.3**.*

119

Statement of comprehensive income for the year ended 31 December 2015

	Continuing operations	Discontinued operations	Total	Continuing operations	Discontinued operations	Total
	Year ended 31/12/15 £000			**Year ended 31/12/14 (as restated) £000**		
Revenue	X	X	X	X	X	X
Cost of sales	X	X	X	X	X	X
Gross profit	X	X	X	X	X	X
Other income	X	X	X	X	X	X
Distribution costs	X	X	X	X	X	X
Administrative expenses	X	X	X	X	X	X
Other expenses	X	X	X	X	X	X
Results from operating activities[5]	X	X	X	X	X	X
Finance costs[6]	X	X	X	X	X	X
Finance income[7]	X	X	X	X	X	X
Net finance costs	X	X	X	X	X	X
Profit before tax	X	X	X	X	X	X
Income tax expense[9]	X	X	X	X	X	X
Profit for the year	X	X	X	X	X	X
Other comprehensive income (loss)						
Revaluation of property, plant and equipment			X			X
Effective portion of changes in fair value of cash flow hedges			X			X
Defined benefit plan actuarial gains (losses)			X			X
Tax on other comprehensive income			X			X
Other comprehensive income for the year, net of tax			**X**			**X**
Total comprehensive income for the year			**X**			**X**
Profit for the year attributable to owners of the Company			X			X
Total comprehensive income attributable to owners of the Company			X			X

Statement of financial position at 31 December 2015

	Note	2015 £'000	2014 (as restated) £'000
Assets			
Non-current assets			
Property, plant and equipment	11	X	X
Investment property	12	X	X
Goodwill	13	X	X
Other intangible assets	14	X	X
Investments	15	X	X
Deferred tax assets	28	X	X
Current assets			
Inventories	16	X	X
Trade receivables	17	X	X
Other current assets	17	X	X
Investments	15	X	X
Cash and cash equivalents	17	X	X
Non-current assets classified as held for sale	19	X	X
Total assets		**X**	**X**
Equity and liabilities			
Equity attributable to equity holders of the parent			
Share capital	20	X	X
Capital reserves	22	X	X
Revaluation reserves	23	X	X
Other reserves	24	X	X
Retained earnings	25	X	X
Non-current liabilities			
Long-term borrowings	26	X	X
Convertible loan notes	27	X	X
Employee benefits	35	X	X
Deferred tax	28	X	X
Obligations under finance leases – due after one year	29	X	X
Long-term provisions	31	X	X

	Note	2015 £'000	2014 (as restated) £'000
Current liabilities			
Trade and other payables	30	X	X
Current portion of long-term borrowings	26	X	X
Employee benefits	35	X	X
Current tax payable	28	X	X
Obligations under finance leases – due within one year	29	X	X
Bank overdrafts and loans – due within one year	26	X	X
Short-term provisions	31	X	X
Liabilities directly associated with non-current assets classified as held for sale	19	X	X
Total liabilities		**X**	**X**
Total equity and liabilities		**X**	**X**

The financial statements on pages to were approved by the board of directors and authorised for issue on

and are signed on its behalf by

_____ Director _____ Director

Statement of changes in equity for the year ended 31 December 2015

Attributable to owners of the Company

	Share capital	Capital reserves	Revaluation reserve	Hedging and translation reserve	Retained earnings	Total
	£000	£000	£000	£000	£000	£000
Balance at 31 December 2015						
– as originally restated	X	X	X	X	X	X
– changes in accounting policy relating to first time adoption of FRS 101					X	X
– restated	X	X	X	X	X	X
Changes in equity for 2014:						
Total comprehensive income for the year			X	X	X	X
Dividends					X	X
Issue of share capital	X	X				X
Balance at 31 December 2014	X	X	X	X	X	X
Changes in equity for 2015:						
Total comprehensive income for the year			X	X	X	X
Dividends					X	X
Issue of share capital	X	X				X
Balance at 31 December 2015	X	X	X	X	X	X

Notes to the consolidated financial statements for the year ended 31 December 2015

1. Basis of preparation of financial statements

The financial statements have been prepared in accordance with FRS 101, *Reduced Disclosure Framework – Disclosure exemptions from EU-adopted IFRS for qualifying entities*. This means that they use the recognition and measurement principles of International Accounting and Financial Reporting Standards (IFRS) as adopted for use in the EU, but with disclosure exemptions as set out in FRS 101. In cases where accounting changes mandated by FRS 101 have also been applied, these are disclosed case by case.

The ultimate parent company which produces true and fair consolidated accounts including this company's results is Y Plc [ADD ADDRESS].

The financial statements are presented in pounds sterling since this is the currency in which the majority of the Company's transactions are denominated.

As at the date of approval of these financial statements, the following standards and interpretations were in issue but not yet effective:

GIVE LIST OF STANDARDS AND INTERPRETATIONS

The Directors do not anticipate that the adoption of these standards and interpretations in future reporting periods will have a material impact on the Company's results.

1. Basis of measurement

The financial statements have been prepared on the historical cost basis, except for the following material items in the statement of financial position:

- derivative financial instruments are measured at fair value;
- non-derivative financial instruments at fair value through profit or loss are measured at fair value;
- available-for-sale financial assets are measured at fair value;
- investment property is measured at fair value;
- liabilities for cash-settled share-based payment arrangements are measured at fair value; and
- the defined benefit liability is recognised as plan assets, plus unrecognised past service cost, less the present value of the defined benefit obligation.

2. Going concern

The Company has a history of profitable operations and has successfully raised financing in the past to provide funding for its activities and to augment its working capital. Having regard to the Company's existing working capital position and its ability to raise potential financing, if required, the Directors are of the opinion that the Company has adequate resources to enable it to undertake its planned activities over the next twelve months.

3. First-time adoption of FRS 101

In the current year, the Company has adopted FRS 101 for the first time, applying the recognition, measurement and disclosure requirements of EU-adopted IFRS with certain amendments and disclosure exemptions.

The Company has applied IFRS 1 *First time adoption of International Financial Reporting Standards* to provide a starting point for reporting under FRS 101. The date of transition to FRS 101 is 1 January 2014 and all comparative information in these financial statements has been restated to reflect the Company's adoption of FRS 101.

The adoption of FRS 101 has resulted in the following changes to the Company's accounting policies.

[Give details of changes to accounting policies.]

Reconciliation of equity at 1 January 2014

The effect of the changes to the Company's accounting policies on the equity of the Company at the date of transition, 1 January 2014, was as follows.

	Note	*As reported under previous GAAP*	*Effect of transition to FRS 101*	*FRS 101*
Property, plant and equipment	1	X	X	X
Goodwill	2	X	X	X
Intangible assets	2	X	X	X

Appendix 1

	Note	As reported under previous GAAP	Effect of transition to FRS 101	FRS 101
Financial assets	3	X	X	X
Total non-current assets		X	X	X
Trade and other receivables		X	X	X
Inventories	4	X	X	X
Other receivables	5	X	X	X
Cash and cash equivalents		X	X	X
Total current assets		X	X	X
Total assets		X	X	X
Interest-bearing loans		X	X	X
Trade and other payables		X	X	X
Employee benefits		X	X	X
Restructuring provision	6	X	X	X
Current tax liability		X	X	X
Deferred tax liability	7	X	X	X
Total liabilities		X	X	X
Total assets less total liabilities		X	X	X
Issued capital		X	X	X
Revaluation reserve	3	X	X	X
Hedging reserve	5	X	X	X
Retained earnings	9	X	X	X
Total equity		X	X	X

Notes to the reconciliation of equity at 1 January 2014

1   Depreciation was influenced by tax requirements under previous GAAP, but under IAS 16 reflects the useful life of the assets. The cumulative adjustment increased the carrying amount of property, plant and equipment by x.

2   Intangible assets under previous GAAP included x for items that are transferred to goodwill because they do not qualify for recognition as intangible assets under IAS 38.

3   Financial assets are all classified as available-for-sale under IAS 39 and are carried at their fair value of x. They were carried at cost of x under previous GAAP. The resulting gains of x (x, less related deferred tax of x) are included in the revaluation reserve.

4   Inventories include fixed and variable production overhead of x under IAS 2 but this overhead was excluded under previous GAAP.

5   Unrealised gains of x on unmatured forward foreign exchange contracts are recognised under IAS 39, but were not recognised under previous GAAP. The resulting gains of x (x, less related deferred tax of x) are included in the hedging reserve because the contracts hedge forecast sales.

6   A restructuring provision of x relating to head office activities was recognised under previous GAAP, but does not qualify for recognition as a liability under IAS 37.

7   The above changes increased the deferred tax liability as follows:

Revaluation reserve (note 3)	X
Hedging reserve (note 5)	X
Retained earnings	X
Increase in deferred tax liability	X

Because the tax base at 1 January 2014 of the items reclassified from intangible assets to goodwill (note 2) equalled their carrying amount at that date, the reclassification did not affect deferred tax liabilities.

8   The adjustments to retained earnings are as follows:

Depreciation (note 1)	X
Production overhead (note 4)	X
Restructuring provision (note 6)	X
Tax effect of the above	X
Total adjustment to retained earnings	X

Reconciliation of equity at 31 December 2014

The effect of the changes to the Company's accounting policies on the equity of the Company at the date of the date of the last financial statements presented under previous GAAP, 31 December 2014 was as follows.

	Note	As reported under previous GAAP	Effect of transition to FRS 101	FRS 101
Property, plant and equipment	1	X	X	X
Goodwill	2	X	X	X
Intangible assets	2	X	X	X
Financial assets	3	X	X	X
Total non-current assets		X	X	X
Trade and other receivables		X	X	X
Inventories	4	X	X	X
Other receivables	5	X	X	X
Cash and cash equivalents		X	X	X
Total current assets		X	X	X
Total assets		X	X	X
Interest-bearing loans		X	X	X
Trade and other payables		X	X	X
Employee benefits		X	X	X
Restructuring provision	6	X	X	X
Current tax liability		X	X	X
Deferred tax liability	7	X	X	X
Total liabilities		X	X	X
Total assets less total liabilities		X	X	X
Issued capital		X	X	X
Revaluation reserve	3	X	X	X
Hedging reserve	5	X	X	X
Retained earnings	9	X	X	X
Total equity		X	X	X

Notes to the reconciliation of equity at 31 December 2014

1   Depreciation was influenced by tax requirements under previous GAAP, but under IAS 16 reflects the useful life of the assets. The cumulative adjustment increased the carrying amount of property, plant and equipment by x.

2   Intangible assets under previous GAAP included x for items that are transferred to goodwill because they do not qualify for recognition as intangible assets under IAS 38.

3   Financial assets are all classified as available-for-sale under IAS 39 and are carried at their fair value of x. They were carried at cost of x under previous GAAP. The resulting gains of x (x, less related deferred tax of x) are included in the revaluation reserve.

4   Inventories include fixed and variable production overhead of x under IAS 2 but this overhead was excluded under previous GAAP.

5   Unrealised gains of x on unmatured forward foreign exchange contracts are recognised under IAS 39, but were not recognised under previous GAAP. The resulting gains of x (x, less related deferred tax of x) are included in the hedging reserve because the contracts hedge forecast sales.

6   A restructuring provision of x relating to head office activities was recognised under previous GAAP, but does not qualify for recognition as a liability under IAS 37.

7   The above changes increased the deferred tax liability as follows:

Revaluation reserve (note 3)	X
Hedging reserve (note 5)	X
Retained earnings	X
Increase in deferred tax liability	X

Because the tax base at 1 January 2014 of the items reclassified from intangible assets to goodwill (note 2) equalled their carrying amount at that date, the reclassification did not affect deferred tax liabilities.

8   The adjustments to retained earnings are as follows:

Depreciation (note 1)	X
Production overhead (note 4)	X
Restructuring provision (note 6)	X
Tax effect of the above	X
Total adjustment to retained earnings	X

Reconciliation of profit for 2014

The changes in accounting policies had the following effect on the profit reported for the year ended 31 December 2014.

	Note	As reported under previous GAAP	Effect of transition to FRS 101	FRS 101
Revenue		X	X	X
Cost of sales	1,2,3	X	X	X
Gross profit		X	X	X
Distribution costs	1	X	X	X
Administrative expenses	1,4	X	X	X
Finance income		X	X	X
Finance costs		X	X	X
Profit before tax		X	X	X
Tax expense	5	X	X	X
Net profit (loss)		X	X	X

Notes to the reconciliation of profit or loss for 2014

1   A pension liability is recognised under IAS 19 but was not recognised under previous GAAP. The pension liability increased by x during 2010, which caused increases in cost of sales (x), distribution costs (x) and administrative expenses (x).

2   Cost of sales is higher by x under FRS 101 because inventories include fixed and variable production overheads under IFRSs but not under previous GAAP.

3   Depreciation was influenced by tax requirements under previous GAAP, but reflects the useful life of the assets under IAS 16. The effect on the profit for 2010 was not material.

4   A restructuring provision of x was recognised under previous GAAP at 1 January 2010 but did not qualify for recognition under IAS 37 until the year ended 31 December 2010. This increases administrative expenses for 2010 under FRS 101.

5   Adjustments 1–4 above lead to a reduction of x in deferred tax expense.

4. Summary of significant accounting policies

Disclosure exemptions

The accounts are prepared under FRS 101, which requires use of the accounting requirements set out in EU-adopted IFRS but gives certain disclosure exemptions. The disclosure exemptions taken relate to the following areas:

- share-based payments, where most details of the scheme are not provided because they appear in the parent's consolidated accounts;
- no cash flow statement is presented, and so neither are any of the associated notes;
- financial instruments – none of IFRS 7's disclosure requirements have been met, because equivalent disclosures appear in the group accounts;
- comparatives are not given in respect of movements in tangible and intangible assets;
- detail is not provided on the calculation of impairment charges, because the equivalent information is included in the group accounts.

The principal accounting policies adopted are set out below.

Revenue recognition

Sales of goods are recognised when goods are delivered and title has passed.

Interest income is accrued on a time basis, by reference to the principal outstanding and at the interest rate applicable.

Dividend income from investments is recognised when the shareholders' rights to receive payment have been established.

[ADD SPECIFIC TAILORED REVENUE POLICY RELEVANT FOR THE COMPANY AND ITS OPERATIONS]

Construction contracts

Where the outcome of a construction contract can be estimated reliably, revenue and costs are recognised by reference to the stage of completion activity at the balance sheet, as measured by the proportion that contract costs incurred for work performed to date bear to the estimated total contract costs. Variations in contract work, claims and incentive payments are included to the extent that they have been agreed with the customer.

Where the income of a construction contract cannot be estimated reliably, contract revenue is recognised to the extent of contract costs incurred that it is probable will be recoverable. Contract costs are recognised as expenses in the period in which they are incurred.

Where it is probable that total contract costs will exceed total contract revenue, the expected loss is recognised as an expense immediately.

Leasing

Leases are classified as finance leases whenever the terms of the lease transfer substantially all the risks and rewards of ownership to the lessee. All other leases are classified as operating leases.

Assets held under finance leases are recognised as assets of the Company at their fair value at the date of acquisition. The corresponding liability to the lessor is included in the balance sheet as a finance lease obligation. Finance costs, which represent the difference between the total leasing commitments and the fair value of the assets acquired, are charged to the income statement over the term of the relevant lease so as to produce a constant periodic rate of charge on the remaining balance of the obligations for each accounting period.

Rentals payable under operating leases are charged to income on a straight-line basis over the term of the relevant lease.

Foreign currencies

Transactions in foreign currencies are initially recorded at the rates of exchange prevailing on the dates of the transactions. Monetary assets and liabilities denominated in such currencies are retranslated at the rates prevailing on the balance sheet date. Profits and losses arising on exchange are included in the net profit or loss for the period.

In order to hedge its exposure to certain foreign exchange risks, the Company enters into forward contracts and options (see below for details of the Company's accounting policies in respect of such derivative financial investments).

Borrowing costs

Borrowing costs directly attributable to the acquisition, construction or production of qualifying assets, which are assets that necessarily take a substantial period of time to get ready for their intended use or sale, are added to the cost of those assets, until such time as the assets are substantially ready for their intended use or sale. Investment income earned on the temporary investment of specific borrowing pending its expenditure on qualifying assets is deducted from the cost of these assets.

All other borrowing costs are recognised in the profit or loss in the period in which they are incurred.

Government grants

Government grants towards staff retraining costs are recognised as income over the periods necessary to match them with the related costs and are deducted in reporting the related expense.

Retirement benefit costs

The Company participates in a group plan run by its parent, Y Plc. In accordance with IAS 19, the Company recognises an allocation of the net defined benefit cost. The Y Group's net obligation in respect of defined benefit plans is calculated separately for each plan by estimating the amount of future benefit that employees have earned in return for their service in the current and prior periods. That benefit is discounted to determine its present value. Any unrecognised past service costs and the fair value of any plan assets are deducted. The discount rate is the yield at the reporting date on corporate bonds, that have a credit rating of at least AA from a rating agency, that have maturity dates approximating the terms of the Y Group's obligations and that are denominated in the currency in which the benefits are expected to be paid.

The calculation is performed annually by a qualified actuary using the projected unit credit method. When the calculation results in a benefit to the Y Group, the recognised asset is limited to the total of any unrecognised past service costs and the present value of economic benefits available in the form of any future refunds from the plan or reductions in future contributions to the plan. In order to calculate the present value of economic benefits, consideration is given to any minimum funding requirements that apply to any plan in the Y Group. An economic benefit is available to the Y Group if it is realisable during the life of the plan, or on settlement of the plan liabilities. When the benefits of a plan are improved, the portion of the increased benefit related to past service by employees is recognised in profit or loss on a straight-line basis over the average period until the benefits become vested. To the extent that the benefits vest immediately, the expense is recognised immediately in profit or loss.

The Y Group recognises all actuarial gains and losses arising from defined benefit plans immediately in other comprehensive income and all expenses related to defined benefit plans in employee benefit expense in profit or loss.

The Y Group recognises gains and losses on the curtailment or settlement of a defined benefit plan when the curtailment or settlement occurs. The gain or loss on curtailment or settlement comprises any resulting change in the fair value of plan assets, any change in the present value of the defined benefit obligation, any related actuarial gains and losses and past service cost that had not previously been recognised.

The Company's share of the defined benefit cost, and the contribution paid, are both determined by its number of employees participating in the plan as a proportion of the total number across the Y Group.

Taxation

The charge for current tax is based on the results for the year as adjusted for items which are non-assessable or disallowed. It is calculated using rates that have been enacted or substantively enacted by the balance sheet date.

Deferred tax is accounted for using the balance sheet liability method in respect of temporary differences arising from differences between the carrying amount of assets and liabilities in the financial statements and the corresponding tax basis used in the computation of taxable profit. In principle, deferred tax liabilities are recognised for all taxable temporary differences and deferred tax assets are recognised to the extent that it is probable that taxable profits will be available against which deductible temporary differences can be utilised. Such assets and liabilities are not recognised if the temporary difference arises from goodwill (or negative goodwill) or from the initial recognition (other than in a business combination) of other assets and liabilities in a transaction which affects neither the tax profit nor the accounting profit.

Deferred tax is calculated at the rates that are expected to apply when the asset or liability is settled. Deferred tax is charged or credited in the income statement, except when it relates to items credited or charged directly to equity, in which case the deferred tax is also dealt with in equity.

Deferred tax assets and liabilities are offset when they relate to income taxes levied by the same taxation authority and the Company intends to settle its current tax assets and liabilities on a net basis.

Property, plant and equipment

Land and buildings held for use in the production or supply of goods or services, or for administration purposes, are stated in the balance sheet at their revalued amounts, being the fair value on the basis of their existing use at the date of revaluation, less any subsequent accumulated depreciation. Revaluations are performed with sufficient regularity such that the carrying amount does not differ materially from that which would be determined using fair values at the balance sheet date.

Any revaluation increase arising on the revaluation of such land and buildings is credited to the properties revaluation reserve, except to the extent that it reverses a revaluation decrease for the same asset previously recognised as an expense, in which case the increase is credited to the income statement to the extent of the decrease previously charged. A decrease in carrying amount arising on the revaluation of land and buildings is charged as an expense to the extent that it exceeds the balance, if any, held in the properties revaluation reverse relating to a previous revaluation of that asset.

On the subsequent sale or retirement of a revalued property, the attributable revaluation surplus remaining in the revaluation reserve is transferred to accumulated profits.

Properties in the course of construction for production, rental or administrative expenses, or for purposes not yet determined, are carried at cost, less any identified impairment loss. Cost includes professional fees and, for qualifying assets, borrowing costs capitalised in accordance with the Company's accounting policy. Depreciation of these assets, on the same basis as other property costs, commences when the assets are ready for their intended use.

Fixtures and equipment are stated at cost less accumulated depreciation.

Depreciation is charged so as to write off the cost or valuation or assets, other than land and properties under construction, over their estimated useful lives, using the straight-line method, on the following bases.

| Buildings | 50 years |
| Fixtures and equipment | 4–10 years |

Assets held under finance leases are depreciated over their expected useful lives on the same basis as owned assets or, where shorter, the term of the relevant lease.

The gain or loss arising on the disposal or retirement of an asset is determined as the difference between the sales proceeds and the carrying amount of the asset and is recognised in income.

Investment property

Investment property, which is property held to earn rentals and/or for the capital appreciation, is stated at its fair value at the balance sheet date. Gains or losses arising from changes in the fair value of investment property are included in net profit or loss for the period in which they arise.

Internally-generated intangible assets – research and development expenditure

Expenditure on research activities is recognised as an expense in the period in which it is incurred.

An internally-generated intangible asset arising from the Company's software development is recognised only if all of the following conditions are met:

- an asset is created that can be identified (such as software and new processes);
- it is probable that the asset created will generate future economic benefits; and
- the development cost of the asset can be measured reliably.

Where no internally-generated intangible asset can be recognised, development expenditure is recognised as an expense in the period in which it is incurred. Internally-generated intangible assets are amortised on a straight-line basis over the useful lives, which is usually no more than five years.

Patents and trademarks

Patents and trademarks are measured initially at purchase cost and amortised on a straight-line basis over their estimated useful lives, which is on average ten years.

Impairment

At each balance sheet date, the Company reviews the carrying amounts of its tangible and intangible assets with finite lives to determine whether there is any indication that those assets have suffered an impairment loss. If any such indication exists, the recoverable amount of the asset is estimated in order to determine the extent of the impairment loss (if any). Where it is not possible to estimate the recoverable amount of an individual asset, the Company estimates the recoverable amount of the cash-generating unit to which the asset belongs.

Goodwill arising on acquisition of a business is allocated to cash-generating units. The recoverable amount of the cash-generating unit to which goodwill has been allocated is tested for impairment annually, or on such other occasions that events or changes in circumstances indicate that it might be impaired.

If the recoverable amount of an asset (or cash-generating unit) is estimated to be less than its carrying amount, the carrying amount of the asset (cash-generating unit) is reduced to its recoverable amount. Impairment losses are recognised as an expense immediately, unless the relevant asset is land or buildings at a revalued amount, in which case the impairment loss is treated as a revaluation decrease.

Where an impairment loss subsequently reverses, the carrying amount of the asset (cash-generating unit) is increased to the revised estimate of its recoverable amount, but so that the increased carrying amount does not exceed the carrying amount that would have been determined had no impairment loss been recognised for the asset (cash-generating unit) in prior years. A reversal of an impairment loss is recognised as income immediately, unless the relevant asset is carried at a revalued amount, in which case the reversal of the impairment loss is treated as a revaluation increase. However, impairment losses relating to goodwill are not reversed.

Inventories

Inventories are stated at the lower of cost and net realisable value. Cost comprises direct materials and, where applicable, direct labour costs and those overheads that have been incurred in bringing the inventories to their present location and condition. Cost is calculated using the weighted average method. Net realisable value represents the estimated selling price less all estimated costs to completion and costs to be incurred in marketing, selling and distribution.

Provisions

Provisions are recognised when the Company has a present obligation as a result of a past event which it is probable will result in an outflow of economic benefits that can be reasonably estimated.

Provisions for restructuring costs are recognised when the Company has a detailed formal plan for the restructuring which has been notified to affected parties.

Financial instruments

Non-derivative financial assets

The Company initially recognises loans and receivables on the date that they are originated. All other financial assets (including assets designated as at fair value through profit or loss) are recognised initially on the trade date, which is the date that the Company becomes a party to the contractual provisions of the instrument.

The Company derecognises a financial asset when the contractual rights to the cash flows from the asset expire, or it transfers the rights to receive the contractual cash flows in a transaction in which substantially all the risks and rewards of ownership of the financial asset are transferred.

Any interest in such transferred financial assets that is created or retained by the Company is recognised as a separate asset or liability.

Financial assets and liabilities are offset and the net amount presented in the statement of financial position when, and only when, the Company has a legal right to offset the amounts and intends either to settle them on a net basis or to realise the asset and settle the liability simultaneously.

The Company classifies non-derivative financial assets into the following categories: financial assets at fair value through profit or loss, held-to-maturity financial assets, loans and receivables and available-for-sale financial assets.

Financial assets at fair value through profit or loss

A financial asset is classified as at fair value through profit or loss if it is classified as held-for-trading. Attributable transaction costs are recognised in profit or loss as incurred. Financial assets at fair value through profit or loss are measured at fair value and changes therein, which takes into account any dividend income, are recognised in profit or loss.

Held-to-maturity financial assets

If the Company has the positive intent and ability to hold debt securities to maturity, then such financial assets are classified as held-to-maturity. Held-to-maturity financial assets are recognised initially at fair value plus any directly attributable transaction costs. Subsequent to initial recognition, held-to-maturity financial assets are measured at amortised cost using the effective interest method, less any impairment losses.

Loans and receivables

Loans and receivables are financial assets with fixed or determinable payments that are not quoted in an active market. Such assets are recognised initially at fair value plus any directly attributable transaction costs. Subsequent to initial recognition, loans and receivables are measured at amortised cost using the effective interest method, less any impairment losses.

Loans and receivables comprise cash and cash equivalents, and trade and other receivables.

Cash and cash equivalents

Cash and cash equivalents comprise cash balances and call deposits with maturities of three months or less from the acquisition date that are subject to an insignificant risk of changes in their fair value, and are used by the Company in the management of its short-term commitments.

Available-for-sale financial assets

Available-for-sale financial assets are non-derivative financial assets that are designated as available-for-sale or are not classified in any of the above categories of financial assets. Available-for-sale financial assets are recognised initially at fair value plus any directly attributable transaction costs.

Subsequent to initial recognition, they are measured at fair value and changes therein, other than impairment losses and foreign currency differences on available-for-sale debt instruments, are recognised in other comprehensive income and presented in the fair value reserve in equity. When an investment is derecognised, the gain or loss accumulated in equity is reclassified to profit or loss.

Non-derivative financial liabilities

The Company initially recognises debt securities issued and subordinated liabilities on the date that they are originated. All other financial liabilities are recognised initially on the trade date, which is the date that the Company becomes a party to the contractual provisions of the instrument.

The Company derecognises a financial liability when its contractual obligations are discharged, cancelled or expire.

The Company classifies non-derivative financial liabilities into the other financial liabilities category. Such financial liabilities are recognised initially at fair value less any directly attributable transaction costs. Subsequent to initial recognition, these financial liabilities are measured at amortised cost using the effective interest method.

Other financial liabilities comprise loans and borrowings, debt securities issued, bank overdrafts, and trade and other payables.

Bank overdrafts that are repayable on demand and form an integral part of the Company's cash management are included as a component of cash and cash equivalents for the statement of cash flows.

Equity instruments

Equity instruments are recorded at the proceeds received, net of direct issue costs.

Derivative financial instruments

Derivative financial instruments are initially recorded at cost and are remeasured to fair value at subsequent reporting dates.

Changes in the fair value of derivative financial instruments that are designated and effective as cash flow hedges are recognised directly in equity. Amounts deferred in equity are recognised in the income statement in the same period in which the hedged firm commitments or forecasted transaction affects net profit or loss.

Changes in the fair value of derivative financial instruments that do not qualify for hedge accounting are recognised in the income statement as they arise.

Critical accounting estimates and judgments

Estimates and judgments are continually evaluated and are based on historical experience and other factors, including expectations of future events that are believed to be reasonable under the circumstances.

The Company makes estimates and assumptions concerning the future. The resulting accounting estimates may differ from the related actual results. The estimates and assumptions that have a significant risk of causing a material adjustment to the carrying amounts of assets and liabilities within the next financial year are addressed below.

GIVE DETAILS OF CRITICAL ACCOUNTING ESTIMATES AND JUDGMENTS

5. Results from operating activity

Profit from operations has been arrived at after charging (crediting).

	Year ended 31/12/15 £000	Year ended 31/12/14 £000
Net foreign exchange losses/(gains)	X	X
Research and development costs	X	X
Government grants towards training costs	X	X
Amortisation of intangible assets	X	X

Total staff costs incurred during the period amounted to £xxx million (2014: £xxx million) and total depreciation amounted to £xxx million (2014: £xxx million).

6. Finance costs

	Year ended 31/12/15 £000	Year ended 31/12/14 £000
Interest on bank overdrafts and loans	X	X
Interest on convertible loan notes (note 34)	X	X
Interest on obligations under finance leases	X	X
Total borrowing costs	X	X
Less: amounts included in the cost of qualifying assets	X	X

Borrowing costs included in the cost of qualifying assets during the year arose on the general borrowing pool and are calculated by applying a capitalisation rate of 5% to expenditure on such assets.

7. Finance income

	Year ended 31/12/15 £000	Year ended 31/12/14 £000
Interest on bank deposits	X	X
Dividends from trading Investments	X	X
Loss on disposal of trading Investments	X	X
Unrealised loss on trading Investments	X	X
Profit on disposal of available-for-sale investments	X	X

8. Discontinued operations

On 21 May 2015, the Company entered into a sale agreement to dispose of its A division, which carried out all of the Company's furniture manufacturing operations. The disposal was effected in order to generate cash flow for the expansion of the Company's other business. The disposal was completed on 3 November 2015, on which date control of the division's trade, assets and operations passed to the acquirer.

A profit of £xxx arose on the disposal of the A division, being the proceeds of disposal less the carrying amount of the division's net assets. No tax charge or credit arose from the transaction.

9. **Income tax expense**

	Year ended 31/12/15 £000	Year ended 31/12/14 £000
Current tax:		
Domestic	X	X
Foreign	X	X
Deferred tax (note 28):		
Current year	X	X
Attributable to a reduction in the rate of domestic income tax	X	X
Total	X	X

Domestic income tax is calculated at 20% (2014: 20%) of the estimated assessable profit for the year.

Taxation for other jurisdictions is calculated at the rates prevailing in the respective jurisdictions.

Of the charge to domestic income tax, approximately £xxx (2014: £xxx) related to profits arising in the furniture division, which was disposed of during the year. No tax charge or credit arose on the disposal of the relevant subsidiary.

The charge for the year can be reconciled to the profit per the income statement as follows.

	Year ended 31/12/15 £000	Year ended 31/12/15 %	Year ended 31/12/14 £000	Year ended 31/12/14 %
Profit before tax	x	x	x	x
Tax on the domestic income tax rate of 20% (2014: 20%)	x	x	x	x
Tax effect of expenses that are not deductible in determining taxable profit	x	x	x	x
Tax effect of utilisation of tax losses not previously recognised	x	x	x	x
Decrease in opening deferred tax liability resulting from a reduction in tax rates	x	x	x	x
Tax expense and effective tax rate for the year	x	x	x	x

In addition to the amount charged to the income statement, deferred tax relating to the revaluation of the Company's properties amounting to £xxx million and to the equity component of convertible bonds issued amounting to £xxx million has been charged directly to equity (see note 28).

10. Dividends

On 23 May 2015, a dividend of xxx pence (2014: xxx pence) per share was paid to shareholders.

In respect of the current year, the directors proposed that a dividend of xxx pence per share will be paid to shareholders on 27 May 2016. This dividend is subject to approval by shareholders at the Annual General Meeting and has not been included as a liability in these financial statements.

The proposed dividend for 2015 is payable to all shareholders on the Register of Members on 27 May 2016. The total estimated dividend to be paid is £xxx million.

11. Property, plant and equipment

	Land and buildings	Property under construction	Fixtures and equipment	Total
	£000	£000	£000	£000
Cost or valuation				
At 1 January 2015	x	x	x	x
Additions	x	x	x	x
Disposals	x	x	x	x
Revaluation increase	x	x	x	x
At 31 December 2015	**x**	**x**	**x**	**x**
Comprising:				
At cost	x	x	x	x
At valuation	x	x	x	x
	x	**x**	**x**	**x**
Accumulated depreciation				
At 1 January 2015	x	x	x	x
Charge for the year	x	x	x	x
Impairment loss	x	x	x	x
Eliminated on disposals	x	x	x	x
Eliminated on revaluation	x	x	x	x
At 31 December 2015	**x**	**x**	**x**	**x**
Carrying amount				
At 31 December 2015	**x**	**x**	**x**	**x**
At 31 December 2014	**x**	**x**	**x**	**x**

The impairment loss on fixtures and fittings and equipment arose in connection with the restructuring following the disposal of the A division (see note 6).

The carrying amount of the Company's fixtures and equipment includes an amount of £xxx million (2014: £xxx million) in respect of assets held under finance leases.

Additions to fixtures and equipment during the year amounting to £xxx million were financed by new finance leases.

The Company has pledged land and buildings having a carrying value of approximately £xxx million (2014: £xxx million) to secure banking facilities granted to the Company.

Land and buildings were revalued at 31 December 2015 by Forth & Clyde, Chartered Surveyors. Forth & Clyde, Chartered Surveyors are not connected with the Company.

At 31 December 2015, had the land and buildings of the Company been carried at historical cost less accumulated depreciation, their carrying amount would have been approximately £xxx million (2014: £xxx million).

12. Investment property

	£000
Fair value	
At 1 January 2014	X
Increase in fair value during the year	X
At 31 December 2014	X
Increase in fair value during the year	X
At 31 December 2015	X

The fair value of the Company's investment property at 31 December 2015 has been arrived at on the basis of a valuation carried out at that date by Severn & Tyne, Chartered Surveyors, on an open market value basis. The valuation was arrived at by reference to market evidence of transaction prices for similar properties.

The Company has pledged all of its investment property to secure general banking facilities granted to the Company.

The property rental income earned by the Company from its investment property, all of which is leased out under operating leases, amounted to £xxx million (2014: £xxx million). Direct operating expenses arising on the investment property in the period amounted to £xxx million (2014: £xxx million).

13. Goodwill

	£000
Cost	
At 1 January 2014	X
Exchange differences	X
At 31 December 2014	X
Exchange differences	X
At 31 December 2015	X
Impairment losses	
At 1 January 2014	X
Impairment in the period	X
At 31 December 2014	X
Impairment in the period	X
At 31 December 2015	X
Carrying amount	
At 31 December 2015	X
At 31 December 2014	X

Impairment reviews were performed on the carrying amount of goodwill in December 2015. An impairment loss of £x was recognised in respect of goodwill arising from the acquisition of the trade and assets of R Ltd in 2012. As a result of this impairment all goodwill arising on the acquisition of the R division is fully written off.

14. Other Intangible assets

	Development costs	Patents and trademarks	Total
	£000	£000	£000
Cost			
At 1 January 2015	x	x	x
Additions	x	x	x
At 31 December 2015	x	x	x
Amortisation			
At 1 January 2015	x	x	x
Charge for the year	x	x	x
At 31 December 2015	x	x	x
Carrying amount			
At 31 December 2015	x	x	x
At 31 December 2014	x	x	x

15. Investments

Investments comprise Available for sale investments, which are reported as Non current assets and trading investments, which are reported as current assets.

Available for sale investments

	£000
At 1 January 2014	X
Disposed of in the year	X
Increase in fair value	X
At 31 December 2014	X
Disposed of in the year	X
Increase in fair value	X
Fair value at 31 December 2015	X

The investments in securities included above represent investments in listed equity securities which present the Company with opportunity for return through dividend income and trading gains. The fair values of these securities are based on quoted market prices.

Trading investments

	2015	2014
	£000	£000
Fair value at 31 December	X	X

The investments in securities included above represent investments in listed equity securities, which present the Company with opportunity for return through dividend income and trading gains. The fair values of these securities are based on quoted market prices.

16. Inventories

	2015	2014
	£000	£000
Raw materials	X	X
Work-in-progress	X	X
Finished goods	X	X

Included above are raw materials of £xxx million (2014: £xxx million) and work in progress of £xxx million (2014: nil) carried at a net realisable value.

Inventories with a carrying amount of £xxx million (2014: £xxx million) have been pledged as security for certain of the Company's bank overdrafts.

17. Other financial assets

Trade receivables comprise amounts receivable from the sale of goods of £xxx million (2014: £xxx million), amounts due from construction contract customers of £xxx million (2014: £xxx million).

Other current assets include deferred consideration for the disposal of the A division of £xxx million (see note 39), and currency and interest rate derivatives with a fair value of £xxx million (see note 33).

Cash and cash equivalents comprise cash and short-term deposits.

18. Construction contracts

	2015	2014
	£000	£000
Contracts in progress at balance sheet date:	X	X
Amounts due from contract customers included in trade and other receivables	X	X
Amounts due to contract customers included in accounts payable	X	X
Contract costs incurred plus recognised profits less recognised losses to date	X	X
Less: progress billings	X	X

At 31 December 2015, retentions held by customers for contract work amounted to £xxx million (2014: £xxx million). Advances received from customers for contract work amounted to £xxx million (2014: £nil).

At 31 December 2015, amounts of £xxx million (2014: £xxx million) included in trade and other receivables and arising from construction contracts are due for settlement after more than 12 months.

19. Disposal groups classified as held for sale

At 31 December 2015, part of the Company's property investment and construction division was classified as a disposal group held for sale following the decision of the board to enter into negotiations leading to the sale of this part of the business. The disposal group is represented by the following assets and liabilities.

	£000
Property, plant and equipment	X
Inventories	X
Other current assets	X
Liabilities	X
Net carrying value of disposal group	X

20. Share capital

	2015 £000	2014 £000
Authorised:		
Ordinary shares of £1 each	X	X
Issued and fully paid:		
Ordinary shares of £1 each	X	X
Reported as at 1 January	X	X
Issue of share options (see note 21)	X	X
Reported as at 31 December	X	X

The Company has one class of ordinary shares which carry no rights to fixed income.

21. Share-based payment

During the year ended 31 December 2015, the Company's employees participated in a share-based payment scheme relating to the shares of its parent, Y Plc.

Participating employees must remain in service for the whole vesting period, which varies between three and five years, and there is then a five-year exercise period. All arrangements are equity-settled, so options that vest are taken advantage of by employees' purchasing shares in Y for cash at the agreed option price. The expense recognised in the current and prior periods is also measured as equity-settled because the parent has the obligation to issue shares to the employees.

22. Capital reserves

	Share premium £000	Equity reserve £000	Total £000
Balance at 1 January and 31 December 2014	X	X	X
Equity component of convertible loan notes issue (see note 34)	X	X	X
Balance at 31 December 2015	X	X	X

EXPLAIN THE PURPOSE OF THE CAPITAL RESERVES.

23. Revaluation reserve

	£000
Balance at 1 January 2014	X
Revaluation decrease on land and buildings	X
Balance at 31 December 2014	X
Revaluation increase on land and buildings	X
Deferred tax liability on revaluation of land and buildings	X
Balance at 31 December 2015	X

EXPLAIN THE PURPOSE OF THE REVALUATION RESERVE.

24. Hedging reserve

	£000
Balance at 1 January 2014	X
Cash flow hedges	X
Transferred to profit or loss for the period	X
Gains/losses taken to equity	X
Transferred to initial carrying amount of hedged items	X
Balance at 31 December 2014	X
Cash flow hedges	X
Gains/losses taken to equity	X
Transferred to profit or loss for the period	X
Transferred to initial carrying amount of hedged items	X
Balance at 31 December 2015	X

EXPLAIN THE PURPOSE OF THE HEDGING RESERVE.

25. Accumulated profits

	£000
Balance at 1 January 2014	
– as originally stated	X
– prior period adjustment arising from first-time adoption of FRS 101 (see note 2)	X
as restated	X
Dividends paid	X
Net profit for the year	X
Balance at 31 December 2014	X
Dividends paid	X
Net profit for the year	X
Balance at 31 December 2015	X

EXPLAIN WHY THE COMPANY HOLDS ACCUMULATED PROFITS.

26. Bank overdrafts and loans

	2015 £000	2014 £000
Bank overdrafts	X	X
Bank loans	X	X

27. Convertible loan notes

The convertible loan notes were issued on 1 April 2015. The notes are convertible into ordinary shares of the Company at any time between the date of issue of the notes and their settlement date. On issue, the loan notes were convertible at 15 shares per £10 loan note.

If the notes have not been converted they will be redeemed on 1 April 2015 at par. Interest of 4% will be paid annually up until that settlement date.

28. Deferred tax

	2015 £000	2014 £000
Analysis for financial reporting purposes		
Deferred tax liabilities	X	X
Deferred tax assets	X	X
Net position at 31 December	X	X

The movement for the year in the Company's net deferred tax position was as follows.

	31/12/15 £000	31/12/14 £000
At 1 January	X	X
Charge to income for the year	X	X
Charge to equity for the year	X	X
Effect of change in tax rate	X	X
At 31 December	X	X

The following are in deferred tax liabilities and assets recognised by the Company and movements thereon during the period.

	2015 £000	2014 £000
Deferred tax liabilities	X	X
Accelerated tax depreciation	X	X
Deferred development costs	X	X
Revaluation of properties	X	X
Convertible bond-equity component	X	X
Total	X	X

	2015	2014
	£000	£000
Deferred tax assets	X	X
Retirement benefit obligations	X	X
Tax losses	X	X
Total	X	X

At the year end date, the Company has unused tax losses of £xxx million (2014: £xxx million) available for offset against future profits. A deferred tax asset has been recognised in respect of £xxx million (2014: £xxx million) of such losses. No deferred tax assets had been recognised in respect of the remaining £xxx million (2014: £xxx million) due to the unpredictability of future profit streams. Included in unrecognised tax losses are losses of £xxx million (2014: £xxx million) which will expire in 2016. Other losses may be carried forward indefinitely.

29. Obligations under finance leases

	Minimum lease payments		Present value lease payments	
	2015	2014	2015	2014
	£000	£000	£000	£000
Amounts payable under finance leases				
Within one year	X	X	X	X
In the second to fifth years inclusive	X	X	X	X
Less: future finance charges	X	X	X	X
Present value of lease obligations	X	X	X	X
Less: Amount due to settlement within 12 months (shown under current liabilities)	X	X	X	X
Amount due to settlement after 12 months	X	X	X	X

It is the Company's policy to lease certain of its plant and equipment under finance leases. The average lease term is 3–4 years. For the year ended 31 December 2015, the average effective borrowing rate was 4.5%. Interest rates are fixed at the contract date. All leases are on a fixed repayment basis and no arrangements have been entered into for contingent rental payments.

The fair value of the Company's lease obligations approximates their carrying amount.

The Company's obligations under finance lease are secured by the lessor's charge over the leased assets.

30. Other financial liabilities

Trade and other payables principally comprise amounts outstanding for trade purchases and ongoing costs. The average credit period taken for trade purchases is 35 days.

31. Provisions

	Restructuring £000	Warranty £000	Other £000	Total £000
At 1 January 2014	X	X	X	X
Additional provision in the year	X	X	X	X
Utilisation of provision	X	X	X	X
At 31 December 2014	X	X	X	X
Additional provision in the year	X	X	X	X
Utilisation of provision	X	X	X	X
At 31 December 2015	X	X	X	X

The warranty provision represents management's best estimate of the Company's liability under two-year warranties given on office equipment based on past experience and the testing of new products. It is expected that £x of the provision will be incurred in 2015.

The restructuring provision relates to redundancy costs incurred on the disposal of E Limited (see note 6). As at 31 December 2015, approximately half the employees had ceased to be employed by the Company, with the remaining departing in January 2015.

32. Contingent liabilities

During the reporting period, a customer of the Company instigated proceedings against it for alleged defects in a product which, it is claimed, was the cause of a major fire in their premises in February 2013. Total losses to the customer have been estimated at £xxx million and this amount is being claimed from the Company.

The Company's solicitors have advised that they did not consider that the suit has merit, and they have recommended that it be contested. No provision has been made in these financial statements as the Company's management do not consider that there is any probable loss.

33. Capital commitments

	2015 £000	2014 £000
Commitments for the acquisition of property, plant and equipment	X	X

In addition, the Company has entered into a contract for the maintenance of its investment property for the next five years, which will give rise to an annual charge of £xxx million.

34. Operating lease commitments

At the balance sheet date, the Company had outstanding commitments under non-cancellable leases, which fall due as follows.

	2015 £000	2014 £000
Within one year	X	X
In the second to fifth years inclusive	X	X
After five years	X	X

Operating lease payments represent rentals payable by the Company for certain of its office properties. Leases are negotiated for an average term of seven years and rentals are fixed for an average of three years.

35. Employee benefits

Employee benefits are represented by the Company's participation in the Y Group defined benefit plan for eligible employees.

In accordance with IAS 19 paragraph 150, the information required to be disclosed about the group defined benefit plan is all provided in the Y Group's financial statements, which are publicly available.

36. Subsequent events

On 14 February 2016, the Company made a bonus issue of shares.

37. Related party transactions

Trading transactions

During the year the Company entered into the following transactions with related parties.

	2015	2014
	£000	£000
Sales of goods	X	X
Purchases of goods	X	X
Amounts owed by related parties	X	X
Amounts owed to related parties	X	X

Sales of goods to related parties were made at the Company's usual list prices, less average discounts of 5%. Purchases were made at market price discounts of 5%. Purchases were made at market price discounted to reflect the quantity of goods purchased and the relationship between the parties.

Directors' and executives' remuneration

Remuneration paid to directors and other members of key management during the year was as follows.

	Year ended 31/12/15	Year ended 31/12/14
	£000	£000
Salaries	X	X
Discretionary bonuses	X	X
Post retirement benefits	X	X

The remuneration of directors and key executives is decided by the remuneration committee of the parent Company having regard to comparable market statistics.

In addition to the above, B Holdings Limited performed certain administrative services for the Company, for which a management fee of £xxx million (2014: £xxx million) was charged, being an appropriate allocation of costs incurred by relevant administrative departments.

Appendix 2

SI 2008/410 – Large and Medium-sized Companies and Groups (Accounts and Reports) Regulations 2008

Part 1   Introduction

Part 2   Form and content of accounts

Part 3   Directors' report

Part 4   Directors' remuneration report

Part 5   Interpretation

Schedule 1 – Companies Act individual accounts: companies which are not banking or insurance companies

Schedule 2 – Banking companies: Companies Act individual accounts

Schedule 3 – Insurance companies: Companies Act individual accounts

Schedule 4 – Information on related undertakings required whether preparing Companies Act or IAS accounts

Schedule 5 – Information about benefits of directors

Schedule 6 – Companies Act group accounts

Schedule 7 – Matters to be dealt with in Directors' Report

Schedule 8 – Quoted companies: Directors' Remuneration Report

Schedule 9 – Interpretation of term "provisions"

Schedule 10 – General interpretation

Large and Medium-sized Companies and Groups (Accounts and Reports) Regulations 2008

(SI 2008/410 as amended by SI 2015/980 The Companies, Partnerships and Groups (Accounts and Reports) Regulations 2015)

Made on 19 February 2008 by the Secretary of State, in exercise of the powers conferred by s. 396(3), 404(3), 409(1) to (3), 412(1) to (3), 416(4), 421(1) and (2), 445(3)(a) and (b), 677(3)(a), 712(2)(b)(i), 831(3)(a), 832(4)(a), 836(1)(b)(i) and 1292(1) (a) and (c) of the Companies Act 2006. In accordance with s. 473(3) and 1290 of the Companies Act 2006 a draft of this instrument was laid before Parliament and approved by a resolution of each House of Parliament. Operative from 6 April 2008.

PART 1 – INTRODUCTION
CITATION AND INTERPRETATION

1(1) These Regulations may be cited as the Large and Medium-sized Companies and Groups (Accounts and Reports) Regulations 2008.

1(2) In these Regulations **"the 2006 Act"** means the Companies Act 2006.

Commencement and application

2(1) These Regulations come into force on 6th April 2008.

2(2) Subject to paragraph (3), they apply in relation to financial years beginning on or after 6th April 2008.

2(3) The requirement for disclosure in paragraph 4 of Schedule 8 to these Regulations (directors' remuneration report: disclosure relating to consideration of conditions in company and group) applies in relation to financial years beginning on or after 6th April 2009.

2(4) These Regulations apply to companies other than those which are subject to the small companies regime under Part 15 of the 2006 Act.

PART 2 – FORM AND CONTENT OF ACCOUNTS

Companies Act individual accounts (companies other than banking and insurance companies)

3(1) Subject to regulation 4, the directors of a company–

(a) for which they are preparing Companies Act individual accounts under section 396396 of the 2006 Act (Companies Act: individual accounts), and
(b) which is not a banking company or an insurance company, must comply with the provisions of Schedule 1 to these Regulations as to the form and content of the balance sheet and profit and loss account, and additional information to be provided by way of notes to the accounts.

3(2) The profit and loss account of a company that falls within section 408 of the 2006 Act (individual profit and loss account where group accounts prepared) need not contain the information specified in paragraphs 65 to 69 of Schedule 1 to these Regulations (information supplementing the profit and loss account).

Medium-sized companies: exemptions for Companies Act individual accounts

4(1) This regulation applies to a company–

(a) which qualifies as medium-sized in relation to a financial year under section 465 of the 2006 Act, and

(b) the directors of which are preparing Companies Act individual accounts under section 396 of that Act for that year.

4(2A) The individual accounts for the year need not comply with paragraph 45 (disclosure with respect to compliance with accounting standards) of Schedule 1 to these Regulations.

4(2B) Paragraph 72 (related party transactions) applies with the modification that only particulars of transactions which have not been concluded under normal market conditions with the following must be disclosed–

(a) owners holding a participating interest in the company;

(b) companies in which the company itself has a participating interest; and

(c) the company's directors.

4(3) [Omitted by SI 2015/980, reg. 26(3).]

History – Reg. 4(2A) and (2B) substituted for reg. 4(2) by SI 2015/980, reg. 26(2), with effect in relation to–

    (a) financial years beginning on or after 1 January 2016, and

    (b) a financial year of a company beginning on or after 1 January 2015, but before 1 January 2016, if the directors of the company so decide.

Reg. 4(3) omitted by SI 2015/980, reg. 26(3), with effect in relation to–

    (a) financial years beginning on or after 1 January 2016, and

    (b) a financial year of a company beginning on or after 1 January 2015, but before 1 January 2016, if the directors of the company so decide.

Former reg. 4(3) read as follows:

    "**4(3)** The directors of the company may deliver to the registrar of companies a copy of the accounts for the year–

        (a) which includes a profit and loss account in which the following items listed in the profit and loss account formats set out in Schedule 1 are combined as one item – items 2, 3 and 6 in format 1; items 2 to 5 in format 2; items A.1 and B.2 in format 3; items A.1, A.2 and B.2 to B.4 in format 4;

        (b) which does not contain the information required by paragraph 68 of Schedule 1 (particulars of turnover)."

Companies Act individual accounts: banking companies

5(1) The directors of a company–

(a) for which they are preparing Companies Act individual accounts under section 396 of the 2006 Act, and

(b) which is a banking company, must comply with the provisions of Schedule 2 to these Regulations as to the form and content of the balance sheet and profit and loss account, and additional information to be provided by way of notes to the accounts.

5(2) The profit and loss account of a banking company that falls within section 408 of the 2006 Act (individual profit and loss account where group accounts prepared) need not contain the information specified in paragraphs 85 to 91 of Schedule 2 to these Regulations (information supplementing the profit and loss account).

5(3) Accounts prepared in accordance with this regulation must contain a statement that they are prepared in accordance with the provisions of these Regulations relating to banking companies.

Companies Act individual accounts: insurance companies

6(1) The directors of a company–

(a) for which they are preparing Companies Act individual accounts under section 396 of the 2006 Act, and
(b) which is an insurance company, must comply with the provisions of Schedule 3 to these Regulations as to the form and content of the balance sheet and profit and loss account, and additional information to be provided by way of notes to the accounts.

6(2) The profit and loss account of a company that falls within section 408 of the 2006 Act (individual profit and loss account where group accounts prepared)(a) need not contain the information specified in paragraphs 83 to 89 of Schedule 3 to these Regulations (information supplementing the profit and loss account).

6(3) Accounts prepared in accordance with this regulation must contain a statement that they are prepared in accordance with the provisions of these Regulations relating to insurance companies.

Information about related undertakings (Companies Act or IAS individual or group accounts)

7(1) Companies Act or IAS individual or group accounts must comply with the provisions of Schedule 4 to these Regulations as to information about related undertakings to be given in notes to the company's accounts.

7(2) In Schedule 4–

Part 1 contains provisions applying to all companies
Part 2 contains provisions applying only to companies not required to prepare group accounts
Part 3 contains provisions applying only to companies required to prepare group accounts
Part 4 contains additional disclosures for banking companies and groups
Part 5 contains interpretative provisions.

7(3) Information otherwise required to be given by Schedule 4 need not be disclosed with respect to an undertaking that–

(a) is established under the law of a country outside the United Kingdom, or
(b) carries on business outside the United Kingdom,

if the conditions specified in section 409(4) of the 2006 Act are met (see section 409(5) of the 2006 Act for disclosure required where advantage taken of this exemption).

This paragraph does not apply in relation to the information otherwise required by paragraph 3, 7 or 21 of Schedule 4.

Information about directors' benefits: remuneration (Companies Act or IAS individual or group accounts: quoted and unquoted companies)

8(1) Companies Act or IAS individual or group accounts must comply with the provisions of Schedule 5 to these Regulations as to information about directors' remuneration to be given in notes to the company's accounts.

8(2) In Schedule 5–

Part 1 contains provisions applying to quoted and unquoted companies,
Part 2 contains provisions applying only to unquoted companies, and
Part 3 contains supplementary provisions.

Companies Act group accounts

9(1) Subject to paragraphs (2) and (3), where the directors of a parent company prepare Companies Act group accounts under section 403 of the 2006 Act (group accounts: applicable accounting framework), those accounts must comply with the provisions of Part 1 of Schedule 6 to these Regulations as to the form and content of the consolidated balance sheet and consolidated profit and loss account, and additional information to be provided by way of notes to the accounts.

9(2) The directors of the parent company of a banking group preparing Companies Act group accounts must do so in accordance with the provisions of Part 1 of Schedule 6 as modified by Part 2 of that Schedule.

9(3) The directors of the parent company of an insurance group preparing Companies Act group accounts must do so in accordance with the provisions of Part 1 of Schedule 6 as modified by Part 3 of that Schedule.

9(4) Accounts prepared in accordance with paragraph (2) or (3) must contain a statement that they are prepared in accordance with the provisions of these Regulations relating to banking groups or to insurance groups, as the case may be.

PART 3 – DIRECTORS' REPORT
DIRECTORS' REPORT

10(1) The report which the directors of a company are required to prepare under section 415 of the 2006 Act (duty to prepare directors' report) must disclose the matters specified in Schedule 7 to these Regulations.

10(2) In Schedule 7–

Part 1 relates to matters of a general nature including political donations and expenditure,
Part 2 relates to the acquisition by a company of its own shares or a charge on them,
Part 3 relates to the employment, training and advancement of disabled persons,
Part 4 relates to the involvement of employees in the affairs, policy and performance of the company,
Part 6 relates to certain disclosures required by publicly traded companies, and
Part 7 relates to disclosures in relation to greenhouse gas emissions.

History – Reg. 10(2) substituted by SI 2013/1970, reg. 7(1) and (2), with effect from 1 October 2013 in respect of financial years ending on or after 30 September 2013.

This version of reg. 10 applies to financial years ending on or after 30 September 2013. The version applying to financial years ending before 30 September 2013 read as follows:

"**10(1)** The report which the directors of a company are required to prepare under section 415 of the 2006 Act (duty to prepare directors' report) must disclose the matters specified in Schedule 7 to these Regulations.

10(2) In Schedule 7–

Part 1 relates to matters of a general nature, including changes in asset values and contributions for political and charitable purposes,
Part 2 relates to the acquisition by a company of its own shares or a charge on them,
Part 3 relates to the employment, training and advancement of disabled persons,
Part 4 relates to the involvement of employees in the affairs, policy and performance of the company, and
Part 5 relates to the company's policy and practice on the payment of creditors."

PART 4 – DIRECTORS' REMUNERATION REPORT
DIRECTORS' REMUNERATION REPORT (QUOTED COMPANIES)

11(1) The remuneration report which the directors of a quoted company are required to prepare under section 420 of the 2006 Act (duty to prepare directors' remuneration report) must contain the information specified in Schedule 8 to these Regulations, and must comply with any requirement of that Schedule as to how information is to be set out in the report.

11(1A) The document setting out a revised directors' remuneration policy in accordance with section 422A of the 2006 Act must contain the information specified in Schedule 8 to these Regulations, and must comply with any requirements in that Schedule as to how that information is to be set out.

11(2) [Revoked.]

11(3) For the purposes of section 497 in Part 16 of the 2006 Act (auditor's report on auditable part of directors' remuneration report), "the auditable part" of a directors' remuneration report is the information set out in the report as identified in Part 5 of Schedule 8 to these Regulations.

History – Reg. 11(1A) inserted, 11(2) revoked and, in reg. 11(3), "the information set out in the report as identified in Part 5" substituted for "the part containing the information required by Part 3" by SI 2013/1981, reg. 2, with effect from 1 October 2013 in relation to a company's financial year ending on or after 30 September 2013.

This version of reg. 11 applies to financial years ending on or after 30 September 2013. The version applying to financial years ending before 30 September 2013 read as follows:

"**11(1)** The remuneration report which the directors of a quoted company are required to prepare under section 420 of the 2006 Act (duty to prepare directors' remuneration report) must contain the information specified in Schedule 8 to these Regulations, and must comply with any requirement of that Schedule as to how information is to be set out in the report.

11(2) In Schedule 8–

Part 1 is introductory,
Part 2 relates to information about remuneration committees, performance related remuneration, consideration of conditions elsewhere in company and group and liabilities in respect of directors' contracts,
Part 3 relates to detailed information about directors' remuneration (information included under Part 3 is required to be reported on by the auditor (see subsection (3)), and
Part 4 contains interpretative and supplementary provisions.

11(3) For the purposes of section 497 in Part 16 of the 2006 Act (auditor's report on auditable part of directors' remuneration report), **"the auditable part"** of a directors' remuneration report is the part containing the information required by Part 3 of Schedule 8 to these Regulations."

PART 5 – INTERPRETATION
DEFINITION OF "PROVISIONS"

12 Schedule 9 to these Regulations defines **"provisions"** for the purposes of these Regulations and for the purposes of–

(a) section 677(3)(a) (Companies Act accounts: relevant provisions for purposes of financial assistance) in Part 18 of the 2006 Act,
(b) section 712(2)(b)(i) (Companies Act accounts: relevant provisions to determine available profits for redemption or purchase by private company out of capital) in that Part,
(c) sections 831(3)(a) (Companies Act accounts: net asset restriction on public company distributions), 832(4)(a) (Companies Act accounts: investment companies distributions) and 836(1)(b)(i) (Companies Act accounts: relevant provisions for distribution purposes) in Part 23 of that Act, and
(d) section 841(2)(a) (Companies Act accounts: provisions to be treated as realised losses) in that Part.

History – Para. (d) inserted by SI 2009/1581 reg 12(1) and (2): 27 June 2009 applying in relation to financial years beginning on or after 6 April 2008 which have not ended before 27 June 2009.

General interpretation

13 Schedule 10 to these Regulations contains general definitions for the purposes of these Regulations.

SCHEDULES

SCHEDULE 1   Regulation 3(1)

COMPANIES ACT INDIVIDUAL ACCOUNTS: COMPANIES WHICH ARE NOT BANKING OR INSURANCE COMPANIES

PART 1 – GENERAL RULES AND FORMATS

SECTION A – GENERAL RULES

1(1) Subject to the following provisions of this Schedule–

(a) every balance sheet of a company must show the items listed in either of the balance sheet formats in Section B of this Part, and

(b) every profit and loss account must show the items listed in either of the profit and loss account formats in Section B.

1(2) References in this Schedule to the items listed in any of the formats in Section B are to those items read together with any of the notes following the formats which apply to those items.

1(3) Subject to paragraph 1A, the items must be shown in the order and under the headings and sub-headings given in the particular format used, but–

(a) the notes to the formats may permit alternative positions for any particular items, and

(b) the heading or sub-heading for any item does not have to be distinguished by any letter or number assigned to that item in the format used.

History – In para. 1(1)(b), the word "either" substituted for the words "any one" by SI 2015/980, reg. 27(2)(a), with effect in relation to–

(a) financial years beginning on or after 1 January 2016, and

(b) a financial year of a company beginning on or after 1 January 2015, but before 1 January 2016, if the directors of the company so decide.

In para. 1(3), the words "Subject to paragraph 1A," inserted by SI 2015/980, reg. 27(2)(b), with effect in relation to–

(a) financial years beginning on or after 1 January 2016, and

(b) a financial year of a company beginning on or after 1 January 2015, but before 1 January 2016, if the directors of the company so decide.

1A(1) The company's directors may adapt one of the balance sheet formats in Section B so to distinguish between current and non-current items in a different way, provided that–

(a) the information given is at least equivalent to that which would have been required by the use of such format had it not been thus adapted, and

(b) the presentation of those items is in accordance with generally accepted accounting principles or practice.

1A(2) The company's directors may adapt one of the profit and loss account formats in Section B, provided that–

(a) the information given is at least equivalent to that which would have been required by the use of such format had it not been thus adapted, and

(b) the presentation is in accordance with generally accepted accounting principles or practice.

1A(3) So far as is practicable, the following provisions of Section A of this Part of this Schedule apply to the balance sheet or profit or loss account of a company notwithstanding any such adaptation pursuant to this paragraph.

History – Para. 1A inserted by SI 2015/980, reg. 27(2)(c), with effect in relation to–

    (a)   financial years beginning on or after 1 January 2016, and

    (b)   a financial year of a company beginning on or after 1 January 2015, but before 1 January 2016, if the directors of the company so decide.

2(1) Where in accordance with paragraph 1 a company's balance sheet or profit and loss account for any financial year has been prepared by reference to one of the formats in Section B, the company's directors must use the same format in preparing Companies Act individual accounts for subsequent financial years, unless in their opinion there are special reasons for a change.

2(2) Particulars of any such change must be given in a note to the accounts in which the new format is first used, and the reasons for the change must be explained.

3(1) Any item required to be shown in a company's balance sheet or profit and loss account may be shown in greater detail than required by the particular format used.

3(2) The balance sheet or profit and loss account may include an item representing or covering the amount of any asset or liability, income or expenditure not otherwise covered by any of the items listed in the format used, save that none of the following may be treated as assets in any balance sheet–

    (a) preliminary expenses,
    (b) expenses of, and commission on, any issue of shares or debentures, and
    (c) costs of research.

4(1) Where the special nature of the company's business requires it, the company's directors must adapt the arrangement, headings and sub-headings otherwise required in respect of items given an Arabic number in the balance sheet or profit and loss account format used.

4(2) The directors may combine items to which Arabic numbers are given in any of the formats in Section B if–

    (a) their individual amounts are not material to assessing the state of affairs or profit or loss of the company for the financial year in question, or
    (b) the combination facilitates that assessment.

4(3) Where sub-paragraph (2)(b) applies, the individual amounts of any items which have been combined must be disclosed in a note to the accounts.

5(1) Subject to sub-paragraph (2), the directors must not include a heading or sub-heading corresponding to an item in the balance sheet or profit and loss account format used if there is no amount to be shown for that item for the financial year to which the balance sheet or profit and loss account relates.

5(2) Where an amount can be shown for the item in question for the immediately preceding financial year that amount must be shown under the heading or sub-heading required by the format for that item.

6 Every profit and loss account must show the amount of a company's profit or loss before taxation.

History – In para. 6, the words "on ordinary activities" omitted by SI 2015/980, reg. 27(2)(d), with effect in relation to–

    (a)   financial years beginning on or after 1 January 2016, and

    (b)   a financial year of a company beginning on or after 1 January 2015, but before 1 January 2016, if the directors of the company so decide.

7(1) For every item shown in the balance sheet or profit and loss account the corresponding amount for the immediately preceding financial year must also be shown.

7(2) Where that corresponding amount is not comparable with the amount to be shown for the item in question in respect of the financial year to which the balance sheet or profit and loss account relates, the former amount may be adjusted, and particulars of the non-comparability and of any adjustment must be disclosed in a note to the accounts.

8 Amounts in respect of items representing assets or income may not be set off against amounts in respect of items representing liabilities or expenditure (as the case may be), or vice versa.

9 The company's directors must, in determining how amounts are presented within items in the profit and loss account and balance sheet, have regard to the substance of the reported transaction or arrangement, in accordance with generally accepted accounting principles or practice.

9A Where an asset or liability relates to more than one item in the balance sheet, the relationship of such asset or liability to the relevant items must be disclosed either under those items or in the notes to the accounts.

History – Para. 9A inserted by SI 2015/980, reg. 27(2)(e), with effect in relation to–

    (a)   financial years beginning on or after 1 January 2016, and

    (b)   a financial year of a company beginning on or after 1 January 2015, but before 1 January 2016, if the directors of the company so decide.

SECTION B – THE REQUIRED FORMATS FOR ACCOUNTS
Balance sheet formats – Format 1

A.   Called up share capital not paid *(1)*

B.   Fixed assets

    I.   Intangible assets

        1.   Development costs
        2.   Concessions, patents, licences, trade marks and similar rights and assets *(2)*
        3.   Goodwill *(3)*
        4.   Payments on account

    II.   Tangible assets

        1. Land and buildings
        2. Plant and machinery
        3. Fixtures, fittings, tools and equipment
        4. Payments on account and assets in course of construction

    III.   Investments

        1. Shares in group undertakings
        2. Loans to group undertakings
        3. Participating interests
        4. Loans to undertakings in which the company has a participating interest
        5. Other investments other than loans
        6. Other loans
        7. Own shares *(4)*

C.   Current assets

  I.   Stocks

      1.   Raw materials and consumables
      2.   Work in progress
      3.   Finished goods and goods for resale
      4.   Payments on account

  II.   Debtors *(5)*

      1.   Trade debtors
      2.   Amounts owed by group undertakings
      3.   Amounts owed by undertakings in which the company has a participating interest
      4.   Other debtors
      5.   Called up share capital not paid *(1)*
      6.   Prepayments and accrued income *(6)*

  III. Investments

      1.   Shares in group undertakings
      2.   Own shares *(4)*
      3.   Other investments

  IV. Cash at bank and in hand

D.   Prepayments and accrued income *(6)*

E.   Creditors: amounts falling due within one year

      1.   Debenture loans *(7)*
      2.   Bank loans and overdrafts
      3.   Payments received on account *(8)*
      4.   Trade creditors
      5.   Bills of exchange payable
      6.   Amounts owed to group undertakings
      7.   Amounts owed to undertakings in which the company has a participating interest
      8.   Other creditors including taxation and social security *(9)*
      9.   Accruals and deferred income *(10)*

F.   Net current assets (liabilities) *(11)*

G.   Total assets less current liabilities

H.   Creditors: amounts falling due after more than one year

      1.   Debenture loans *(7)*
      2.   Bank loans and overdrafts
      3.   Payments received on account *(8)*
      4.   Trade creditors
      5.   Bills of exchange payable
      6.   Amounts owed to group undertakings
      7.   Amounts owed to undertakings in which the company has a participating interest
      8.   Other creditors including taxation and social security *(9)*
      9.   Accruals and deferred income *(10)*

  I.   Provisions for liabilities

      1.   Pensions and similar obligations
      2.   Taxation, including deferred taxation

3. Other provisions

J. Accruals and deferred income *(10)*

K. Capital and reserves

    I. Called up share capital *(12)*
    II. Share premium account
    III. Revaluation reserve
    IV. Other reserves

        1. Capital redemption reserve
        2. Reserve for own shares
        3. Reserves provided for by the articles of association
        4. Other reserves, including the fair value reserve

V. Profit and loss account

Balance sheet formats – Format 2

ASSETS

A. Called up share capital not paid *(1)*

B. Fixed assets

    I. Intangible assets

        1. Development costs
        2. Concessions, patents, licences, trade marks and similar rights and assets *(2)*
        3. Goodwill *(3)*
        4. Payments on account

    II. Tangible assets

        1. Land and buildings
        2. Plant and machinery
        3. Fixtures, fittings, tools and equipment
        4. Payments on account and assets in course of construction

    III. Investments

        1. Shares in group undertakings
        2. Loans to group undertakings
        3. Participating interests
        4. Loans to undertakings in which the company has a participating interest
        5. Other investments other than loans
        6. Other loans
        7. Own shares *(4)*

C. Current assets

    I. Stocks

        1. Raw materials and consumables
        2. Work in progress
        3. Finished goods and goods for resale
        4. Payments on account

II.   Debtors *(5)*

    1.   Trade debtors
    2.   Amounts owed by group undertakings
    3.   Amounts owed by undertakings in which the company has a participating interest
    4.   Other debtors
    5.   Called up share capital not paid *(1)*
    6.   Prepayments and accrued income *(6)*

III.   Investments

    1.   Shares in group undertakings
    2.   Own shares *(4)*
    3.   Other investments

IV.   Cash at bank and in hand

D.   Prepayments and accrued income *(6)*

CAPITAL, RESERVES AND LIABILITIES

A.   Capital and reserves

    I.   Called up share capital *(12)*
    II.   Share premium account
    III.   Revaluation reserve
    IV.   Other reserves

    1.   Capital redemption reserve
    2.   Reserve for own shares
    3.   Reserves provided for by the articles of association
    4.   Other reserves, including the fair value reserve

    V.   Profit and loss account

B.   Provisions for liabilities

    1.   Pensions and similar obligations
    2.   Taxation, including deferred taxation
    3.   Other provisions

C.   Creditors *(13)*

    1.   Debenture loans *(7)*
    2.   Bank loans and overdrafts
    3.   Payments received on account *(8)*
    4.   Trade creditors
    5.   Bills of exchange payable
    6.   Amounts owed to group undertakings
    7.   Amounts owed to undertakings in which the company has a participating interest
    8.   Other creditors including taxation and social security *(9)*
    9.   Accruals and deferred income *(10)*

D.   Accruals and deferred income *(10)*

Notes on the balance sheet formats

(1) Called up share capital not paid

(Formats 1 and 2, items A and C.II.5.)
This item may be shown in either of the two positions given in formats 1 and 2.

(2) Concessions, patents, licences, trade marks and similar rights and assets

(Formats 1 and 2, item B.I.2.)

Amounts in respect of assets are only to be included in a company's balance sheet under this item if either–

(a) the assets were acquired for valuable consideration and are not required to be shown under goodwill, or
(b) the assets in question were created by the company itself.

(3) Goodwill

(Formats 1 and 2, item B.I.3.)
Amounts representing goodwill are only to be included to the extent that the goodwill was acquired for valuable consideration.

(4) Own shares

(Formats 1 and 2, items B.III.7 and C.III.2.)
The nominal value of the shares held must be shown separately.

(5) Debtors

(Formats 1 and 2, items C.II.1 to 6.)
The amount falling due after more than one year must be shown separately for each item included under debtors.

(6) Prepayments and accrued income

(Formats 1 and 2, items C.II.6 and D.)
This item may be shown in either of the two positions given in formats 1 and 2.

(7) Debenture loans

(Format 1, items E.1 and H.1 and format 2, item C.1.)
The amount of any convertible loans must be shown separately.

(8) Payments received on account

(Format 1, items E.3 and H.3 and format 2, item C.3.)

Payments received on account of orders must be shown for each of these items in so far as they are not shown as deductions from stocks.

(9) Other creditors including taxation and social security

(Format 1, items E.8 and H.8 and format 2, item C.8.)

The amount for creditors in respect of taxation and social security must be shown separately from the amount for other creditors.

(10) Accruals and deferred income

(Format 1, items E.9, H.9 and J and format 2, items C.9 and D.)

The two positions given for this item in format 1 at E.9 and H.9 are an alternative to the position at J, but if the item is not shown in a position corresponding to that at J it may be shown in either or both of the other two positions (as the case may require).

The two positions given for this item in format 2 are alternatives.

(11) Net current assets (liabilities)

(Format 1, item F.)

In determining the amount to be shown for this item any amounts shown under "prepayments and accrued income" must be taken into account wherever shown.

(12) Called up share capital

(Format 1, item K.I and format 2, item A.I.)

The amount of allotted share capital and the amount of called up share capital which has been paid up must be shown separately.

(13) Creditors

(Format 2, items C.1 to 9.)

Amounts falling due within one year and after one year must be shown separately for each of these items and for the aggregate of all of these items.

Profit and loss account formats – Format 1
(See note (17) Below)

1. Turnover

2. Cost of sales *(14)*

3. Gross profit or loss

4. Distribution costs *(14)*

5. Administrative expenses *(14)*

6. Other operating income

7. Income from shares in group undertakings

8. Income from participating interests

9. Income from other fixed asset investments *(15)*

10. Other interest receivable and similar income *(15)*

11. Amounts written off investments

12. Interest payable and similar expenses *(16)*

13. Tax on profit or loss

14. Profit or loss after taxation

15. Omitted

16. Omitted

17. Omitted

18. Omitted

19. Other taxes not shown under the above items

20. Profit or loss for the financial year

Profit and loss account formats – Format 2

1. Turnover

2. Change in stocks of finished goods and in work in progress

3. Own work capitalised

4. Other operating income

5. (a) Raw materials and consumables
   (b) Other external expenses

6. Staff costs

   (a) wages and salaries
   (b) social security costs
   (c) other pension costs

7. (a) Depreciation and other amounts written off tangible and intangible fixed assets
   (b) Amounts written off current assets, to the extent that they exceed write-offs which are normal in the undertaking concerned

8. Other operating expenses

9. Income from shares in group undertakings

10. Income from participating interests

11. Income from other fixed asset investments *(15)*

12. Other interest receivable and similar income *(15)*

13. Amounts written off investments

14. Interest payable and similar expenses *(16)*

15. Tax on profit or loss

16. Profit or loss after taxation

17. Omitted

18. Omitted

19. Omitted

20. Omitted

21. Other taxes not shown under the above items

22. Profit or loss for the financial year

Notes on the profit and loss account formats

(14) *Cost of sales: distribution costs: administrative expenses*

(Format 1, items 2, 4 and 5.)

These items must be stated after taking into account any necessary provisions for depreciation or diminution in value of assets.

(15) *Income from other fixed asset investments: other interest receivable and similar income*

(Format 1, items 9 and 10; format 2, items 11 and 12.)

Income and interest derived from group undertakings must be shown separately from income and interest derived from other sources.

(16) *Interest payable and similar expenses*

(Format 1, item 12; format 2, item 14.)

The amount payable to group undertakings must be shown separately.

(17) *Format 1*

The amount of any provisions for depreciation and diminution in value of tangible and intangible fixed assets falling to be shown under item 7(a) in format 2 must be disclosed in a note to the accounts in any case where the profit and loss account is prepared using format 1.

History – In section B, the following amendments were made by SI 2015/980, reg. 27(3), with effect in relation to– (a) financial years beginning on or after 1 January 2016, and (b) a financial year of a company beginning on or after 1 January 2015, but before 1 January 2016, if the directors of the company so decide:

- in balance sheet format 1, item "4 Other reserves, including the fair value reserve" substitute for "4 Other reserves".
- the heading "CAPITAL, RESERVES AND LIABILITIES" substituted for the word "LIABILITIES".
- in balance sheet format 2, item "4 Other reserves, including the fair value reserve" substitute for "4 Other reserves".
- in profit and loss account format 1–
    - at item 12, the word "expenses" substitute for "charges";
    - at item 13, the words "on ordinary activities" omitted;
    - at item 14, the words "on ordinary activities" omitted;
    - items 15–18 omit.
- in profit and loss account format 2–
    - at item 5(b), the word "expenses" substitute for "charges";
    - item 7(b) substituted;
    - at item 8, the word "expenses" substitute for "charges";
    - at item 14, the word "expenses" substitute for "charges";
    - at item 15, the words "on ordinary activities" omitted;
    - at item 16, the words "on ordinary activities" omitted;
    - items 17–20 omitted.
- profit and loss account format 3 omitted.
- profit and loss account format 4 omitted.
- in note (14) of "Notes on the profit and loss account formats", the words "and format 3, items A.1, 2 and 3" omitted.
- in note (15), the words "format 3, items B.5 and 6 and format 4, items B.7 and 8" omitted.
- in note (16) title, the word "expenses" substitute for "charges"; and the words "format 3, item A.5 and format 4, item A.7" omitted.
- note (17) title, "Format 1" substituted; the words "item 7(a) in format 2" substitute for "items 7(a) and A.4(a) respectively in formats 2 and 4"; and the words "or format 3" omitted.

PART 2 – ACCOUNTING PRINCIPLES AND RULES
SECTION A – ACCOUNTING PRINCIPLES

Preliminary

10(1) The amounts to be included in respect of all items shown in a company's accounts must be determined in accordance with the principles set out in this Section.

10(2) But if it appears to the company's directors that there are special reasons for departing from any of those principles in preparing the company's accounts in respect of any financial year they may do so, in which case particulars of the departure, the reasons for it and its effect must be given in a note to the accounts.

Accounting principles

11 The company is presumed to be carrying on business as a going concern.

12 Accounting policies and measurement bases must be applied consistently within the same accounts and from one financial year to the next.

History – In para. 12, the words "and measurement bases" inserted by SI 2015/980, reg. 28(2)(a), with effect in relation to–

    (a)   financial years beginning on or after 1 January 2016, and
    (b)   a financial year of a company beginning on or after 1 January 2015, but before 1 January 2016, if the directors of the company so decide.

13 The amount of any item must be determined on a prudent basis, and in particular–

    (a)   only profits realised at the balance sheet date are to be included in the profit and loss account,
    (b)   all liabilities which have arisen in respect of the financial year to which the accounts relate or a previous financial year must be taken into account, including those which only become apparent between the balance sheet date and the date on which it is signed on behalf of the board of directors in accordance with Section 414 of the 2006 Act (approval and signing of accounts) and
    (c)   all provisions for diminution of value must be recognised, whether the result of the financial year is a profit or a loss.

History – Para. 13(c), (and the word "and" preceding it) inserted; the word "and" in para. (a) omitted by SI 2015/980, reg. 28(2)(b), with effect in relation to–

    (a)   financial years beginning on or after 1 January 2016, and
    (b)   a financial year of a company beginning on or after 1 January 2015, but before 1 January 2016, if the directors of the company so decide.

14 All income and charges relating to the financial year to which the accounts relate must be taken into account, without regard to the date of receipt or payment.

15 In determining the aggregate amount of any item, the amount of each individual asset or liability that falls to be taken into account must be determined separately.

15A The opening balance sheet for each financial year shall correspond to the closing balance sheet for the preceding financial year.

History – Para. 15A inserted by SI 2015/980, reg. 28(2)(c), with effect in relation to–

    (a)   financial years beginning on or after 1 January 2016, and
    (b)   a financial year of a company beginning on or after 1 January 2015, but before 1 January 2016, if the directors of the company so decide.

SECTION B – HISTORICAL COST ACCOUNTING RULES

Preliminary

16 Subject to Sections C and D of this Part of this Schedule, the amounts to be included in respect of all items shown in a company's accounts must be determined in accordance with the rules set out in this Section.

Fixed assets

General rules

17(1) The amount to be included in respect of any fixed asset must be its purchase price or production cost.

17(2) This is subject to any provision for depreciation or diminution in value made in accordance with paragraphs 18 to 20.

Rules for depreciation and diminution in value

18 In the case of any fixed asset which has a limited useful economic life, the amount of–

(a) its purchase price or production cost, or
(b) where it is estimated that any such asset will have a residual value at the end of the period of its useful economic life, its purchase price or production cost less that estimated residual value, must be reduced by provisions for depreciation calculated to write off that amount systematically over the period of the asset's useful economic life.

19(1) Where a fixed asset investment falling to be included under item B.III of either of the balance sheet formats set out in Part 1 of this Schedule has diminished in value, provisions for diminution in value may be made in respect of it and the amount to be included in respect of it may be reduced accordingly.

19(2) Provisions for diminution in value must be made in respect of any fixed asset which has diminished in value if the reduction in its value is expected to be permanent (whether its useful economic life is limited or not), and the amount to be included in respect of it must be reduced accordingly.

19(3) Provisions made under sub-paragraph (1) or (2) must be charged to the profit and loss account and disclosed separately in a note to the accounts if not shown separately in the profit and loss account.

History – Para. 19(3) substituted by SI 2015/980, reg. 28(3)(a), with effect in relation to–
(a) financial years beginning on or after 1 January 2016, and
(b) a financial year of a company beginning on or after 1 January 2015, but before 1 January 2016, if the directors of the company so decide.
Former para. 19(3) read as follows:
"**19(3)** Any provisions made under sub-paragraph (1) or (2) which are not shown in the profit and loss account must be disclosed (either separately or in aggregate) in a note to the accounts."

20(1) Where the reasons for which any provision was made in accordance with paragraph 19 have ceased to apply to any extent, that provision must be written back to the extent that it is no longer necessary.

20(2) Any amounts written back under sub-paragraph (1) must be recognised in the profit and loss account and disclosed separately in a note to the accounts if not shown separately in the profit and loss account.

History – Para. 20(2) substituted by SI 2015/980, reg. 28(3)(b), with effect in relation to–

    (a)   financial years beginning on or after 1 January 2016, and

    (b)   a financial year of a company beginning on or after 1 January 2015, but before 1 January 2016, if the directors of the company so decide.

Former para. 20(2) read as follows:

"**20(2)** Any amounts written back in accordance with sub-paragraph (1) which are not shown in the profit and loss account must be disclosed (either separately or in aggregate) in a note to the accounts."

Intangible Assets

21(1) Where this is in accordance with generally accepted accounting principles or practice, development costs may be included in "other intangible assets" under "fixed assets" in the balance sheet formats set out in Section B of Part 1 of this Schedule.

21(2) If any amount is included in a company's balance sheet in respect of development costs, the note on accounting policies (see paragraph 44 of this Schedule) must include the following information–

    (a)   the period over which the amount of those costs originally capitalised is being or is to be written off, and

    (b)   the reasons for capitalising the development costs in question.

History – Para. 21 and the heading preceding it substituted by SI 2015/980, reg. 28(3)(c), with effect in relation to–

    (a)   financial years beginning on or after 1 January 2016, and

    (b)   a financial year of a company beginning on or after 1 January 2015, but before 1 January 2016, if the directors of the company so decide.

Former para. 21 read as follows:

"Development costs

21(1) Notwithstanding that an item in respect of **"development costs"** is included under **"fixed assets"** in the balance sheet formats set out in Part 1 of this Schedule, an amount may only be included in a company's balance sheet in respect of development costs in special circumstances.

21(2) If any amount is included in a company's balance sheet in respect of development costs the following information must be given in a note to the accounts–

    (a)   the period over which the amount of those costs originally capitalised is being or is to be written off, and

    (b)   the reasons for capitalising the development costs in question."

22(1) Intangible assets must be written off over the useful economic life of the intangible asset.

22(2) Where in exceptional cases the useful life of intangible assets cannot be reliably estimated, such assets must be written off over a period chosen by the directors of the company.

22(3) The period referred to in sub-paragraph (2) must not exceed ten years.

22(4) There must be disclosed in a note to the accounts the period referred to in sub-paragraph (2) and the reasons for choosing that period.

History – Para. 22 substituted by SI 2015/980, reg. 28(3)(c), with effect in relation to–

    (a)   financial years beginning on or after 1 January 2016, and

    (b)   a financial year of a company beginning on or after 1 January 2015, but before 1 January 2016, if the directors of the company so decide.

Former para. 22 read as follows:

"**22(1)** The application of paragraphs 17 to 20 in relation to goodwill (in any case where goodwill is treated as an asset) is subject to the following.

22(2) Subject to sub-paragraph (3), the amount of the consideration for any goodwill acquired by a company must be reduced by provisions for depreciation calculated to write off that amount systematically over a period chosen by the directors of the company.

22(3) The period chosen must not exceed the useful economic life of the goodwill in question.

22(4) In any case where any goodwill acquired by a company is shown or included as an asset in the company's balance sheet there must be disclosed in a note to the accounts–

(a)   the period chosen for writing off the consideration for that goodwill, and

(b)   the reasons for choosing that period."

Current assets

23 Subject to paragraph 24, the amount to be included in respect of any current asset must be its purchase price or production cost.

24(1) If the net realisable value of any current asset is lower than its purchase price or production cost, the amount to be included in respect of that asset must be the net realisable value.

24(2) Where the reasons for which any provision for diminution in value was made in accordance with sub-paragraph (1) have ceased to apply to any extent, that provision must be written back to the extent that it is no longer necessary.

Miscellaneous and supplementary provisions

Excess of money owed over value received as an asset item

25(1) Where the amount repayable on any debt owed by a company is greater than the value of the consideration received in the transaction giving rise to the debt, the amount of the difference may be treated as an asset.

25(2) Where any such amount is so treated–

(a)   it must be written off by reasonable amounts each year and must be completely written off before repayment of the debt, and

(b)   if the current amount is not shown as a separate item in the company's balance sheet, it must be disclosed in a note to the accounts.

Assets included at a fixed amount

26(1) Subject to sub-paragraph (2), assets which fall to be included–

(a)   amongst the fixed assets of a company under the item "tangible assets", or

(b)   amongst the current assets of a company under the item "raw materials and consumables", may be included at a fixed quantity and value.

26(2) Sub-paragraph (1) applies to assets of a kind which are constantly being replaced where–

(a)   their overall value is not material to assessing the company's state of affairs, and

(b)   their quantity, value and composition are not subject to material variation.

Determination of purchase price or production cost

27(1) The purchase price of an asset is to be determined by adding to the actual price paid any expenses incidental to its acquisition and then subtracting any incidental reductions in the cost of acquisition.

27(2) The production cost of an asset is to be determined by adding to the purchase price of the raw materials and consumables used the amount of the costs incurred by the company which are directly attributable to the production of that asset.

27(3) In addition, there may be included in the production cost of an asset–

(a) a reasonable proportion of the costs incurred by the company which are only indirectly attributable to the production of that asset, but only to the extent that they relate to the period of production, and

(b) interest on capital borrowed to finance the production of that asset, to the extent that it accrues in respect of the period of production, provided, however, in a case within paragraph (b), that the inclusion of the interest in determining the cost of that asset and the amount of the interest so included is disclosed in a note to the accounts.

27(4) In the case of current assets distribution costs may not be included in production costs.

History – In para. 27(1), the words "and then subtracting any incidental reductions in the cost of acquisition" inserted by SI 2015/980, reg. 28(3)(d), with effect in relation to–

(a) financial years beginning on or after 1 January 2016, and

(b) a financial year of a company beginning on or after 1 January 2015, but before 1 January 2016, if the directors of the company so decide.

28(1) The purchase price or production cost of–

(a) any assets which fall to be included under any item shown in a company's balance sheet under the general item "stocks", and

(b) any assets which are fungible assets (including investments), may be determined by the application of any of the methods mentioned in sub-paragraph (2) in relation to any such assets of the same class, provided that the method chosen is one which appears to the directors to be appropriate in the circumstances of the company.

28(2) Those methods are–

(a) the method known as "first in, first out" (FIFO),

(b) the method known as "last in, first out" (LIFO),

(c) a weighted average price, and

(d) any other method reflecting generally accepted best practice.

28(3) Where in the case of any company–

(a) the purchase price or production cost of assets falling to be included under any item shown in the company's balance sheet has been determined by the application of any method permitted by this paragraph, and

(b) the amount shown in respect of that item differs materially from the relevant alternative amount given below in this paragraph, the amount of that difference must be disclosed in a note to the accounts.

28(4) Subject to sub-paragraph (5), for the purposes of sub-paragraph (3)(b), the relevant alternative amount, in relation to any item shown in a company's balance sheet, is the amount which would have been shown in respect of that item if assets of any class included under that item at an amount determined by any method permitted by this paragraph had instead been included at their replacement cost as at the balance sheet date.

28(5) The relevant alternative amount may be determined by reference to the most recent actual purchase price or production cost before the balance sheet date of assets of any class included under the item in question instead of by reference to their replacement cost as at that date, but only if the former appears to the directors of the company to constitute the more appropriate standard of comparison in the case of assets of that class.

History – In para. 28(2)(d), the words "reflecting generally accepted best practice" substituted for the words "similar to any of the methods mentioned above" by SI 2015/980, reg. 28(3)(e), with effect in relation to–

(a) financial years beginning on or after 1 January 2016, and

(b) a financial year of a company beginning on or after 1 January 2015, but before 1 January 2016, if the directors of the company so decide.

Substitution of original stated amount where price or cost unknown

29(1) This paragraph applies where–

    (a) there is no record of the purchase price or production cost of any asset of a company or of any price, expenses or costs relevant for determining its purchase price or production cost in accordance with paragraph 27, or

    (b) any such record cannot be obtained without unreasonable expense or delay.

29(2) In such a case, the purchase price or production cost of the asset must be taken, for the purposes of paragraphs 17 to 24, to be the value ascribed to it in the earliest available record of its value made on or after its acquisition or production by the company.

Equity method in respect of participating interests

29A(1) Participating interests may be accounted for using the equity method.

29A(2) If participating interests are accounted for using the equity method–

    (a) the proportion of profit or loss attributable to a participating interest and recognised in the profit and loss account may be that proportion which corresponds to the amount of any dividends, and

    (b) where the profit attributable to a participating interest and recognised in the profit and loss account exceeds the amount of any dividends, the difference must be placed in a reserve which cannot be distributed to shareholders.

29A(3) The reference to **"dividends"** in sub-paragraph (2) includes dividends already paid and those whose payment can be claimed.

History – Para. 29A and the heading preceding it inserted by SI 2015/980, reg. 28(3)(f), with effect in relation to–

    (a) financial years beginning on or after 1 January 2016, and

    (b) a financial year of a company beginning on or after 1 January 2015, but before 1 January 2016, if the directors of the company so decide.

SECTION C – ALTERNATIVE ACCOUNTING RULES

Preliminary

30(1) The rules set out in Section B are referred to below in this Schedule as the historical cost accounting rules.

30(2) Those rules, with the omission of paragraphs 16, 22 and 26 to 29, are referred to below in this Part of this Schedule as the depreciation rules; and references below in this Schedule to the historical cost accounting rules do not include the depreciation rules as they apply by virtue of paragraph 33.

31 Subject to paragraphs 33 to 35, the amounts to be included in respect of assets of any description mentioned in paragraph 32 may be determined on any basis so mentioned.

Alternative accounting rules

32(1) Intangible fixed assets, other than goodwill, may be included at their current cost.

32(2) Tangible fixed assets may be included at a market value determined as at the date of their last valuation or at their current cost.

32(3) Investments of any description falling to be included under item B III of either of the balance sheet formats set out in Part 1 of this Schedule may be included either–

(a) at a market value determined as at the date of their last valuation, or
(b) at a value determined on any basis which appears to the directors to be appropriate in the circumstances of the company.

But in the latter case particulars of the method of valuation adopted and of the reasons for adopting it must be disclosed in a note to the accounts.

32(4) [Omitted by SI 2015/980, reg. 17(4)(a).]

32(5) [Omitted by SI 2015/980, reg. 17(4)(a).]

History – Para. 32(4) and (5) omitted by SI 2015/980, reg. 28(4)(a), with effect in relation to–

(a) financial years beginning on or after 1 January 2016, and
(b) a financial year of a company beginning on or after 1 January 2015, but before 1 January 2016, if the directors of the company so decide.

Former para. 32(4) and (5) read as follows:

"**32(4)** Investments of any description falling to be included under item C III of either of the balance sheet formats set out in Part 1 of this Schedule may be included at their current cost.

32(5) Stocks may be included at their current cost."

Application of the depreciation rules

33(1) Where the value of any asset of a company is determined on any basis mentioned in paragraph 32, that value must be, or (as the case may require) be the starting point for determining, the amount to be included in respect of that asset in the company's accounts, instead of its purchase price or production cost or any value previously so determined for that asset.

The depreciation rules apply accordingly in relation to any such asset with the substitution for any reference to its purchase price or production cost of a reference to the value most recently determined for that asset on any basis mentioned in paragraph 32.

33(2) The amount of any provision for depreciation required in the case of any fixed asset by paragraphs 18 to 20 as they apply by virtue of sub-paragraph (1) is referred to below in this paragraph as the adjusted amount, and the amount of any provision which would be required by any of those paragraphs in the case of that asset according to the historical cost accounting rules is referred to as the historical cost amount.

33(3) Where sub-paragraph (1) applies in the case of any fixed asset the amount of any provision for depreciation in respect of that asset–

(a) included in any item shown in the profit and loss account in respect of amounts written off assets of the description in question, or
(b) taken into account in stating any item so shown which is required by note (14) of the notes on the profit and loss account formats set out in Part 1 of this Schedule to be stated after taking into account any necessary provision for depreciation or diminution in value of assets included under it,

may be the historical cost amount instead of the adjusted amount, provided that the amount of any difference between the two is shown separately in the profit and loss account or in a note to the accounts.

Additional information to be provided in case of departure from historical cost accounting rules

34(1) This paragraph applies where the amounts to be included in respect of assets covered by any items shown in a company's accounts have been determined on any basis mentioned in paragraph 32.

34(2) The items affected and the basis of valuation adopted in determining the amounts of the assets in question in the case of each such item must be disclosed in the note on accounting policies (see paragraph 44 of this Schedule).

34(3) In the case of each balance sheet item affected, the comparable amounts determined according to the historical cost accounting rules must be shown in a note to the accounts.

34(4) In sub-paragraph (3), references in relation to any item to the comparable amounts determined as there mentioned are references to–

 (a) the aggregate amount which would be required to be shown in respect of that item if the amounts to be included in respect of all the assets covered by that item were determined according to the historical cost accounting rules, and
 (b) the aggregate amount of the cumulative provisions for depreciation or diminution in value which would be permitted or required in determining those amounts according to those rules.

History – In para. 34(2), the words "the note on accounting policies (see paragraph 44 of this Schedule)" substituted for the words "a note to the accounts" by SI 2015/980, reg. 28(4)(b), with effect in relation to–

 (a) financial years beginning on or after 1 January 2016, and
 (b) a financial year of a company beginning on or after 1 January 2015, but before 1 January 2016, if the directors of the company so decide.

Para. 34(3) substituted by SI 2015/980, reg. 28(4)(c), with effect in relation to–

 (a) financial years beginning on or after 1 January 2016, and
 (b) a financial year of a company beginning on or after 1 January 2015, but before 1 January 2016, if the directors of the company so decide.

Former para. 34(3) read as follows:

"**34(3)** In the case of each balance sheet item affected (except stocks) either–

 (a) the comparable amounts determined according to the historical cost accounting rules, or
 (b) the differences between those amounts and the corresponding amounts actually shown in the balance sheet in respect of that item, must be shown separately in the balance sheet or in a note to the accounts."

Revaluation reserve

35(1) With respect to any determination of the value of an asset of a company on any basis mentioned in paragraph 32, the amount of any profit or loss arising from that determination (after allowing, where appropriate, for any provisions for depreciation or diminution in value made otherwise than by reference to the value so determined and any adjustments of any such provisions made in the light of that determination) must be credited or (as the case may be) debited to a separate reserve ("the revaluation reserve").

35(2) The amount of the revaluation reserve must be shown in the company's balance sheet under a separate sub-heading in the position given for the item "revaluation reserve" under "Capital and reserves" in format 1 or 2 of the balance sheet formats set out in Part 1 of this Schedule.

35(3) An amount may be transferred–

 (a) from the revaluation reserve–

  (i) to the profit and loss account, if the amount was previously charged to that account or represents realised profit, or
  (ii) on capitalisation,

(b)   to or from the revaluation reserve in respect of the taxation relating to any profit or loss credited or debited to the reserve.

The revaluation reserve must be reduced to the extent that the amounts transferred to it are no longer necessary for the purposes of the valuation method used.

35(4) In sub-paragraph (3)(a)(ii) **"capitalisation"**, in relation to an amount standing to the credit of the revaluation reserve, means applying it in wholly or partly paying up unissued shares in the company to be allotted to members of the company as fully or partly paid shares.

35(5) The revaluation reserve must not be reduced except as mentioned in this paragraph.

35(6) The treatment for taxation purposes of amounts credited or debited to the revaluation reserve must be disclosed in a note to the accounts.

History – In para. 35(2), the words 'under "Capital and reserves"' inserted; and the words "but need not be shown under that name" omitted by SI 2015/980, reg. 28(4)(d), with effect in relation to–

(a)   financial years beginning on or after 1 January 2016, and

(b)   a financial year of a company beginning on or after 1 January 2015, but before 1 January 2016, if the directors of the company so decide.

SECTION D – FAIR VALUE ACCOUNTING

Inclusion of financial instruments at fair value

36(1) Subject to sub-paragraphs (2) to (5), financial instruments (including derivatives) may be included at fair value.

36(2) Sub-paragraph (1) does not apply to financial instruments that constitute liabilities unless–

(a)   they are held as Part of a trading portfolio,
(b)   they are derivatives, or
(c)   they are financial instruments falling within sub-paragraph (4).

36(3) Unless they are financial instruments falling within sub-paragraph (4), sub-paragraph (1) does not apply to–

(a)   financial instruments (other than derivatives) held to maturity,
(b)   loans and receivables originated by the company and not held for trading purposes,
(c)   interests in subsidiary undertakings, associated undertakings and joint ventures,
(d)   equity instruments issued by the company,
(e)   contracts for contingent consideration in a business combination, or
(f)   other financial instruments with such special characteristics that the instruments, according to generally accepted accounting principles or practice, should be accounted for differently from other financial instruments.

36(4) Financial instruments which under international accounting standards may be included in accounts at fair value, may be so included, provided that the disclosures required by such accounting standards are made.

36(5) If the fair value of a financial instrument cannot be determined reliably in accordance with paragraph 37, sub-paragraph (1) does not apply to that financial instrument.

36(6) In this paragraph–

"associated undertaking" has the meaning given by paragraph 19 of Schedule 6 to these Regulations;
"joint venture" has the meaning given by paragraph 18 of that Schedule.

History – Para. 36(4) substituted by SI 2015/980, reg. 28(5)(a), with effect in relation to–

   (a)   financial years beginning on or after 1 January 2016, and

   (b)   a financial year of a company beginning on or after 1 January 2015, but before 1 January 2016, if the directors of the company so decide.

Former para. 36(4) read as follows:

"**36(4)** Financial instruments that, under international accounting standards adopted by the European Commission on or before 5th September 2006 in accordance with the IAS Regulation, may be included in accounts at fair value, may be so included, provided that the disclosures required by such accounting standards are made."

Determination of fair value

37(1) The fair value of a financial instrument is its value determined in accordance with this paragraph.

37(2) If a reliable market can readily be identified for the financial instrument, its fair value is determined by reference to its market value.

37(3) If a reliable market cannot readily be identified for the financial instrument but can be identified for its components or for a similar instrument, its fair value is determined by reference to the market value of its components or of the similar instrument.

37(4) If neither sub-paragraph (2) nor (3) applies, the fair value of the financial instrument is a value resulting from generally accepted valuation models and techniques.

37(5) Any valuation models and techniques used for the purposes of sub-paragraph (4) must ensure a reasonable approximation of the market value.

Hedged items

38 A company may include any assets and liabilities, or identified portions of such assets or liabilities, that qualify as hedged items under a fair value hedge accounting system at the amount required under that system.

Other assets that may be included at fair value

39(1) This paragraph applies to–

   (a)   stocks,

   (b)   investment property, and

   (c)   living animals and plants.

39(2) Such stocks, investment property, and living animals and plants may be included at fair value, provided that, as the case may be, all such stocks, investment property, and living animals and plants are so included where their fair value can reliably be determined.

39(3) In this paragraph, **"fair value"** means fair value determined in accordance with generally accepted accounting principles or practice.

History – Para. 39 substituted by SI 2015/980, reg. 28(5)(b), with effect in relation to–

   (a)   financial years beginning on or after 1 January 2016, and

   (b)   a financial year of a company beginning on or after 1 January 2015, but before 1 January 2016, if the directors of the company so decide.

Former para. 39 read as follows:

"**39(1)** This paragraph applies to–

(a)   investment property, and

(b)   living animals and plants, that, under international accounting standards, may be included in accounts at fair value.

39(2) Such investment property and such living animals and plants may be included at fair value, provided that all such investment property or, as the case may be, all such living animals and plants are so included where their fair value can reliably be determined.

39(3) In this paragraph, **"fair value"** means fair value determined in accordance with relevant international accounting standards."

Accounting for changes in value

40(1) This paragraph applies where a financial instrument is valued in accordance with paragraph 36 or 38 or an asset is valued in accordance with paragraph 39.

40(2) Notwithstanding paragraph 13 in this Part of this Schedule, and subject to sub-paragraphs (3) and (4), a change in the value of the financial instrument or of the investment property or living animal or plant must be included in the profit and loss account.

40(3) Where–

(a)   the financial instrument accounted for is a hedging instrument under a hedge accounting system that allows some or all of the change in value not to be shown in the profit and loss account, or

(b)   the change in value relates to an exchange difference arising on a monetary item that forms Part of a company's net investment in a foreign entity, the amount of the change in value must be credited to or (as the case may be) debited from a separate reserve ("the fair value reserve").

40(4) Where the instrument accounted for–

(a)   is an available for sale financial asset, and

(b)   is not a derivative, the change in value may be credited to or (as the case may be) debited from the fair value reserve.

The fair value reserve

41(1) The fair value reserve must be adjusted to the extent that the amounts shown in it are no longer necessary for the purposes of paragraph 40(3) or (4).

41(2) The treatment for taxation purposes of amounts credited or debited to the fair value reserve must be disclosed in a note to the accounts.

PART 3 – NOTES TO THE ACCOUNTS

Preliminary

42(1) Any information required in the case of a company by the following provisions of this Part of this Schedule must be given by way of a note to the accounts.

42(2) These notes must be presented in the order in which, where relevant, the items to which they relate are presented in the balance sheet and in the profit and loss account.

History – Para. 42 substituted by SI 2015/980, reg. 29(2), with effect in relation to–

    (a)   financial years beginning on or after 1 January 2016, and

    (b)   a financial year of a company beginning on or after 1 January 2015, but before 1 January 2016, if the directors of the company so decide.

Former para. 42 read as follows:

    "**42** Any information required in the case of any company by the following provisions of this Part of this Schedule must (if not given in the company's accounts) be given by way of a note to the accounts."

General

Reserves and dividends

43 There must be stated–

    (a)   any amount set aside or proposed to be set aside to, or withdrawn or proposed to be withdrawn from, reserves,

    (b)   the aggregate amount of dividends paid in the financial year (other than those for which a liability existed at the immediately preceding balance sheet date),

    (c)   the aggregate amount of dividends that the company is liable to pay at the balance sheet date, and

    (d)   the aggregate amount of dividends that are proposed before the date of approval of the accounts, and not otherwise disclosed under sub-paragraph (b) or (c).

Disclosure of accounting policies

44 The accounting policies adopted by the company in determining the amounts to be included in respect of items shown in the balance sheet and in determining the profit or loss of the company must be stated (including such policies with respect to the depreciation and diminution in value of assets).

45 It must be stated whether the accounts have been prepared in accordance with applicable accounting standards and particulars of any material departure from those standards and the reasons for it must be given (see regulation 4(2) for exemption for medium-sized companies).

Information supplementing the balance sheet

46 Paragraphs 47 to 64 require information which either supplements the information given with respect to any particular items shown in the balance sheet or is otherwise relevant to assessing the company's state of affairs in the light of the information so given.

Share capital and debentures

47(1) The following information must be given with respect to the company's share capital–

    (a)   where shares of more than one class have been allotted, the number and aggregate nominal value of shares of each class allotted, and

    (b)   where shares are held as treasury shares, the number and aggregate nominal value of the treasury shares and, where shares of more than one class have been allotted, the number and aggregate nominal value of the shares of each class held as treasury shares.

47(2) In the case of any Part of the allotted share capital that consists of redeemable shares, the following information must be given–

    (a)   the earliest and latest dates on which the company has power to redeem those shares,

    (b)   whether those shares must be redeemed in any event or are liable to be redeemed at the option of the company or of the shareholder, and

    (c)   whether any (and, if so, what) premium is payable on redemption.

48 If the company has allotted any shares during the financial year, the following information must be given–

    (a)   the classes of shares allotted, and

    (b)   as respects each class of shares, the number allotted, their aggregate nominal value, and the consideration received by the company for the allotment.

49(1) With respect to any contingent right to the allotment of shares in the company the following particulars must be given–

    (a)   the number, description and amount of the shares in relation to which the right is exercisable,

    (b)   the period during which it is exercisable, and

    (c)   the price to be paid for the shares allotted.

49(2) In sub-paragraph (1) **"contingent right to the allotment of shares"** means any option to subscribe for shares and any other right to require the allotment of shares to any person whether arising on the conversion into shares of securities of any other description or otherwise.

50(1) If the company has issued any debentures during the financial year to which the accounts relate, the following information must be given–

    (a)   the classes of debentures issued, and

    (b)   as respects each class of debentures, the amount issued and the consideration received by the company for the issue.

50(2) Where any of the company's debentures are held by a nominee of or trustee for the company, the nominal amount of the debentures and the amount at which they are stated in the accounting records kept by the company in accordance with Section 386 of the 2006 Act (duty to keep accounting records) must be stated.

Fixed assets

51(1) In respect of each item which is or would but for paragraph 4(2)(b) be shown under the general item "fixed assets" in the company's balance sheet the following information must be given–

    (a)   the appropriate amounts in respect of that item as at the date of the beginning of the financial year and as at the balance sheet date respectively,

    (b)   the effect on any amount shown in the balance sheet in respect of that item of–

        (i)   any revision of the amount in respect of any assets included under that item made during that year on any basis mentioned in paragraph 32,

        (ii)   acquisitions during that year of any assets,

        (iii)   disposals during that year of any assets, and

        (iv)   any transfers of assets of the company to and from that item during that year.

51(2) The reference in sub-paragraph (1)(a) to the appropriate amounts in respect of any item as at any date there mentioned is a reference to amounts representing the aggregate amounts determined, as at that date, in respect of assets falling to be included under that item on either of the following bases, that is to say–

    (a)   on the basis of purchase price or production cost (determined in accordance with paragraphs 27 and 28), or

(b) on any basis mentioned in paragraph 32, (leaving out of account in either case any provisions for depreciation or diminution in value).

51(3) In respect of each item within sub-paragraph (1) there must also be stated–

(a) the cumulative amount of provisions for depreciation or diminution in value of assets included under that item as at each date mentioned in sub-paragraph (1)(a),
(b) the amount of any such provisions made in respect of the financial year,
(c) the amount of any adjustments made in respect of any such provisions during that year in consequence of the disposal of any assets, and
(d) the amount of any other adjustments made in respect of any such provisions during that year.

52 Where any fixed assets of the company (other than listed investments) are included under any item shown in the company's balance sheet at an amount determined on any basis mentioned in paragraph 32, the following information must be given–

(a) the years (so far as they are known to the directors) in which the assets were severally valued and the several values, and
(b) in the case of assets that have been valued during the financial year, the names of the persons who valued them or particulars of their qualifications for doing so and (whichever is stated) the bases of valuation used by them.

53 In relation to any amount which is or would but for paragraph 4(2)(b) be shown in respect of the item "land and buildings" in the company's balance sheet there must be stated–

(a) how much of that amount is ascribable to land of freehold tenure and how much to land of leasehold tenure, and
(b) how much of the amount ascribable to land of leasehold tenure is ascribable to land held on long lease and how much to land held on short lease.

Investments

54(1) In respect of the amount of each item which is or would but for paragraph 4(2)(b) be shown in the company's balance sheet under the general item "investments" (whether as fixed assets or as current assets) there must be stated how much of that amount is ascribable to listed investments.

54(2) Where the amount of any listed investments is stated for any item in accordance with subparagraph (1), the following amounts must also be stated–

(a) the aggregate market value of those investments where it differs from the amount so stated, and
(b) both the market value and the stock exchange value of any investments of which the former value is, for the purposes of the accounts, taken as being higher than the latter.

Information about fair value of assets and liabilities

55(1) This paragraph applies where financial instruments or other assets have been valued in accordance with, as appropriate, paragraph 36, 38 or 39.

55(2) There must be stated–

(a) the significant assumptions underlying the valuation models and techniques used to determine the fair value of the instruments or other assets,
(b) for each category of financial instrument or other asset, the fair value of the assets in that category and the changes in value–

(i) included directly in the profit and loss account, or

(ii) credited to or (as the case may be) debited from the fair value reserve,

in respect of those assets, and

(c) for each class of derivatives, the extent and nature of the instruments, including significant terms and conditions that may affect the amount, timing and certainty of future cash flows.

55(3) Where any amount is transferred to or from the fair value reserve during the financial year, there must be stated in tabular form–

(a) the amount of the reserve as at the date of the beginning of the financial year and as at the balance sheet date respectively,

(b) the amount transferred to or from the reserve during the year, and

(c) the source and application respectively of the amounts so transferred.

History – Para. 55 substituted by SI 2015/980, reg. 29(3), with effect in relation to–

(a) financial years beginning on or after 1 January 2016, and

(b) a financial year of a company beginning on or after 1 January 2015, but before 1 January 2016, if the directors of the company so decide.

Former para. 55 read as follows:

"**55(1)** This paragraph applies where financial instruments have been valued in accordance with paragraph 36 or 38.

55(2) There must be stated–

(a) the significant assumptions underlying the valuation models and techniques used where the fair value of the instruments has been determined in accordance with paragraph 37(4),

(b) for each category of financial instrument, the fair value of the instruments in that category and the changes in value–

(i) included in the profit and loss account, or

(ii) credited to or (as the case may be) debited from the fair value reserve, in respect of those instruments, and

(c) for each class of derivatives, the extent and nature of the instruments, including significant terms and conditions that may affect the amount, timing and certainty of future cash flows.

55(3) Where any amount is transferred to or from the fair value reserve during the financial year, there must be stated in tabular form–

(a) the amount of the reserve as at the date of the beginning of the financial year and as at the balance sheet date respectively,

(b) the amount transferred to or from the reserve during that year, and

(c) the source and application respectively of the amounts so transferred."

56 Where the company has derivatives that it has not included at fair value, there must be stated for each class of such derivatives–

(a) the fair value of the derivatives in that class, if such a value can be determined in accordance with paragraph 37, and

(b) the extent and nature of the derivatives.

57(1) This paragraph applies if–

(a) the company has financial fixed assets that could be included at fair value by virtue of paragraph 36,

(b) the amount at which those items are included under any item in the company's accounts is in excess of their fair value, and

(c) the company has not made provision for diminution in value of those assets in accordance with paragraph 19(1) of this Schedule.

57(2) There must be stated–

(a) the amount at which either the individual assets or appropriate groupings of those individual assets are included in the company's accounts,

(b) the fair value of those assets or groupings, and

(c)   the reasons for not making a provision for diminution in value of those assets, including the nature of the evidence that provides the basis for the belief that the amount at which they are stated in the accounts will be recovered.

Information where investment property and living animals and plants included at fair value

58(1) This paragraph applies where the amounts to be included in a company's accounts in respect of stocks, investment property or living animals and plants have been determined in accordance with paragraph 39.

58(2) The balance sheet items affected and the basis of valuation adopted in determining the amounts of the assets in question in the case of each such item must be disclosed in a note to the accounts.

58(3) In the case of investment property, for each balance sheet item affected there must be shown, either separately in the balance sheet or in a note to the accounts–

(a)   the comparable amounts determined according to the historical cost accounting rules, or
(b)   the differences between those amounts and the corresponding amounts actually shown in the balance sheet in respect of that item.

58(4) In sub-paragraph (3), references in relation to any item to the comparable amounts determined in accordance with that sub-paragraph are to–

(a)   the aggregate amount which would be required to be shown in respect of that item if the amounts to be included in respect of all the assets covered by that item were determined according to the historical cost accounting rules, and
(b)   the aggregate amount of the cumulative provisions for depreciation or diminution in value which would be permitted or required in determining those amounts according to those rules.

History – In para. 58(1), the word "stocks," inserted by SI 2015/980, reg. 29(4), with effect in relation to–

(a)   financial years beginning on or after 1 January 2016, and
(b)   a financial year of a company beginning on or after 1 January 2015, but before 1 January 2016, if the directors of the company so decide.

Reserves and provisions

59(1) This paragraph applies where any amount is transferred–

(a)   to or from any reserves, or
(b)   to any provision for liabilities, or
(c)   from any provision for liabilities otherwise than for the purpose for which the provision was established, and the reserves or provisions are or would but for paragraph 4(2)(b) be shown as separate items in the company's balance sheet.

59(2) The following information must be given in respect of the aggregate of reserves or provisions included in the same item in tabular form–

(a)   the amount of the reserves or provisions as at the date of the beginning of the financial year and as at the balance sheet date respectively,
(b)   any amounts transferred to or from the reserves or provisions during that year, and
(c)   the source and application respectively of any amounts so transferred.

59(3) Particulars must be given of each provision included in the item "other provisions" in the company's balance sheet in any case where the amount of that provision is material.

History – In para. 59(2), the words "in tabular form" inserted by SI 2015/980, reg. 29(5), with effect in relation to–

(a) financial years beginning on or after 1 January 2016, and
(b) a financial year of a company beginning on or after 1 January 2015, but before 1 January 2016, if the directors of the company so decide.

Provision for taxation

60 The amount of any provision for deferred taxation must be stated separately from the amount of any provision for other taxation.

Details of indebtedness

61(1) For the aggregate of all items shown under "creditors" in the company's balance sheet there must be stated the aggregate of the following amounts–

(a) the amount of any debts included under "creditors" which are payable or repayable otherwise than by instalments and fall due for payment or repayment after the end of the period of five years beginning with the day next following the end of the financial year, and
(b) in the case of any debts so included which are payable or repayable by instalments, the amount of any instalments which fall due for payment after the end of that period.

61(2) Subject to sub-paragraph (3), in relation to each debt falling to be taken into account under sub-paragraph (1), the terms of payment or repayment and the rate of any interest payable on the debt must be stated.

61(3) If the number of debts is such that, in the opinion of the directors, compliance with subparagraph (2) would result in a statement of excessive length, it is sufficient to give a general indication of the terms of payment or repayment and the rates of any interest payable on the debts.

61(4) In respect of each item shown under "creditors" in the company's balance sheet there must be stated–

(a) the aggregate amount of any debts included under that item in respect of which any security has been given by the company, and
(b) an indication of the nature and form of the securities so given.

61(5) References above in this paragraph to an item shown under "creditors" in the company's balance sheet include references, where amounts falling due to creditors within one year and after more than one year are distinguished in the balance sheet–

(a) in a case within sub-paragraph (1), to an item shown under the latter of those categories, and
(b) in a case within sub-paragraph (4), to an item shown under either of those categories. References to items shown under "creditors" include references to items which would but for paragraph 4(2)(b) be shown under that heading.

History – In para. 61(4)(b), the words "and form" inserted by SI 2015/980, reg. 29(6), with effect in relation to–

(a) financial years beginning on or after 1 January 2016, and
(b) a financial year of a company beginning on or after 1 January 2015, but before 1 January 2016, if the directors of the company so decide.

62 If any fixed cumulative dividends on the company's shares are in arrear, there must be stated–

(a) the amount of the arrears, and
(b) the period for which the dividends or, if there is more than one class, each class of them are in arrear.

Guarantees and other financial commitments

63(1) Particulars must be given of any charge on the assets of the company to secure the liabilities of any other person including the amount secured.

63(2) Particulars and the total amount of any financial commitments, guarantees and contingencies that are not included in the balance sheet must be disclosed.

63(3) An indication of the nature and form of any valuable security given by the company in respect of commitments, guarantees and contingencies within sub-paragraph (2) must be given.

63(4) The total amount of any commitments within sub-paragraph (2) concerning pensions must be separately disclosed.

63(5) Particulars must be given of pension commitments which are included in the balance sheet.

63(6) Where any commitment within sub-paragraph (4) or (5) relates wholly or partly to pensions payable to past directors of the company separate particulars must be given of that commitment.

63(7) The total amount of any commitments, guarantees and contingencies within sub-paragraph (2) which are undertaken on behalf of or for the benefit of–

  (a) any parent undertaking or fellow subsidiary undertaking of the company,
  (b) any subsidiary undertaking of the company, or
  (c) any undertaking in which the company has a participating interest

must be separately stated and those within each of paragraphs (a), (b) and (c) must also be stated separately from those within any other of those paragraphs.

History – Para. 63 substituted by SI 2015/980, reg. 29(7), with effect in relation to–

  (a) financial years beginning on or after 1 January 2016, and
  (b) a financial year of a company beginning on or after 1 January 2015, but before 1 January 2016, if the directors of the company so decide.

Former para. 63 read as follows:

"Guarantees and other financial commitments

63(1) Particulars must be given of any charge on the assets of the company to secure the liabilities of any other person, including, where practicable, the amount secured.

63(2) The following information must be given with respect to any other contingent liability not provided for–

  (a) the amount or estimated amount of that liability,
  (b) its legal nature, and
  (c) whether any valuable security has been provided by the company in connection with that liability and if so, what.

63(3) There must be stated, where practicable, the aggregate amount or estimated amount of contracts for capital expenditure, so far as not provided for.

63(4) Particulars must be given of–

  (a) any pension commitments included under any provision shown in the company's balance sheet, and
  (b) any such commitments for which no provision has been made, and where any such commitment relates wholly or partly to pensions payable to past directors of the company separate particulars must be given of that commitment so far as it relates to such pensions.

63(5) Particulars must also be given of any other financial commitments that–

  (a) have not been provided for, and
  (b) are relevant to assessing the company's state of affairs."

Miscellaneous matters

64(1) Particulars must be given of any case where the purchase price or production cost of any asset is for the first time determined under paragraph 29.

64(2) Where any outstanding loans made under the authority of Section 682(2)(b), (c) or (d) of the 2006 Act (various cases of financial assistance by a company for purchase of its own shares) are included under any item shown in the company's balance sheet, the aggregate amount of those loans must be disclosed for each item in question.

Information supplementing the profit and loss account

65 Paragraphs 66 to 69 require information which either supplements the information given with respect to any particular items shown in the profit and loss account or otherwise provides particulars of income or expenditure of the company or of circumstances affecting the items shown in the profit and loss account (see regulation 3(2) for exemption for companies falling within Section 408 of the 2006 Act (individual profit and loss account where group accounts prepared)).

Separate statement of certain items of income and expenditure

66(1) Subject to sub-paragraph (2), there must be stated the amount of the interest on or any similar charges in respect of bank loans and overdrafts, and loans of any other kind made to the company.

66(2) Sub-paragraph (1) does not apply to interest or charges on loans to the company from group undertakings, but, with that exception, it applies to interest or charges on all loans, whether made on the security of debentures or not.

Particulars of tax

67(1) Particulars must be given of any special circumstances which affect liability in respect of taxation of profits, income or capital gains for the financial year or liability in respect of taxation of profits, income or capital gains for succeeding financial years.

67(2) The following amounts must be stated–

    (a)   the amount of the charge for United Kingdom corporation tax,

    (b)   if that amount would have been greater but for relief from double taxation, the amount which it would have been but for such relief,

    (c)   the amount of the charge for United Kingdom income tax, and

    (d)   the amount of the charge for taxation imposed outside the United Kingdom of profits, income and (so far as charged to revenue) capital gains.

These amounts must be stated separately in respect of each of the amounts which is or would but for paragraph 4(2)(b) be shown under the item "tax on profit or loss" in the profit and loss account.

History – In para. 67(2), the words 'These amounts must be stated separately in respect of each of the amounts which is or would but for paragraph 4(2)(b) be shown under the item "tax on profit or loss" in the profit and loss account.' substituted for the words 'These amounts must be stated separately in respect of each of the amounts which is or would but for paragraph 4(2)(b) be shown under the items "tax on profit or loss on ordinary activities" and "tax in extraordinary profit or loss" in the profit and loss account.' by SI 2015/980, reg. 29(8), with effect in relation to–

    (a)   financial years beginning on or after 1 January 2016, and

    (b)   a financial year of a company beginning on or after 1 January 2015, but before 1 January 2016, if the directors of the company so decide.

Particulars of turnover

68(1) If in the course of the financial year the company has carried on business of two or more classes that, in the opinion of the directors, differ substantially from each other, the amount of the turnover attributable to each class must be stated and the class described (see regulation 4(3)(b) for exemption for medium-sized companies in accounts delivered to registrar).

68(2) If in the course of the financial year the company has supplied markets that, in the opinion of the directors, differ substantially from each other, the amount of the turnover attributable to each such market must also be stated.

In this paragraph **"market"** means a market delimited by geographical bounds.

68(3) In analysing for the purposes of this paragraph the source (in terms of business or in terms of market) of turnover, the directors of the company must have regard to the manner in which the company's activities are organised.

68(4) For the purposes of this paragraph–

    (a) classes of business which, in the opinion of the directors, do not differ substantially from each other must be treated as one class, and

    (b) markets which, in the opinion of the directors, do not differ substantially from each other must be treated as one market, and any amounts properly attributable to one class of business or (as the case may be) to one market which are not material may be included in the amount stated in respect of another.

68(5) Where in the opinion of the directors the disclosure of any information required by this paragraph would be seriously prejudicial to the interests of the company, that information need not be disclosed, but the fact that any such information has not been disclosed must be stated.

Miscellaneous matters

69(1) Where any amount relating to any preceding financial year is included in any item in the profit and loss account, the effect must be stated.

69(2) The amount, nature and effect of any individual items of income or expenditure which are of exceptional size or incidence must be stated.

History – Para. 69(2) substituted for para. 69(2) and (3) by SI 2015/980, reg. 29(9), with effect in relation to–

    (a) financial years beginning on or after 1 January 2016, and

    (b) a financial year of a company beginning on or after 1 January 2015, but before 1 January 2016, if the directors of the company so decide.

Sums denominated in foreign currencies

70 Where any sums originally denominated in foreign currencies have been brought into account under any items shown in the balance sheet format or profit and loss account formats, the basis on which those sums have been translated into sterling (or the currency in which the accounts are drawn up) must be stated.

Dormant companies acting as agents

71 Where the directors of a company take advantage of the exemption conferred by Section 480 of the 2006 Act (dormant companies: exemption from audit), and the company has during the financial year in question acted as an agent for any person, the fact that it has so acted must be stated.

Related party transactions

72(1) Particulars may be given of transactions which the company has entered into with related parties, and must be given if such transactions are material and have not been concluded under normal market conditions (see regulation 4(2B) for a modification for medium-sized companies).

72(2) The particulars of transactions required to be disclosed by sub-paragraph (1) must include–

(a) the amount of such transactions,

(b) the nature of the related party relationship, and

(c) other information about the transactions necessary for an understanding of the financial position of the company.

72(3) Information about individual transactions may be aggregated according to their nature, except where separate information is necessary for an understanding of the effects of related party transactions on the financial position of the company.

72(4) Particulars need not be given of transactions entered into between two or more members of a group, provided that any subsidiary undertaking which is a party to the transaction is whollyowned by such a member.

72(5) In this paragraph, **"related party"** has the same meaning as in international accounting standards.

History – In para. 72(1), the words "regulation 4(2B) for a modification" substituted for the words "regulation 4(2) for exemption" by SI 2015/980, reg. 29(10), with effect in relation to–

(a) financial years beginning on or after 1 January 2016, and

(b) a financial year of a company beginning on or after 1 January 2015, but before 1 January 2016, if the directors of the company so decide.

Post balance sheet events

72A The nature and financial effect of material events arising after the balance sheet date which are not reflected in the profit and loss account or balance sheet must be stated.

History – Para. 72A and the heading preceding it inserted by SI 2015/980, reg. 29(11), with effect in relation to–

(a) financial years beginning on or after 1 January 2016, and

(b) a financial year of a company beginning on or after 1 January 2015, but before 1 January 2016, if the directors of the company so decide.

Appropriations

72B Particulars must be given of the proposed appropriation of profit or treatment of loss or, where applicable, particulars of the actual appropriation of the profits or treatment of the losses.

History – Para. 72B and the heading preceding it inserted by SI 2015/980, reg. 29(11), with effect in relation to–

(a) financial years beginning on or after 1 January 2016, and

(b) a financial year of a company beginning on or after 1 January 2015, but before 1 January 2016, if the directors of the company so decide.

PART 4 – SPECIAL PROVISION WHERE
COMPANY IS A PARENT COMPANY OR SUBSIDIARY UNDERTAKING
COMPANY'S OWN ACCOUNTS: GUARANTEES AND OTHER FINANCIAL COMMITMENTS IN FAVOUR OF GROUP UNDERTAKINGS

73 [Omitted by SI 2015/980, reg. 30.]

History – Para. 73 omitted by SI 2015/980, reg. 30, with effect in relation to–

(a) financial years beginning on or after 1 January 2016, and

(b) a financial year of a company beginning on or after 1 January 2015, but before 1 January 2016, if the directors of the company so decide.

Former para. 73 read as follows:

"**73** Commitments within any of sub-paragraphs (1) to (5) of paragraph 63 (guarantees and other financial commitments) which are undertaken on behalf of or for the benefit of–

(a) any parent undertaking or fellow subsidiary undertaking, or

(b) any subsidiary undertaking of the company, must be stated separately from the other commitments within that paragraph, and commitments within paragraph

(a) must also be stated separately from those within paragraph (b)."

PART 5 – SPECIAL PROVISIONS WHERE THE COMPANY IS AN INVESTMENT COMPANY

74(1) Paragraph 35 does not apply to the amount of any profit or loss arising from a determination of the value of any investments of an investment company on any basis mentioned in paragraph 32(3).

74(2) Any provisions made by virtue of paragraph 19(1) or (2) in the case of an investment company in respect of any fixed asset investments need not be charged to the company's profit and loss account provided they are either–

(a) charged against any reserve account to which any amount excluded by sub-paragraph (1) from the requirements of paragraph 35 has been credited, or

(b) shown as a separate item in the company's balance sheet under the sub-heading "other reserves".

74(3) For the purposes of this paragraph, as it applies in relation to any company, **"fixed asset investment"** means any asset falling to be included under any item shown in the company's balance sheet under the subdivision "investments" under the general item "fixed assets".

75(1) Any distribution made by an investment company which reduces the amount of its net assets to less than the aggregate of its called-up share capital and undistributable reserves shall be disclosed in a note to the company's accounts.

75(2) For purposes of this paragraph, a company's net assets are the aggregate of its assets less the aggregate of its liabilities (including any provision for liabilities within paragraph 2 of Schedule 9 to these Regulations that is made in Companies Act accounts and any provision that is made in IAS accounts); and **"undistributable reserves"** has the meaning given by Section 831(4) of the 2006 Act.

75(3) A company shall be treated as an investment company for the purposes of this Part of this Schedule in relation to any financial year of the company if–

(a) during the whole of that year it was an investment company as defined by Section 833 of the 2006 Act, and

(b) it was not at any time during that year prohibited from making a distribution by virtue of Section 832 of the 2006 Act due to either or both of the conditions specified in Section 832(4) (a) or (b) (no distribution where capital profits have been distributed etc) not being met.

SCHEDULE 2

Regulation 5(1)

BANKING COMPANIES: COMPANIES ACT INDIVIDUAL ACCOUNTS

PART 1 – GENERAL RULES AND FORMATS

SECTION A – GENERAL RULES

1 Subject to the following provisions of this Part of this Schedule–

(a) every balance sheet of a company must show the items listed in the balance sheet format set out in Section B of this Part, and

(b) every profit and loss account must show the items listed in either of the profit and loss account formats in Section B.

2(1) References in this Part of this Schedule to the items listed in any of the formats set out in Section B, are to those items read together with any of the notes following the formats which apply to those items.

2(2) The items must be shown in the order and under the headings and sub-headings given in the particular format used, but–

(a) the notes to the formats may permit alternative positions for any particular items,
(b) the heading or sub-heading for any item does not have to be distinguished by any letter or number assigned to that item in the format used, and
(c) where the heading of an item in the format used contains any wording in square brackets, that wording may be omitted if not applicable to the company.

3(1) Where in accordance with paragraph 1 a company's profit and loss account for any financial year has been prepared by reference to one of the formats in Section B, the company's directors must use the same format in preparing the profit and loss account for subsequent financial years, unless in their opinion there are special reasons for a change.

3(2) Particulars of any change must be given in a note to the accounts in which the new format is first used, and the reasons for the change must be explained.

4(1) Any item required to be shown in a company's balance sheet or profit and loss account may be shown in greater detail than required by the particular format used.

4(2) The balance sheet or profit and loss account may include an item representing or covering the amount of any asset or liability, income or expenditure not specifically covered by any of the items listed in the format used, save that none of the following may be treated as assets in any balance sheet–

(a) preliminary expenses,
(b) expenses of, and commission on, any issue of shares or debentures, and
(c) costs of research.

5(1) Items to which lower case letters are assigned in any of the formats in Section B may be combined in a company's accounts for any financial year if–

(a) their individual amounts are not material for the purpose of giving a true and fair view, or
(b) the combination facilitates the assessment of the state of affairs or profit or loss of the company for that year.

5(2) Where sub-paragraph (1)(b) applies, the individual amounts of any items so combined must be disclosed in a note to the accounts and any notes required by this Schedule to the items so combined must, not with standing the combination, be given.

6(1) Subject to sub-paragraph (2), the directors must not include a heading or sub-heading corresponding to an item in the balance sheet or profit and loss account format used if there is no amount to be shown for that item for the financial year to which the balance sheet or profit and loss account relates.

6(2) Where an amount can be shown for the item in question for the immediately preceding financial year, that amount must be shown under the heading or sub-heading required by the format for that item.

7(1) For every item shown in the balance sheet or profit and loss account the corresponding amount for the immediately preceding financial year must also be shown.

7(2) Where that corresponding amount is not comparable with the amount to be shown for the item in question in respect of the financial year to which the balance sheet or profit and loss account relates, the former amount may be adjusted, and particulars of the non-comparability and of any adjustment must be disclosed in a note to the accounts.

8(1) Subject to the following provisions of this paragraph and without prejudice to note (6) to the balance sheet format, amounts in respect of items representing assets or income may not be set off against amounts in respect of items representing liabilities or expenditure (as the case may be), or vice versa.

8(2) Charges required to be included in profit and loss account format 1, items 11(a) and 11(b) or format 2, items A7(a) and A7(b) may be set off against income required to be included in format 1, items 12(a) and 12(b) or format 2, items B5(a) and B5(b) and the resulting figure shown as a single item (in format 2 at position A7 if negative and at position B5 if positive).

8(3) Charges required to be included in profit and loss account format 1, item 13 or format 2, item A8 may also be set off against income required to be included in format 1, item 14 or format 2, item B6 and the resulting figure shown as a single item (in format 2 at position A8 if negative and at position B6 if positive).

9(1) Assets must be shown under the relevant balance sheet headings even where the company has pledged them as security for its own liabilities or for those of third parties or has otherwise assigned them as security to third parties.

9(2) A company may not include in its balance sheet assets pledged or otherwise assigned to it as security unless such assets are in the form of cash in the hands of the company.

9(3) Assets acquired in the name of and on behalf of third parties must not be shown in the balance sheet.

10 The company's directors must, in determining how amounts are presented within items in the profit and loss account and balance sheet, have regard to the substance of the reported transaction or arrangement, in accordance with generally accepted accounting principles or practice.

10A Where an asset or liability relates to more than one item in the balance sheet, the relationship of such asset or liability to the relevant items must be disclosed either under those items or in the notes to the accounts.

History – Para. 10A inserted by SI 2015/980, reg. 31(2), with effect in relation to–

    (a)   financial years beginning on or after 1 January 2016, and

    (b)   a financial year of a company beginning on or after 1 January 2015, but before 1 January 2016, if the directors of the company so decide.

SECTION B – THE REQUIRED FORMATS

Balance sheet format
ASSETS

1.   Cash and balances at central [or post office] banks *(1)*
2.   Treasury bills and other eligible bills *(20)*

    (a)   Treasury bills and similar securities *(2)*
    (b)   Other eligible bills *(3)*

3. Loans and advances to banks *(4)*, *(20)*

   (a) Repayable on demand
   (b) Other loans and advances

4. Loans and advances to customers *(5)*, *(20)*

5. Debt securities [and other fixed-income securities] *(6)*, *(20)*

   (a) Issued by public bodies
   (b) Issued by other issuers

6. Equity shares [and other variable-yield securities]

7. Participating interests

8. Shares in group undertakings

9. Intangible fixed assets *(7)*

10. Tangible fixed assets *(8)*

11. Called up capital not paid *(9)*

12. Own shares *(10)*

13. Other assets

14. Called up capital not paid *(9)*

15. Prepayments and accrued income

Total assets

LIABILITIES

1. Deposits by banks *(11)*, *(20)*

   (a) Repayable on demand
   (b) With agreed maturity dates or periods of notice

2. Customer accounts *(12)*, *(20)*

   (a) Repayable on demand
   (b) With agreed maturity dates or periods of notice

3. Debt securities in issue *(13)*, *(20)*

   (a) Bonds and medium term notes
   (b) Others

4. Other liabilities

5. Accruals and deferred income

6. Provisions for liabilities

   (a) Provisions for pensions and similar obligations
   (b) Provisions for tax

(c)   Other provisions

7.   Subordinated liabilities *(14)*, *(20)*

8.   Called up share capital *(15)*

9.   Share premium account

10. Reserves

    (a)   Capital redemption reserve
    (b)   Reserve for own shares
    (c)   Reserves provided for by the articles of association
    (d)   Other reserves

11. Revaluation reserve

12. Profit and loss account

Total liabilities

MEMORANDUM ITEMS

1.   Contingent liabilities *(16)*

    (1)   Acceptances and endorsements
    (2)   Guarantees and assets pledged as collateral security *(17)*
    (3)   Other contingent liabilities

2.   Commitments *(18)*

    (1)   Commitments arising out of sale and option to resell transactions *(19)*
    (2)   Other commitments

Notes on the balance sheet format and memorandum items

(1)   *Cash and balances at central [or post office]*

(Assets item 1.)

Cash is to comprise all currency including foreign notes and coins.

Only those balances which may be withdrawn without notice and which are deposited with central or post office banks of the country or countries in which the company is established may be included in this item. All other claims on central or post office banks must be shown under assets items 3 or 4.

(2)   *Treasury bills and other eligible bills: Treasury bills and similar securities*

(Assets item 2.(a).)

Treasury bills and similar securities are to comprise treasury bills and similar debt instruments issued by public bodies which are eligible for refinancing with central banks of the country or countries in which the company is established. Any treasury bills or similar debt instruments not so eligible must be included under assets item 5(a).

(3)   *Treasury bills and other eligible bills: Other eligible bills*

(Assets item 2.(b).)

Other eligible bills are to comprise all bills purchased to the extent that they are eligible, under national law, for refinancing with the central banks of the country or countries in which the company is established.

(4) *Loans and advances to banks*

(Assets item 3.)

Loans and advances to banks are to comprise all loans and advances to domestic or foreign credit institutions made by the company arising out of banking transactions. However loans and advances to credit institutions represented by debt securities or other fixed-income securities must be included under assets item 5 and not this item.

(5) *Loans and advances to customers*

(Assets item 4.)

Loans and advances to customers are to comprise all types of assets in the form of claims on domestic and foreign customers other than credit institutions. However loans and advances represented by debt securities or other fixed-income securities must be included under assets item 5 and not this item.

(6) *Debt securities [and other fixed-income securities]*

(Assets item 5.)

This item is to comprise transferable debt securities and any other transferable fixed-income securities issued by credit institutions, other undertakings or public bodies. Debt securities and other fixed-income securities issued by public bodies are, however, only to be included in this item if they may not be shown under assets item 2.

Where a company holds its own debt securities these must not be included under this item but must be deducted from liabilities item 3.(a) or (b), as appropriate.

Securities bearing interest rates that vary in accordance with specific factors, for example the interest rate on the inter-bank market or on the Euromarket, are also to be regarded as fixed-income securities to be included under this item.

(7) *Intangible fixed assets*

(Assets item 9.)

This item is to comprise–

    (a) development costs,
    (b) concessions, patents, licences, trade marks and similar rights and assets,
    (c) goodwill, and
    (d) payments on account.

Amounts are, however, to be included in respect of (b) only if the assets were acquired for valuable consideration or the assets in question were created by the company itself.

Amounts representing goodwill are only to be included to the extent that the goodwill was acquired for valuable consideration.

The amount of any goodwill included in this item must be disclosed in a note to the accounts.

(8) *Tangible fixed assets*

(Assets item 10.)

This item is to comprise—

    (a) land and buildings,
    (b) plant and machinery,
    (c) fixtures and fittings, tools and equipment, and
    (d) payments on account and assets in the course of construction.

The amount included in this item with respect to land and buildings occupied by the company for its own activities must be disclosed in a note to the accounts.

(9) *Called up capital not paid*

(Assets items 11 and 14.)

The two positions shown for this item are alternatives.

(10) *Own shares*

(Assets item 12.)

The nominal value of the shares held must be shown separately under this item.

(11) *Deposits by banks*

(Liabilities item 1.)

Deposits by banks are to comprise all amounts arising out of banking transactions owed to other domestic or foreign credit institutions by the company. However liabilities in the form of debt securities and any liabilities for which transferable certificates have been issued must be included under liabilities item 3 and not this item.

(12) *Customer accounts*

(Liabilities item 2.)

This item is to comprise all amounts owed to creditors that are not credit institutions. However liabilities in the form of debt securities and any liabilities for which transferable certificates have been issued must be shown under liabilities item 3 and not this item.

(13) *Debt securities in issue*

(Liabilities item 3.)

This item is to include both debt securities and debts for which transferable certificates have been issued, including liabilities arising out of own acceptances and promissory notes. (Only acceptances which a company has issued for its own refinancing and in respect of which it is the first party liable are to be treated as own acceptances.)

(14) *Subordinated liabilities*

(Liabilities item 7.)

This item is to comprise all liabilities in respect of which there is a contractual obligation that, in the event of winding up or bankruptcy, they are to be repaid only after the claims of other creditors have been met.

This item must include all subordinated liabilities, whether or not a ranking has been agreed between the subordinated creditors concerned.

(15) *Called up share capital*

(Liabilities item 8.)

The amount of allotted share capital and the amount of called up share capital which has been paid up must be shown separately.

(16) *Contingent liabilities*

(Memorandum item 1.)

This item is to include all transactions whereby the company has underwritten the obligations of a third party.

Liabilities arising out of the endorsement of rediscounted bills must be included in this item. Acceptances other than own acceptances must also be included.

(17) *Contingent liabilities: Guarantees and assets pledged as collateral security*

(Memorandum item 1(2).)

This item is to include all guarantee obligations incurred and assets pledged as collateral security on behalf of third parties, particularly in respect of sureties and irrevocable letters of credit.

(18) *Commitments*

(Memorandum item 2.)

This item is to include every irrevocable commitment which could give rise to a credit risk.

(19) *Commitments: Commitments arising out of sale and option to resell transactions*

(Memorandum item 2(1).)

This item is to comprise commitments entered into by the company in the context of sale and option to resell transactions.

(20) *Claims on, and liabilities to, undertakings in which a participating interest is held or group undertakings*

(Assets items 2 to 5, liabilities items 1 to 3 and 7.)

The following information must be given either by way of subdivision of the relevant items or by way of notes to the accounts.

The amount of the following must be shown for each of assets items 2 to 5–

(a) claims on group undertakings included therein, and
(b) claims on undertakings in which the company has a participating interest included therein.

The amount of the following must be shown for each of liabilities items 1, 2, 3 and 7–

(i) liabilities to group undertakings included therein, and
(ii) liabilities to undertakings in which the company has a participating interest included therein.

Special rules

Subordinated assets

11(1) The amount of any assets that are subordinated must be shown either as a subdivision of any relevant asset item or in the notes to the accounts; in the latter case disclosure must be by reference to the relevant asset item or items in which the assets are included.

11(2) In the case of assets items 2 to 5 in the balance sheet format, the amounts required to be shown by note (20) to the format as sub-items of those items must be further subdivided so as to show the amount of any claims included therein that are subordinated.

11(3) For this purpose, assets are subordinated if there is a contractual obligation to the effect that, in the event of winding up or bankruptcy, they are to be repaid only after the claims of other creditors have been met, whether or not a ranking has been agreed between the subordinated creditors concerned.

Syndicated loans

12(1) Where a company is a party to a syndicated loan transaction the company must include only that part of the total loan which it itself has funded.

12(2) Where a company is a party to a syndicated loan transaction and has agreed to reimburse (in whole or in part) any other party to the syndicate any funds advanced by that party or any interest thereon upon the occurrence of any event, including the default of the borrower, any additional liability by reason of such a guarantee must be included as a contingent liability in Memorandum item 1(2).

Sale and repurchase transactions

13(1) The following rules apply where a company is a party to a sale and repurchase transaction.

13(2) Where the company is the transferor of the assets under the transaction–

   (a) the assets transferred must, notwithstanding the transfer, be included in its balance sheet,
   (b) the purchase price received by it must be included in its balance sheet as an amount owed to the transferee, and
   (c) the value of the assets transferred must be disclosed in a note to its accounts.

13(3) Where the company is the transferee of the assets under the transaction, it must not include the assets transferred in its balance sheet but the purchase price paid by it to the transferor must be so included as an amount owed by the transferor.

Sale and option to resell transactions

14(1) The following rules apply where a company is a party to a sale and option to resell transaction.

14(2) Where the company is the transferor of the assets under the transaction, it must not include in its balance sheet the assets transferred but it must enter under Memorandum item 2 an amount equal to the price agreed in the event of repurchase.

14(3) Where the company is the transferee of the assets under the transaction it must include those assets in its balance sheet.

Managed funds

15(1) For the purposes of this paragraph, "managed funds" are funds which the company administers in its own name but on behalf of others and to which it has legal title.

15(2) The company must, in any case where claims and obligations arising in respect of managed funds fall to be treated as claims and obligations of the company, adopt the following accounting treatment.

15(3) Claims and obligations representing managed funds are to be included in the company's balance sheet, with the notes to the accounts disclosing the total amount included with respect to such assets and liabilities in the balance sheet and showing the amount included under each relevant balance sheet item in respect of such assets or (as the case may be) liabilities.

Profit and loss account formats – Format 1: Vertical layout

1. Interest receivable *(1)*

    (1) Interest receivable and similar income arising from debt securities [and other fixed-income securities]
    (2) Other interest receivable and similar income

2. Interest payable *(2)*

3. Dividend income

    (a) Income from equity shares [and other variable-yield securities]
    (b) Income from participating interests
    (c) Income from shares in group undertakings

4. Fees and commissions receivable *(3)*

5. Fees and commissions payable *(4)*

6. Dealing [profits] [losses] *(5)*

7. Other operating income

8. Administrative expenses

    (a) Staff costs

        (i) Wages and salaries
        (ii) Social security costs
        (iii) Other pension costs

    (b) Other administrative expenses

9. Depreciation and amortisation *(6)*

10. Other operating charges

11. Provisions

    (a) Provisions for bad and doubtful debts *(7)*
    (b) Provisions for contingent liabilities and commitments *(8)*

12. Adjustments to provisions

    (a) Adjustments to provisions for bad and doubtful debts *(9)*
    (b) Adjustments to provisions for contingent liabilities and commitments *(10)*

13. Amounts written off fixed asset investments *(11)*

14. Adjustments to amounts written off fixed asset investments *(12)*

15. [Profit] [loss] on ordinary activities before tax

16. Tax on [profit] [loss] on ordinary activities

17. [Profit] [loss] on ordinary activities after tax

18. Extraordinary income

19. Extraordinary charges

20. Extraordinary [profit] [loss]

21. Tax on extraordinary [profit] [loss]

22. Extraordinary [profit] [loss] after tax

23. Other taxes not shown under the preceding items

24. [Profit] [loss] for the financial year

Profit and loss account formats – Format 2: Horizontal layout

A. Charges

1. Interest payable *(2)*

2. Fees and commissions payable *(4)*

3. Dealing losses *(5)*

4. Administrative expenses

    (a) Staff costs

        (i) Wages and salaries
        (ii) Social security costs
        (iii) Other pension costs

    (b) Other administrative expenses

5. Depreciation and amortisation *(6)*

6. Other operating charges

7. Provisions

    (a) Provisions for bad and doubtful debts *(7)*
    (b) Provisions for contingent liabilities and commitments *(8)*

8. Amounts written off fixed asset investments *(11)*

9. Profit on ordinary activities before tax

10. Tax on [profit] [loss] on ordinary activities

11. Profit on ordinary activities after tax

12. Extraordinary charges

13. Tax on extraordinary [profit] [loss]

14. Extraordinary loss after tax

15. Other taxes not shown under the preceding items

16. Profit for the financial year

B. Income

1. Interest receivable *(1)*

    (1) Interest receivable and similar income arising from debt securities [and other fixed-income securities]

    (2) Other interest receivable and similar income

2. Dividend income

    (a) Income from equity shares [and other variable-yield securities]
    (b) Income from participating interests
    (c) Income from shares in group undertakings

3. Fees and commissions receivable *(3)*

4. Dealing profits *(5)*

5. Adjustments to provisions

    (a) Adjustments to provisions for bad and doubtful debts *(9)*
    (b) Adjustments to provisions for contingent liabilities and commitments *(10)*

6. Adjustments to amounts written off fixed asset investments *(12)*

7. Other operating income

8. Loss on ordinary activities before tax

9. Loss on ordinary activities after tax

10. Extraordinary income

11. Extraordinary profit after tax

12. Loss for the financial year

Notes on the profit and loss account formats

(1) *Interest receivable*

(Format 1, item 1; format 2, item B1.)

This item is to include all income arising out of banking activities, including–

(a) income from assets included in assets items 1 to 5 in the balance sheet format, however calculated,
(b) income resulting from covered forward contracts spread over the actual duration of the contract and similar in nature to interest, and

    (c)   fees and commissions receivable similar in nature to interest and calculated on a time basis or by reference to the amount of the claim (but not other fees and commissions receivable).

(2) *Interest payable*

(Format 1, item 2; format 2, item A1.)

    This item is to include all expenditure arising out of banking activities, including–

    (a)   charges arising out of liabilities included in liabilities items 1, 2, 3 and 7 in the balance sheet format, however calculated,

    (b)   charges resulting from covered forward contracts, spread over the actual duration of the contract and similar in nature to interest, and

    (c)   fees and commissions payable similar in nature to interest and calculated on a time basis or by reference to the amount of the liability (but not other fees and commissions payable).

(3) *Fees and commissions receivable*

(Format 1, item 4; format 2, item B3.)

    Fees and commissions receivable are to comprise income in respect of all services supplied by the company to third parties, but not fees or commissions required to be included under interest receivable (format 1, item 1; format 2, item B1).

    In particular the following fees and commissions receivable must be included (unless required to be included under interest receivable)–

    (a)   fees and commissions for guarantees, loan administration on behalf of other lenders and securities transactions,

    (b)   fees, commissions and other income in respect of payment transactions, account administration charges and commissions for the safe custody and administration of securities,

    (c)   fees and commissions for foreign currency transactions and for the sale and purchase of coin and precious metals, and

    (d)   fees and commissions charged for brokerage services in connection with savings and insurance contracts and loans.

(4) *Fees and commissions payable*

(Format 1, item 5; format 2, item A2.)

    Fees and commissions payable are to comprise charges for all services rendered to the company by third parties but not fees or commissions required to be included under interest payable (format 1, item 2; format 2, item A1).

    In particular the following fees and commissions payable must be included (unless required to be included under interest payable)–

    (a)   fees and commissions for guarantees, loan administration and securities transactions;

    (b)   fees, commissions and other charges in respect of payment transactions, account administration charges and commissions for the safe custody and administration of securities;

    (c)   fees and commissions for foreign currency transactions and for the sale and purchase of coin and precious metals; and

    (d)   fees and commissions for brokerage services in connection with savings and insurance contracts and loans.

(5) *[Dealing [profits] [losses]]*

(Format 1, item 6; format 2, items B4 and A3.)

This item is to comprise–

(a) the net profit or net loss on transactions in securities which are not held as financial fixed assets together with amounts written off or written back with respect to such securities, including amounts written off or written back as a result of the application of paragraph 33(1),

(b) the net profit or loss on exchange activities, save in so far as the profit or loss is included in interest receivable or interest payable (format 1, items 1 or 2; format 2, items B1 or A1), and

(c) the net profits and losses on other dealing operations involving financial instruments, including precious metals.

(6) *Depreciation and amortisation*

(Format 1, item 9; format 2, item A5.)

This item is to comprise depreciation and other amounts written off in respect of balance sheet assets items 9 and 10.

(7) *Provisions: Provisions for bad and doubtful debts*

(Format 1, item 11(a); format 2, item A7(a).)

Provisions for bad and doubtful debts are to comprise charges for amounts written off and for provisions made in respect of loans and advances shown under balance sheet assets items 3 and 4.

(8) *Provisions: Provisions for contingent liabilities and commitments*

(Format 1, item 11(b); format 2, item A7(b).)

This item is to comprise charges for provisions for contingent liabilities and commitments of a type which would, if not provided for, be shown under Memorandum items 1 and 2.

(9) *Adjustments to provisions: Adjustments to provisions for bad and doubtful debts*

(Format 1, item 12(a); format 2, item B5(a).)

This item is to include credits from the recovery of loans that have been written off, from other advances written back following earlier write offs and from the reduction of provisions previously made with respect to loans and advances.

(10) *Adjustments to provisions: Adjustments to provisions for contingent liabilities and commitments*

(Format 1, item 12(b); format 2, item B5(b).)

This item comprises credits from the reduction of provisions previously made with respect to contingent liabilities and commitments.

(11) *Amounts written off fixed asset investments*

(Format 1, item 13; format 2, item A8.)

Amounts written off fixed asset investments are to comprise amounts written off in respect of assets which are transferable securities held as financial fixed assets, participating interests and shares in group undertakings and which are included in assets items 5 to 8 in the balance sheet format.

(12) *Adjustments to amounts written off fixed asset investments*

(Format 1, item 14; format 2, item B6.)

Adjustments to amounts written off fixed asset investments are to include amounts written back following earlier write offs and provisions in respect of assets which are transferable securities held as financial fixed assets, participating interests and group undertakings and which are included in assets items 5 to 8 in the balance sheet format.

PART 2 – ACCOUNTING PRINCIPLES AND RULES
SECTION A – ACCOUNTING PRINCIPLES

Preliminary

16(1) The amounts to be included in respect of all items shown in a company's accounts must be determined in accordance with the principles set out in this Section.

16(2) But if it appears to the company's directors that there are special reasons for departing from any of those principles in preparing the company's accounts in respect of any financial year they may do so, in which case particulars of the departure, the reasons for it and its effect must be given in a note to the accounts.

Accounting principles

17 The company is presumed to be carrying on business as a going concern.

18 Accounting policies and measurement bases must be applied consistently within the same accounts and from one financial year to the next.

History – In para. 18, the words "and measurement bases" inserted by SI 2015/980, reg. 32(2)(a), with effect in relation to–
  (a)   financial years beginning on or after 1 January 2016, and
  (b)   a financial year of a company beginning on or after 1 January 2015, but before 1 January 2016, if the directors of the company so decide.

19 The amount of any item must be determined on a prudent basis, and in particular–

  (a)   only profits realised at the balance sheet date are to be included in the profit and loss account,
  (b)   all liabilities which have arisen in respect of the financial year to which the accounts relate or a previous financial year must be taken into account, including those which only become apparent between the balance sheet date and the date on which it is signed on behalf of the board of directors in accordance with section 414 of the 2006 Act (approval and signing of accounts) and
  (c)   all provisions for diminution of value must be recognised, whether the result of the financial year is a profit or a loss.

History – Para. 19(c), (and the word "and" preceding it) inserted; the word "and" in para. (a) omitted by SI 2015/980, reg. 32(2)(b), with effect in relation to–
  (a)   financial years beginning on or after 1 January 2016, and
  (b)   a financial year of a company beginning on or after 1 January 2015, but before 1 January 2016, if the directors of the company so decide.

20 All income and charges relating to the financial year to which the accounts relate must be taken into account, without regard to the date of receipt or payment.

21 In determining the aggregate amount of any item, the amount of each individual asset or liability that falls to be taken into account must be determined separately.

21A The opening balance sheet for each financial year shall correspond to the closing balance sheet for the preceding financial year.

History – Para. 21A inserted by SI 2015/980, reg. 32(2)(c), with effect in relation to–

(a)   financial years beginning on or after 1 January 2016, and
(b)   a financial year of a company beginning on or after 1 January 2015, but before 1 January 2016, if the directors of the company so decide.

SECTION B – HISTORICAL COST ACCOUNTING RULES

Preliminary

22 Subject to Sections C and D of this Part of this Schedule, the amounts to be included in respect of all items shown in a company's accounts must be determined in accordance with the rules set out in this Section.

Fixed assets

General rules

23(1) The amount to be included in respect of any fixed asset is its cost.

23(2) This is subject to any provision for depreciation or diminution in value made in accordance with paragraphs 24 to 26.

Rules for depreciation and diminution in value

24 In the case of any fixed asset which has a limited useful economic life, the amount of–

(a)   its cost, or
(b)   where it is estimated that any such asset will have a residual value at the end of the period of its useful economic life, its cost less that estimated residual value, must be reduced by provisions for depreciation calculated to write off that amount systematically over the period of the asset's useful economic life.

25(1) Where a fixed asset investment to which sub-paragraph (2) applies has diminished in value, provisions for diminution in value may be made in respect of it and the amount to be included in respect of it may be reduced accordingly.

25(2) This sub-paragraph applies to fixed asset investments of a description falling to be included under assets item 7 (participating interests) or 8 (shares in group undertakings) in the balance sheet format, or any other holding of securities held as a financial fixed asset.

25(3) Provisions for diminution in value must be made in respect of any fixed asset which has diminished in value if the reduction in its value is expected to be permanent (whether its useful economic life is limited or not), and the amount to be included in respect of it must be reduced accordingly.

25(4) Provisions made under this paragraph must be charged to the profit and loss account and disclosed separately in a note to the accounts if they have not been shown separately in the profit and loss account.

History – Para. 25(4) substituted by SI 2015/980, reg. 32(3)(a), with effect in relation to–

   (a)   financial years beginning on or after 1 January 2016, and

   (b)   a financial year of a company beginning on or after 1 January 2015, but before 1 January 2016, if the directors of the company so decide.

Former para. 25(4) read as follows:

"**25(4)** Any provisions made under this paragraph which are not shown in the profit and loss account must be disclosed (either separately or in aggregate) in a note to the accounts."

26(1) Where the reasons for which any provision was made in accordance with paragraph 25 have ceased to apply to any extent, that provision must be written back to the extent that it is no longer necessary.

26(2) Any amounts written back under sub-paragraph (1) must be recognised in the profit and loss account and disclosed separately in a note to the accounts if not shown separately in the profit and loss account.

History – Para. 26(2) substituted by SI 2015/980, reg. 32(3)(b), with effect in relation to–

   (a)   financial years beginning on or after 1 January 2016, and

   (b)   a financial year of a company beginning on or after 1 January 2015, but before 1 January 2016, if the directors of the company so decide.

Former para. 26(2) read as follows:

"**26(2)** Any amounts written back in accordance with sub-paragraph (1) which are not shown in the profit and loss account must be disclosed (either separately or in aggregate) in a note to the accounts."

Intangible assets

27(1) Where this is in accordance with generally accepted accounting principles or practice, development costs may be included under assets item 9 in the balance sheet format.

27(2) If any amount is included in a company's balance sheet in respect of development costs, the note on accounting policies (see paragraph 53 of this Schedule) must include the following information–

   (a)   the period over which the amount of those costs originally capitalised is being or is to be written off, and

   (b)   the reasons for capitalising the development costs in question.

History – Para. 27 and the heading preceding it substituted by SI 2015/980, reg. 32(3)(c), with effect in relation to–

   (a)   financial years beginning on or after 1 January 2016, and

   (b)   a financial year of a company beginning on or after 1 January 2015, but before 1 January 2016, if the directors of the company so decide.

Former para. 27 read as follows:

"**Development costs**

27(1) Notwithstanding that amounts representing "development costs" may be included under assets item 9 in the balance sheet format, an amount may only be included in a company's balance sheet in respect of development costs in special circumstances.

27(2) If any amount is included in a company's balance sheet in respect of development costs the following information must be given in a note to the accounts–

   (a)   the period over which the amount of those costs originally capitalised is being or is to be written off, and

   (b)   the reasons for capitalising the development costs in question."

Goodwill

28(1) Intangible assets must be written off over the useful economic life of the intangible asset.

28(2) Where in exceptional cases the useful life of intangible assets cannot be reliably estimated, such assets must be written off over a period chosen by the directors of the company.

28(3) The period referred to in sub-paragraph (2) must not exceed ten years.

28(4) There must be disclosed in a note to the accounts the period referred to in sub-paragraph (2) and the reasons for choosing that period.

History – Para. 28 substituted by SI 2015/980, reg. 32(3)(c), with effect in relation to–

    (a)   financial years beginning on or after 1 January 2016, and

    (b)   a financial year of a company beginning on or after 1 January 2015, but before 1 January 2016, if the directors of the company so decide.

Former para. 28 read as follows:

"**28(1)** The application of paragraphs 23 to 26 in relation to goodwill (in any case where goodwill is treated as an asset) is subject to the following.

28(2) Subject to sub-paragraph (3), the amount of the consideration for any goodwill acquired by a company must be reduced by provisions for depreciation calculated to write off that amount systematically over a period chosen by the directors of the company.

28(3) The period chosen must not exceed the useful economic life of the goodwill in question.

28(4) In any case where any goodwill acquired by a company is included as an asset in the company's balance sheet there must be disclosed in a note to the accounts–

    (a)   the period chosen for writing off the consideration for that goodwill, and

    (b)   the reasons for choosing that period."

Treatment of fixed assets

29(1) Assets included in assets items 9 (intangible fixed assets) and 10 (tangible fixed assets) in the balance sheet format must be valued as fixed assets.

29(2) Other assets falling to be included in the balance sheet must be valued as fixed assets where they are intended for use on a continuing basis in the company's activities.

Financial fixed assets

30(1) Debt securities, including fixed-income securities, held as financial fixed assets must be included in the balance sheet at an amount equal to their maturity value plus any premium, or less any discount, on their purchase, subject to the following provisions of this paragraph.

30(2) The amount included in the balance sheet with respect to such securities purchased at a premium must be reduced each financial year on a systematic basis so as to write the premium off over the period to the maturity date of the security and the amounts so written off must be charged to the profit and loss account for the relevant financial years.

30(3) The amount included in the balance sheet with respect to such securities purchased at a discount must be increased each financial year on a systematic basis so as to extinguish the discount over the period to the maturity date of the security and the amounts by which the amount is increased must be credited to the profit and loss account for the relevant years.

30(4) The notes to the accounts must disclose the amount of any unamortized premium or discount not extinguished which is included in the balance sheet by virtue of sub-paragraph (1).

30(5) For the purposes of this paragraph **"premium"** means any excess of the amount paid for a security over its maturity value and **"discount"** means any deficit of the amount paid for a security over its maturity value.

Current assets

31 The amount to be included in respect of loans and advances, debt or other fixed-income securities and equity shares or other variable yield securities not held as financial fixed assets must be their cost, subject to paragraphs 32 and 33.

32(1) If the net realisable value of any asset referred to in paragraph 31 is lower than its cost, the amount to be included in respect of that asset is the net realisable value.

32(2) Where the reasons for which any provision for diminution in value was made in accordance with sub-paragraph (1) have ceased to apply to any extent, that provision must be written back to the extent that it is no longer necessary.

33(1) Subject to paragraph 32, the amount to be included in the balance sheet in respect of transferable securities not held as financial fixed assets may be the higher of their cost or their market value at the balance sheet date.

33(2) The difference between the cost of any securities included in the balance sheet at a valuation under sub-paragraph (1) and their market value must be shown (in aggregate) in the notes to the accounts.

Miscellaneous and supplementary provisions

Excess of money owed over value received as an asset item

34(1) Where the amount repayable on any debt owed by a company is greater than the value of the consideration received in the transaction giving rise to the debt, the amount of the difference may be treated as an asset.

34(2) Where any such amount is so treated–

(a) it must be written off by reasonable amounts each year and must be completely written off before repayment of the debt, and

(b) if the current amount is not shown as a separate item in the company's balance sheet, it must be disclosed in a note to the accounts.

Determination of cost

35(1) The cost of an asset that has been acquired by the company is to be determined by adding to the actual price paid any expenses incidental to its acquisition and then subtracting any incidental reductions in the cost of acquisition.

35(2) The cost of an asset constructed by the company is to be determined by adding to the purchase price of the raw materials and consumables used the amount of the costs incurred by the company which are directly attributable to the construction of that asset.

35(3) In addition, there may be included in the cost of an asset constructed by the company–

(a) a reasonable proportion of the costs incurred by the company which are only indirectly attributable to the construction of that asset, but only to the extent that they relate to the period of construction, and

(b) interest on capital borrowed to finance the construction of that asset, to the extent that it accrues in respect of the period of construction, provided, however, in a case within paragraph (b), that the inclusion of the interest in determining the cost of that asset and the amount of the interest so included is disclosed in a note to the accounts.

History – In para. 35(1), the words "and then subtracting any incidental reductions in the cost of acquisition" inserted by SI 2015/980, reg. 32(3)(d), with effect in relation to–

(a) financial years beginning on or after 1 January 2016, and

(b) a financial year of a company beginning on or after 1 January 2015, but before 1 January 2016, if the directors of the company so decide.

36(1) The cost of any assets which are fungible assets (including investments), may be determined by the application of any of the methods mentioned in sub-paragraph (2) in relation to any such assets of the same class, provided that the method chosen is one which appears to the directors to be appropriate in the circumstances of the company.

36(2) Those methods are–

    (a)   the method known as "first in, first out" (FIFO),
    (b)   the method known as "last in, first out" (LIFO),
    (c)   a weighted average price, and
    (d)   any other method reflecting generally accepted best practice.

36(3) Where in the case of any company–

    (a)   the cost of assets falling to be included under any item shown in the company's balance sheet has been determined by the application of any method permitted by this paragraph, and
    (b)   the amount shown in respect of that item differs materially from the relevant alternative amount given below in this paragraph, the amount of that difference must be disclosed in a note to the accounts.

36(4) Subject to sub-paragraph (5), for the purposes of sub-paragraph (3)(b), the relevant alternative amount, in relation to any item shown in a company's balance sheet, is the amount which would have been shown in respect of that item if assets of any class included under that item at an amount determined by any method permitted by this paragraph had instead been included at their replacement cost as at the balance sheet date.

36(5) The relevant alternative amount may be determined by reference to the most recent actual purchase price before the balance sheet date of assets of any class included under the item in question instead of by reference to their replacement cost as at that date, but only if the former appears to the directors of the company to constitute the more appropriate standard of comparison in the case of assets of that class.

History – In para. 36(2)(d), the words "reflecting generally accepted best practice" substituted for the words "similar to any of the methods mentioned above" by SI 2015/980, reg. 32(3)(e), with effect in relation to–

    (a)   financial years beginning on or after 1 January 2016, and
    (b)   a financial year of a company beginning on or after 1 January 2015, but before 1 January 2016, if the directors of the company so decide.Substitution of original stated amount where price or cost unknown.

37(1) This paragraph applies where–

    (a)   there is no record of the purchase price of any asset acquired by a company or of any price, expenses or costs relevant for determining its cost in accordance with paragraph 35, or
    (b)   any such record cannot be obtained without unreasonable expense or delay.

37(2) In such a case, its cost is to be taken, for the purposes of paragraphs 23 to 33, to be the value ascribed to it in the earliest available record of its value made on or after its acquisition by the company.

SECTION C – ALTERNATIVE ACCOUNTING RULES

Preliminary

38(1) The rules set out in Section B are referred to below in this Schedule as the historical cost accounting rules.

38(2) Paragraphs 23 to 26 and 30 to 34 are referred to below in this Section as the depreciation rules; and references below in this Schedule to the historical cost accounting rules do not include the depreciation rules as they apply by virtue of paragraph 41.

39 Subject to paragraphs 41 to 43, the amounts to be included in respect of assets of any description mentioned in paragraph 40 may be determined on any basis so mentioned.

Alternative accounting rules

40(1) Intangible fixed assets, other than goodwill, may be included at their current cost.

40(2) Tangible fixed assets may be included at a market value determined as at the date of their last valuation or at their current cost.

40(3) Investments of any description falling to be included under assets items 7 (participating interests) or 8 (shares in group undertakings) of the balance sheet format and any other securities held as financial fixed assets may be included either–

    (a) at a market value determined as at the date of their last valuation, or

    (b) at a value determined on any basis which appears to the directors to be appropriate in the circumstances of the company.But in the latter case particulars of the method of valuation adopted and of the reasons for adopting it must be disclosed in a note to the accounts.

40(4) [Omitted by SI 2015/980, reg. 32(4).]

History – Para. 40(4) omitted by SI 2015/980, reg. 32(4)(a), with effect in relation to–

    (a)   financial years beginning on or after 1 January 2016, and

    (b)   a financial year of a company beginning on or after 1 January 2015, but before 1 January 2016, if the directors of the company so decide.

Former para. 40(4) read as follows:

"**40(4)** Securities of any description not held as financial fixed assets (if not valued in accordance with paragraph 33) may be included at their current cost."

Application of the depreciation rules

41(1) Where the value of any asset of a company is determined in accordance with paragraph 40, that value must be, or (as the case may require) be the starting point for determining, the amount to be included in respect of that asset in the company's accounts, instead of its cost or any value previously so determined for that asset.

The depreciation rules apply accordingly in relation to any such asset with the substitution for any reference to its cost of a reference to the value most recently determined for that asset in accordance with paragraph 40.

41(2) The amount of any provision for depreciation required in the case of any fixed asset by paragraphs 24 to 26 as they apply by virtue of sub-paragraph (1) is referred to below in this paragraph as the adjusted amount, and the amount of any provision which would be required by any of those paragraphs in the case of that asset according to the historical cost accounting rules is referred to as the historical cost amount.

41(3) Where sub-paragraph (1) applies in the case of any fixed asset the amount of any provision for depreciation in respect of that asset included in any item shown in the profit and loss account in respect of amounts written off assets of the description in question may be the historical cost amount instead of the adjusted amount, provided that the amount of any difference between the two is shown separately in the profit and loss account or in a note to the accounts.

**Additional information to be provided in case of departure
from historical cost accounting rules**

42(1) This paragraph applies where the amounts to be included in respect of assets covered by any items shown in a company's accounts have been determined in accordance with paragraph 40.

42(2) The items affected and the basis of valuation adopted in determining the amounts of the assets in question in the case of each such item must be disclosed in the note on accounting policies (see paragraph 53 of this Schedule).

42(3) In the case of each balance sheet item affected, the comparable amounts determined according to the historical cost accounting rules must be shown in a note to the accounts.

42(4) In sub-paragraph (3), references in relation to any item to the comparable amounts determined as there mentioned are references to–

    (a) the aggregate amount which would be required to be shown in respect of that item if the amounts to be included in respect of all the assets covered by that item were determined according to the historical cost accounting rules, and

    (b) the aggregate amount of the cumulative provisions for depreciation or diminution in value which would be permitted or required in determining those amounts according to those rules.

History – In para. 42(2), the words "the note on accounting policies (see paragraph 53 of this Schedule)" substituted for the words "a note to the accounts" by SI 2015/980, reg. 32(4)(b), with effect in relation to–

    (a) financial years beginning on or after 1 January 2016, and

    (b) a financial year of a company beginning on or after 1 January 2015, but before 1 January 2016, if the directors of the company so decide.

Para. 42(3) substituted by SI 2015/980, reg. 32(4)(c), with effect in relation to–

    (a) financial years beginning on or after 1 January 2016, and

    (b) a financial year of a company beginning on or after 1 January 2015, but before 1 January 2016, if the directors of the company so decide.

Former para. 42(3) read as follows:

    "**42(3)** In the case of each balance sheet item affected either–

        (a) the comparable amounts determined according to the historical cost accounting rules, or

        (b) the differences between those amounts and the corresponding amounts actually shown in the balance sheet in respect of that item, must be shown separately in the balance sheet or in a note to the accounts."

Revaluation reserve

43(1) With respect to any determination of the value of an asset of a company in accordance with paragraph 40, the amount of any profit or loss arising from that determination (after allowing, where appropriate, for any provisions for depreciation or diminution in value made otherwise than by reference to the value so determined and any adjustments of any such provisions made in the light of that determination) must be credited or (as the case may be) debited to a separate reserve ("the revaluation reserve").

43(2) The amount of the revaluation reserve must be shown in the company's balance sheet under liabilities item 11 in the balance sheet format.

43(3) An amount may be transferred–

    (a) from the revaluation reserve–

        (i) to the profit and loss account, if the amount was previously charged to that account or represents realised profit, or

        (ii) on capitalisation,

(b) to or from the revaluation reserve in respect of the taxation relating to any profit or loss credited or debited to the reserve.

The revaluation reserve must be reduced to the extent that the amounts transferred to it are no longer necessary for the purposes of the valuation method used.

43(4) In sub-paragraph (3)(a)(ii) **"capitalisation"**, in relation to an amount standing to the credit of the revaluation reserve, means applying it in wholly or partly paying up unissued shares in the company to be allotted to members of the company as fully or partly paid shares.

43(5) The revaluation reserve must not be reduced except as mentioned in this paragraph.

43(6) The treatment for taxation purposes of amounts credited or debited to the revaluation reserve must be disclosed in a note to the accounts.

History – In para. 43(2), the words "but need not be shown under that name" omitted by SI 2015/980, reg. 32(4)(d), with effect in relation to–

(a) financial years beginning on or after 1 January 2016, and
(b) a financial year of a company beginning on or after 1 January 2015, but before 1 January 2016, if the directors of the company so decide.

SECTION D – FAIR VALUE ACCOUNTING

Inclusion of financial instruments at fair value

44(1) Subject to sub-paragraphs (2) to (5), financial instruments (including derivatives) may be included at fair value.

44(2) Sub-paragraph (1) does not apply to financial instruments that constitute liabilities unless–

(a) they are held as part of a trading portfolio,
(b) they are derivatives, or
(c) they are financial instruments falling within sub-paragraph (4).

44(3) Unless they are financial instruments falling within sub-paragraph (4), sub-paragraph (1) does not apply to–

(a) financial instruments (other than derivatives) held to maturity,
(b) loans and receivables originated by the company and not held for trading purposes,
(c) interests in subsidiary undertakings, associated undertakings and joint ventures,
(d) equity instruments issued by the company,
(e) contracts for contingent consideration in a business combination, or
(f) other financial instruments with such special characteristics that the instruments, according to generally accepted accounting principles or practice, should be accounted for differently from other financial instruments.

44(4) Financial instruments which under international accounting standards may be included in accounts at fair value, may be so included, provided that the disclosures required by such accounting standards are made.

44(5) If the fair value of a financial instrument cannot be determined reliably in accordance with paragraph 45, sub-paragraph (1) does not apply to that financial instrument.

44(6) In this paragraph–

"associated undertaking" has the meaning given by paragraph 19 of Schedule 6 to these Regulations;
"joint venture" has the meaning given by paragraph 18 of that Schedule.

History – Para. 44(4) substituted by SI 2015/980, reg. 32(5)(a), with effect in relation to–

   (a)   financial years beginning on or after 1 January 2016, and

   (b)   a financial year of a company beginning on or after 1 January 2015, but before 1 January 2016, if the directors of the company so decide.

Former para. 44(4) read as follows:

"**44(4)** Financial instruments that, under international accounting standards adopted by the European Commission on or before 5th September 2006 in accordance with the IAS Regulation, may be included in accounts at fair value, may be so included, provided that the disclosures required by such accounting standards are made."

Determination of fair value

45(1) The fair value of a financial instrument is its value determined in accordance with this paragraph.

45(2) If a reliable market can readily be identified for the financial instrument, its fair value is determined by reference to its market value.

45(3) If a reliable market cannot readily be identified for the financial instrument but can be identified for its components or for a similar instrument, its fair value is determined by reference to the market value of its components or of the similar instrument.

45(4) If neither sub-paragraph (2) nor (3) applies, the fair value of the financial instrument is a value resulting from generally accepted valuation models and techniques.

45(5) Any valuation models and techniques used for the purposes of sub-paragraph (4) must ensure a reasonable approximation of the market value.

Hedged items

46 A company may include any assets and liabilities, or identified portions of such assets or liabilities, that qualify as hedged items under a fair value hedge accounting system at the amount required under that system.

Other assets that may be included at fair value

47(1) This paragraph applies to–

   (a)   investment property, and
   (b)   living animals and plants.

47(2) Such investment property and living animals and plants may be included at fair value, provided that, as the case may be, all such investment property or living animals and plants are so included where their fair value can be reliably determined.

47(3) In this paragraph, **"fair value"** means fair value determined in accordance with generally accepted accounting principles or practice.

History – Para. 47 substituted by SI 2015/980, reg. 32(5)(b), with effect in relation to–

   (a)   financial years beginning on or after 1 January 2016, and

   (b)   a financial year of a company beginning on or after 1 January 2015, but before 1 January 2016, if the directors of the company so decide.

Former para. 47 read as follows:

"**47(1)** This paragraph applies to–

   (a)   investment property, and

   (b)   living animals and plants, that, under international accounting standards, may be included in accounts at fair value.

47(2) Such investment property and such living animals and plants may be included at fair value, provided that all such investment property or, as the case may be, all such living animals and plants are so included where their fair value can reliably be determined.

47(3) In this paragraph, **"fair value"** means fair value determined in accordance with relevant international accounting standards."

Accounting for changes in value

48(1) This paragraph applies where a financial instrument is valued in accordance with paragraph 44 or 46 or an asset is valued in accordance with paragraph 47.

48(2) Notwithstanding paragraph 19 in this Part of this Schedule, and subject to sub-paragraphs (3) and (4), a change in the value of the financial instrument or of the investment property or living animal or plant must be included in the profit and loss account.

48(3) Where–

   (a)   the financial instrument accounted for is a hedging instrument under a hedge accounting system that allows some or all of the change in value not to be shown in the profit and loss account, or

   (b)   the change in value relates to an exchange difference arising on a monetary item that forms part of a company's net investment in a foreign entity, the amount of the change in value must be credited to or (as the case may be) debited from a separate reserve ("the fair value reserve").

48(4) Where the instrument accounted for–

   (a)   is an available for sale financial asset, and

   (b)   is not a derivative, the change in value may be credited to or (as the case may be) debited from the fair value reserve.

The fair value reserve

49(1) The fair value reserve must be adjusted to the extent that the amounts shown in it are no longer necessary for the purposes of paragraph 48(3) or (4).

49(2) The treatment for taxation purposes of amounts credited or debited to the fair value reserve must be disclosed in a note to the accounts.

Assets and liabilities denominated in foreign currencies

50(1) Subject to the following sub-paragraphs, amounts to be included in respect of assets and liabilities denominated in foreign currencies must be in sterling (or the currency in which the accounts are drawn up) after translation at an appropriate spot rate of exchange prevailing at the balance sheet date.

50(2) An appropriate rate of exchange prevailing on the date of purchase may however be used for assets held as financial fixed assets and assets to be included under assets items 9 (intangible fixed assets) and 10 (tangible fixed assets) in the balance sheet format, if they are not covered or not specifically covered in either the spot or forward currency markets.

50(3) An appropriate spot rate of exchange prevailing at the balance sheet date must be used for translating uncompleted spot exchange transactions.

50(4) An appropriate forward rate of exchange prevailing at the balance sheet date must be used for translating uncompleted forward exchange transactions.

50(5) This paragraph does not apply to any assets or liabilities held, or any transactions entered into, for hedging purposes or to any assets or liabilities which are themselves hedged.

51(1) Subject to sub-paragraph (2), any difference between the amount to be included in respect of an asset or liability under paragraph 50 and the book value, after translation into sterling (or the currency in which the accounts are drawn up) at an appropriate rate, of that asset or liability must be credited or, as the case may be, debited to the profit and loss account.

51(2) In the case, however, of assets held as financial fixed assets, of assets to be included under assets items 9 (intangible fixed assets) and 10 (tangible fixed assets) in the balance sheet format and of transactions undertaken to cover such assets, any such difference may be deducted from or credited to any non-distributable reserve available for the purpose.

PART 3 – NOTES TO THE ACCOUNTS
PRELIMINARY

52(1) Any information required in the case of a company by the following provisions of this Part of this Schedule must be given by way of a note to the accounts.

52(2) These notes must be presented in the order in which, where relevant, the items to which they relate are presented in the balance sheet and in the profit and loss account.

History – Para. 52 substituted by SI 2015/980, reg. 33(2), with effect in relation to–

    (a)   financial years beginning on or after 1 January 2016, and

    (b)   a financial year of a company beginning on or after 1 January 2015, but before 1 January 2016, if the directors of the company so decide.

Former para. 52 read as follows:

"**52** Any information required in the case of any company by the following provisions of this Part of this Schedule must (if not given in the company's accounts) be given by way of a note to the accounts."

General

Disclosure of accounting policies

53 The accounting policies adopted by the company in determining the amounts to be included in respect of items shown in the balance sheet and in determining the profit or loss of the company must be stated (including such policies with respect to the depreciation and diminution in value of assets).

54 It must be stated whether the accounts have been prepared in accordance with applicable accounting standards and particulars of any material departure from those standards and the reasons for it must be given.

Sums denominated in foreign currencies

55 Where any sums originally denominated in foreign currencies have been brought into account under any items shown in the balance sheet format or profit and loss account formats, the basis on which those sums have been translated into sterling (or the currency in which the accounts are drawn up) must be stated.

Reserves and dividends

56 There must be stated–

    (a)   any amount set aside or proposed to be set aside to, or withdrawn or proposed to be withdrawn from, reserves,

(b)   the aggregate amount of dividends paid in the financial year (other than those for which a liability existed at the immediately preceding balance sheet date),

(c)   the aggregate amount of dividends that the company is liable to pay at the balance sheet date, and

(d)   the aggregate amount of dividends that are proposed before the date of approval of the accounts, and not otherwise disclosed under sub-paragraph (b) or (c).

Information supplementing the balance sheet

57 Paragraphs 58 to 84 require information which either supplements the information given with respect to any particular items shown in the balance sheet or is otherwise relevant to assessing the company's state of affairs in the light of the information so given.

Share capital and debentures

58(1) Where shares of more than one class have been allotted, the number and aggregate nominal value of shares of each class allotted must be given.

58(2) In the case of any part of the allotted share capital that consists of redeemable shares, the following information must be given–

(a)   the earliest and latest dates on which the company has power to redeem those shares,

(b)   whether those shares must be redeemed in any event or are liable to be redeemed at the option of the company or of the shareholder, and

(c)   whether any (and, if so, what) premium is payable on redemption.

59 If the company has allotted any shares during the financial year, the following information must be given–

(a)   the classes of shares allotted, and

(b)   as respects each class of shares, the number allotted, their aggregate nominal value and the consideration received by the company for the allotment.

60(1) With respect to any contingent right to the allotment of shares in the company the following particulars must be given–

(a)   the number, description and amount of the shares in relation to which the right is exercisable,

(b)   the period during which it is exercisable, and

(c)   the price to be paid for the shares allotted.

60(2) In sub-paragraph (1) **"contingent right to the allotment of shares"** means any option to subscribe for shares and any other right to require the allotment of shares to any person whether arising on the conversion into shares of securities of any other description or otherwise.

61(1) If the company has issued any debentures during the financial year to which the accounts relate, the following information must be given–

(a)   the classes of debentures issued, and

(b)   as respects each class of debentures, the amount issued and the consideration received by the company for the issue.

61(2) Where any of the company's debentures are held by a nominee of or trustee for the company, the nominal amount of the debentures and the amount at which they are stated in the accounting records kept by the company in accordance with section 386 of the 2006 Act (duty to keep accounting records) must be stated.

Fixed assets

62(1) In respect of any fixed assets of the company included in any assets item in the company's balance sheet the following information must be given by reference to each such item–

- (a) the appropriate amounts in respect of those assets included in the item as at the date of the beginning of the financial year and as at the balance sheet date respectively,
- (b) the effect on any amount shown included in the item in respect of those assets of–

  - (i) any determination during that year of the value to be ascribed to any of those assets in accordance with paragraph 40,
  - (ii) acquisitions during that year of any fixed assets,
  - (iii) disposals during that year of any fixed assets, and
  - (iv) any transfers of fixed assets of the company to and from that item during that year.

62(2) The reference in sub-paragraph (1)(a) to the appropriate amounts in respect of any fixed assets (included in an assets item) as at any date there mentioned is a reference to amounts representing the aggregate amounts determined, as at that date, in respect of fixed assets falling to be included under the item on either of the following bases–

- (a) on the basis of cost (determined in accordance with paragraphs 35 and 36), or
- (b) on any basis permitted by paragraph 40, (leaving out of account in either case any provisions for depreciation or diminution in value).

62(3) In addition, in respect of any fixed assets of the company included in any assets item in the company's balance sheet, there must be stated (by reference to each such item)–

- (a) the cumulative amount of provisions for depreciation or diminution in value of those assets included under that item as at each date mentioned in sub-paragraph (1)(a),
- (b) the amount of any such provisions made in respect of the financial year,
- (c) the amount of any adjustments made in respect of any such provisions during that year in consequence of the disposal of any of those assets, and
- (d) the amount of any other adjustments made in respect of any such provisions during that year.

62(4) The requirements of this paragraph need not be complied with to the extent that a company takes advantage of the option of setting off charges and income afforded by paragraph 8(3) in Part 1 of this Schedule.

63 Where any fixed assets of the company (other than listed investments) are included under any item shown in the company's balance sheet at an amount determined in accordance with paragraph 40, the following information must be given–

- (a) the years (so far as they are known to the directors) in which the assets were severally valued and the several values, and
- (b) in the case of assets that have been valued during the financial year, the names of the persons who valued them or particulars of their qualifications for doing so and (whichever is stated) the bases of valuation used by them.

64 In relation to any amount which is included under assets item 10 in the balance sheet format (tangible fixed assets) with respect to land and buildings there must be stated–

- (a) how much of that amount is ascribable to land of freehold tenure and how much to land of leasehold tenure, and
- (b) how much of the amount ascribable to land of leasehold tenure is ascribable to land held on long lease and how much to land held on short lease.

65 There must be disclosed separately the amount of–

- (a) any participating interests, and
- (b) any shares in group undertakings that are held in credit institutions.

Information about fair value of assets and liabilities

66(1) This paragraph applies where financial instruments or other assets have been valued in accordance with, as appropriate, paragraph 44, 46 or 47.

66(2) There must be stated–

    (a)   the significant assumptions underlying the valuation models and techniques used to determine the fair value of the financial instruments or other assets,

    (b)   for each category of financial instrument or other asset, the fair value of the assets in that category and the changes in value–

        (i)   included directly in the profit and loss account, or

        (ii) credited to or (as the case may be) debited from the fair value reserve, in respect of those assets, and

    (c)   for each class of derivatives, the extent and nature of the instruments, including significant terms and conditions that may affect the amount, timing and certainty of future cash flows.

66(3) Where any amount is transferred to or from the fair value reserve during the financial year, there must be stated in tabular form–

    (a)   the amount of the reserve as at the date of the beginning of the financial year and as at the balance sheet date respectively,

    (b)   the amount transferred to or from the reserve during the year, and

    (c)   the source and application respectively of the amounts so transferred.

History – Para. 66 substituted by SI 2015/980, reg. 33(3), with effect in relation to–

    (a)   financial years beginning on or after 1 January 2016, and

    (b)   a financial year of a company beginning on or after 1 January 2015, but before 1 January 2016, if the directors of the company so decide.

Former para. 66 read as follows:

"**66(1)** This paragraph applies where financial instruments have been valued in accordance with paragraph 44 or 46.

66(2) There must be stated–

    (a)   the significant assumptions underlying the valuation models and techniques used where the fair value of the instruments has been determined in accordance with paragraph 45(4),

    (b)   for each category of financial instrument, the fair value of the instruments in that category and the changes in value–

        (i)   included in the profit and loss account, or

        (ii) credited to or (as the case may be) debited from the fair value reserve, in respect of those instruments, and

    (c)   for each class of derivatives, the extent and nature of the instruments, including significant terms and conditions that may affect the amount, timing and certainty of future cash flows.

66(3) Where any amount is transferred to or from the fair value reserve during the financial year, there must be stated in tabular form–

    (a)   the amount of the reserve as at the date of the beginning of the financial year and as at the balance sheet date respectively,

    (b)   the amount transferred to or from the reserve during that year, and

    (c)   the source and application respectively of the amounts so transferred."

67 Where the company has derivatives that it has not included at fair value, there must be stated for each class of such derivatives–

    (a)   the fair value of the derivatives in that class, if such a value can be determined in accordance with paragraph 45, and

    (b)   the extent and nature of the derivatives.

68(1) This paragraph applies if–

   (a) the company has financial fixed assets that could be included at fair value by virtue of paragraph 44,

   (b) the amount at which those items are included under any item in the company's accounts is in excess of their fair value, and

   (c) the company has not made provision for diminution in value of those assets in accordance with paragraph 25(1) in Part 2 of this Schedule.

68(2) There must be stated–

   (a) the amount at which either the individual assets or appropriate groupings of those individual assets are included in the company's accounts,

   (b) the fair value of those assets or groupings, and

   (c) the reasons for not making a provision for diminution in value of those assets, including the nature of the evidence that provides the basis for the belief that the amount at which they are stated in the accounts will be recovered.

Information where investment property and living animals and plants included at fair value

69(1) This paragraph applies where the amounts to be included in a company's accounts in respect of investment property or living animals and plants have been determined in accordance with paragraph 47.

69(2) The balance sheet items affected and the basis of valuation adopted in determining the amounts of the assets in question in the case of each such item must be disclosed in a note to the accounts.

69(3) In the case of investment property, for each balance sheet item affected there must be shown, either separately in the balance sheet or in a note to the accounts–

   (a) the comparable amounts determined according to the historical cost accounting rules, or

   (b) the differences between those amounts and the corresponding amounts actually shown in the balance sheet in respect of that item.

69(4) In sub-paragraph (3), references in relation to any item to the comparable amounts determined in accordance with that sub-paragraph are to–

   (a) the aggregate amount which would be required to be shown in respect of that item if the amounts to be included in respect of all the assets covered by that item were determined according to the historical cost accounting rules, and

   (b) the aggregate amount of the cumulative provisions for depreciation or diminution in value which would be permitted or required in determining those amounts according to those rules.

Reserves and provisions

70(1) This paragraph applies where any amount is transferred–

   (a) to or from any reserves, or

   (b) to any provision for liabilities, or

   (c) from any provision for liabilities otherwise than for the purpose for which the provision was established, and the reserves or provisions are or would but for paragraph 5(1) in Part 1 of this Schedule be shown as separate items in the company's balance sheet.

70(2) The following information must be given in respect of the aggregate of reserves or provisions included in the same item in tabular form–

(a) the amount of the reserves or provisions as at the date of the beginning of the financial year and as at the balance sheet date respectively,

(b) any amounts transferred to or from the reserves or provisions during that year, and

(c) the source and application respectively of any amounts so transferred.

70(3) Particulars must be given of each provision included in liabilities item 6.(c) (other provisions) in the company's balance sheet in any case where the amount of that provision is material.

History – In para. 70(2), the words "in tabular form" inserted by SI 2015/980, reg. 33(4), with effect in relation to–

(a) financial years beginning on or after 1 January 2016, and

(b) a financial year of a company beginning on or after 1 January 2015, but before 1 January 2016, if the directors of the company so decide.

Provision for taxation

71 The amount of any provision for deferred taxation must be stated separately from the amount of any provision for other taxation.

Maturity analysis

72(1) A company must disclose separately for each of assets items 3.(b) and 4 and liabilities items 1.(b), 2.(b) and 3.(b) the aggregate amount of the loans and advances and liabilities included in those items broken down into the following categories–

(a) those repayable in not more than three months,

(b) those repayable in more than three months but not more than one year,

(c) those repayable in more than one year but not more than five years,

(d) those repayable in more than five years, from the balance sheet date.

72(2) A company must also disclose the aggregate amounts of all loans and advances falling within assets item 4 (loans and advances to customers) which are–

(a) repayable on demand, or

(b) are for an indeterminate period, being repayable upon short notice.

72(3) For the purposes of sub-paragraph (1), where a loan or advance or liability is repayable by instalments, each such instalment is to be treated as a separate loan or advance or liability.

Debt and other fixed-income securities

73 A company must disclose the amount of debt and fixed-income securities included in assets item 5 (debt securities [and other fixed-income securities]) and the amount of such securities included in liabilities item 3.(a) (bonds and medium term notes) that (in each case) will become due within one year of the balance sheet date.

Subordinated liabilities

74(1) The following information must be disclosed in relation to any borrowing included in liabilities item 7 (subordinated liabilities) that exceeds 10% of the total for that item–

(a) its amount,

(b) the currency in which it is denominated,

(c) the rate of interest and the maturity date (or the fact that it is perpetual),

(d) the circumstances in which early repayment may be demanded,

(e) the terms of the subordination, and

(f)   the existence of any provisions whereby it may be converted into capital or some other form of liability and the terms of any such provisions.

74(2) The general terms of any other borrowings included in liabilities item 7 must also be stated.

Fixed cumulative dividends

75 If any fixed cumulative dividends on the company's shares are in arrear, there must be stated–

(a)   the amount of the arrears, and
(b)   the period for which the dividends or, if there is more than one class, each class of them are in arrear.

Details of assets charged

76(1) There must be disclosed, in relation to each liabilities and memorandum item of the balance sheet format–

(a)   the aggregate amount of any assets of the company which have been charged to secure any liability or potential liability included under that item,
(b)   the aggregate amount of the liabilities or potential liabilities so secured, and
(c)   an indication of the nature of the security given.

76(2) Particulars must also be given of any other charge on the assets of the company to secure the liabilities of any other person, including, where practicable, the amount secured.

Guarantees and other financial commitments

77(1) Particulars and the total amount of any financial commitments, guarantees and contingencies that are not included in the balance sheet must be disclosed.

77(2) An indication of the nature and form of any valuable security given by the company in respect of commitments, guarantees and contingencies within sub-paragraph (1) must be given.

77(3) The total amount of any commitments within sub-paragraph (1) concerning pensions must be separately disclosed.

77(4) Particulars must be given of pension commitments which are included in the balance sheet.

77(5) Where any commitment within sub-paragraph (3) or (4) relates wholly or partly to pensions payable to past directors of the company separate particulars must be given of that commitment.

77(6) The total amount of any commitments, guarantees and contingencies within sub-paragraph (1) which are undertaken on behalf of or for the benefit of–

(a)   any parent undertaking or fellow subsidiary undertaking of the company,
(b)   any subsidiary undertaking of the company, or
(c)   any undertaking in which the company has a participating interest

must be separately stated and those within each of paragraphs (a), (b) and (c) must also be stated separately from those within any other of those paragraphs.

77(7) There must be disclosed the nature and amount of any contingent liabilities and commitments included in Memorandum items 1 and 2 which are material in relation to the company's activities.

History – Para. 77 substituted by SI 2015/980, reg. 33(5), with effect in relation to–

    (a)   financial years beginning on or after 1 January 2016, and

    (b)   a financial year of a company beginning on or after 1 January 2015, but before 1 January 2016, if the directors of the company so decide.

Former para. 77 read as follows:

"**77(1)** There must be stated, where practicable, the aggregate amount or estimated amount of contracts for capital expenditure, so far as not provided for.

77(2) Particulars must be given of–

    (a)   any pension commitments included under any provision shown in the company's balance sheet, and

    (b)   any such commitments for which no provision has been made, and where any such commitment relates wholly or partly to pensions payable to past directors of the company separate particulars must be given of that commitment so far as it relates to such pensions.

77(3) Particulars must also be given of any other financial commitments, including any contingent liabilities, that–

    (a)   have not been provided for,

    (b)   have not been included in the memorandum items in the balance sheet format, and

    (c)   are relevant to assessing the company's state of affairs.

77(4) Commitments within any of the preceding sub-paragraphs undertaken on behalf of or for the benefit of–

    (a)   any parent company or fellow subsidiary undertaking of the company, or

    (b)   any subsidiary undertaking of the company, must be stated separately from the other commitments within that sub-paragraph (and commitments within paragraph(a) must be stated separately from those within paragraph (b)).

77(5) There must be disclosed the nature and amount of any contingent liabilities and commitments included in Memorandum items 1 and 2 which are material in relation to the company's activities."

Memorandum items: Group undertakings

78(1) With respect to contingent liabilities required to be included under Memorandum item 1 in the balance sheet format, there must be stated in a note to the accounts the amount of such contingent liabilities incurred on behalf of or for the benefit of–

    (a) any parent undertaking or fellow subsidiary undertaking, or

    (b) any subsidiary undertaking,

of the company; in addition the amount incurred in respect of the undertakings referred to in paragraph (a) must be stated separately from the amount incurred in respect in respect of the undertakings referred to in paragraph (b).

78(2) With respect to commitments required to be included under Memorandum item 2 in the balance sheet format, there must be stated in a note to the accounts the amount of such commitments undertaken on behalf of or for the benefit of–

    (a) any parent undertaking or fellow subsidiary undertaking, or

    (b) any subsidiary undertaking, of the company; in addition the amount incurred in respect of the undertakings referred to in paragraph

    (a) must be stated separately from the amount incurred in respect of the undertakings referred to in paragraph (b).

Transferable securities

79(1) There must be disclosed for each of assets items 5 to 8 in the balance sheet format the amount of transferable securities included under those items that are listed and the amount of those that are unlisted.

79(2) In the case of each amount shown in respect of listed securities under sub-paragraph (1), there must also be disclosed the aggregate market value of those securities, if different from the amount shown.

79(3) There must also be disclosed for each of assets items 5 and 6 the amount of transferable securities included under those items that are held as financial fixed assets and the amount of those that are not so held, together with the criterion used by the directors to distinguish those held as financial fixed assets.

Leasing transactions

80 The aggregate amount of all property (other than land) leased by the company to other persons must be disclosed, broken down so as to show the aggregate amount included in each relevant balance sheet item.

Assets and liabilities denominated in a currency other than sterling (or the currency in which the accounts are drawn up)

81(1) The aggregate amount, in sterling (or the currency in which the accounts are drawn up), of all assets denominated in a currency other than sterling (or the currency used) together with the aggregate amount, in sterling (or the currency used), of all liabilities so denominated, is to be disclosed.

81(2) For the purposes of this paragraph an appropriate rate of exchange prevailing at the balance sheet date must be used to determine the amounts concerned.

Sundry assets and liabilities

82 Where any amount shown under either of the following items is material, particulars must be given of each type of asset or liability included in that item, including an explanation of the nature of the asset or liability and the amount included with respect to assets or liabilities of that type–

(a)   assets item 13 (other assets),
(b)   liabilities item 4 (other liabilities).

Unmatured forward transactions

83(1) The following must be disclosed with respect to unmatured forward transactions outstanding at the balance sheet date–

(a)   the categories of such transactions, by reference to an appropriate system of classification,
(b)   whether, in the case of each such category, they have been made, to any material extent, for the purpose of hedging the effects of fluctuations in interest rates, exchange rates and market prices or whether they have been made, to any material extent, for dealing purposes.

83(2) Transactions falling within sub-paragraph (1) must include all those in relation to which income or expenditure is to be included in–

(a)   format 1, item 6 or format 2, items B4 or A3 (dealing [profits][losses]),
(b)   format 1, items 1 or 2, or format 2, items B1 or A1, by virtue of notes (1)(b) and (2)(b) to the profit and loss account formats (forward contracts, spread over the actual duration of the contract and similar in nature to interest).

Miscellaneous matters

84(1) Particulars must be given of any case where the cost of any asset is for the first time determined under paragraph 37 in Part 2 of this Schedule.

84(2) Where any outstanding loans made under the authority of section 682(2)(b), (c) or (d) of the 2006 Act (various cases of financial assistance by a company for purchase of its own shares) are included under any item shown in the company's balance sheet, the aggregate amount of those loans must be disclosed for each item in question.

Information supplementing the profit and loss account

85 Paragraphs 86 to 91 require information which either supplements the information given with respect to any particular items shown in the profit and loss account or otherwise provides particulars of income or expenditure of the company or of circumstances affecting the items shown in the profit and loss account (see regulation 5(2) for exemption for companies falling within section 408 of the 2006 Act (individual profit and loss account where group accounts prepared)).

Particulars of tax

86(1) Particulars must be given of any special circumstances which affect liability in respect of taxation of profits, income or capital gains for the financial year or liability in respect of taxation of profits, income or capital gains for succeeding financial years.

86(2) The following amounts must be stated–

   (a)   the amount of the charge for United Kingdom corporation tax,
   (b)   if that amount would have been greater but for relief from double taxation, the amount which it would have been but for such relief,
   (c)   the amount of the charge for United Kingdom income tax, and
   (d)   the amount of the charge for taxation imposed outside the United Kingdom of profits, income and (so far as charged to revenue) capital gains.

These amounts must be stated separately in respect of each of the amounts which is shown under the following items in the profit and loss account, that is to say format 1 item 16, format 2 item A10 (tax on [profit][loss] on ordinary activities) and format 1 item 21, format 2 item A13 (tax on extraordinary [profit][loss]).

Particulars of income

87(1) A company must disclose, with respect to income included in the following items in the profit and loss account formats, the amount of that income attributable to each of the geographical markets in which the company has operated during the financial year–

   (a)   format 1 item 1, format 2 item B1 (interest receivable),
   (b)   format 1 item 3, format 2 item B2 (dividend income),
   (c)   format 1 item 4, format 2 item B3 (fees and commissions receivable),
   (d)   format 1 item 6, format 2 item B4 (dealing profits), and
   (e)   format 1 item 7, format 2 item B7 (other operating income).

87(2) In analysing for the purposes of this paragraph the source of any income, the directors must have regard to the manner in which the company's activities are organised.

87(3) For the purposes of this paragraph, markets which do not differ substantially from each other shall be treated as one market.

87(4) Where in the opinion of the directors the disclosure of any information required by this paragraph would be seriously prejudicial to the interests of the company, that information need not be disclosed, but the fact that any such information has not been disclosed must be stated.

Management and agency services

88 A company providing any management and agency services to customers must disclose that fact, if the scale of such services provided is material in the context of its business as a whole.

Subordinated liabilities

89 Any amounts charged to the profit and loss account representing charges incurred during the year with respect to subordinated liabilities must be disclosed.

Sundry income and charges

90 Where any amount to be included in any of the following items is material, particulars must be given of each individual component of the figure, including an explanation of their nature and amount–

    (a) in format 1–

        (i)   items 7 and 10 (other operating income and charges),
        (ii) items 18 and 19 (extraordinary income and charges);

    (b) in format 2–

        (i)   items A6 and B7 (other operating charges and income),
        (ii) items A12 and B10 (extraordinary charges and income).

Miscellaneous matters

91(1) Where any amount relating to any preceding financial year is included in any item in the profit and loss account, the effect must be stated.

91(2) The amount, nature and effect of any individual items of income or expenditure which are of exceptional size or incidence must be stated.

History – Para. 91(2) substituted by SI 2015/980, reg. 33(6), with effect in relation to–

    (a)   financial years beginning on or after 1 January 2016, and
    (b)   a financial year of a company beginning on or after 1 January 2015, but before 1 January 2016, if the directors of the company so decide.

Former para. 91(2) read as follows:

"**91(2)** The effect must be stated of any transactions that are exceptional by virtue of size or incidence though they fall within the ordinary activities of the company."

Related party transactions

92(1) Particulars may be given of transactions which the company has entered into with related parties, and must be given if such transactions are material and have not been concluded under normal market conditions.

92(2) The particulars of transactions required to be disclosed by sub-paragraph (1) must include–

    (a) the amount of such transactions,
    (b) the nature of the related party relationship, and
    (c) other information about the transactions necessary for an understanding of the financial position of the company.

92(3) Information about individual transactions may be aggregated according to their nature, except where separate information is necessary for an understanding of the effects of related party transactions on the financial position of the company.

92(4) Particulars need not be given of transactions entered into between two or more members of a group, provided that any subsidiary undertaking which is a party to the transaction is whollyowned by such a member.

92(5) In this paragraph, **"related party"** has the same meaning as in international accounting standards.

Post balance sheet events

92A The nature and financial effect of material events arising after the balance sheet date which are not reflected in the profit and loss account of balance sheet must be stated.

History – Para. 92A and the heading preceding it inserted by SI 2015/980, reg. 33(7), with effect in relation to–

  (a)   financial years beginning on or after 1 January 2016, and
  (b)   a financial year of a company beginning on or after 1 January 2015, but before 1 January 2016, if the directors of the company so decide.

Appropriations

92B Particulars must be given of the proposed appropriation of profit or treatment of loss or, where applicable, particulars of the actual appropriation of the profits or treatment of the losses.

History – Para. 92B and the heading preceding it inserted by SI 2015/980, reg. 33(7), with effect in relation to–

  (a)   financial years beginning on or after 1 January 2016, and
  (b)   a financial year of a company beginning on or after 1 January 2015, but before 1 January 2016, if the directors of the company so decide.

PART 4 – INTERPRETATION OF THIS SCHEDULE
DEFINITIONS FOR THIS SCHEDULE

93 The following definitions apply for the purposes of this Schedule.

Financial fixed assets

94 "Financial fixed assets" means loans and advances and securities held as fixed assets; participating interests and shareholdings in group undertakings are to be regarded as financial fixed assets.

Financial instruments

95 For the purposes of this Schedule, references to "derivatives" include commodity-based contracts that give either contracting party the right to settle in cash or in some other financial instrument, except when such contracts–

  (a)   were entered into for the purpose of, and continue to meet, the company's expected purchase, sale or usage requirements,
  (b)   were designated for such purpose at their inception, and
  (c)   are expected to be settled by delivery of the commodity.

96(1) The expressions listed in sub-paragraph (2) have the same meaning in paragraphs 44 to 49, 66 to 68 and 95 of this Schedule as they have in Council Directives 2013/34/EU on the annual financial statements etc of certain types of undertaking and 86/635/EEC on the annual accounts and consolidated accounts of banks and other financial institutions.

96(2) Those expressions are "available for sale financial asset", "business combination", "commodity-based contracts", "derivative", "equity instrument", "exchange difference", "fair value hedge accounting system", "financial fixed asset", "financial instrument", "foreign entity", "hedge accounting", "hedge accounting system", "hedged items", "hedging instrument", "held for trading purposes", "held to maturity", "monetary item", "receivables", "reliable market" and "trading portfolio".

History – In para. 96(1), the words "2013/34/EU on the annual financial statements etc of certain types of undertaking" substituted for the words "78/660/EEC on the annual accounts of certain types of companies" by SI 2015/980, reg. 33(8), with effect in relation to–

(a) financial years beginning on or after 1 January 2016, and

(b) a financial year of a company beginning on or after 1 January 2015, but before 1 January 2016, if the directors of the company so decide.

Repayable on demand

97 "Repayable on demand", in connection with deposits, loans or advances, means that they can at any time be withdrawn or demanded without notice or that a maturity or period of notice of not more than 24 hours or one working day has been agreed for them.

Sale and repurchase transaction

98(1) "Sale and repurchase transaction" means a transaction which involves the transfer by a credit institution or customer ("the transferor") to another credit institution or customer ("the transferee") of assets subject to an agreement that the same assets, or (in the case of fungible assets) equivalent assets, will subsequently be transferred back to the transferor at a specified price on a date specified or to be specified by the transferor.

98(2) The following are not to be regarded as sale and repurchase transactions for the purposes of sub-paragraph (1)–

(a) forward exchange transactions,

(b) options,

(c) transactions involving the issue of debt securities with a commitment to repurchase all or part of the issue before maturity, or

(d) any similar transactions.

Sale and option to resell transaction

99 "Sale and option to resell transaction" means a transaction which involves the transfer by a credit institution or customer ("the transferor") to another credit institution or customer ("the transferee") of assets subject to an agreement that the transferee is entitled to require the subsequent transfer of the same assets, or (in the case of fungible assets) equivalent assets, back to the transferor at the purchase price or another price agreed in advance on a date specified or to be specified.

SCHEDULE 3   Regulation 6(1)

INSURANCE COMPANIES: COMPANIES ACT INDIVIDUAL ACCOUNTS

PART 1 – GENERAL RULES AND FORMATS

SECTION A – GENERAL RULES

1(1) Subject to the following provisions of this Schedule–

   (a) every balance sheet of a company must show the items listed in the balance sheet format in Section B of this Part, and

   (b) every profit and loss account must show the items listed in the profit and loss account format in Section B.

1(2) References in this Schedule to the items listed in any of the formats in Section B are to those items read together with any of the notes following the formats which apply to those items.

1(3) The items must be shown in the order and under the headings and sub-headings given in the particular format, but–

   (a) the notes to the formats may permit alternative positions for any particular items, and

   (b) the heading or sub-heading for any item does not have to be distinguished by any letter or number assigned to that item in the format used.

2(1) Any item required to be shown in a company's balance sheet or profit and loss account may be shown in greater detail than required by the particular format.

2(2) The balance sheet or profit and loss account may include an item representing or covering the amount of any asset or liability, income or expenditure not specifically covered by any of the items listed in the formats set out in Section B, save that none of the following may be treated as assets in any balance sheet–

   (a) preliminary expenses,

   (b) expenses of, and commission on, any issue of shares or debentures, and

   (c) costs of research.

3(1) The directors may combine items to which Arabic numbers are given in the balance sheet format set out in Section B (except for items concerning technical provisions and the reinsurers' share of technical provisions), and items to which lower case letters in parentheses are given in the profit and loss account format so set out (except for items within items I.1 and 4 and II.1, 5 and 6) if–

   (a) their individual amounts are not material for the purpose of giving a true and fair view, or

   (b) the combination facilitates the assessment of the state of affairs or profit or loss of the company for the financial year in question.

3(2) Where sub-paragraph (1)(b) applies–

   (a) the individual amounts of any items which have been combined must be disclosed in a note to the accounts, and

   (b) any notes required by this Schedule to the items so combined must, notwithstanding the combination, be given.

4(1) Subject to sub-paragraph (2), the directors must not include a heading or sub-heading corresponding to an item in the balance sheet or profit and loss account format used if there is no amount to be shown for that item for the financial year to which the balance sheet or profit and loss account relates.

4(2) Where an amount can be shown for the item in question for the immediately preceding financial year that amount must be shown under the heading or sub-heading required by the format for that item.

5(1) For every item shown in the balance sheet or profit and loss account the corresponding amount for the immediately preceding financial year must also be shown.

5(2) Where that corresponding amount is not comparable with the amount to be shown for the item in question in respect of the financial year to which the balance sheet or profit and loss account relates, the former amount may be adjusted, and particulars of the non-comparability and of any adjustment must be disclosed in a note to the accounts.

6 Subject to the provisions of this Schedule, amounts in respect of items representing assets or income may not be set off against amounts in respect of items representing liabilities or expenditure (as the case may be), or vice versa.

7(1) The provisions of this Schedule which relate to long-term business apply, with necessary modifications, to business which consists of effecting or carrying out relevant contracts of general insurance which–

    (a) is transacted exclusively or principally according to the technical principles of long-term business, and

    (b) is a significant amount of the business of the company.

7(2) For the purposes of paragraph (1), a contract of general insurance is a relevant contract if the risk insured against relates to–

    (a) accident, or

    (b) sickness.

7(3) Sub-paragraph (2) must be read with–

    (a) section 22 of the Financial Services and Markets Act 2000,

    (b) the Financial Services and Markets Act 2000 (Regulated Activities) Order 2001, and

    (c) Schedule 2 to that Act.

8 The company's directors must, in determining how amounts are presented within items in the profit and loss account and balance sheet, have regard to the substance of the reported transaction or arrangement, in accordance with generally accepted accounting principles or practice.

8A Where an asset or liability relates to more than one item in the balance sheet, the relationship of such asset or liability to the relevant items must be disclosed either under those items or in the notes to the accounts.

History – Para. 8A inserted by SI 2015/980, reg. 34(2), with effect in relation to–

    (a) financial years beginning on or after 1 January 2016, and

    (b) a financial year of a company beginning on or after 1 January 2015, but before 1 January 2016, if the directors of the company so decide.

SECTION B – THE REQUIRED FORMATS

Preliminary

9(1) Where in respect of any item to which an Arabic number is assigned in the balance sheet or profit and loss account format, the gross amount and reinsurance amount or reinsurers' share are required to be shown, a sub-total of those amounts must also be given.

9(2) Where in respect of any item to which an Arabic number is assigned in the profit and loss account format, separate items are required to be shown, then a separate sub-total of those items must also be given in addition to any sub-total required by sub-paragraph (1).

10(1) In the profit and loss account format set out below–

(a) the heading "Technical account – General business" is for business which consists of effecting or carrying out contracts of general business; and

(b) the heading "Technical account – Long-term business" is for business which consists of effecting or carrying out contracts of long-term insurance.

10(2) In sub-paragraph (1), references to–

(a) contracts of general or long-term insurance, and

(b) the effecting or carrying out of such contracts, must be read with section 22 of the Financial Services and Markets Act 2000, the Financial Services and Markets Act 2000 (Regulated Activities) Order 2001, and Schedule 2 to that Act.

Balance sheet format

ASSETS

A. Called up share capital not paid *(1)*

B. Intangible assets

    1. Development costs
    2. Concessions, patents, licences, trade marks and similar rights and assets *(2)*
    3. Goodwill *(3)*
    4. Payments on account

C. Investments

    I. Land and buildings *(4)*
    II. Investments in group undertakings and participating interests

        1. Shares in group undertakings
        2. Debt securities issued by, and loans to, group undertakings
        3. Participating interests
        4. Debt securities issued by, and loans to, undertakings in which the company has a participating interest

    III. Other financial investments

        1. Shares and other variable-yield securities and units in unit trusts
        2. Debt securities and other fixed-income securities *(5)*
        3. Participation in investment pools *(6)*
        4. Loans secured by mortgages *(7)*
        5. Other loans *(7)*

6.   Deposits with credit institutions *(8)*
7.   Other *(9)*

   IV. Deposits with ceding undertakings *(10)*

D.   Assets held to cover linked liabilities *(11)*

Da. Reinsurers' share of technical provisions *(12)*

1.   Provision for unearned premiums
2.   Long-term business provision
3.   Claims outstanding
4.   Provisions for bonuses and rebates
5.   Other technical provisions
6.   Technical provisions for unit-linked liabilities

E.   Debtors *(13)*

I.   Debtors arising out of direct insurance operations

1.   Policyholders
2.   Intermediaries

II.   Debtors arising out of reinsurance operations
III. Other debtors
IV. Called up share capital not paid *(1)*

F.   Other assets

I.   Tangible assets

1.   Plant and machinery
2.   Fixtures, fittings, tools and equipment
3.   Payments on account (other than deposits paid on land and buildings) and assets (other than buildings) in course of construction

II.   Stocks

1.   Raw materials and consumables
2.   Work in progress
3.   Finished goods and goods for resale
4.   Payments on account

III. Cash at bank and in hand
IV. Own shares *(14)*
V.   Other *(15)*

G.   Prepayments and accrued income

I.   Accrued interest and rent *(16)*
II.   Deferred acquisition costs *(17)*
III. Other prepayments and accrued income

LIABILITIES

A.   Capital and reserves

I.   Called up share capital or equivalent funds
II.   Share premium account

    III. Revaluation reserve
    IV. Reserves

        1. Capital redemption reserve
        2. Reserve for own shares
        3. Reserves provided for by the articles of association
        4. Other reserves

    V. Profit and loss account

B. Subordinated liabilities *(18)*

Ba. Fund for future appropriations *(19)*

C. Technical provisions

    1. Provision for unearned premiums *(20)*

      (a) gross amount
      (b) reinsurance amount *(12)*

    2. Long-term business provision *(20) (21) (26)*

      (a) gross amount
      (b) reinsurance amount *(12)*

    3. Claims outstanding *(22)*

      (a) gross amount
      (b) reinsurance amount *(12)*

    4. Provision for bonuses and rebates *(23)*

      (a) gross amount
      (b) reinsurance amount *(12)*

    5. Equalisation provision *(24)*

    6. Other technical provisions *(25)*

      (a) gross amount
      (b) reinsurance amount *(12)*

D. Technical provisions for linked liabilities *(26)*

      (a) gross amount
      (b) reinsurance amount *(12)*

E. Provisions for other risks

    1. Provisions for pensions and similar obligations
    2. Provisions for taxation
    3. Other provisions

F. Deposits received from reinsurers *(27)*

G. Creditors *(28)*

    I. Creditors arising out of direct insurance operations
    II. Creditors arising out of reinsurance operations

    III.   Debenture loans *(29)*
    IV. Amounts owed to credit institutions
    V.   Other creditors including taxation and social security

H.   Accruals and deferred income

Notes on the balance sheet format

(1) Called up share capital not paid

(Assets items A and E.IV.)

   This item may be shown in either of the positions given in the format.

(2) *Concessions, patents, licences, trade marks and similar rights and assets*

(Assets item B.2.)

   Amounts in respect of assets are only to be included in a company's balance sheet under this item if either–

    (a) the assets were acquired for valuable consideration and are not required to be shown under goodwill, or
    (b) the assets in question were created by the company itself.

(3) *Goodwill*

(Assets item B.3.)

   Amounts representing goodwill are only to be included to the extent that the goodwill was acquired for valuable consideration.

(4) *Land and buildings*

(Assets item C.I.)

   The amount of any land and buildings occupied by the company for its own activities must be shown separately in the notes to the accounts.

(5) *Debt securities and other fixed-income securities*

(Assets item C.III.2.)

   This item is to comprise transferable debt securities and any other transferable fixed-income securities issued by credit institutions, other undertakings or public bodies, in so far as they are not covered by assets item C.II.2 or C.II.4.

   Securities bearing interest rates that vary in accordance with specific factors, for example the interest rate on the inter-bank market or on the Euromarket, are also to be regarded as debt securities and other fixed-income securities and so be included under this item.

(6) *Participation in investment pools*

(Assets item C.III.3.)

   This item is to comprise shares held by the company in joint investments constituted by several undertakings or pension funds, the management of which has been entrusted to one of those undertakings or to one of those pension funds.

(7) *Loans secured by mortgages and other loans*

(Assets items C.III.4 and C.III.5.)

Loans to policyholders for which the policy is the main security are to be included under "Other loans" and their amount must be disclosed in the notes to the accounts. Loans secured by mortgage are to be shown as such even where they are also secured by insurance policies. Where the amount of "Other loans" not secured by policies is material, an appropriate breakdown must be given in the notes to the accounts.

(8) *Deposits with credit institutions*

(Assets item C.III.6.)

This item is to comprise sums the withdrawal of which is subject to a time restriction. Sums deposited with no such restriction must be shown under assets item F.III even if they bear interest.

(9) *Other*

(Assets item C.III.7.)

This item is to comprise those investments which are not covered by assets items C.III.1 to 6. Where the amount of such investments is significant, they must be disclosed in the notes to the accounts.

(10) *Deposits with ceding undertakings*

(Assets item C.IV.)

Where the company accepts reinsurance this item is to comprise amounts, owed by the ceding undertakings and corresponding to guarantees, which are deposited with those ceding undertakings or with third parties or which are retained by those undertakings.

These amounts may not be combined with other amounts owed by the ceding insurer to the reinsurer or set off against amounts owed by the reinsurer to the ceding insurer.

Securities deposited with ceding undertakings or third parties which remain the property of the company must be entered in the company's accounts as an investment, under the appropriate item.

(11) *Assets held to cover linked liabilities*

(Assets item D.)

In respect of long-term business, this item is to comprise investments made pursuant to long-term policies under which the benefits payable to the policyholder are wholly or partly to be determined by reference to the value of, or the income from, property of any description (whether or not specified in the contract) or by reference to fluctuations in, or in an index of, the value of property of any description (whether or not so specified).

This item is also to comprise investments which are held on behalf of the members of a tontine and are intended for distribution among them.

(12) *Reinsurance amounts*

(Assets item Da: liabilities items C.1.(b), 2.(b), 3.(b), 4.(b) and 6.(b) and D.(b).)

The reinsurance amounts may be shown either under assets item Da or under liabilities items C.1.(b), 2.(b), 3.(b), 4.(b) and 6.(b) and D.(b).

The reinsurance amounts are to comprise the actual or estimated amounts which, under contractual reinsurance arrangements, are deducted from the gross amounts of technical provisions.

As regards the provision for unearned premiums, the reinsurance amounts must be calculated according to the methods referred to in paragraph 50 below or in accordance with the terms of the reinsurance policy.

(13) *Debtors*

(Assets item E.)

Amounts owed by group undertakings and undertakings in which the company has a participating interest must be shown separately as sub-items of assets items E.I, II and III.

(14) *Own shares*

(Assets item F.IV.)

The nominal value of the shares must be shown separately under this item.

(15) *Other*

(Assets item F.V.)

This item is to comprise those assets which are not covered by assets items F.I to IV. Where such assets are material they must be disclosed in the notes to the accounts.

(16) *Accrued interest and rent*

(Assets item G.I.)

This item is to comprise those items that represent interest and rent that have been earned up to the balance-sheet date but have not yet become receivable.

(17) *Deferred acquisition costs*

(Assets item G.II.)

This item is to comprise the costs of acquiring insurance policies which are incurred during a financial year but relate to a subsequent financial year ("deferred acquisition costs"), except in so far as–

(a) allowance has been made in the computation of the long-term business provision made under paragraph 52 below and shown under liabilities item C2 or D in the balance sheet, for–

(i) the explicit recognition of such costs, or
(ii) the implicit recognition of such costs by virtue of the anticipation of future income from which such costs may prudently be expected to be recovered, or

(b) allowance has been made for such costs in respect of general business policies by a deduction from the provision for unearned premiums made under paragraph 50 below and shown under liabilities item C.I in the balance sheet.

Deferred acquisition costs arising in general business must be distinguished from those arising in long-term business.

In the case of general business, the amount of any deferred acquisition costs must be established on a basis compatible with that used for unearned premiums.

There must be disclosed in the notes to the accounts–

(c) how the deferral of acquisition costs has been treated (unless otherwise expressly stated in the accounts), and

(d) where such costs are included as a deduction from the provisions at liabilities item C.I, the amount of such deduction, or

(e) where the actuarial method used in the calculation of the provisions at liabilities item C.2 or D has made allowance for the explicit recognition of such costs, the amount of the costs so recognised.

(18) *Subordinated liabilities*

(Liabilities item B.)

This item is to comprise all liabilities in respect of which there is a contractual obligation that, in the event of winding up or of bankruptcy, they are to be repaid only after the claims of all other creditors have been met (whether or not they are represented by certificates).

(19) *Fund for future appropriations*

(Liabilities item Ba.)

This item is to comprise all funds the allocation of which either to policyholders or to shareholders has not been determined by the end of the financial year.

Transfers to and from this item must be shown in item II.12a in the profit and loss account.

(20) *Provision for unearned premiums*

(Liabilities item C.1.)

In the case of long-term business the provision for unearned premiums may be included in liabilities item C.2 rather than in this item.

The provision for unearned premiums is to comprise the amount representing that part of gross premiums written which is estimated to be earned in the following financial year or to subsequent financial years.

(21) *Long-term business provision*

(Liabilities item C.2.)

This item is to comprise the actuarially estimated value of the company's liabilities (excluding technical provisions included in liabilities item D), including bonuses already declared and after deducting the actuarial value of future premiums.

This item is also to comprise claims incurred but not reported, plus the estimated costs of settling such claims.

(22) *Claims outstanding*

(Liabilities item C.3.)

This item is to comprise the total estimated ultimate cost to the company of settling all claims arising from events which have occurred up to the end of the financial year (including, in the case of general business, claims incurred but not reported) less amounts already paid in respect of such claims.

(23) *Provision for bonuses and rebates*

(Liabilities item C.4.)

This item is to comprise amounts intended for policyholders or contract beneficiaries by way of bonuses and rebates as defined in Note *(5)* on the profit and loss account format to the extent that such amounts have not been credited to policyholders or contract beneficiaries or included in liabilities item Ba or in liabilities item C.2.

(24) *Equalisation provision*

(Liabilities item C.5.)

This item is to comprise the amount of any equalisation reserve maintained in respect of general business by the company, in accordance with the rules made by the Financial Conduct Authority or the Prudential Regulation Authority under Part 10 of the Financial Services and Markets Act 2000.

This item is also to comprise any amounts which, in accordance with Council Directive 87/343/ EEC of 22nd June 1987, are required to be set aside by a company to equalise fluctuations in loss ratios in future years or to provide for special risks.

A company which otherwise constitutes reserves to equalise fluctuations in loss ratios in future years or to provide for special risks must disclose that fact in the notes to the accounts.

(25) *Other technical provisions*

(Liabilities item C.6.)

This item is to comprise, inter alia, the provision for unexpired risks as defined in paragraph 91 below. Where the amount of the provision for unexpired risks is significant, it must be disclosed separately either in the balance sheet or in the notes to the accounts.

(26) *Technical provisions for linked liabilities*

(Liabilities item D.)

This item is to comprise technical provisions constituted to cover liabilities relating to investment in the context of long-term policies under which the benefits payable to policyholders are wholly or partly to be determined by reference to the value of, or the income from, property of any description (whether or not specified in the contract) or by reference to fluctuations in, or in an index of, the value of property of any description (whether or not so specified).

Any additional technical provisions constituted to cover death risks, operating expenses or other risks (such as benefits payable at the maturity date or guaranteed surrender values) must be included under liabilities item C.2.

This item must also comprise technical provisions representing the obligations of a tontine's organiser in relation to its members.

(27) *Deposits received from reinsurers*

(Liabilities item F.)

Where the company cedes reinsurance, this item is to comprise amounts deposited by or withheld from other insurance undertakings under reinsurance contracts. These amounts may not be merged with other amounts owed to or by those other undertakings.

Where the company cedes reinsurance and has received as a deposit securities which have been transferred to its ownership, this item is to comprise the amount owed by the company by virtue of the deposit.

(28) *Creditors*

(Liabilities item G.)

Amounts owed to group undertakings and undertakings in which the company has a participating interest must be shown separately as sub-items.

(29) *Debenture loans*

(Liabilities item G.III.)

The amount of any convertible loans must be shown separately.

History – In note (24), "made by the Financial Conduct Authority or the Prudential Regulation Authority" substituted for "in section 1.4 of the Prudential Sourcebook for Insurers made by the Financial Services Authority" by SI 2013/472, Sch. 2, para. 135(a), with effect from 1 April 2013.

Special rules for balance sheet format

Additional items

11(1) Every balance sheet of a company which carries on long-term business must show separately as an additional item the aggregate of any amounts included in liabilities item A (capital and reserves) which are required not to be treated as realised profits under section 843 of the 2006 Act.

11(2) A company which carries on long-term business must show separately, in the balance sheet or in the notes to the accounts, the total amount of assets representing the long-term fund valued in accordance with the provisions of this Schedule.

Managed funds

12(1) For the purposes of this paragraph "managed funds" are funds of a group pension fund–
  (a) the management of which constitutes long-term insurance business, and
  (b) which the company administers in its own name but on behalf of others, and
  (c) to which it has legal title.

12(2) The company must, in any case where assets and liabilities arising in respect of managed funds fall to be treated as assets and liabilities of the company, adopt the following accounting treatment: assets and liabilities representing managed funds are to be included in the company's balance sheet, with the notes to the accounts disclosing the total amount included with respect to such assets and liabilities in the balance sheet and showing the amount included under each relevant balance sheet item in respect of such assets or (as the case may be) liabilities.

Deferred acquisition costs

13 The costs of acquiring insurance policies which are incurred during a financial year but which relate to a subsequent financial year must be deferred in a manner specified in Note *(17)* on the balance sheet format.

Profit and loss account format

I.   Technical account – General business

    1.   Earned premiums, net of reinsurance

        (a)   gross premiums written *(1)*
        (b)   outward reinsurance premiums *(2)*
        (c)   change in the gross provision for unearned premiums
        (d)   change in the provision for unearned premiums, reinsurers' share

    2.   Allocated investment return transferred from the non-technical account (item III.6) *(10)*

    2a.   Investment income *(8) (10)*

        (a)   income from participating interests, with a separate indication of that derived from group undertakings
        (b)   income from other investments, with a separate indication of that derived from group undertakings (aa) income from land and buildings (bb) income from other investments
        (c)   value re-adjustments on investments
        (d)   gains on the realisation of investments

    3.   Other technical income, net of reinsurance

    4.   Claims incurred, net of reinsurance *(4)*

        (a)   claims paid

            (aa) gross amount
            (bb) reinsurers' share

        (b)   change in the provision for claims

            (aa) gross amount
            (bb) reinsurers' share

    5.   Changes in other technical provisions, net of reinsurance, not shown under other headings

    6.   Bonuses and rebates, net of reinsurance *(5)*

    7.   Net operating expenses

        (a)   acquisition costs *(6)*
        (b)   change in deferred acquisition costs
        (c)   administrative expenses *(7)*
        (d)   reinsurance commissions and profit participation

    8.   Other technical charges, net of reinsurance

    8a.   Investment expenses and charges *(8)*

        (a)   investment management expenses, including interest
        (b)   value adjustments on investments
        (c)   losses on the realisation of investments

    9.   Change in the equalisation provision

    10. Sub-total (balance on the technical account for general business) (item III.1)

II. Technical account – Long-term business

    1.   Earned premiums, net of reinsurance

        (a) gross premiums written *(1)*
        (b) outward reinsurance premiums *(2)*
        (c) change in the provision for unearned premiums, net of reinsurance *(3)*

    2.   Investment income *(8) (10)*

        (a) income from participating interests, with a separate indication of that derived from group undertakings
        (b) income from other investments, with a separate indication of that derived from group undertakings (aa) income from land and buildings (bb) income from other investments
        (c) value re-adjustments on investments
        (d) gains on the realisation of investments

    3.   Unrealised gains on investments *(9)*

    4.   Other technical income, net of reinsurance

    5.   Claims incurred, net of reinsurance *(4)*

        (a) claims paid

            (aa) gross amount
            (bb) reinsurers' share

        (b) change in the provision for claims

            (aa) gross amount
            (bb) reinsurers' share

    6.   Change in other technical provisions, net of reinsurance, not shown under other headings

        (a) Long-term business provision, net of reinsurance *(3)*

            (aa) gross amount
            (bb) reinsurers' share

        (b) other technical provisions, net of reinsurance

    7.   Bonuses and rebates, net of reinsurance *(5)*

    8.   Net operating expenses

        (a) acquisition costs *(6)*
        (b) change in deferred acquisition costs
        (c) administrative expenses *(7)*
        (d) reinsurance commissions and profit participation

    9.   Investment expenses and charges *(8)*

        (a) investment management expenses, including interest
        (b) value adjustments on investments
        (c) losses on the realisation of investments

    10. Unrealised losses on investments *(9)*

11. Other technical charges, net of reinsurance

11a. Tax attributable to the long-term business

12. Allocated investment return transferred to the non-technical account (item III.4)

12a. Transfers to or from the fund for future appropriations

13. Sub-total (balance on the technical account – long-term business) (item III.2)

III. Non-technical account

1. Balance on the general business technical account (item I.10)

2. Balance on the long-term business technical account (item II.13)

2a. Tax credit attributable to balance on the long-term business technical account

3. Investment income *(8)*

    (a) income from participating interests, with a separate indication of that derived from group undertakings
    (b) income from other investments, with a separate indication of that derived from group undertakings (aa) income from land and buildings (bb) income from other investments
    (c) value re-adjustments on investments
    (d) gains on the realisation of investments

3a. Unrealised gains on investments *(9)*

4. Allocated investment return transferred from the long-term business technical account (item II.12) *(10)*

5. Investment expenses and charges *(8)*

    (a) investment management expenses, including interest
    (b) value adjustments on investments
    (c) losses on the realisation of investments

5a. Unrealised losses on investments *(9)*

6. Allocated investment return transferred to the general business technical account (item I.2) *(10)*

7. Other income

8. Other charges, including value adjustments

8a. Profit or loss on ordinary activities before tax

9. Tax on profit or loss on ordinary activities

10. Profit or loss on ordinary activities after tax

11. Extraordinary income

12. Extraordinary charges

13. Extraordinary profit or loss

14. Tax on extraordinary profit or loss

15. Other taxes not shown under the preceding items

16. Profit or loss for the financial year

Notes on the profit and loss account format

(1) *Gross premiums written*

(General business technical account: item I.1.(a).

Long-term business technical account: item II.1.(a).)

This item is to comprise all amounts due during the financial year in respect of insurance contracts entered into regardless of the fact that such amounts may relate in whole or in part to a later financial year, and must include inter alia–

(i)   premiums yet to be determined, where the premium calculation can be done only at the end of the year;

(ii) single premiums, including annuity premiums, and, in long-term business, single premiums resulting from bonus and rebate provisions in so far as they must be considered as premiums under the terms of the contract;

(iii) additional premiums in the case of half-yearly, quarterly or monthly payments and additional payments from policyholders for expenses borne by the company;

(iv) in the case of co-insurance, the company's portion of total premiums;

(v)   reinsurance premiums due from ceding and retroceding insurance undertakings, including portfolio entries, after deduction of cancellations and portfolio withdrawals credited to ceding and retroceding insurance undertakings.

The above amounts must not include the amounts of taxes or duties levied with premiums.

(2) *Outward reinsurance premiums*

(General business technical account: item I.1.(b).

Long-term business technical account: item II.1.(b).)

This item is to comprise all premiums paid or payable in respect of outward reinsurance contracts entered into by the company. Portfolio entries payable on the conclusion or amendment of outward reinsurance contracts must be added; portfolio withdrawals receivable must be deducted.

(3) *Change in the provision for unearned premiums, net of reinsurance*

(Long-term business technical account: items II.1.(c) and II.6.(a).)

In the case of long-term business, the change in unearned premiums may be included either in item II.1.(c) or in item II.6.(a) of the long-term business technical account.

(4) *Claims incurred, net of reinsurance*

(General business technical account: item I.4.

Long-term business technical account: item II.5.)

This item is to comprise all payments made in respect of the financial year with the addition of the provision for claims (but after deducting the provision for claims for the preceding financial year).

238

These amounts must include annuities, surrenders, entries and withdrawals of loss provisions to and from ceding insurance undertakings and reinsurers and external and internal claims management costs and charges for claims incurred but not reported such as are referred to in paragraphs 53(2) and 55 below.

Sums recoverable on the basis of subrogation and salvage (within the meaning of paragraph 53 below) must be deducted.

Where the difference between—

(a) the loss provision made at the beginning of the year for outstanding claims incurred in previous years, and

(b) the payments made during the year on account of claims incurred in previous years and the loss provision shown at the end of the year for such outstanding claims, is material, it must be shown in the notes to the accounts, broken down by category and amount.

(5) *Bonuses and rebates, net of reinsurance*

(General business technical account: item I.6.

Long-term business technical account: item II.7.)

Bonuses are to comprise all amounts chargeable for the financial year which are paid or payable to policyholders and other insured parties or provided for their benefit, including amounts used to increase technical provisions or applied to the reduction of future premiums, to the extent that such amounts represent an allocation of surplus or profit arising on business as a whole or a section of business, after deduction of amounts provided in previous years which are no longer required.

Rebates are to comprise such amounts to the extent that they represent a partial refund of premiums resulting from the experience of individual contracts.

Where material, the amount charged for bonuses and that charged for rebates must be disclosed separately in the notes to the accounts.

(6) *Acquisition costs*

(General business technical account: item I.7.(a).

Long-term business technical account: item II.8.(a).)

This item is to comprise the costs arising from the conclusion of insurance contracts. They must cover both direct costs, such as acquisition commissions or the cost of drawing up the insurance document or including the insurance contract in the portfolio, and indirect costs, such as advertising costs or the administrative expenses connected with the processing of proposals and the issuing of policies.

In the case of long-term business, policy renewal commissions must be included under item II.8.(c) in the long-term business technical account.

(7) *Administrative expenses*

(General business technical account: item I.7.(c).

Long-term business technical account: item II.8.(c).)

This item must include the costs arising from premium collection, portfolio administration, handling of bonuses and rebates, and inward and outward reinsurance. They must in particular include staff costs and depreciation provisions in respect of office furniture and equipment in so far as these need not be shown under acquisition costs, claims incurred or investment charges.

Item II.8.(c) must also include policy renewal commissions.

(8) *Investment income, expenses and charges*

(General business technical account: items I.2a and 8a.

Long-term business technical account: items II.2 and 9.

Non-technical account: items III.3 and 5.)

Investment income, expenses and charges must, to the extent that they arise in the long-term fund, be disclosed in the long-term business technical account. Other investment income, expenses and charges must either be disclosed in the non-technical account or attributed between the appropriate technical and non-technical accounts. Where the company makes such an attribution it must disclose the basis for it in the notes to the accounts.

(9) *Unrealised gains and losses on investments*

(Long-term business technical account: items II.3 and 10.

Non-technical account: items III.3a and 5a.)

In the case of investments attributed to the long-term fund, the difference between the valuation of the investments and their purchase price or, if they have previously been valued, their valuation as at the last balance sheet date, may be disclosed (in whole or in part) in item II.3 or II.10 (as the case may be) of the long-term business technical account, and in the case of investments shown as assets under assets item D (assets held to cover linked liabilities) must be so disclosed.

In the case of other investments, the difference between the valuation of the investments and their purchase price or, if they have previously been valued, their valuation as at the last balance sheet date, may be disclosed (in whole or in part) in item III.3a or III.5a (as the case may require) of the non-technical account.

(10) *Allocated investment return*

(General business technical account: item I.2.

Long-term business technical account: item II.2.

Non-technical account: items III.4 and 6.)

The allocated return may be transferred from one part of the profit and loss account to another.

Where part of the investment return is transferred to the general business technical account, the transfer from the non-technical account must be deducted from item III.6 and added to item I.2.

Where part of the investment return disclosed in the long-term business technical account is transferred to the non-technical account, the transfer to the non-technical account shall be deducted from item II.12 and added to item III.4.

The reasons for such transfers (which may consist of a reference to any relevant statutory requirement) and the bases on which they are made must be disclosed in the notes to the accounts.

PART 2 – ACCOUNTING PRINCIPLES AND RULES
SECTION A – ACCOUNTING PRINCIPLES

Preliminary

14 The amounts to be included in respect of all items shown in a company's accounts must be determined in accordance with the principles set out in this Section.

15 But if it appears to the company's directors that there are special reasons for departing from any of those principles in preparing the company's accounts in respect of any financial year they may do so, in which case particulars of the departure, the reasons for it and its effect must be given in a note to the accounts.

Accounting principles

16 The company is presumed to be carrying on business as a going concern.

17 Accounting policies and measurement bases must be applied consistently within the same accounts and from one financial year to the next.

History – In para. 17, the words "and measurement bases" inserted by SI 2015/980, reg. 35(2)(a), with effect in relation to–

    (a)   financial years beginning on or after 1 January 2016, and
    (b)   a financial year of a company beginning on or after 1 January 2015, but before 1 January 2016, if the directors of the company so decide.

18 The amount of any item must be determined on a prudent basis, and in particular–

    (a)   subject to note (9) on the profit and loss account format, only profits realised at the balance sheet date are to be included in the profit and loss account
    (b)   all liabilities which have arisen in respect of the financial year to which the accounts relate or a previous financial year must be taken into account, including those which only become apparent between the balance sheet date and the date on which it is signed on behalf of the board of directors in accordance with section 414 of the 2006 Act (approval and signing of accounts) and
    (c)   all provisions for diminution of value must be recognised, whether the result of the financial year is a profit or a loss.

History – Para. 18(c), (and the word "and" preceding it) inserted; the word "and" in para. (a) omitted by SI 2015/980, reg. 35(2)(b), with effect in relation to–

    (a)   financial years beginning on or after 1 January 2016, and
    (b)   a financial year of a company beginning on or after 1 January 2015, but before 1 January 2016, if the directors of the company so decide.

19 All income and charges relating to the financial year to which the accounts relate are to be taken into account, without regard to the date of receipt or payment.

20 In determining the aggregate amount of any item, the amount of each individual asset or liability that falls to be taken into account must be determined separately.

20A The opening balance sheet for each financial year shall correspond to the closing balance sheet for the preceding financial year.

History – Para. 20A inserted by SI 2015/980, reg. 35(2)(c), with effect in relation to–
    (a)   financial years beginning on or after 1 January 2016, and
    (b)   a financial year of a company beginning on or after 1 January 2015, but before 1 January 2016, if the directors of the company so decide.

Valuation

21(1) The amounts to be included in respect of assets of any description mentioned in paragraph 22 (valuation of assets: general) must be determined either–

    (a)   in accordance with that paragraph and paragraph 24 (but subject to paragraphs 27 to 29), or
    (b)   so far as applicable to an asset of that description, in accordance with Section C (valuation at fair value).

21(2) The amounts to be included in respect of assets of any description mentioned in paragraph 24 (alternative valuation of fixed-income securities) may be determined–

    (a)   in accordance with that paragraph (but subject to paragraphs 27 to 29), or
    (b)   so far as applicable to an asset of that description, in accordance with Section C.

21(3) The amounts to be included in respect of assets which–

    (a)   are not assets of a description mentioned in paragraph 22 or 23, but
    (b)   are assets of a description to which Section C is applicable, may be determined in accordance with that Section.

21(4) Subject to sub-paragraphs (1) to (3), the amounts to be included in respect of all items shown in a company's accounts are determined in accordance with Section C.

SECTION B – CURRENT VALUE ACCOUNTING RULES

Valuation of assets: general

22(1) Subject to paragraph 24, investments falling to be included under assets item C (investments) must be included at their current value calculated in accordance with paragraphs 25 and 26.

22(2) Investments falling to be included under assets item D (assets held to cover linked liabilities) must be shown at their current value calculated in accordance with paragraphs 25 and 26.

23(1) Intangible assets other than goodwill may be shown at their current cost.

23(2) Assets falling to be included under assets items F.I (tangible assets) and F.IV (own shares) in the balance sheet format may be shown at their current value calculated in accordance with paragraphs 25 and 26 or at their current cost.

23(3) Assets falling to be included under assets item F.II (stocks) may be shown at current cost.

Alternative valuation of fixed-income securities

24(1) This paragraph applies to debt securities and other fixed-income securities shown as assets under assets items C.II (investments in group undertakings and participating interests) and C.III (other financial investments).

24(2) Securities to which this paragraph applies may either be valued in accordance with paragraph 22 or their amortised value may be shown in the balance sheet, in which case the provisions of this paragraph apply.

24(3) Subject to sub-paragraph (4), where the purchase price of securities to which this paragraph applies exceeds the amount repayable at maturity, the amount of the difference–

    (a)   must be charged to the profit and loss account, and

    (b)   must be shown separately in the balance sheet or in the notes to the accounts.

24(4) The amount of the difference referred to in sub-paragraph (3) may be written off in instalments so that it is completely written off when the securities are repaid, in which case there must be shown separately in the balance sheet or in the notes to the accounts the difference between the purchase price (less the aggregate amount written off) and the amount repayable at maturity.

24(5) Where the purchase price of securities to which this paragraph applies is less than the amount repayable at maturity, the amount of the difference must be released to income in instalments over the period remaining until repayment, in which case there must be shown separately in the balance sheet or in the notes to the accounts the difference between the purchase price (plus the aggregate amount released to income) and the amount repayable at maturity.

24(6) Both the purchase price and the current value of securities valued in accordance with this paragraph must be disclosed in the notes to the accounts.

24(7) Where securities to which this paragraph applies which are not valued in accordance with paragraph 22 are sold before maturity, and the proceeds are used to purchase other securities to which this paragraph applies, the difference between the proceeds of sale and their book value may be spread uniformly over the period remaining until the maturity of the original investment.

Meaning of "current value"

25(1) Subject to sub-paragraph (5), in the case of investments other than land and buildings, **"current value"** means market value determined in accordance with this paragraph.

25(2) In the case of listed investments, **"market value"** means the value on the balance sheet date or, when the balance sheet date is not a stock exchange trading day, on the last stock exchange trading day before that date.

25(3) Where a market exists for unlisted investments, **"market value"** means the average price at which such investments were traded on the balance sheet date or, when the balance sheet date is not a trading day, on the last trading day before that date.

25(4) Where, on the date on which the accounts are drawn up, listed or unlisted investments have been sold or are to be sold within the short term, the market value must be reduced by the actual or estimated realisation costs.

25(5) Except where the equity method of accounting is applied, all investments other than those referred to in sub-paragraphs (2) and (3) must be valued on a basis which has prudent regard to the likely realisable value.

26(1) In the case of land and buildings, **"current value"** means the market value on the date of valuation, where relevant reduced as provided in sub-paragraphs (4) and (5).

26(2) **"Market value"** means the price at which land and buildings could be sold under private contract between a willing seller and an arm's length buyer on the date of valuation, it being assumed that the property is publicly exposed to the market, that market conditions permit orderly disposal and that a normal period, having regard to the nature of the property, is available for the negotiation of the sale.

26(3) The market value must be determined through the separate valuation of each land and buildings item, carried out at least every five years in accordance with generally recognised methods of valuation.

26(4) Where the value of any land and buildings item has diminished since the preceding valuation under sub-paragraph (3), an appropriate value adjustment must be made.

26(5) The lower value arrived at under sub-paragraph (4) must not be increased in subsequent balance sheets unless such increase results from a new determination of market value arrived at in accordance with sub-paragraphs (2) and (3).

26(6) Where, on the date on which the accounts are drawn up, land and buildings have been sold or are to be sold within the short term, the value arrived at in accordance with sub-paragraphs (2) and (4) must be reduced by the actual or estimated realisation costs.

26(7) Where it is impossible to determine the market value of a land and buildings item, the value arrived at on the basis of the principle of purchase price or production cost is deemed to be its current value.

Application of the depreciation rules

27(1) Where–

    (a) the value of any asset of a company is determined in accordance with paragraph 22 or 23, and

    (b) in the case of a determination under paragraph 22, the asset falls to be included under assets item C.I, that value must be, or (as the case may require) must be the starting point for determining, the amount to be included in respect of that asset in the company's accounts, instead of its cost or any value previously so determined for that asset.

Paragraphs 36 to 41 and 43 apply accordingly in relation to any such asset with the substitution for any reference to its cost of a reference to the value most recently determined for that asset in accordance with paragraph 22 or 23 (as the case may be).

27(2) The amount of any provision for depreciation required in the case of any asset by paragraph 37 or 38 as it applies by virtue of sub-paragraph (1) is referred to below in this paragraph as the adjusted amount, and the amount of any provision which would be required by that paragraph in the case of that asset according to the historical cost accounting rules is referred to as the historical cost amount.

27(3) Where sub-paragraph (1) applies in the case of any asset the amount of any provision for depreciation in respect of that asset included in any item shown in the profit and loss account in respect of amounts written off assets of the description in question may be the historical cost amount instead of the adjusted amount, provided that the amount of any difference between the two is shown separately in the profit and loss account or in a note to the accounts.

Additional information to be provided

28(1) This paragraph applies where the amounts to be included in respect of assets covered by any items shown in a company's accounts have been determined in accordance with paragraph 22 or 23.

28(2) The items affected and the basis of valuation adopted in determining the amounts of the assets in question in the case of each such item must be disclosed in a note to the accounts.

28(3) The purchase price of investments valued in accordance with paragraph 22 must be disclosed in the notes to the accounts.

28(4) In the case of each balance sheet item valued in accordance with paragraph 23 either–

(a) the comparable amounts determined according to the historical cost accounting rules (without any provision for depreciation or diminution in value), or

(b) the differences between those amounts and the corresponding amounts actually shown in the balance sheet in respect of that item, must be shown separately in the balance sheet or in a note to the accounts.

28(5) In sub-paragraph (4), references in relation to any item to the comparable amounts determined as there mentioned are references to–

(a) the aggregate amount which would be required to be shown in respect of that item if the amounts to be included in respect of all the assets covered by that item were determined according to the historical cost accounting rules, and

(b) the aggregate amount of the cumulative provisions for depreciation or diminution in value which would be permitted or required in determining those amounts according to those rules.

Revaluation reserve

29(1) Subject to sub-paragraph (7), with respect to any determination of the value of an asset of a company in accordance with paragraph 22 or 23, the amount of any profit or loss arising from that determination (after allowing, where appropriate, for any provisions for depreciation or diminution in value made otherwise than by reference to the value so determined and any adjustments of any such provisions made in the light of that determination) must be credited or (as the case may be) debited to a separate reserve ("the revaluation reserve").

29(2) The amount of the revaluation reserve must be shown in the company's balance sheet under liabilities item A.III, but need not be shown under the name "revaluation reserve".

29(3) An amount may be transferred–

(a) from the revaluation reserve–

(i) to the profit and loss account, if the amount was previously charged to that account or represents realised profit, or

(ii) on capitalisation,

(b) to or from the revaluation reserve in respect of the taxation relating to any profit or loss credited or debited to the reserve.

The revaluation reserve must be reduced to the extent that the amounts transferred to it are no longer necessary for the purposes of the valuation method used.

29(4) In sub-paragraph (3)(a)(ii) **"capitalisation"**, in relation to an amount standing to the credit of the revaluation reserve, means applying it in wholly or partly paying up unissued shares in the company to be allotted to members of the company as fully or partly paid shares.

29(5) The revaluation reserve must not be reduced except as mentioned in this paragraph.

29(6) The treatment for taxation purposes of amounts credited or debited to the revaluation reserve must be disclosed in a note to the accounts.

29(7) This paragraph does not apply to the difference between the valuation of investments and their purchase price or previous valuation shown in the long-term business technical account or the non-technical account in accordance with note (9) on the profit and loss account format.

SECTION C – VALUATION AT FAIR VALUE

Inclusion of financial instruments at fair value

30(1) Subject to sub-paragraphs (2) to (5), financial instruments (including derivatives) may be included at fair value.

30(2) Sub-paragraph (1) does not apply to financial instruments that constitute liabilities unless–

  (a) they are held as part of a trading portfolio,
  (b) they are derivatives, or
  (c) they are financial instruments falling within paragraph (4).

30(3) Except where they fall within paragraph (4), or fall to be included under assets item D (assets held to cover linked liabilities), sub-paragraph (1) does not apply to–

  (a) financial instruments (other than derivatives) held to maturity,
  (b) loans and receivables originated by the company and not held for trading purposes,
  (c) interests in subsidiary undertakings, associated undertakings and joint ventures,
  (d) equity instruments issued by the company,
  (e) contracts for contingent consideration in a business combination, or
  (f) other financial instruments with such special characteristics that the instruments, according to generally accepted accounting principles or practice, should be accounted for differently from other financial instruments.

30(4) Financial instruments which under international accounting standards may be included in accounts at fair value, may be so included, provided that the disclosures required by such accounting standards are made.

30(5) If the fair value of a financial instrument cannot be determined reliably in accordance with paragraph 31, sub-paragraph (1) does not apply to that financial instrument.

30(6) In this paragraph–

"associated undertaking" has the meaning given by paragraph 19 of Schedule 6 to these Regulations; and
"joint venture" has the meaning given by paragraph 18 of that Schedule.

History – Para. 30(4) substituted by SI 2015/980, reg. 35(3)(a), with effect in relation to–

  (a) financial years beginning on or after 1 January 2016, and
  (b) a financial year of a company beginning on or after 1 January 2015, but before 1 January 2016, if the directors of the company so decide.

Former para. 30(4) read as follows:

  "**30(4)** Financial instruments that, under international accounting standards adopted by the European Commission on or before 5th September 2006 in accordance with the IAS Regulation, may be included in accounts at fair value, may be so included, provided that the disclosures required by such accounting standards are made."

Determination of fair value

31(1) The fair value of a financial instrument is its value determined in accordance with this paragraph.

31(2) If a reliable market can readily be identified for the financial instrument, its fair value is determined by reference to its market value.

31(3) If a reliable market cannot readily be identified for the financial instrument but can be identified for its components or for a similar instrument, its fair value is determined by reference to the market value of its components or of the similar instrument.

31(4) If neither sub-paragraph (2) nor (3) applies, the fair value of the financial instrument is a value resulting from generally accepted valuation models and techniques.

31(5) Any valuation models and techniques used for the purposes of sub-paragraph (4) must ensure a reasonable approximation of the market value.

Hedged items

32 A company may include any assets and liabilities, or identified portions of such assets or liabilities, that qualify as hedged items under a fair value hedge accounting system at the amount required under that system.

Other assets that may be included at fair value

33(1) This paragraph applies to—

- (a) investment property, and
- (b) living animals and plants.

33(2) Such investment property and living animals and plants may be included at fair value provided that, as the case may be, all such investment property or living animals and plants are so included where their fair value can be reliably determined.

33(3) In this paragraph, **"fair value"** means fair value determined in accordance with generally accepted accounting principles or practice.

History – Para. 33 substituted by SI 2015/980, reg. 35(3)(b), with effect in relation to–

- (a) financial years beginning on or after 1 January 2016, and
- (b) a financial year of a company beginning on or after 1 January 2015, but before 1 January 2016, if the directors of the company so decide.

Former para. 33 read as follows:

"**33(1)** This paragraph applies to–

- (a) investment property, and
- (b) living animals and plants, that, under international accounting standards, may be included in accounts at fair value.

33(2) Such investment property and such living animals and plants may be included at fair value, provided that all such investment property or, as the case may be, all such living animals and plants are so included where their fair value can reliably be determined.

33(3) In this paragraph, **"fair value"** means fair value determined in accordance with relevant international accounting standards."

Accounting for changes in value

34(1) This paragraph applies where a financial instrument is valued in accordance with paragraph 30 or 32 or an asset is valued in accordance with paragraph 33.

34(2) Notwithstanding paragraph 18 in this Part of this Schedule, and subject to sub-paragraphs (3) and (4), a change in the value of the financial instrument or of the investment property or living animal or plant must be included in the profit and loss account.

34(3) Where—

- (a) the financial instrument accounted for is a hedging instrument under a hedge accounting system that allows some or all of the change in value not to be shown in the profit and loss account, or

(b) the change in value relates to an exchange difference arising on a monetary item that forms part of a company's net investment in a foreign entity, the amount of the change in value must be credited to or (as the case may be) debited from a separate reserve ("the fair value reserve").

34(4) Where the instrument accounted for–

(a) is an available for sale financial asset, and
(b) is not a derivative, the change in value may be credited to or (as the case may be) debited from the fair value reserve.

The fair value reserve

35(1) The fair value reserve must be adjusted to the extent that the amounts shown in it are no longer necessary for the purposes of paragraph 34(3) or (4).

35(2) The treatment for taxation purposes of amounts credited or debited to the fair value reserve must be disclosed in a note to the accounts.

SECTION D – HISTORICAL COST ACCOUNTING RULES

Valuation of assets

General rules

36(1) The rules in this Section are "the historical cost accounting rules".

36(2) Subject to any provision for depreciation or diminution in value made in accordance with paragraph 37 or 38, the amount to be included in respect of any asset in the balance sheet format is its cost.

37 In the case of any asset included under assets item B (intangible assets), C.I (land and buildings), F.I (tangible assets) or F.II (stocks) which has a limited useful economic life, the amount of–

(a) its cost, or
(b) where it is estimated that any such asset will have a residual value at the end of the period of its useful economic life, its cost less that estimated residual value, must be reduced by provisions for depreciation calculated to write off that amount systematically over the period of the asset's useful economic life.

38(1) This paragraph applies to any asset included under assets item B (intangible assets), C (investments), F.I (tangible assets) or F.IV (own shares).

38(2) Where an asset to which this paragraph applies has diminished in value, provisions for diminution in value may be made in respect of it and the amount to be included in respect of it may be reduced accordingly.

38(3) Provisions for diminution in value must be made in respect of any asset to which this paragraph applies if the reduction in its value is expected to be permanent (whether its useful economic life is limited or not), and the amount to be included in respect of it must be reduced accordingly.

38(4) Any provisions made under sub-paragraph (2) or (3) which are not shown in the profit and loss account must be disclosed (either separately or in aggregate) in a note to the accounts.

39(1) Where the reasons for which any provision was made in accordance with paragraph 38 have ceased to apply to any extent, that provision must be written back to the extent that it is no longer necessary.

39(2) Any amounts written back in accordance with sub-paragraph (1) which are not shown in the profit and loss account must be disclosed (either separately or in aggregate) in a note to the accounts.

40(1) This paragraph applies to assets included under assets items E.I, II and III (debtors) and F.III (cash at bank and in hand) in the balance sheet.

40(2) If the net realisable value of an asset to which this paragraph applies is lower than its cost the amount to be included in respect of that asset is the net realisable value.

40(3) Where the reasons for which any provision for diminution in value was made in accordance with sub-paragraph (2) have ceased to apply to any extent, that provision must be written back to the extent that it is no longer necessary.

Intangible assets

41(1) Where this is in accordance with generally accepted accounting principles or practice, development costs may be included under assets item B (intangible assets) in the balance sheet format.

41(2) If any amount is included in a company's balance sheet in respect of development costs, the note on accounting policies (see paragraph 61 of this Schedule) must include the following information–

    (a)   the period over which the amount of those costs originally capitalised is being or is to be written off, and

    (b)   the reasons for capitalising the development costs in question.

History – Para. 41 and the heading preceding it substituted by SI 2015/980, reg. 35(4)(a), with effect in relation to–

    (a)   financial years beginning on or after 1 January 2016, and

    (b)   a financial year of a company beginning on or after 1 January 2015, but before 1 January 2016, if the directors of the company so decide.

Former para. 41 read as follows:

"Development costs

    41(1) Notwithstanding that amounts representing "development costs" may be included under assets item B (intangible assets) in the balance sheet format, an amount may only be included in a company's balance sheet in respect of development costs in special circumstances.

    41(2) If any amount is included in a company's balance sheet in respect of development costs the following information must be given in a note to the accounts–

    (a)   the period over which the amount of those costs originally capitalised is being or is to be written off, and

    (b)   the reasons for capitalising the development costs in question."

Goodwill

42(1) Intangible assets must be written off over the useful economic life of the intangible asset.

42(2) Where in exceptional cases the useful life of intangible assets cannot be reliably estimated, such assets must be written off over a period chosen by the directors of the company.

42(3) The period referred to in sub-paragraph (2) must not exceed ten years.

42(4) There must be disclosed in a note to the accounts the period referred to in sub-paragraph (2) and the reasons for choosing that period.

History – Para. 42 substituted by SI 2015/980, reg. 35(4)(a), with effect in relation to–

    (a)   financial years beginning on or after 1 January 2016, and

    (b)   a financial year of a company beginning on or after 1 January 2015, but before 1 January 2016, if the directors of the company so decide.

Former para. 42 read as follows:

"**42(1)** The application of paragraphs 36 to 39 in relation to goodwill (in any case where goodwill is treated as an asset) is subject to the following.

42(2) Subject to sub-paragraph (3), the amount of the consideration for any goodwill acquired by a company must be reduced by provisions for depreciation calculated to write off that amount systematically over a period chosen by the directors of the company.

42(3) The period chosen must not exceed the useful economic life of the goodwill in question.

42(4) In any case where any goodwill acquired by a company is included as an asset in the company's balance sheet, there must be disclosed in a note to the accounts–

    (a)   the period chosen for writing off the consideration for that goodwill, and

    (b)   the reasons for choosing that period."

Miscellaneous and supplementary provisions

Excess of money owed over value received as an asset item

43(1) Where the amount repayable on any debt owed by a company is greater than the value of the consideration received in the transaction giving rise to the debt, the amount of the difference may be treated as an asset.

43(2) Where any such amount is so treated–

    (a)   it must be written off by reasonable amounts each year and must be completely written off before repayment of the debt, and

    (b)   if the current amount is not shown as a separate item in the company's balance sheet, it must be disclosed in a note to the accounts.

Assets included at a fixed amount

44(1) Subject to sub-paragraph (2), assets which fall to be included under assets item F.I (tangible assets) in the balance sheet format may be included at a fixed quantity and value.

44(2) Sub-paragraph (1) applies to assets of a kind which are constantly being replaced where–

    (a)   their overall value is not material to assessing the company's state of affairs, and

    (b)   their quantity, value and composition are not subject to material variation.

Determination of cost

45(1) The cost of an asset that has been acquired by the company is to be determined by adding to the actual price paid any expenses incidental to its acquisition and then subtracting any incidental reductions in the cost of acquisition.

45(2) The cost of an asset constructed by the company is to be determined by adding to the purchase price of the raw materials and consumables used the amount of the costs incurred by the company which are directly attributable to the construction of that asset.

45(3) In addition, there may be included in the cost of an asset constructed by the company–

    (a)   a reasonable proportion of the costs incurred by the company which are only indirectly attributable to the construction of that asset, but only to the extent that they relate to the period of construction, and

(b)   interest on capital borrowed to finance the construction of that asset, to the extent that it accrues in respect of the period of construction, provided, however, in a case within paragraph (b), that the inclusion of the interest in determining the cost of that asset and the amount of the interest so included is disclosed in a note to the accounts.

History – In para. 45(1), the words "and then subtracting any incidental reductions in the cost of acquisition" inserted by SI 2015/980, reg. 35(4)(b), with effect in relation to–

(a)   financial years beginning on or after 1 January 2016, and

(b)   a financial year of a company beginning on or after 1 January 2015, but before 1 January 2016, if the directors of the company so decide.

46(1) The cost of any assets which are fungible assets may be determined by the application of any of the methods mentioned in sub-paragraph (2) in relation to any such assets of the same class, provided that the method chosen is one which appears to the directors to be appropriate in the circumstances of the company.

46(2) Those methods are–

(a)   the method known as "first in, first out" (FIFO),

(b)   the method known as "last in, first out" (LIFO),

(c)   a weighted average price, and

(d)   any other method reflecting generally accepted best practice.

46(3) Where in the case of any company–

(a)   the cost of assets falling to be included under any item shown in the company's balance sheet has been determined by the application of any method permitted by this paragraph, and

(b)   the amount shown in respect of that item differs materially from the relevant alternative amount given below in this paragraph, the amount of that difference must be disclosed in a note to the accounts.

46(4) Subject to sub-paragraph (5), for the purposes of sub-paragraph (3)(b), the relevant alternative amount, in relation to any item shown in a company's balance sheet, is the amount which would have been shown in respect of that item if assets of any class included under that item at an amount determined by any method permitted by this paragraph had instead been included at their replacement cost as at the balance sheet date.

46(5) The relevant alternative amount may be determined by reference to the most recent actual purchase price before the balance sheet date of assets of any class included under the item in question instead of by reference to their replacement cost as at that date, but only if the former appears to the directors of the company to constitute the more appropriate standard of comparison in the case of assets of that class.

History – In para. 46(2)(d), the words "reflecting generally accepted best practice" substituted for the words "similar to any of the methods mentioned above" by SI 2015/980, reg. 35(4)(c), with effect in relation to–

(a)   financial years beginning on or after 1 January 2016, and

(b)   a financial year of a company beginning on or after 1 January 2015, but before 1 January 2016, if the directors of the company so decide.

Substitution of original amount where price or cost unknown

47(1) This paragraph applies where–

(a)   there is no record of the purchase price of any asset acquired by a company or of any price, expenses or costs relevant for determining its cost in accordance with paragraph 45, or

(b)   any such record cannot be obtained without unreasonable expense or delay.

47(2) In such a case, the cost of the asset must be taken, for the purposes of paragraphs 36 to 42, to be the value ascribed to it in the earliest available record of its value made on or after its acquisition by the company.

SECTION E – RULES FOR DETERMINING PROVISIONS

Preliminary

48 Provisions which are to be shown in a company's accounts are to be determined in accordance with this Section.

Technical provisions

49 The amount of technical provisions must at all times be sufficient to cover any liabilities arising out of insurance contracts as far as can reasonably be foreseen.

Provision for unearned premiums

50(1) The provision for unearned premiums must in principle be computed separately for each insurance contract, save that statistical methods (and in particular proportional and flat rate methods) may be used where they may be expected to give approximately the same results as individual calculations.

50(2) Where the pattern of risk varies over the life of a contract, this must be taken into account in the calculation methods.

Provision for unexpired risks

51 The provision for unexpired risks (as defined in paragraph 91) must be computed on the basis of claims and administrative expenses likely to arise after the end of the financial year from contracts concluded before that date, in so far as their estimated value exceeds the provision for unearned premiums and any premiums receivable under those contracts.

Long-term business provision

52(1) The long-term business provision must in principle be computed separately for each long-term contract, save that statistical or mathematical methods may be used where they may be expected to give approximately the same results as individual calculations.

52(2) A summary of the principal assumptions in making the provision under sub-paragraph (1) must be given in the notes to the accounts.

52(3) The computation must be made annually by a Fellow of the Institute or Faculty of Actuaries on the basis of recognised actuarial methods, with due regard to the actuarial principles laid down in Directive 2002/83/EC of the European Parliament and of the Council of 5th November 2002 concerning life assurance.

Prospective amendments – In para. 52(3), the words "Directive 2009/138/EC of the European Parliament and of the Council of 25 November 2009 on the taking-up and pursuit of the business of Insurance and Reinsurance (Solvency II)" substituted for the words "Directive 2002/83/EC of the European Parliament and of the Council of 5th November 2002 concerning life assurance" by SI 2015/575, Sch. 2, para. 26, with effect from 1 January 2016.

Provisions for claims outstanding

General business

53(1) A provision must in principle be computed separately for each claim on the basis of the costs still expected to arise, save that statistical methods may be used if they result in an adequate provision having regard to the nature of the risks.

53(2) This provision must also allow for claims incurred but not reported by the balance sheet date, the amount of the allowance being determined having regard to past experience as to the number and magnitude of claims reported after previous balance sheet dates.

53(3) All claims settlement costs (whether direct or indirect) must be included in the calculation of the provision.

53(4) Recoverable amounts arising out of subrogation or salvage must be estimated on a prudent basis and either deducted from the provision for claims outstanding (in which case if the amounts are material they must be shown in the notes to the accounts) or shown as assets.

53(5) In sub-paragraph (4), **"subrogation"** means the acquisition of the rights of policy holders with respect to third parties, and **"salvage"** means the acquisition of the legal ownership of insured property.

53(6) Where benefits resulting from a claim must be paid in the form of annuity, the amounts to be set aside for that purpose must be calculated by recognised actuarial methods, and paragraph 54 does not apply to such calculations.

53(7) Implicit discounting or deductions, whether resulting from the placing of a current value on a provision for an outstanding claim which is expected to be settled later at a higher figure or otherwise effected, is prohibited.

54(1) Explicit discounting or deductions to take account of investment income is permitted, subject to the following conditions–

  (a) the expected average interval between the date for the settlement of claims being discounted and the accounting date must be at least four years;
  (b) the discounting or deductions must be effected on a recognised prudential basis;
  (c) when calculating the total cost of settling claims, the company must take account of all factors that could cause increases in that cost;
  (d) the company must have adequate data at its disposal to construct a reliable model of the rate of claims settlements;
  (e) the rate of interest used for the calculation of present values must not exceed a rate prudently estimated to be earned by assets of the company which are appropriate in magnitude and nature to cover the provisions for claims being discounted during the period necessary for the payment of such claims, and must not exceed either–

    (i) a rate justified by the performance of such assets over the preceding five years, or
    (ii) a rate justified by the performance of such assets during the year preceding the balance sheet date.

54(2) When discounting or effecting deductions, the company must, in the notes to the accounts, disclose–

  (a) the total amount of provisions before discounting or deductions,
  (b) the categories of claims which are discounted or from which deductions have been made,
  (c) for each category of claims, the methods used, in particular the rates used for the estimates referred to in sub-paragraph (1)(d) and (e), and the criteria adopted for estimating the period that will elapse before the claims are settled.

Long-term business

55 The amount of the provision for claims must be equal to the sums due to beneficiaries, plus the costs of settling claims.

Equalisation reserves

56 The amount of any equalisation reserve maintained in respect of general business by the company, in accordance with the rules made by the Financial Conduct Authority or the Prudential Regulation Authority under Part 10 of the Financial Services and Markets Act 2000, must be determined in accordance with such rules.

History – The words "made by the Financial Conduct Authority or the Prudential Regulation Authority" substituted for "in section 1.4 of the Prudential Sourcebook for Insurers made by the Financial Services Authority" by SI 2013/472, Sch. 2, para. 135(b), with effect from 1 April 2013.

Accounting on a non-annual basis

57(1) Either of the methods described in paragraphs 58 and 59 may be applied where, because of the nature of the class or type of insurance in question, information about premiums receivable or claims payable (or both) for the underwriting years is insufficient when the accounts are drawn up for reliable estimates to be made.

57(2) The use of either of the methods referred to in sub-paragraph (1) must be disclosed in the notes to the accounts together with the reasons for adopting it.

57(3) Where one of the methods referred to in sub-paragraph (1) is adopted, it must be applied systematically in successive years unless circumstances justify a change.

57(4) In the event of a change in the method applied, the effect on the assets, liabilities, financial position and profit or loss must be stated in the notes to the accounts.

57(5) For the purposes of this paragraph and paragraph 58, **"underwriting year"** means the financial year in which the insurance contracts in the class or type of insurance in question commenced.

58(1) The excess of the premiums written over the claims and expenses paid in respect of contracts commencing in the underwriting year shall form a technical provision included in the technical provision for claims outstanding shown in the balance sheet under liabilities item C.3.

58(2) The provision may also be computed on the basis of a given percentage of the premiums written where such a method is appropriate for the type of risk insured.

58(3) If necessary, the amount of this technical provision must be increased to make it sufficient to meet present and future obligations.

58(4) The technical provision constituted under this paragraph must be replaced by a provision for claims outstanding estimated in accordance with paragraph 53 as soon as sufficient information has been gathered and not later than the end of the third year following the underwriting year.

58(5) The length of time that elapses before a provision for claims outstanding is constituted in accordance with sub-paragraph (4) must be disclosed in the notes to the accounts.

59(1) The figures shown in the technical account or in certain items within it must relate to a year which wholly or partly precedes the financial year (but by no more than 12 months).

59(2) The amounts of the technical provisions shown in the accounts must if necessary be increased to make them sufficient to meet present and future obligations.

59(3) The length of time by which the earlier year to which the figures relate precedes the financial year and the magnitude of the transactions concerned must be disclosed in the notes to the accounts.

PART 3 – NOTES TO THE ACCOUNTS

Preliminary

60(1) Any information required in the case of a company by the following provisions of this Part of this Schedule must be given by way of a note to the accounts.

60(2) These notes must be presented in the order in which, where relevant, the items to which they relate are presented in the balance sheet and in the profit and loss account.

History – Para. 60 substituted by SI 2015/980, reg. 36(2), with effect in relation to–

    (a)   financial years beginning on or after 1 January 2016, and

    (b)   a financial year of a company beginning on or after 1 January 2015, but before 1 January 2016, if the directors of the company so decide.

Former para. 60 read as follows:

"**60** Any information required in the case of any company by the following provisions of this Part of this Schedule must (if not given in the company's accounts) be given by way of a note to the accounts."

General

Disclosure of accounting policies

61 The accounting policies adopted by the company in determining the amounts to be included in respect of items shown in the balance sheet and in determining the profit or loss of the company must be stated (including such policies with respect to the depreciation and diminution in value of assets).

62 It must be stated whether the accounts have been prepared in accordance with applicable accounting standards and particulars of any material departure from those standards and the reasons for it must be given.

Sums denominated in foreign currencies

63 Where any sums originally denominated in foreign currencies have been brought into account under any items shown in the balance sheet or profit and loss account format, the basis on which those sums have been translated into sterling (or the currency in which the accounts are drawn up) must be stated.

Reserves and dividends

64 There must be stated–

    (a)   any amount set aside or proposed to be set aside to, or withdrawn or proposed to be withdrawn from, reserves,

    (b)   the aggregate amount of dividends paid in the financial year (other than those for which a liability existed at the immediately preceding balance sheet date),

    (c)   the aggregate amount of dividends that the company is liable to pay at the balance sheet date, and

    (d)   the aggregate amount of dividends that are proposed before the date of approval of the accounts, and not otherwise disclosed under sub-paragraph (b) or (c).

Information supplementing the balance sheet

Share capital and debentures

65(1) Where shares of more than one class have been allotted, the number and aggregate nominal value of shares of each class allotted must be given.

65(2) In the case of any part of the allotted share capital that consists of redeemable shares, the following information must be given–

    (a)   the earliest and latest dates on which the company has power to redeem those shares,

    (b)   whether those shares must be redeemed in any event or are liable to be redeemed at the option of the company or of the shareholder, and

    (c)   whether any (and, if so, what) premium is payable on redemption.

66 If the company has allotted any shares during the financial year, the following information must be given–

    (a)   the classes of shares allotted, and

    (b)   as respects each class of shares, the number allotted, their aggregate nominal value and the consideration received by the company for the allotment.

67(1) With respect to any contingent right to the allotment of shares in the company the following particulars must be given–

    (a)   the number, description and amount of the shares in relation to which the right is exercisable,

    (b)   the period during which it is exercisable, and

    (c)   the price to be paid for the shares allotted.

67(2) In sub-paragraph (1) **"contingent right to the allotment of shares"** means any option to subscribe for shares and any other right to require the allotment of shares to any person whether arising on the conversion into shares of securities of any other description or otherwise.

68(1) If the company has issued any debentures during the financial year to which the accounts relate, the following information must be given–

    (a)   the classes of debentures issued, and

    (b)   as respects each class of debentures, the amount issued and the consideration received by the company for the issue.

68(2) Where any of the company's debentures are held by a nominee of or trustee for the company, the nominal amount of the debentures and the amount at which they are stated in the accounting records kept by the company in accordance with section 386 of the 2006 Act (duty to keep accounting records) must be stated.

Assets

69(1) In respect of any assets of the company included in assets items B (intangible assets), C.I (land and buildings) and C.II (investments in group undertakings and participating interests) in the company's balance sheet the following information must be given by reference to each such item–

    (a)   the appropriate amounts in respect of those assets included in the item as at the date of the beginning of the financial year and as at the balance sheet date respectively,

    (b)   the effect on any amount included in assets item B in respect of those assets of–

        (i)   any determination during that year of the value to be ascribed to any of those assets in accordance with paragraph 23,

(ii)   acquisitions during that year of any assets,

(iii)   disposals during that year of any assets, and

(iv)   any transfers of assets of the company to and from the item during that year.

69(2) The reference in sub-paragraph (1)(a) to the appropriate amounts in respect of any assets (included in an assets item) as at any date there mentioned is a reference to amounts representing the aggregate amounts determined, as at that date, in respect of assets falling to be included under the item on either of the following bases–

(a)   on the basis of cost (determined in accordance with paragraphs 45 and 46), or

(b)   on any basis permitted by paragraph 22 or 23, (leaving out of account in either case any provisions for depreciation or diminution in value).

69(3) In addition, in respect of any assets of the company included in any assets item in the company's balance sheet, there must be stated (by reference to each such item)–

(a)   the cumulative amount of provisions for depreciation or diminution in value of those assets included under the item as at each date mentioned in sub-paragraph (1)(a),

(b)   the amount of any such provisions made in respect of the financial year,

(c)   the amount of any adjustments made in respect of any such provisions during that year in consequence of the disposal of any of those assets, and

(d)   the amount of any other adjustments made in respect of any such provisions during that year.

70 Where any assets of the company (other than listed investments) are included under any item shown in the company's balance sheet at an amount determined on any basis mentioned in paragraph 22 or 23, the following information must be given–

(a)   the years (so far as they are known to the directors) in which the assets were severally valued and the several values, and

(b)   in the case of assets that have been valued during the financial year, the names of the persons who valued them or particulars of their qualifications for doing so and (whichever is stated) the bases of valuation used by them.

71 In relation to any amount which is included under assets item C.I (land and buildings) there must be stated–

(a)   how much of that amount is ascribable to land of freehold tenure and how much to land of leasehold tenure, and

(b)   how much of the amount ascribable to land of leasehold tenure is ascribable to land held on long lease and how much to land held on short lease.

Investments

72 In respect of the amount of each item which is shown in the company's balance sheet under assets item C (investments) there must be stated how much of that amount is ascribable to listed investments.

Information about fair value of assets and liabilities

73(1) This paragraph applies where financial instruments or other assets have been valued in accordance with, as appropriate, paragraph 30, 32 or 33.

73(2) There must be stated–

(a)   the significant assumptions underlying the valuation models and techniques used to determine the fair value of the financial instruments or other assets,

(b)   in the case of financial instruments, their purchase price, the items affected and the basis of valuation,

(c) for each category of financial instrument or other asset, the fair value of the assets in that category and the changes in value–

    (i) included directly in the profit and loss account, or

    (ii) credited to or (as the case may be) debited from the fair value reserve, in respect of those assets, and

(c) for each class of derivatives, the extent and nature of the instruments, including significant terms and conditions that may affect the amount, timing and certainty of future cash flows.

73(3) Where any amount is transferred to or from the fair value reserve during the financial year, there must be stated in tabular form–

(a) the amount of the reserve as at the date of the beginning of the financial year and as at the balance sheet date respectively,

(b) the amount transferred to or from the reserve during the year, and

(c) the source and application respectively of the amounts so transferred.

History – Para. 73 substituted by SI 2015/980, reg. 36(3), with effect in relation to–

    (a) financial years beginning on or after 1 January 2016, and

    (b) a financial year of a company beginning on or after 1 January 2015, but before 1 January 2016, if the directors of the company so decide.

Former para. 73 read as follows:

"**73(1)** This paragraph applies where financial instruments have been valued in accordance with paragraph 30 or 32.

73(2) The items affected and the basis of valuation adopted in determining the amounts of the financial instruments must be disclosed.

73(3) The purchase price of the financial instruments must be disclosed.

73(4) There must be stated–

    (a) the significant assumptions underlying the valuation models and techniques used, where the fair value of the instruments has been determined in accordance with paragraph 31(4),

    (b) for each category of financial instrument, the fair value of the instruments in that category and the changes in value–

        (i) included in the profit and loss account, or

        (ii) credited to or (as the case may be) debited from the fair value reserve, in respect of those instruments, and

    (c) for each class of derivatives, the extent and nature of the instruments, including significant terms and conditions that may affect the amount, timing and certainty of future cash flows.

73(5) Where any amount is transferred to or from the fair value reserve during the financial year, there must be stated in tabular form–

    (a) the amount of the reserve as at the date of the beginning of the financial year and as at the balance sheet date respectively,

    (b) the amount transferred to or from the reserve during that year, and

    (c) the source and application respectively of the amounts so transferred."

74 Where the company has derivatives that it has not included at fair value, there must be stated for each class of such derivatives–

(a) the fair value of the derivatives in that class, if such a value can be determined in accordance with paragraph 31, and

(b) the extent and nature of the derivatives.

75(1) This paragraph applies if–

(a) the company has financial fixed assets that could be included at fair value by virtue of paragraph 30,

(b) the amount at which those assets are included under any item in the company's accounts is in excess of their fair value, and

    (c)   the company has not made provision for diminution in value of those assets in accordance with paragraph 38(2) of this Schedule.

75(2) There must be stated–

    (a)   the amount at which either the individual assets or appropriate groupings of those individual assets are included in the company's accounts,

    (b)   the fair value of those assets or groupings, and

    (c)   the reasons for not making a provision for diminution in value of those assets, including the nature of the evidence that provides the basis for the belief that the amount at which they are stated in the accounts will be recovered.

Information where investment property and living animals and plants included at fair value

76(1) This paragraph applies where the amounts to be included in a company's accounts in respect of investment property or living animals and plants have been determined in accordance with paragraph 33.

76(2) The balance sheet items affected and the basis of valuation adopted in determining the amounts of the assets in question in the case of each such item must be disclosed in a note to the accounts.

76(3) In the case of investment property, for each balance sheet item affected there must be shown, either separately in the balance sheet or in a note to the accounts–

    (a)   the comparable amounts determined according to the historical cost accounting rules, or

    (b)   the differences between those amounts and the corresponding amounts actually shown in the balance sheet in respect of that item.

76(4) In sub-paragraph (3), references in relation to any item to the comparable amounts determined in accordance with that sub-paragraph are to–

    (a)   the aggregate amount which would be required to be shown in respect of that item if the amounts to be included in respect of all the assets covered by that item were determined according to the historical cost accounting rules, and

    (b)   the aggregate amount of the cumulative provisions for depreciation or diminution in value which would be permitted or required in determining those amounts according to those rules.

Reserves and provisions

77(1) This paragraph applies where any amount is transferred–

    (a)   to or from any reserves,

    (b)   to any provisions for other risks, or

    (c)   from any provisions for other risks otherwise than for the purpose for which the provision was established, and the reserves or provisions are or would but for paragraph 3(1) be shown as separate items in the company's balance sheet.

77(2) The following information must be given in respect of the aggregate of reserves or provisions included in the same item–

    (a)   the amount of the reserves or provisions as at the date of the beginning of the financial year and as at the balance sheet date respectively,

    (b)   any amounts transferred to or from the reserves or provisions during that year, and

    (c)   the source and application respectively of any amounts so transferred.

77(3) Particulars must be given of each provision included in liabilities item E.3 (other provisions) in the company's balance sheet in any case where the amount of that provision is material.

Provision for taxation

78 The amount of any provision for deferred taxation must be stated separately from the amount of any provision for other taxation.

Details of indebtedness

79(1) In respect of each item shown under "creditors" in the company's balance sheet there must be stated the aggregate of the following amounts—

    (a) the amount of any debts included under that item which are payable or repayable otherwise than by instalments and fall due for payment or repayment after the end of the period of five years beginning with the day next following the end of the financial year, and

    (b) in the case of any debts so included which are payable or repayable by instalments, the amount of any instalments which fall due for payment after the end of that period.

79(2) Subject to sub-paragraph (3), in relation to each debt falling to be taken into account under sub-paragraph (1), the terms of payment or repayment and the rate of any interest payable on the debt must be stated.

79(3) If the number of debts is such that, in the opinion of the directors, compliance with subparagraph (2) would result in a statement of excessive length, it is sufficient to give a general indication of the terms of payment or repayment and the rates of any interest payable on the debts.

79(4) In respect of each item shown under "creditors" in the company's balance sheet there must be stated—

    (a) the aggregate amount of any debts included under that item in respect of which any security has been given by the company, and

    (b) an indication of the nature of the securities so given.

79(5) References above in this paragraph to an item shown under "creditors" in the company's balance sheet include references, where amounts falling due to creditors within one year and after more than one year are distinguished in the balance sheet—

    (a) in a case within sub-paragraph (1), to an item shown under the latter of those categories, and

    (b) in a case within sub-paragraph (4), to an item shown under either of those categories. References to items shown under "creditors" include references to items which would but for paragraph 3(1)(b) be shown under that heading.

80 If any fixed cumulative dividends on the company's shares are in arrear, there must be stated—

    (a) the amount of the arrears, and

    (b) the period for which the dividends or, if there is more than one class, each class of them are in arrear.

Guarantees and other financial commitments

81(1) Particulars must be given of any charge on the assets of the company to secure the liabilities of any other person including the amount secured.

81(2) Particulars and the total amount of any financial commitments, guarantees and contingencies (excluding those which arise out of insurance contracts) that are not included in the balance sheet must be disclosed.

81(3) An indication of the nature and form of any valuable security given by the company in respect of commitments, guarantees and contingencies within sub-paragraph (2) must be given.

81(4) The total amount of any commitments within sub-paragraph (2) concerning pensions must be separately disclosed.

81(5) Particulars must be given of pension commitments which are included in the balance sheet.

81(6) Where any commitment within sub-paragraph (4) or (5) relates wholly or partly to pensions payable to past directors of the company separate particulars must be given of that commitment.

81(7) The total amount of any commitments, guarantees and contingencies within sub-paragraph (2) which are undertaken on behalf of or for the benefit of–

    (a)   any parent undertaking or fellow subsidiary undertaking of the company,
    (b)   any subsidiary undertaking of the company, or
    (c)   any undertaking in which the company has a participating interest

must be separately stated and those within each of paragraphs (a), (b) and (c) must also be stated separately from those within any other of those paragraphs.

History – Para. 81 substituted by SI 2015/980, reg. 36(4), with effect in relation to–

    (a)   financial years beginning on or after 1 January 2016, and

    (b)   a financial year of a company beginning on or after 1 January 2015, but before 1 January 2016, if the directors of the company so decide.

Former para. 81 read as follows:

"**81(1)** Particulars must be given of any charge on the assets of the company to secure the liabilities of any other person, including, where practicable, the amount secured.

81(2) The following information must be given with respect to any other contingent liability not provided for (other than a contingent liability arising out of an insurance contract)–

    (a)   the amount or estimated amount of that liability,
    (b)   its legal nature, and
    (c)   whether any valuable security has been provided by the company in connection with that liability and if so, what.

81(3) There must be stated, where practicable, the aggregate amount or estimated amount of contracts for capital expenditure, so far as not provided for.

81(4) Particulars must be given of–

    (a)   any pension commitments included under any provision shown in the company's balance sheet, and
    (b)   any such commitments for which no provision has been made, and where any such commitment relates wholly or partly to pensions payable to past directors of the company separate particulars must be given of that commitment so far as it relates to such pensions.

81(5) Particulars must also be given of any other financial commitments, other than commitments arising out of insurance contracts, that–

    (a)   have not been provided for, and
    (b)   are relevant to assessing the company's state of affairs.

81(6) Commitments within any of the preceding sub-paragraphs undertaken on behalf of or for the benefit of–

    (a)   any parent undertaking or fellow subsidiary undertaking, or
    (b)   any subsidiary undertaking of the company, must be stated separately from the other commitments within that sub-paragraph, and commitments within paragraph
    (a)   must also be stated separately from those within paragraph (b)."

Miscellaneous matters

82(1) Particulars must be given of any case where the cost of any asset is for the first time determined under paragraph 47.

82(2) Where any outstanding loans made under the authority of section 682(2)(b)), (c) or (d) of the 2006 Act (various cases of financial assistance by a company for purchase of its own shares) are included under any item shown in the company's balance sheet, the aggregate amount of those loans must be disclosed for each item in question.

Information supplementing the profit and loss account

Separate statement of certain items of income and expenditure

83(1) Subject to sub-paragraph (2), there must be stated the amount of the interest on or any similar charges in respect of–

(a) bank loans and overdrafts, and
(b) loans of any other kind made to the company.

83(2) Sub-paragraph (1) does not apply to interest or charges on loans to the company from group undertakings, but, with that exception, it applies to interest or charges on all loans, whether made on the security of debentures or not.

Particulars of tax

84(1) Particulars must be given of any special circumstances which affect liability in respect of taxation of profits, income or capital gains for the financial year or liability in respect of taxation of profits, income or capital gains for succeeding financial years.

84(2) The following amounts must be stated–

(a) the amount of the charge for United Kingdom corporation tax,
(b) if that amount would have been greater but for relief from double taxation, the amount which it would have been but for such relief,
(c) the amount of the charge for United Kingdom income tax, and
(d) the amount of the charge for taxation imposed outside the United Kingdom of profits, income and (so far as charged to revenue) capital gains.

Those amounts must be stated separately in respect of each of the amounts which is shown under the following items in the profit and loss account, that is to say item III.9 (tax on profit or loss on ordinary activities) and item III.14 (tax on extraordinary profit or loss).

Particulars of business

85(1) As regards general business a company must disclose–

(a) gross premiums written,
(b) gross premiums earned,
(c) gross claims incurred,
(d) gross operating expenses, and
(e) the reinsurance balance.

85(2) The amounts required to be disclosed by sub-paragraph (1) must be broken down between direct insurance and reinsurance acceptances, if reinsurance acceptances amount to 10 per cent or more of gross premiums written.

85(3) Subject to sub-paragraph (4), the amounts required to be disclosed by sub-paragraphs (1) and (2) with respect to direct insurance must be further broken down into the following groups of classes–

(a) accident and health,
(b) motor (third party liability),
(c) motor (other classes),
(d) marine, aviation and transport,
(e) fire and other damage to property,
(f) third-party liability,
(g) credit and suretyship,
(h) legal expenses,
(i) assistance, and
(j) miscellaneous, where the amount of the gross premiums written in direct insurance for each such group exceeds 10 million Euros.

85(4) The company must in any event disclose the amounts relating to the three largest groups of classes in its business.

86(1) As regards long-term business, the company must disclose–

(a) gross premiums written, and
(b) the reinsurance balance.

86(2) Subject to sub-paragraph (3)–

(a) gross premiums written must be broken down between those written by way of direct insurance and those written by way of reinsurance, and
(b) gross premiums written by way of direct insurance must be broken down–

    (i) between individual premiums and premiums under group contracts,
    (ii) between periodic premiums and single premiums, and
    (iii) between premiums from non-participating contracts, premiums from participating contracts and premiums from contracts where the investment risk is borne by policyholders.

86(3) Disclosure of any amount referred to in sub-paragraph (2)(a) or (2)(b)(i), (ii) or (iii) is not required if it does not exceed 10 per cent of the gross premiums written or (as the case may be) of the gross premiums written by way of direct insurance.

87(1) Subject to sub-paragraph (2), there must be disclosed as regards both general and long-term business the total gross direct insurance premiums resulting from contracts concluded by the company–

(a) in the member State of its head office,
(b) in the other member States, and
(c) in other countries.

87(2) Disclosure of any amount referred to in sub-paragraph (1) is not required if it does not exceed 5 per cent of total gross premiums.

Commissions

88 There must be disclosed the total amount of commissions for direct insurance business accounted for in the financial year, including acquisition, renewal, collection and portfolio management commissions.

Miscellaneous matters

89(1) Where any amount relating to any preceding financial year is included in any item in the profit and loss account, the effect must be stated.

89(2) The amount, nature and effect of any individual items of income or expenditure which are of exceptional size or incidence must be stated.

History – Para. 89(2) substituted for para. 89(2) and (3) by SI 2015/980, reg. 36(5), with effect in relation to–
   (a)   financial years beginning on or after 1 January 2016, and
   (b)   a financial year of a company beginning on or after 1 January 2015, but before 1 January 2016, if the directors of the company so decide.

Related party transactions

90(1) Particulars may be given of transactions which the company has entered into with related parties, and must be given if such transactions are material and have not been concluded under normal market conditions.

90(2) The particulars of transactions required to be disclosed by sub-paragraph (1) must include–
   (a)   the amount of such transactions,
   (b)   the nature of the related party relationship, and
   (c)   other information about the transactions necessary for an understanding of the financial position of the company.

90(3) Information about individual transactions may be aggregated according to their nature, except where separate information is necessary for an understanding of the effects of related party transactions on the financial position of the company.

90(4) Particulars need not be given of transactions entered into between two or more members of a group, provided that any subsidiary undertaking which is a party to the transaction is whollyowned by such a member.

90(5) In this paragraph, **"related party"** has the same meaning as in international accounting standards.

Post balance sheet events

90A The nature and financial effect of material events arising after the balance sheet date which are not reflected in the profit and loss account of balance sheet must be stated.

History – Para. 90A and the heading preceding it inserted by SI 2015/980, reg. 36(6), with effect in relation to–
   (a)   financial years beginning on or after 1 January 2016, and
   (b)   a financial year of a company beginning on or after 1 January 2015, but before 1 January 2016, if the directors of the company so decide.

Appropriations

90B Particulars must be given of the proposed appropriation of profit or treatment of loss or, where applicable, particulars of the actual appropriation of the profits or treatment of the losses.

History – Para. 90B and the heading preceding it inserted by SI 2015/980, reg. 36(6), with effect in relation to–
   (a)   financial years beginning on or after 1 January 2016, and
   (b)   a financial year of a company beginning on or after 1 January 2015, but before 1 January 2016, if the directors of the company so decide.

PART 4 – INTERPRETATION OF THIS SCHEDULE

Definitions for this schedule

91 The following definitions apply for the purposes of this Schedule and its interpretation–

"general business" means business which consists of effecting or carrying out contracts of general insurance;

"long-term business" means business which consists of effecting or carrying out contracts of long-term insurance;

"long-term fund" means the fund or funds maintained by a company in respect of its long-term business in accordance with rules made by the Financial Conduct Authority or the Prudential Regulation Authority under Part 10 of the Financial Services and Markets Act 2000;

"policyholder" has the meaning given by article 3 of the Financial Services and Markets Act 2000 (Meaning of "Policy" and "Policyholder") Order 2001;

"provision for unexpired risks" means the amount set aside in addition to unearned premiums in respect of risks to be borne by the company after the end of the financial year, in order to provide for all claims and expenses in connection with insurance contracts in force in excess of the related unearned premiums and any premiums receivable on those contracts.

History – In the definition of "long-term fund", "rules made by the Financial Conduct Authority or the Prudential Regulation Authority" substituted for "rule 1.5.22 in the Prudential Sourcebook for Insurers made by the Financial Services Authority" by SI 2013/472, Sch. 2, para. 135(c), with effect from 1 April 2013.

SCHEDULE 4

Regulation 7

INFORMATION ON RELATED UNDERTAKINGS REQUIRED WHETHER PREPARING COMPANIES ACT OR IAS ACCOUNTS
PART 1 – PROVISIONS APPLYING TO ALL COMPANIES

Subsidiary undertakings

1(1) The following information must be given where at the end of the financial year the company has subsidiary undertakings.

1(2) The name of each subsidiary undertaking must be stated.

1(3) There must be stated with respect to each subsidiary undertaking–

(a) the address of the undertaking's registered office (whether in or outside the United Kingdom),

(b) if it is unincorporated, the address of its principal place of business.

History – Para. 1(3)(a) substituted by SI 2015/980, reg. 37(2), with effect in relation to–

(a) financial years beginning on or after 1 January 2016, and

(b) a financial year of a company beginning on or after 1 January 2015, but before 1 January 2016, if the directors of the company so decide.

Financial information about subsidiary undertakings

2(1) There must be disclosed with respect to each subsidiary undertaking not included in consolidated accounts by the company–

(a) the aggregate amount of its capital and reserves as at the end of its relevant financial year, and

(b) its profit or loss for that year.

2(2) That information need not be given if the company is exempt by virtue of section 400 or 401 of the 2006 Act from the requirement to prepare group accounts (parent company included in accounts of larger group).

2(3) That information need not be given if the company's investment in the subsidiary undertaking is included in the company's accounts by way of the equity method of valuation.

2(4) That information need not be given if–

    (a) the subsidiary undertaking is not required by any provision of the 2006 Act to deliver a copy of its balance sheet for its relevant financial year and does not otherwise publish that balance sheet in the United Kingdom or elsewhere, and

    (b) the company's holding is less than 50% of the nominal value of the shares in the undertaking.

2(5) Information otherwise required by this paragraph need not be given if it is not material.

2(6) For the purposes of this paragraph the **"relevant financial year"** of a subsidiary undertaking is–

    (a) if its financial year ends with that of the company, that year, and

    (b) if not, its financial year ending last before the end of the company's financial year.

Shares and debentures of company held by subsidiary undertakings

3(1) The number, description and amount of the shares in the company held by or on behalf of its subsidiary undertakings must be disclosed.

3(2) Sub-paragraph (1) does not apply in relation to shares in the case of which the subsidiary undertaking is concerned as personal representative or, subject as follows, as trustee.

3(3) The exception for shares in relation to which the subsidiary undertaking is concerned as trustee does not apply if the company, or any of its subsidiary undertakings, is beneficially interested under the trust, otherwise than by way of security only for the purposes of a transaction entered into by it in the ordinary course of a business which includes the lending of money.

3(4) Part 5 of this Schedule has effect for the interpretation of the reference in sub-paragraph (3) to a beneficial interest under a trust.

Significant holdings in undertakings other than subsidiary undertakings

4(1) The information required by paragraphs 5 and 6 must be given where at the end of the financial year the company has a significant holding in an undertaking which is not a subsidiary undertaking of the company, and which does not fall within paragraph 18 (joint ventures) or 19 (associated undertakings).

4(2) A holding is significant for this purpose if–

    (a) it amounts to 20% or more of the nominal value of any class of shares in the undertaking, or

    (b) the amount of the holding (as stated or included in the company's individual accounts) exceeds one-fifth of the amount (as so stated) of the company's assets.

5(1) The name of the undertaking must be stated.

5(2) There must be stated–

(a) the address of the undertaking's registered office (whether in or outside the United Kingdom),

(b) if it is unincorporated, the address of its principal place of business.

5(3) There must also be stated–

(a) the identity of each class of shares in the undertaking held by the company, and

(b) the proportion of the nominal value of the shares of that class represented by those shares.

History – Para. 5(2)(a) substituted by SI 2015/980, reg. 37(3), with effect in relation to–

(a) financial years beginning on or after 1 January 2016, and

(b) a financial year of a company beginning on or after 1 January 2015, but before 1 January 2016, if the directors of the company so decide.

6(1) Subject to paragraph 14, there must also be stated–

(a) the aggregate amount of the capital and reserves of the undertaking as at the end of its relevant financial year, and

(b) its profit or loss for that year.

6(2) That information need not be given in respect of an undertaking if–

(a) the undertaking is not required by any provision of the 2006 Act to deliver a copy of its balance sheet for its relevant financial year and does not otherwise publish that balance sheet in the United Kingdom or elsewhere, and

(b) the company's holding is less than 50% of the nominal value of the shares in the undertaking.

6(3) Information otherwise required by this paragraph need not be given if it is not material.

6(4) For the purposes of this paragraph the **"relevant financial year"** of an undertaking is–

(a) if its financial year ends with that of the company, that year, and

(b) if not, its financial year ending last before the end of the company's financial year.

Membership of certain undertakings

7(1) The information required by this paragraph must be given where at the end of the financial year the company is a member of an undertaking having unlimited liability.

7(2) There must be stated–

(a) the name and legal form of the undertaking, and

(b) the address of the undertaking's registered office (whether in or outside the United Kingdom) or, if it does not have such an office, its head office (whether in or outside the United Kingdom).

7(3) Where the undertaking is a qualifying partnership there must also be stated either–

(a) that a copy of the latest accounts of the undertaking has been or is to be appended to the copy of the company's accounts sent to the registrar under section 444 of the 2006 Act, or

(b) the name of at least one body corporate (which may be the company) in whose group accounts the undertaking has been or is to be dealt with on a consolidated basis.

7(4) Information otherwise required by sub-paragraph (2) need not be given if it is not material.

7(5) Information otherwise required by sub-paragraph (3)(b) need not be given if the notes to the company's accounts disclose that advantage has been taken of the exemption conferred by regulation 7 of the Partnerships (Accounts) Regulations 2008.

7(6) [Omitted by SI 2015/980, reg. 37(4)(b).]

7(7) In this paragraph–

"dealt with on a consolidated basis" and **"qualifying partnership"** have the same meanings as in the Partnerships (Accounts) Regulations 2008;

7(8) [Omitted by SI 2015/980, reg. 37(4)(d).]

7(9) [Omitted by SI 2015/980, reg. 37(4)(e).]

7(10) [Omitted by SI 2015/980, reg. 37(4)(f).]

History – In para. 7(5) "Partnerships (Accounts) Regulations 2008" substituted for "Partnerships and Unlimited Companies (Accounts) Regulations 1993" by SI 2008/569, reg. 17(2), with effect from 6 April 2008.

Para. 7(6) substituted and para. 7(7)–(10) inserted by SI 2013/2005, reg. 6, with effect from 1 September 2013 applying in relation to a financial year of a company beginning on or after 1 October 2013.

This version of para. 7 applies to financial years beginning on or after 1 October 2013. The version applying to financial years beginning before 1 October 2013 read as follows:

"**7(1)** The information required by this paragraph must be given where at the end of the financial year the company is a member of a qualifying undertaking.

7(2) There must be stated–

   (a)   the name and legal form of the undertaking, and

   (b)   the address of the undertaking's registered office (whether in or outside the United (Kingdom) or, if it does not have such an office, its head office (whether in or outside the United Kingdom).

7(3) Where the undertaking is a qualifying partnership there must also be stated either–

   (a)   that a copy of the latest accounts of the undertaking has been or is to be appended to the copy of the company's accounts sent to the registrar under section 444 of the 2006 Act, or

   (b)   the name of at least one body corporate (which may be the company) in whose group accounts the undertaking has been or is to be dealt with on a consolidated basis.

7(4) Information otherwise required by sub-paragraph (2) need not be given if it is not material.

7(5) Information otherwise required by sub-paragraph (3)(b) need not be given if the notes to the company's accounts disclose that advantage has been taken of the exemption conferred by regulation 7 of the Partnerships (Accounts) Regulations 2008.

7(6) In this paragraph–

"dealt with on a consolidated basis", **"member"** and **"qualifying partnership"** have the same meanings as in the Partnerships (Accounts) Regulations 2008;
"qualifying undertaking" means–

   (a)   a qualifying partnership, or

   (b)   an unlimited company each of whose members is–

      (i)   a limited company,

      (ii)   another unlimited company each of whose members is a limited company, or

      (iii)   a Scottish partnership each of whose members is a limited company, and references in this paragraph to a limited company, another unlimited company or a Scottish partnership include a comparable undertaking incorporated in or formed under the law of a country or territory outside the United Kingdom."

In para. 7(1), the words "an undertaking having unlimited liability" substituted for the words "a qualifying undertaking" by SI 2015/980, reg. 37(4)(a), with effect in relation to–

   (a)   financial years beginning on or after 1 January 2016, and

   (b)   a financial year of a company beginning on or after 1 January 2015, but before 1 January 2016, if the directors of the company so decide.

Para. 7(6) omitted by SI 2015/980, reg. 37(4)(b), with effect in relation to–

    (a)   financial years beginning on or after 1 January 2016, and

    (b)   a financial year of a company beginning on or after 1 January 2015, but before 1 January 2016, if the directors of the company so decide.

Former para. 7(6) read as follows:

"**7(6)** In sub-paragraph (1) **"member"**, in relation to a qualifying undertaking which is a qualifying partnership, has the same meaning as in the Partnerships (Accounts) Regulations 2008."

In para. 7(7), the definition of "qualifying undertaking" omitted by SI 2015/980, reg. 37(4)(c), with effect in relation to–

    (a)   financial years beginning on or after 1 January 2016, and

    (b)   a financial year of a company beginning on or after 1 January 2015, but before 1 January 2016, if the directors of the company so decide.

Para. 7(8)–(10) omitted by SI 2015/980, reg. 37(4)(d)–(f), with effect in relation to–

    (a)   financial years beginning on or after 1 January 2016, and

    (b)   a financial year of a company beginning on or after 1 January 2015, but before 1 January 2016, if the directors of the company so decide.

Former para. 7(8)–(10) read as follows:

"**7(8)** In sub-paragraph (7) the references to a limited company, another unlimited company, a Scottish partnership which is not a limited partnership or a Scottish partnership which is a limited partnership include a comparable undertaking incorporated in or formed under the law of a country or territory outside the United Kingdom.

7(9) In sub-paragraph (7) **"general partner"** means–

    (a)   in relation to a Scottish partnership which is a limited partnership, a person who is a general partner within the meaning of the Limited Partnerships Act 1907, and

    (b)   in relation to an undertaking incorporated in or formed under the law of any country or territory outside the United Kingdom and which is comparable to a Scottish partnership which is a limited partnership, a person comparable to such a general partner.

7(10) In sub-paragraphs (7), (8) and (9) **"limited partnership"** means a partnership registered under the Limited Partnerships Act 1907."

Parent undertaking drawing up accounts for larger group

8(1) Where the company is a subsidiary undertaking, the following information must be given with respect to the parent undertaking of–

    (a)   the largest group of undertakings for which group accounts are drawn up and of which the company is a member, and

    (b)   the smallest such group of undertakings.

8(2) The name of the parent undertaking must be stated.

8(3) There must be stated–

    (a)   the address of the undertaking's registered office (whether in or outside the United Kingdom),

    (b)   if it is unincorporated, the address of its principal place of business.

8(4) If copies of the group accounts referred to in sub-paragraph (1) are available to the public, there must also be stated the addresses from which copies of the accounts can be obtained.

History – Para. 8(3)(a) substituted by SI 2015/980, reg. 37(5), with effect in relation to–

    (a)   financial years beginning on or after 1 January 2016, and

    (b)   a financial year of a company beginning on or after 1 January 2015, but before 1 January 2016, if the directors of the company so decide.

Identification of ultimate parent company

9(1) Where the company is a subsidiary undertaking, the following information must be given with respect to the company (if any) regarded by the directors as being the company's ultimate parent company.

9(2) The name of that company must be stated.

9(3) If that company is incorporated outside the United Kingdom, the country in which it is incorporated must be stated (if known to the directors).

9(4) In this paragraph **"company"** includes any body corporate.

PART 2 – COMPANIES NOT REQUIRED TO PREPARE GROUP ACCOUNTS
REASON FOR NOT PREPARING GROUP ACCOUNTS

10(1) The reason why the company is not required to prepare group accounts must be stated.

10(2) If the reason is that all the subsidiary undertakings of the company fall within the exclusions provided for in section 405 of the 2006 Act (Companies Act group accounts: subsidiary undertakings included in the consolidation), it must be stated with respect to each subsidiary undertaking which of those exclusions applies.

Holdings in subsidiary undertakings

11(1) There must be stated in relation to shares of each class held by the company in a subsidiary undertaking–

    (a) the identity of the class, and
    (b) the proportion of the nominal value of the shares of that class represented by those shares.

11(2) The shares held by or on behalf of the company itself must be distinguished from those attributed to the company which are held by or on behalf of a subsidiary undertaking.

Financial years of subsidiary undertakings

12 Where–

    (a) disclosure is made under paragraph 2(1) with respect to a subsidiary undertaking, and
    (b) that undertaking's financial year does not end with that of the company, there must be stated in relation to that undertaking the date on which its last financial year ended (last before the end of the company's financial year).

Exemption from giving information about significant holdings in non-subsidiary undertakings

13(1) The information otherwise required by paragraph 6 (significant holdings in undertakings other than subsidiary undertaking) need not be given if–

    (a) the company is exempt by virtue of section 400 or 401 of the 2006 Act from the requirement to prepare group accounts (parent company included in accounts of larger group), and
    (b) the investment of the company in all undertakings in which it has such a holding as is mentioned in sub-paragraph (1) is shown, in aggregate, in the notes to the accounts by way of the equity method of valuation.

Construction of references to shares held by company

14(1) References in Parts 1 and 2 of this Schedule to shares held by a company are to be construed as follows.

14(2) For the purposes of paragraphs 2, 11 and 12 (information about subsidiary undertakings)–

   (a) there must be attributed to the company any shares held by a subsidiary undertaking, or by a person acting on behalf of the company or a subsidiary undertaking; but

   (b) there must be treated as not held by the company any shares held on behalf of a person other than the company or a subsidiary undertaking.

14(3) For the purposes of paragraphs 4 to 6 (information about undertakings other than subsidiary undertakings)–

   (a) there must be attributed to the company shares held on its behalf by any person; but

   (b) there must be treated as not held by a company shares held on behalf of a person other than the company.

14(4) For the purposes of any of those provisions, shares held by way of security must be treated as held by the person providing the security–

   (a) where apart from the right to exercise them for the purpose of preserving the value of the security, or of realising it, the rights attached to the shares are exercisable only in accordance with that person's instructions, and

   (b) where the shares are held in connection with the granting of loans as part of normal business activities and apart from the right to exercise them for the purpose of preserving the value of the security, or of realising it, the rights attached to the shares are exercisable only in that person's interests.

PART 3 – COMPANIES REQUIRED TO PREPARE GROUP ACCOUNTS

Introductory

15 In this Part of this Schedule **"the group"** means the group consisting of the parent company and its subsidiary undertakings.

Subsidiary undertakings

16(1) In addition to the information required by paragraph 2, the following information must also be given with respect to the undertakings which are subsidiary undertakings of the parent company at the end of the financial year.

16(2) It must be stated whether the subsidiary undertaking is included in the consolidation and, if it is not, the reasons for excluding it from consolidation must be given.

16(3) It must be stated with respect to each subsidiary undertaking by virtue of which of the conditions specified in section 1162(2) or (4) of the 2006 Act it is a subsidiary undertaking of its immediate parent undertaking.

That information need not be given if the relevant condition is that specified in subsection (2)(a) of that section (holding of a majority of the voting rights) and the immediate parent undertaking holds the same proportion of the shares in the undertaking as it holds voting rights.

Holdings in subsidiary undertakings

17(1) The following information must be given with respect to the shares of a subsidiary undertaking held–

- (a) by the parent company, and
- (b) by the group, and the information under paragraphs
- (a) and
- (b) must (if different) be shown separately.

17(2) There must be stated–

- (a) the identity of each class of shares held, and
- (b) the proportion of the nominal value of the shares of that class represented by those shares.

Joint ventures

18(1) The following information must be given where an undertaking is dealt with in the consolidated accounts by the method of proportional consolidation in accordance with paragraph 18 of Schedule 6 to these Regulations (joint ventures)–

- (a) the address of the undertaking's registered office (whether in or outside the United Kingdom),
- (b) the address of the principal place of business of the undertaking,
- (c) the factors on which joint management of the undertaking is based, and
- (d) the proportion of the capital of the undertaking held by undertakings included in the consolidation.

18(2) Where the financial year of the undertaking did not end with that of the company, there must be stated the date on which a financial year of the undertaking last ended before that date.

History – Para. 18(1)(a) substituted by SI 2015/980, reg. 38(2), with effect in relation to–

- (a) financial years beginning on or after 1 January 2016, and
- (b) a financial year of a company beginning on or after 1 January 2015, but before 1 January 2016, if the directors of the company so decide.

Associated undertakings

19(1) The following information must be given where an undertaking included in the consolidation has an interest in an associated undertaking.

19(2) The name of the associated undertaking must be stated.

19(3) There must be stated–

- (a) if the undertaking is incorporated outside the United Kingdom, the country in which it is incorporated,
- (b) the address of the undertaking's registered office (whether in or outside the United Kingdom),

19(4) The following information must be given with respect to the shares of the undertaking held–

- (a) by the parent company, and
- (b) by the group, and the information under paragraphs (a) and (b) must be shown separately.

19(5) There must be stated–

(a) the identity of each class of shares held, and

(b) the proportion of the nominal value of the shares of that class represented by those shares.

19(6) In this paragraph **"associated undertaking"** has the meaning given by paragraph 19 of Schedule 6 to these Regulations; and the information required by this paragraph must be given notwithstanding that paragraph 21(3) of that Schedule (materiality) applies in relation to the accounts themselves.

History – Para. 19(3)(b) substituted by SI 2015/980, reg. 38(3), with effect in relation to–

(a) financial years beginning on or after 1 January 2016, and

(b) a financial year of a company beginning on or after 1 January 2015, but before 1 January 2016, if the directors of the company so decide.

Requirement to give information about other significant holdings of parent company or group

20(1) The information required by paragraphs 5 and 6 must also be given where at the end of the financial year the group has a significant holding in an undertaking which is not a subsidiary undertaking of the parent company and does not fall within paragraph 18 (joint ventures) or 19 (associated undertakings), as though the references to the company in those paragraphs were a reference to the group.

20(2) A holding is significant for this purpose if–

(a) it amounts to 20% or more of the nominal value of any class of shares in the undertaking, or

(b) the amount of the holding (as stated or included in the group accounts) exceeds one-fifth of the amount of the group's assets (as so stated).

20(3) For the purposes of those paragraphs as applied to a group the **"relevant financial year"** of an outside undertaking is–

(a) if its financial year ends with that of the parent company, that year, and

(b) if not, its financial year ending last before the end of the parent company's financial year.

Group's membership of certain undertakings

21 The information required by paragraph 7 must also be given where at the end of the financial year the group is a member of an undertaking having unlimited liability.

History – In para. 21, the words "an undertaking having unlimited liability" substituted for the words "a qualifying undertaking" by SI 2015/980, reg. 38(4), with effect in relation to–

(a) financial years beginning on or after 1 January 2016, and

(b) a financial year of a company beginning on or after 1 January 2015, but before 1 January 2016, if the directors of the company so decide.

Construction of references to shares held by parent company or group

22(1) References in Parts 1 and 3 of this Schedule to shares held by that parent company or group are to be construed as follows.

22(2) For the purposes of paragraphs 4 to 6, 17, 19(4) and (5) and 12 (information about holdings in subsidiary and other undertakings)–

(a) there must be attributed to the parent company shares held on its behalf by any person; but

(b) there must be treated as not held by the parent company shares held on behalf of a person other than the company.

22(3) References to shares held by the group are to any shares held by or on behalf of the parent company or any of its subsidiary undertakings; but any shares held on behalf of a person other than the parent company or any of its subsidiary undertakings are not to be treated as held by the group.

22(4) Shares held by way of security must be treated as held by the person providing the security–

(a) where apart from the right to exercise them for the purpose of preserving the value of the security, or of realising it, the rights attached to the shares are exercisable only in accordance with his instructions, and

(b) where the shares are held in connection with the granting of loans as part of normal business activities and apart from the right to exercise them for the purpose of preserving the value of the security, or of realising it, the rights attached to the shares are exercisable only in his interests.

PART 4 – ADDITIONAL DISCLOSURES FOR BANKING COMPANIES AND GROUPS

23(1) This paragraph applies where accounts are prepared in accordance with the special provisions of Schedules 2 and 6 relating to banking companies or groups.

23(2) The information required by paragraph 5 of this Schedule, modified where applicable by paragraph 20 (information about significant holdings of the company or group in undertakings other than subsidiary undertakings) need only be given in respect of undertakings (otherwise falling within the class of undertakings in respect of which disclosure is required) in which the company or group has a significant holding amounting to 20% or more of the nominal value of the shares in the undertaking.

In addition any information required by those paragraphs may be omitted if it is not material.

23(3) Paragraphs 14(3) and (4) and 22(3) and (4) of this Schedule apply with necessary modifications for the purposes of this paragraph.

PART 5 – INTERPRETATION OF REFERENCES TO "BENEFICIAL INTEREST"

Residual interests under pension and employees' share schemes

24(1) Where shares in an undertaking are held on trust for the purposes of a pension scheme or an employees' share scheme, there must be disregarded any residual interest which has not vested in possession, being an interest of the undertaking or any of its subsidiary undertakings.

24(2) In this paragraph a **"residual interest"** means a right of the undertaking in question (the "residual beneficiary") to receive any of the trust property in the event of–

(a) all the liabilities arising under the scheme having been satisfied or provided for, or

(b) the residual beneficiary ceasing to participate in the scheme, or

(c) the trust property at any time exceeding what is necessary for satisfying the liabilities arising or expected to arise under the scheme.

24(3) In sub-paragraph (2) references to a right include a right dependent on the exercise of a discretion vested by the scheme in the trustee or any other person; and references to liabilities arising under a scheme include liabilities that have resulted or may result from the exercise of any such discretion.

24(4) For the purposes of this paragraph a residual interest vests in possession–

(a) in a case within sub-paragraph (2)(a), on the occurrence of the event there mentioned, whether or not the amount of the property receivable pursuant to the right mentioned in that sub-paragraph is then ascertained,

(b) in a case within sub-paragraph (2)(b) or (c), when the residual beneficiary becomes entitled to require the trustee to transfer to that beneficiary any of the property receivable pursuant to that right.

Employer's charges and other rights of recovery

25(1) Where shares in an undertaking are held on trust there must be disregarded–

(a) if the trust is for the purposes of a pension scheme, any such rights as are mentioned in sub-paragraph (2),

(b) if the trust is for the purposes of an employees' share scheme, any such rights as are mentioned in paragraph(a) of that sub-paragraph, being rights of the undertaking or any of its subsidiary undertakings.

25(2) The rights referred to are–

(a) any charge or lien on, or set-off against, any benefit or other right or interest under the scheme for the purpose of enabling the employer or former employer of a member of the scheme to obtain the discharge of a monetary obligation due to him from the member, and

(b) any right to receive from the trustee of the scheme, or as trustee of the scheme to retain, an amount that can be recovered or retained under section 61 of the Pension Schemes Act 1993 or section 57 of the Pension Schemes (Northern Ireland) Act 1993 (deduction of contributions equivalent premium from refund of scheme contributions) or otherwise as reimbursement or partial reimbursement for any contributions equivalent premium paid in connection with the scheme under Chapter 3 of Part 3 of that Act.

Trustee's right to expenses, remuneration, indemnity etc.

26 Where an undertaking is a trustee, there must be disregarded any rights which the undertaking has in its capacity as trustee including, in particular, any right to recover its expenses or be remunerated out of the trust property and any right to be indemnified out of that property for any liability incurred by reason of any act or omission of the undertaking in the performance of its duties as trustee.

Supplementary

27(1) This Schedule applies in relation to debentures as it applies in relation to shares.

27(2) **"Pension scheme"** means any scheme for the provision of benefits consisting of or including relevant benefits for or in respect of employees or former employees; and **"relevant benefits"** means any pension, lump sum, gratuity or other like benefit given or to be given on retirement or on death or in anticipation of retirement or, in connection with past service, after retirement or death.

27(3) In sub-paragraph (2) of this paragraph and in paragraph 25(2) **"employee"** and **"employer"** are to be read as if a director of an undertaking were employed by it.

SCHEDULE 5

Regulation 8

INFORMATION ABOUT BENEFITS OF DIRECTORS
PART 1 – PROVISIONS APPLYING TO QUOTED AND UNQUOTED COMPANIES

Total amount of directors' remuneration etc.

1(1) There must be shown–

   (a) the aggregate amount of remuneration paid to or receivable by directors in respect of qualifying services;

   (b) the aggregate of the amount of gains made by directors on the exercise of share options;

   (c) the aggregate of the amount of money paid to or receivable by directors, and the net value of assets (other than money and share options) received or receivable by directors, under long term incentive schemes in respect of qualifying services; and

   (d) the aggregate value of any company contributions–

      (i) paid, or treated as paid, to a pension scheme in respect of directors' qualifying services, and

      (ii) by reference to which the rate or amount of any money purchase benefits that may become payable will be calculated.

1(2) There must be shown the number of directors (if any) to whom retirement benefits are accruing in respect of qualifying services–

   (a) under money purchase schemes, and

   (b) under defined benefit schemes.

1(3) In the case of a company which is not a quoted company and whose equity share capital is not listed on the market known as AIM–

   (a) sub-paragraph (1) has effect as if paragraph (b) were omitted and, in paragraph (c), "assets" did not include shares; and

   (b) the number of each of the following (if any) must be shown, namely–

      (i) the directors who exercised share options, and

      (ii) the directors in respect of whose qualifying services shares were received or receivable under long term incentive schemes.

PART 2 – PROVISIONS APPLYING
ONLY TO UNQUOTED COMPANIES

Details of highest paid director's emoluments etc.

2(1) Where the aggregates shown under paragraph 1(1)(a), (b) and (c) total £200,000 or more, there must be shown–

   (a) so much of the total of those aggregates as is attributable to the highest paid director, and

   (b) so much of the aggregate mentioned in paragraph 1(1)(d) as is so attributable.

2(2) Where sub-paragraph (1) applies and the highest paid director has performed qualifying services during the financial year by reference to which the rate or amount of any defined benefits that may become payable will be calculated, there must also be shown–

(a) the amount at the end of the year of his accrued pension, and

(b) where applicable, the amount at the end of the year of his accrued lump sum.

2(3) Subject to sub-paragraph (4), where sub-paragraph (1) applies in the case of a company which is not a listed company, there must also be shown–

(a) whether the highest paid director exercised any share options, and

(b) whether any shares were received or receivable by that director in respect of qualifying services under a long term incentive scheme.

2(4) Where the highest paid director has not been involved in any of the transactions specified in sub-paragraph (3), that fact need not be stated.

Excess retirement benefits of directors and past directors

3(1) Subject to sub-paragraph (2), there must be shown the aggregate amount of–

(a) so much of retirement benefits paid to or receivable by directors under pension schemes, and

(b) so much of retirement benefits paid to or receivable by past directors under such schemes, as (in each case) is in excess of the retirement benefits to which they were respectively entitled on the date on which the benefits first became payable or 31st March 1997, whichever is the later.

3(2) Amounts paid or receivable under a pension scheme need not be included in the aggregate amount if–

(a) the funding of the scheme was such that the amounts were or, as the case may be, could have been paid without recourse to additional contributions, and

(b) amounts were paid to or receivable by all pensioner members of the scheme on the same basis.

3(3) In sub-paragraph (2), **"pensioner member"**, in relation to a pension scheme, means any person who is entitled to the present payment of retirement benefits under the scheme.

3(4) In this paragraph–

(a) references to retirement benefits include benefits otherwise than in cash, and

(b) in relation to so much of retirement benefits as consists of a benefit otherwise than in cash, references to their amount are to the estimated money value of the benefit, and the nature of any such benefit must also be disclosed.

Compensation to directors for loss of office

4(1) There must be shown the aggregate amount of any compensation to directors or past directors in respect of loss of office.

4(2) This includes compensation received or receivable by a director or past director–

(a) for loss of office as director of the company, or

(b) for loss, while director of the company or on or in connection with his ceasing to be a director of it, of–

(i) any other office in connection with the management of the company's affairs, or

    (ii)   any office as director or otherwise in connection with the management of the affairs of any subsidiary undertaking of the company.

4(3) In this paragraph references to compensation for loss of office include–

    (a)   compensation in consideration for, or in connection with, a person's retirement from office, and

    (b)   where such a retirement is occasioned by a breach of the person's contract with the company or with a subsidiary undertaking of the company–

        (i)   payments made by way of damages for the breach, or

        (ii)   payments made by way of settlement or compromise of any claim in respect of the breach.

4(4) In this paragraph–

    (a)   references to compensation include benefits otherwise than in cash, and

    (b)   in relation to such compensation references to its amount are to the estimated money value of the benefit.

The nature of any such compensation must be disclosed.

Sums paid to third parties in respect of directors' services

5(1) There must be shown the aggregate amount of any consideration paid to or receivable by third parties for making available the services of any person–

    (a)   as a director of the company, or

    (b)   while director of the company–

        (i)   as director of any of its subsidiary undertakings, or

        (ii)   otherwise in connection with the management of the affairs of the company or any of its subsidiary undertakings.

5(2) In sub-paragraph (1)–

    (a)   the reference to consideration includes benefits otherwise than in cash, and

    (b)   in relation to such consideration the reference to its amount is to the estimated money value of the benefit.

The nature of any such consideration must be disclosed.

5(3) For the purposes of this paragraph a **"third party"** means a person other than–

    (a)   the director himself or a person connected with him or a body corporate controlled by him, or

    (b)   the company or any of its subsidiary undertakings.

PART 3 – SUPPLEMENTARY PROVISIONS

General nature of obligations

6(1) This Schedule requires information to be given only so far as it is contained in the company's books and papers or the company has the right to obtain it from the persons concerned.

6(2) For the purposes of this Schedule any information is treated as shown if it is capable of being readily ascertained from other information which is shown.

Provisions as to amounts to be shown

7(1) The following provisions apply with respect to the amounts to be shown under this Schedule.

7(2) The amount in each case includes all relevant sums, whether paid by or receivable from the company, any of the company's subsidiary undertakings or any other person.

7(3) References to amounts paid to or receivable by a person include amounts paid to or receivable by a person connected with him or a body corporate controlled by him (but not so as to require an amount to be counted twice).

7(4) Except as otherwise provided, the amounts to be shown for any financial year are–

    (a) the sums receivable in respect of that year (whenever paid), or
    (b) in the case of sums not receivable in respect of a period, the sums paid during that year.

7(5) Sums paid by way of expenses allowance that are charged to United Kingdom income tax after the end of the relevant financial year must be shown in a note to the first accounts in which it is practicable to show them and must be distinguished from the amounts to be shown apart from this provision.

7(6) Where it is necessary to do so for the purpose of making any distinction required in complying with this Schedule, the directors may apportion payments between the matters in respect of which they have been paid or are receivable in such manner as they think appropriate.

Exclusion of sums liable to be accounted for to company etc.

8(1) The amounts to be shown under this Schedule do not include any sums that are to be accounted for–

    (a) to the company or any of its subsidiary undertakings, or
    (b) by virtue of sections 219 and 222(3) of the 2006 Act (payments in connection with share transfers: duty to account) to persons who sold their shares as a result of the offer made.

8(2) Where–

    (a) any such sums are not shown in a note to the accounts for the relevant financial year on the ground that the person receiving them is liable to account for them, and
    (b) the liability is afterwards wholly or partly released or is not enforced within a period of two years, those sums, to the extent to which the liability is released or not enforced, must be shown in a note to the first accounts in which it is practicable to show them and must be distinguished from the amounts to be shown apart from this provision.

Meaning of "remuneration"

9(1) In this Schedule **"remuneration"** of a director includes–

    (a) salary, fees and bonuses, sums paid by way of expenses allowance (so far as they are chargeable to United Kingdom income tax), and
    (b) subject to sub-paragraph (2), the estimated money value of any other benefits received by the director otherwise than in cash.

9(2) The expression does not include–

    (a) the value of any share options granted to the director or the amount of any gains made on the exercise of any such options,
    (b) any company contributions paid, or treated as paid, under any pension scheme or any benefits to which the director is entitled under any such scheme, or

    (c)   any money or other assets paid to or received or receivable by the director under any long term incentive scheme.

Meaning of "highest paid director"

10 In this Schedule, **"the highest paid director"** means the director to whom is attributable the greatest part of the total of the aggregates shown under paragraph 1(1)(a),(b) and (c).

Meaning of "long term incentive scheme"

11(1) In this Schedule **"long term incentive scheme"** means an agreement or arrangement–

    (a)   under which money or other assets may become receivable by a director, and
    (b)   which includes one or more qualifying conditions with respect to service or performance which cannot be fulfilled within a single financial year.

11(2) For this purpose the following must be disregarded–

    (a)   bonuses the amount of which falls to be determined by reference to service or performance within a single financial year;
    (b)   compensation for loss of office, payments for breach of contract and other termination payments; and
    (c)   retirement benefits.

Meaning of "shares" and "share option" and related expressions

12 In this Schedule–

    (a)   **"shares"** means shares (whether allotted or not) in the company, or any undertaking which is a group undertaking in relation to the company, and includes a share warrant as defined by section 779(1) of the 2006 Act; and
    (b)   **"share option"** means a right to acquire shares.

Meaning of "pension scheme" and related expressions

13(1) In this Schedule–

"pension scheme" means a retirement benefits scheme as defined by section 611 of the Income and Corporation Taxes Act 1988; and
"retirement benefits" has the meaning given by section 612(1) of that Act.

13(2) In this Schedule **"accrued pension"** and **"accrued lump sum"**, in relation to any pension scheme and any director, mean respectively the amount of the annual pension, and the amount of the lump sum, which would be payable under the scheme on his attaining normal pension age if–

    (a)   he had left the company's service at the end of the financial year,
    (b)   there was no increase in the general level of prices in the United Kingdom during the period beginning with the end of that year and ending with his attaining that age,
    (c)   no question arose of any commutation of the pension or inverse commutation of the lump sum, and
    (d)   any amounts attributable to voluntary contributions paid by the director to the scheme, and any money purchase benefits which would be payable under the scheme, were disregarded.

13(3) In this Schedule, **"company contributions"**, in relation to a pension scheme and a director, means any payments (including insurance premiums) made, or treated as made, to the scheme in respect of the director by a person other than the director.

13(4) In this Schedule, in relation to a director–

"defined benefits" means retirement benefits payable under a pension scheme that are not money purchase benefits;

"defined benefit scheme" means a pension scheme that is not a money purchase scheme;

"money purchase benefits" means retirement benefits payable under a pension scheme the rate or amount of which is calculated by reference to payments made, or treated as made, by the director or by any other person in respect of the director and which are not average salary benefits; and

"money purchase scheme" means a pension scheme under which all of the benefits that may become payable to or in respect of the director are money purchase benefits.

13(5) In this Schedule, **"normal pension age"**, in relation to any pension scheme and any director, means the age at which the director will first become entitled to receive a full pension on retirement of an amount determined without reduction to take account of its payment before a later age (but disregarding any entitlement to pension upon retirement in the event of illness, incapacity or redundancy).

13(6) Where a pension scheme provides for any benefits that may become payable to or in respect of any director to be whichever are the greater of–

(a) money purchase benefits as determined by or under the scheme; and
(b) defined benefits as so determined, the company may assume for the purposes of this paragraph that those benefits will be money purchase benefits, or defined benefits, according to whichever appears more likely at the end of the financial year.

13(7) For the purpose of determining whether a pension scheme is a money purchase or defined benefit scheme, any death in service benefits provided for by the scheme are to be disregarded.

References to subsidiary undertakings

14(1) Any reference in this Schedule to a subsidiary undertaking of the company, in relation to a person who is or was, while a director of the company, a director also, by virtue of the company's nomination (direct or indirect) of any other undertaking, includes that undertaking, whether or not it is or was in fact a subsidiary undertaking of the company.

14(2) Any reference to a subsidiary undertaking of the company–

(a) for the purposes of paragraph 1 (remuneration etc.) is to an undertaking which is a subsidiary undertaking at the time the services were rendered, and
(b) for the purposes of paragraph 4 (compensation for loss of office) is to a subsidiary undertaking immediately before the loss of office as director.

Other minor definitions

15(1) In this Schedule–

"net value", in relation to any assets received or receivable by a director, means value after deducting any money paid or other value given by the director in respect of those assets;

"qualifying services", in relation to any person, means his services as a director of the company, and his services while director of the company–

(a) as director of any of its subsidiary undertakings; or
(b) otherwise in connection with the management of the affairs of the company or any of its subsidiary undertakings.

15(2) References in this Schedule to a person being "connected" with a director, and to a director "controlling" a body corporate, are to be construed in accordance with sections 252 to 255 of the 2006 Act.

15(3) For the purposes of this Schedule, remuneration paid or receivable or share options granted in respect of a person's accepting office as a director are treated as emoluments paid or receivable or share options granted in respect of his services as a director.

SCHEDULE 6

Regulation 9

COMPANIES ACT GROUP ACCOUNTS
PART 1 – GENERAL RULES

General rules

1(1) Group accounts must comply so far as practicable with the provisions of Schedule 1 to these Regulations as if the undertakings included in the consolidation ("the group") were a single company (see Parts 2 and 3 of this Schedule for modifications for banking and insurance groups).

1(2) Where the parent company is treated as an investment company for the purposes of Part 5 of Schedule 1 (special provisions for investment companies) the group must be similarly treated.

2(1) The consolidated balance sheet and profit and loss account must incorporate in full the information contained in the individual accounts of the undertakings included in the consolidation, subject to the adjustments authorised or required by the following provisions of this Schedule and to such other adjustments (if any) as may be appropriate in accordance with generally accepted accounting principles or practice.

2(1A) Group accounts must be drawn up as at the same date as the accounts of the parent company.

2(2) If the financial year of a subsidiary undertaking included in the consolidation does not end with that of the parent company, the group accounts must be made up–

   (a) from the accounts of the subsidiary undertaking for its financial year last ending before the end of the parent company's financial year, provided that year ended no more than three months before that of the parent company, or

   (b) from interim accounts prepared by the subsidiary undertaking as at the end of the parent company's financial year.

History – Para. 2(1A) inserted by SI 2015/980, reg. 39(2), with effect in relation to–

   (a) financial years beginning on or after 1 January 2016, and

   (b) a financial year of a company beginning on or after 1 January 2015, but before 1 January 2016, if the directors of the company so decide.

3(1) Where assets and liabilities to be included in the group accounts have been valued or otherwise determined by undertakings according to accounting rules differing from those used for the group accounts, the values or amounts must be adjusted so as to accord with the rules used for the group accounts.

3(2) If it appears to the directors of the parent company that there are special reasons for departing from sub-paragraph (1) they may do so, but particulars of any such departure, the reasons for it and its effect must be given in a note to the accounts.

3(3) The adjustments referred to in this paragraph need not be made if they are not material for the purpose of giving a true and fair view.

4 Any differences of accounting rules as between a parent company's individual accounts for a financial year and its group accounts must be disclosed in a note to the latter accounts and the reasons for the difference given.

5 Amounts that in the particular context of any provision of this Schedule are not material may be disregarded for the purposes of that provision.

Elimination of group transactions

6(1) Debts and claims between undertakings included in the consolidation, and income and expenditure relating to transactions between such undertakings, must be eliminated in preparing the group accounts.

6(2) Where profits and losses resulting from transactions between undertakings included in the consolidation are included in the book value of assets, they must be eliminated in preparing the group accounts.

6(3) The elimination required by sub-paragraph (2) may be effected in proportion to the group's interest in the shares of the undertakings.

6(4) Sub-paragraphs (1) and (2) need not be complied with if the amounts concerned are not material for the purpose of giving a true and fair view.

Acquisition and merger accounting

7(1) The following provisions apply where an undertaking becomes a subsidiary undertaking of the parent company.

7(2) That event is referred to in those provisions as an "acquisition", and references to the "undertaking acquired" are to be construed accordingly.

8 An acquisition must be accounted for by the acquisition method of accounting unless the conditions for accounting for it as a merger are met and the merger method of accounting is adopted.

9(1) The acquisition method of accounting is as follows.

9(2) The identifiable assets and liabilities of the undertaking acquired must be included in the consolidated balance sheet at their fair values as at the date of acquisition.

9(3) The income and expenditure of the undertaking acquired must be brought into the group accounts only as from the date of the acquisition.

9(4) There must be set off against the acquisition cost of the interest in the shares of the undertaking held by the parent company and its subsidiary undertakings the interest of the parent company and its subsidiary undertakings in the adjusted capital and reserves of the undertaking acquired.

9(5) The resulting amount if positive must be treated as goodwill, and if negative as a negative consolidation difference.

9(6) Negative goodwill may be transferred to the consolidated profit and loss account where such a treatment is in accordance with the principles and rules of Part 2 of Schedule 1 to these Regulations.

History – Para. 9(6) inserted by SI 2015/980, reg. 39(3), with effect in relation to–

    (a)   financial years beginning on or after 1 January 2016, and

    (b)   a financial year of a company beginning on or after 1 January 2015, but before 1 January 2016, if the directors of the company so decide.

10 The conditions for accounting for an acquisition as a merger are–

    (a)   that the undertaking whose shares are acquired is ultimately controlled by the same party both before and after the acquisition,

    (b)   that the control referred to in paragraph (a) is not transitory, and

    (c)   that adoption of the merger method accords with generally accepted accounting principles or practice.

History – Para. 10 substituted by SI 2015/980, reg. 39(4), with effect in relation to–

    (a)   financial years beginning on or after 1 January 2016, and

    (b)   a financial year of a company beginning on or after 1 January 2015, but before 1 January 2016, if the directors of the company so decide.

Former para. 10 read as follows:

"**10(1)** The conditions for accounting for an acquisition as a merger are–

    (a)   that at least 90% of the nominal value of the relevant shares in the undertaking acquired (excluding any shares in the undertaking held as treasury shares) is held by or on behalf of the parent company and its subsidiary undertakings,

    (b)   that the proportion referred to in paragraph (a) was attained pursuant to an arrangement providing for the issue of equity shares by the parent company or one or more of its subsidiary undertakings,

    (c)   that the fair value of any consideration other than the issue of equity shares given pursuant to the arrangement by the parent company and its subsidiary undertakings did not exceed 10% of the nominal value of the equity shares issued, and

    (d)   that adoption of the merger method of accounting accords with generally accepted accounting principles or practice.

10(2) The reference in sub-paragraph (1)(a) to the **"relevant shares"** in an undertaking acquired is to those carrying unrestricted rights to participate both in distributions and in the assets of the undertaking upon liquidation."

11(1) The merger method of accounting is as follows.

11(2) The assets and liabilities of the undertaking acquired must be brought into the group accounts at the figures at which they stand in the undertaking's accounts, subject to any adjustment authorised or required by this Schedule.

11(3) The income and expenditure of the undertaking acquired must be included in the group accounts for the entire financial year, including the period before the acquisition.

11(4) The group accounts must show corresponding amounts relating to the previous financial year as if the undertaking acquired had been included in the consolidation throughout that year.

11(5) There must be set off against the aggregate of–

    (a)   the appropriate amount in respect of qualifying shares issued by the parent company or its subsidiary undertakings in consideration for the acquisition of shares in the undertaking acquired, and

    (b)   the fair value of any other consideration for the acquisition of shares in the undertaking acquired, determined as at the date when those shares were acquired, the nominal value of the issued share capital of the undertaking acquired held by the parent company and its subsidiary undertakings.

11(6) The resulting amount must be shown as an adjustment to the consolidated reserves.

11(7) In sub-paragraph (5)(a) **"qualifying shares"** means–

    (a)   in relation to which any of the following provisions applies (merger relief), and in respect of which the appropriate amount is the nominal value–

        (i)   section 131 of the Companies Act 1985,
        (ii)   Article 141 of the Companies (Northern Ireland) Order 1986, or
        (iii)   section 612 of the 2006 Act, or

    (b)   shares in relation to which any of the following provisions applies (group reconstruction relief), and in respect of which the appropriate amount is the nominal value together with any minimum premium value within the meaning of that section–

        (i)   section 132 of the Companies Act 1985,
        (ii)   Article 142 of the Companies (Northern Ireland) Order 1986, or
        (iii)   section 611 of the 2006 Act.

12(1) Where a group is acquired, paragraphs 9 to 11 apply with the following adaptations.

12(2) References to shares of the undertaking acquired are to be construed as references to shares of the parent undertaking of the group.

12(3) Other references to the undertaking acquired are to be construed as references to the group; and references to the assets and liabilities, income and expenditure and capital and reserves of the undertaking acquired must be construed as references to the assets and liabilities, income and expenditure and capital and reserves of the group after making the set-offs and other adjustments required by this Schedule in the case of group accounts.

13(1) The following information with respect to acquisitions taking place in the financial year must be given in a note to the accounts.

13(2) There must be stated–

    (a)   the name of the undertaking acquired or, where a group was acquired, the name of the parent undertaking of that group, and
    (b)   whether the acquisition has been accounted for by the acquisition or the merger method of accounting; and in relation to an acquisition which significantly affects the figures shown in the group accounts, the following further information must be given.

13(3) The composition and fair value of the consideration for the acquisition given by the parent company and its subsidiary undertakings must be stated.

13(4) Where the acquisition method of accounting has been adopted, the book values immediately prior to the acquisition, and the fair values at the date of acquisition, of each class of assets and liabilities of the undertaking or group acquired must be stated in tabular form, including a statement of the amount of any goodwill or negative consolidation difference arising on the acquisition, together with an explanation of any significant adjustments made.

13(5) In ascertaining for the purposes of sub-paragraph (4) the profit or loss of a group, the book values and fair values of assets and liabilities of a group or the amount of the assets and liabilities of a group, the set-offs and other adjustments required by this Schedule in the case of group accounts must be made.

14(1) There must also be stated in a note to the accounts the cumulative amount of goodwill resulting from acquisitions in that and earlier financial years which has been written off otherwise than in the consolidated profit and loss account for that or any earlier financial year.

14(2) That figure must be shown net of any goodwill attributable to subsidiary undertakings or businesses disposed of prior to the balance sheet date.

15 Where during the financial year there has been a disposal of an undertaking or group which significantly affects the figure shown in the group accounts, there must be stated in a note to the accounts—

(a) the name of that undertaking or, as the case may be, of the parent undertaking of that group, and

(b) the extent to which the profit or loss shown in the group accounts is attributable to profit or loss of that undertaking or group.

16 The information required by paragraph 13, 14 or 15 need not be disclosed with respect to an undertaking which—

(a) is established under the law of a country outside the United Kingdom, or

(b) carries on business outside the United Kingdom, if in the opinion of the directors of the parent company the disclosure would be seriously prejudicial to the business of that undertaking or to the business of the parent company or any of its subsidiary undertakings and the Secretary of State agrees that the information should not be disclosed.

16A Where an acquisition has taken place in the financial year and the merger method of accounting has been adopted, the notes to the accounts must also disclose—

(a) the address of the registered office of the undertaking acquired (whether in or outside the United Kingdom),

(b) the name of the party referred to in paragraph 10(a),

(c) the address of the registered office of that party (whether in or outside the United Kingdom), and

(d) the information referred to in paragraph 11(6).

History – Para. 16A inserted by SI 2015/980, reg. 39(5), with effect in relation to—

(a) financial years beginning on or after 1 January 2016, and

(b) a financial year of a company beginning on or after 1 January 2015, but before 1 January 2016, if the directors of the company so decide.

Non-controlling interests

17(1) The formats set out in Schedule 1 to these Regulations have effect in relation to group accounts with the following additions.

17(2) In the balance sheet formats there must be shown, as a separate item and under the heading "non-controlling interests", the amount of capital and reserves attributable to shares in subsidiary undertakings included in the consolidation held by or on behalf of persons other than the parent company and its subsidiary undertakings.

17(3) In the profit and loss account formats there must be shown, as a separate item and under the heading "non-controlling interests", the amount of any profit or loss attributable to shares in subsidiary undertakings included in the consolidation held by or on behalf of persons other than the parent company and its subsidiary undertakings.

17(4) For the purposes of paragraph 4(1) and (2) of Schedule 1 (power to adapt or combine items)—

(a) the additional item required by sub-paragraph (2) above is treated as one to which a letter is assigned, and

(b) the additional item required by sub-paragraph (3) above is treated as one to which an Arabic number is assigned.

History – Para. 17 and the heading preceding it substituted by SI 2015/980, reg. 39(6), with effect in relation to–

(a) financial years beginning on or after 1 January 2016, and

(b) a financial year of a company beginning on or after 1 January 2015, but before 1 January 2016, if the directors of the company so decide.

Former para. 17 read as follows:

"**Minority interests**

17(1) The formats set out in Schedule 1 to these Regulations have effect in relation to group accounts with the following additions.

17(2) In the balance sheet formats there must be shown, as a separate item and under an appropriate heading, the amount of capital and reserves attributable to shares in subsidiary undertakings included in the consolidation held by or on behalf of persons other than the parent company and its subsidiary undertakings.

17(3) In the profit and loss account formats there must be shown, as a separate item and under an appropriate heading–

(a) the amount of any profit or loss on ordinary activities, and

(b) the amount of any profit or loss on extraordinary activities, attributable to shares in subsidiary undertakings included in the consolidation held by or on behalf of persons other than the parent company and its subsidiary undertakings.

17(4) For the purposes of paragraph 4(1) and (2) of Schedule 1 (power to adapt or combine items)–

(a) the additional item required by sub-paragraph (2) above is treated as one to which a letter is assigned, and

(b) the additional items required by sub-paragraph (3)(a) and (b) above are treated as ones to which an Arabic number is assigned."

Joint ventures

18(1) Where an undertaking included in the consolidation manages another undertaking jointly with one or more undertakings not included in the consolidation, that other undertaking ("the joint venture") may, if it is not–

(a) a body corporate, or

(b) a subsidiary undertaking of the parent company, be dealt with in the group accounts by the method of proportional consolidation.

18(2) The provisions of this Schedule relating to the preparation of consolidated accounts and sections 402 and 405 of the 2006 Act apply, with any necessary modifications, to proportional consolidation under this paragraph.

18(3) In addition to the disclosure of the average number of employees employed during the financial year (see section 411(7) of the 2006 Act), there must be a separate disclosure in the notes to the accounts of the average number of employees employed by undertakings that are proportionately consolidated.

History – In para. 18(2), the words "and sections 402 and 405 of the 2006 Act" inserted by SI 2015/980, reg. 39(7), with effect in relation to–

(a) financial years beginning on or after 1 January 2016, and

(b) a financial year of a company beginning on or after 1 January 2015, but before 1 January 2016, if the directors of the company so decide.

Para. 18(3) inserted by SI 2015/980, reg. 39(8), with effect in relation to–

(a) financial years beginning on or after 1 January 2016, and

(b) a financial year of a company beginning on or after 1 January 2015, but before 1 January 2016, if the directors of the company so decide.

Associated undertakings

19(1) An **"associated undertaking"** means an undertaking in which an undertaking included in the consolidation has a participating interest and over whose operating and financial policy it exercises a significant influence, and which is not–

   (a) a subsidiary undertaking of the parent company, or
   (b) a joint venture dealt with in accordance with paragraph 18.

19(2) Where an undertaking holds 20% or more of the voting rights in another undertaking, it is presumed to exercise such an influence over it unless the contrary is shown.

19(3) The voting rights in an undertaking means the rights conferred on shareholders in respect of their shares or, in the case of an undertaking not having a share capital, on members, to vote at general meetings of the undertaking on all, or substantially all, matters.

19(4) The provisions of paragraphs 5 to 11 of Schedule 7 to the 2006 Act (parent and subsidiary undertakings: rights to be taken into account and attribution of rights) apply in determining for the purposes of this paragraph whether an undertaking holds 20% or more of the voting rights in another undertaking.

20(1) The formats set out in Schedule 1 to these Regulations have effect in relation to group accounts with the following modifications.

20(2) In the balance sheet formats replace the items headed "Participating interests", that is–

   (a) in format 1, item B.III.3, and
   (b) in format 2, item B.III.3 under the heading "ASSETS", by two items: "Interests in associated undertakings" and "Other participating interests".

20(3) In the profit and loss account formats replace the items headed "Income from participating interests", that is–

   (a) in format 1, item 8, and
   (b) in format 2, item 10.

History – Para. 20(3)(c) and (d) omitted; and the word "and" in para. (a) inserted by SI 2015/980, reg. 39(9), with effect in relation to–

   (a)   financial years beginning on or after 1 January 2016, and
   (b)   a financial year of a company beginning on or after 1 January 2015, but before 1 January 2016, if the directors of the company so decide.

21(1) The interest of an undertaking in an associated undertaking, and the amount of profit or loss attributable to such an interest, must be shown by the equity method of accounting (including dealing with any goodwill arising in accordance with paragraphs 17 to 20 and 22 of Schedule 1 to these Regulations).

21(2) Where the associated undertaking is itself a parent undertaking, the net assets and profits or losses to be taken into account are those of the parent and its subsidiary undertakings (after making any consolidation adjustments).

21(3) The equity method of accounting need not be applied if the amounts in question are not material for the purpose of giving a true and fair view.

Related party transactions

22 Paragraph 72 of Schedule 1 to these Regulations applies to transactions which the parent company, or other undertakings included in the consolidation, have entered into with related parties, unless they are intra group transactions.

Total amount of directors' remuneration etc

22A Paragraph 1 of Schedule 5 to these Regulations applies to group accounts with the modification that only the amounts and values referred to in that paragraph received or receivable by the directors of the parent company from the parent company and any of its subsidiary undertakings must be disclosed in the notes to the accounts.

History – Para. 22A inserted by SI 2015/980, reg. 39(10), with effect in relation to–

    (a)   financial years beginning on or after 1 January 2016, and
    (b)   a financial year of a company beginning on or after 1 January 2015, but before 1 January 2016, if the directors of the company so decide.

Deferred tax balances

22B Deferred tax balances must be recognised on consolidation where it is probable that a charge to tax will arise within the foreseeable future for one of the undertakings included in the consolidation.

History – Para. 22B inserted by SI 2015/980, reg. 39(10), with effect in relation to–

    (a)   financial years beginning on or after 1 January 2016, and
    (b)   a financial year of a company beginning on or after 1 January 2015, but before 1 January 2016, if the directors of the company so decide.

PART 2 – MODIFICATIONS FOR BANKING GROUPS
GENERAL APPLICATION OF PROVISIONS APPLICABLE TO INDIVIDUAL ACCOUNTS

23 In its application to banking groups, Part 1 of this Schedule has effect with the following modifications.

24 In paragraph 1 of this Schedule–

    (a)   the reference in sub-paragraph (1) to the provisions of Schedule 1 to these Regulations is to be construed as a reference to the provisions of Schedule 2 to these Regulations, and
    (b)   sub-paragraph (2) is to be omitted.

24A In paragraph 9 of this Schedule, the reference in sub-paragraph (6) to Schedule 1 is to these Regulations is to be construed as a reference to Schedule 2.

History – Para. 24A inserted by SI 2015/980, reg. 39(11), with effect in relation to–

    (a)   financial years beginning on or after 1 January 2016, and
    (b)   a financial year of a company beginning on or after 1 January 2015, but before 1 January 2016, if the directors of the company so decide.

Non-controlling interests and associated undertakings

History – In heading, the words "Non-controlling interests and associated undertakings" substituted for the words "Minority interests and associated undertakings" by SI 2015/980, reg. 39(12), with effect in relation to–

    (a)   financial years beginning on or after 1 January 2016, and
    (b)   a financial year of a company beginning on or after 1 January 2015, but before 1 January 2016, if the directors of the company so decide.

25(1) This paragraph adapts paragraphs 17 and 20 (which require items in respect of "non-controlling interests" and associated undertakings to be added to the formats set out in Schedule 1 to these Regulations) to the formats prescribed by Schedule 2 to these Regulations.

25(2) In paragraph 17–

(a) in sub-paragraph (1), for the reference to Schedule 1 to these Regulations, substitute a reference to Schedule 2,

(b) sub-paragraph (3) is to apply as if the reference to **"a separate item"** were a reference to **"separate items"** and the reference to **"the amount of any profit or loss"** were a reference to the following–

    (i) the amount of any profit or loss on ordinary activities, and

    (ii) the amount of any profit or loss on extraordinary activities, and

(c) sub-paragraph (4) is not to apply, but for the purposes of paragraph 5(1) of Part 1 of Schedule 2 to these Regulations (power to combine items) the additional items required by the foregoing provisions of this paragraph are to be treated as items to which a letter is assigned.

25(3) Paragraph 20(2) is to apply with respect to a balance sheet prepared under Schedule 2 to these Regulations as if it required assets item 7 (participating interests) in the balance sheet format to be replaced by the two replacement items referred to in that paragraph.

25(4) Paragraph 20(3) is not to apply, but the following items in the profit and loss account formats–

(a) format 1 item 3(b) (income from participating interests),

(b) format 2 item B2(b) (income from participating interests),

are replaced by the following–

    (i) "Income from participating interests other than associated undertakings", to be shown at position 3(b) in format 1 and position B2(b) in format 2, and

    (ii) "Income from associated undertakings", to be shown at an appropriate position.

History – Para. 25 substituted by SI 2015/980, reg. 39(12), with effect in relation to–

(a) financial years beginning on or after 1 January 2016, and

(b) a financial year of a company beginning on or after 1 January 2015, but before 1 January 2016, if the directors of the company so decide.

Former para. 25 read as follows:

"**25(1)** This paragraph adapts paragraphs 17 and 20 (which require items in respect of "Minority interests" and associated undertakings to be added to the formats set out in Schedule 1 to these Regulations) to the formats prescribed by Schedule 2 to these Regulations.

25(2) In paragraph 17–

(a) in sub-paragraph (1), for the reference to Schedule 1 to these Regulations, substitute a reference to Schedule 2, and

(b) paragraph 17(4) is not to apply, but for the purposes of paragraph 5(1) of Part I of

Schedule 2 to these Regulations (power to combine items) the additional items required by the foregoing provisions of this paragraph are to be treated as items to which a letter is assigned.

25(3) Paragraph 20(2) is to apply with respect to a balance sheet prepared under Schedule 2 to these Regulations as if it required assets item 7 (participating interests) in the balance sheet format to be replaced by the two replacement items referred to in that paragraph.

25(4) Paragraph 20(3) is not to apply, but the following items in the profit and loss account formats–

(a) format 1 item 3(b) (income from participating interests),

(b) format 2 item B2(b) (income from participating interests), are replaced by the following–

    (i) "Income from participating interests other than associated undertakings", to be shown at position 3(b) in format 1 and position B2(b) in format 2, and

    (ii) "Income from associated undertakings", to be shown at an appropriate position."

26 In paragraph 21(1) of this Schedule, for the references to paragraphs 17 to 20 and 22 of Schedule 1 to these Regulations substitute references to paragraphs 23 to 26 and 28 of Schedule 2 to these Regulations.

Related party transactions

27 In paragraph 22 of this Schedule, for the reference to paragraph 72 of Schedule 1 to these Regulations substitute a reference to paragraph 92 of Schedule 2 to these Regulations.

Foreign currency translation

28 Any difference between–

(a) the amount included in the consolidated accounts for the previous financial year with respect to any undertaking included in the consolidation or the group's interest in any associated undertaking, together with the amount of any transactions undertaken to cover any such interest, and

(b) the opening amount for the financial year in respect of those undertakings and in respect of any such transactions, arising as a result of the application of paragraph 50 of Schedule 2 to these Regulations may be credited to (where (a) is less than (b)), or deducted from (where (a) is greater than (b)), (as the case may be) consolidated reserves.

29 Any income and expenditure of undertakings included in the consolidation and associated undertakings in a foreign currency may be translated for the purposes of the consolidated accounts at the average rates of exchange prevailing during the financial year.

Information as to undertaking in which shares held as a result of financial assistance operation

30(1) The following provisions apply where the parent company of a banking group has a subsidiary undertaking which–

(a) is a credit institution of which shares are held as a result of a financial assistance operation with a view to its reorganisation or rescue, and

(b) is excluded from consolidation under section 405(3)(c) of the 2006 Act (interest held with a view to resale).

30(2) Information as to the nature and terms of the operations must be given in a note to the group accounts, and there must be appended to the copy of the group accounts delivered to the registrar in accordance with section 441 of the 2006 Act a copy of the undertaking's latest individual accounts and, if it is a parent undertaking, its latest group accounts.

If the accounts appended are required by law to be audited, a copy of the auditor's report must also be appended.

30(3) Any requirement of Part 35 of the 2006 Act as to the delivery to the registrar of a certified translation into English must be met in relation to any document required to be appended by subparagraph (2).

30(4) The above requirements are subject to the following qualifications–

(a) an undertaking is not required to prepare for the purposes of this paragraph accounts which would not otherwise be prepared, and if no accounts satisfying the above requirements are prepared none need be appended;

(b) the accounts of an undertaking need not be appended if they would not otherwise be required to be published, or made available for public inspection, anywhere in the world, but in that case the reason for not appending the accounts must be stated in a note to the consolidated accounts.

30(5) Where a copy of an undertaking's accounts is required to be appended to the copy of the group accounts delivered to the registrar, that fact must be stated in a note to the group accounts.

PART 3 – MODIFICATIONS FOR INSURANCE GROUPS

GENERAL APPLICATION OF PROVISIONS APPLICABLE TO INDIVIDUAL ACCOUNTS

31 In its application to insurance groups, Part 1 of this Schedule has effect with the following modifications.

32 In paragraph 1 of this Schedule–

(a) the reference in sub-paragraph (1) to the provisions of Schedule 1 to these Regulations is to be construed as a reference to the provisions of Schedule 3 to these Regulations, and
(b) sub-paragraph (2) is to be omitted.

Financial years of subsidiary undertakings

33 In paragraph 2(2)(a), for "three months" substitute "six months".

Assets and liabilities to be included in group accounts

34 In paragraph 3, after sub-paragraph (1) insert–

"3(1A) Sub-paragraph (1) is not to apply to those liabilities items the valuation of which by the undertakings included in a consolidation is based on the application of provisions applying only to insurance undertakings, nor to those assets items changes in the values of which also affect or establish policyholders' rights.

3(1B) Where sub-paragraph (1A) applies, that fact must be disclosed in the notes to the consolidated accounts.".

Elimination of group transactions

35 For sub-paragraph (4) of paragraph 6 substitute–

"6(4) Sub-paragraphs (1) and (2) need not be complied with–

(a) where a transaction has been concluded according to normal market conditions and a policyholder has rights in respect of the transaction, or
(b) if the amounts concerned are not material for the purpose of giving a true and fair view.

6(5) Where advantage is taken of sub-paragraph (4)(a) that fact must be disclosed in the notes to the accounts, and where the transaction in question has a material effect on the assets, liabilities, financial position and profit or loss of all the undertakings included in the consolidation that fact must also be so disclosed.".

35A In paragraph 9 of this Schedule, the reference in sub-paragraph (6) to Schedule 1 to these Regulations is to be construed as a reference to Schedule 3 to these Regulations.

History – Para. 35A inserted by SI 2015/980, reg. 39(13), with effect in relation to–

(a) financial years beginning on or after 1 January 2016, and
(b) a financial year of a company beginning on or after 1 January 2015, but before 1 January 2016, if the directors of the company so decide.

Non-controlling interests

36 In paragraph 17–

    (a) in sub-paragraph (1), for the reference to Schedule 1 to these Regulations, substitute a reference to Schedule 3,

    (b) sub-paragraph (3) is to apply as if the reference to **"a separate item"** were a reference to **"separate items"** and as if the reference to **"the amount of any profit or loss"** were a reference to the following–

        (i) the amount of any profit or loss on ordinary activities, and

        (ii) the amount of any profit or loss on extraordinary activities, and

    (c) for sub-paragraph (4), substitute–

"17(4) Paragraph 3(1) of Schedule 3 to these Regulations (power to combine items) does not apply in relation to the additional items required by the above provisions of this paragraph."

History – Para. 36 and the heading preceding it substituted by SI 2015/980, reg. 39(14), with effect in relation to–

    (a) financial years beginning on or after 1 January 2016, and

    (b) a financial year of a company beginning on or after 1 January 2015, but before 1 January 2016, if the directors of the company so decide.

Former para. 36 read as follows:

"Minority interests

36 In paragraph 17–

    (a) in sub-paragraph (1), for the reference to Schedule 1 to these Regulations, substitute a reference to Schedule 3, and

    (b) for sub-paragraph (4) substitute–

"17(4) Paragraph 3(1) of Schedule 3 to these Regulations (power to combine items) does not apply in relation to the additional items required by the above provisions of this paragraph"."

Associated undertakings

37 In paragraph 20–

    (a) in sub-paragraph (1), for the reference to Schedule 1 to these Regulations substitute a reference to Schedule 3 to these Regulations, and

    (b) for sub-paragraphs (2) and (3) substitute–

"20(2) In the balance sheet format, replace asset item C.II.3 (participating interests) with two items, "Interests in associated undertakings" and "Other participating interests".

20(3) In the profit and loss account format, replace items II.2.(a) and III.3.(a) (income from participating interests, with a separate indication of that derived from group undertakings) with–

    (a) "Income from participating interests other than associated undertakings, with a separate indication of that derived from group undertakings", to be shown as items II.2.(a) and III.3.(a), and

    (b) "Income from associated undertakings", to be shown as items II.2.(aa) and III.3.(aa).

38 In paragraph 21(1) of this Schedule, for the references to paragraphs 17 to 20 and 22 of Schedule 1 to these Regulations, substitute references to paragraphs 36 to 39 and 42 of Schedule 3 to these Regulations.

Related party transactions

39 In paragraph 22 of this Schedule, for the reference to paragraph 72 of Schedule 1 to these Regulations substitute a reference to paragraph 90 of Schedule 3 to these Regulations.

Modifications of schedule 3 to these regulations for purposes of paragraph 31

40(1) For the purposes of paragraph 31 of this Schedule, Schedule 3 to these Regulations is to be modified as follows.

40(2) The information required by paragraph 11 (additional items) need not be given.

40(3) In the case of general business, investment income, expenses and charges may be disclosed in the non-technical account rather than in the technical account.

40(4) In the case of subsidiary undertakings which are not authorised to carry on long-term business in the United Kingdom, notes (8) and (9) to the profit and loss account format have effect as if references to investment income, expenses and charges arising in the long-term fund or to investments attributed to the long-term fund were references to investment income, expenses and charges or (as the case may be) investments relating to long-term business.

40(5) In the case of subsidiary undertakings which do not have a head office in the United Kingdom, the computation required by paragraph 52 must be made annually by an actuary or other specialist in the field on the basis of recognised actuarial methods.

40(6) The information required by paragraphs 85 to 88 need not be shown.

SCHEDULE 7

Regulation 10

MATTERS TO BE DEALT WITH IN DIRECTORS' REPORT
PART 1 – MATTERS OF A GENERAL NATURE

Introduction

1 In addition to the information required by section 416 of the 2006 Act, the directors' report must contain the following information.

1A Where a company has chosen in accordance with section 414C(11) to set out in the company's strategic report information required by this Schedule to be contained in the directors' report it shall state in the directors' report that it has done so and in respect of which information it has done so.

History – Para. 1A inserted by SI 2013/1970, reg. 7(1) and (3)(a), with effect from 1 October 2013 in respect of financial years ending on or after 30 September 2013.

Asset values

2 [Repealed.]

History – Para. 2 repealed by SI 2013/1970, reg. 7(1) and (3)(b), with effect from 1 October 2013 in respect of financial years ending on or after 30 September 2013. Prior to repeal, para. 2 read as follows:

"**2(1)** If, in the case of such of the fixed assets of the company as consist in interests in land, their market value (as at the end of the financial year) differs substantially from the amount at which they are included in the balance sheet, and the difference is, in the directors' opinion, of such significance as to require that the attention of members of the company or of holders of its debentures should be drawn to it, the report must indicate the difference with such degree of precision as is practicable.

2(2) In relation to a group directors' report sub-paragraph (1) has effect as if the reference to the fixed assets of the company was a reference to the fixed assets of the company and of its subsidiary undertakings included in the consolidation."

Political donations and expenditure

3(1) If–

    (a)   the company (not being the wholly-owned subsidiary of a company incorporated in the United Kingdom) has in the financial year–

        (i)   made any political donation to any political party or other political organisation,

        (ii)   made any political donation to any independent election candidate, or

        (iii)   incurred any political expenditure, and

    (b)   the amount of the donation or expenditure, or (as the case may be) the aggregate amount of all donations and expenditure falling within paragraph (a), exceeded £2000, the directors' report for the year must contain the following particulars.

3(2) Those particulars are–

    (a)   as respects donations falling within sub-paragraph (1)(a)(i) or (ii)–

        (i)   the name of each political party, other political organisation or independent election candidate to whom any such donation has been made, and

        (ii)   the total amount given to that party, organisation or candidate by way of such donations in the financial year; and

    (b)   as respects expenditure falling within sub-paragraph (1)(a)(iii), the total amount incurred by way of such expenditure in the financial year.

3(3) If–

    (a)   at the end of the financial year the company has subsidiaries which have, in that year, made any donations or incurred any such expenditure as is mentioned in sub-paragraph (1)(a), and

    (b)   it is not itself the wholly-owned subsidiary of a company incorporated in the United Kingdom, the directors' report for the year is not, by virtue of sub-paragraph (1), required to contain the particulars specified in sub-paragraph (2).

But, if the total amount of any such donations or expenditure (or both) made or incurred in that year by the company and the subsidiaries between them exceeds £2000, the directors' report for the year must contain those particulars in relation to each body by whom any such donation or expenditure has been made or incurred.

3(4) Any expression used in this paragraph which is also used in Part 14 of the 2006 Act (control of political donations and expenditure) has the same meaning as in that Part.

4(1) If the company (not being the wholly-owned subsidiary of a company incorporated in the United Kingdom) has in the financial year made any contribution to a non-EU political party, the directors' report for the year must contain–

    (a)   a statement of the amount of the contribution, or

    (b)   (if it has made two or more such contributions in the year) a statement of the total amount of the contributions.

4(2) If–

    (a)   at the end of the financial year the company has subsidiaries which have, in that year, made any such contributions as are mentioned in sub-paragraph (1), and

    (b)   it is not itself the wholly-owned subsidiary of a company incorporated in the United Kingdom, the directors' report for the year is not, by virtue of sub-paragraph (1), required to contain any such statement as is there mentioned, but it must instead contain a statement of the total amount of the contributions made in the year by the company and the subsidiaries between them.

4(3) In this paragraph, **"contribution"**, in relation to an organisation, means–

(a) any gift of money to the organisation (whether made directly or indirectly);
(b) any subscription or other fee paid for affiliation to, or membership of, the organisation; or
(c) any money spent (otherwise than by the organisation or a person acting on its behalf) in paying any expenses incurred directly or indirectly by the organisation.

4(4) In this paragraph, **"non-EU political party"** means any political party which carries on, or proposes to carry on, its activities wholly outside the member States.

Charitable donations

5 [Repealed.]

History – Para. 5 repealed by SI 2013/1970, reg. 7(1) and (3)(b), with effect from 1 October 2013 in respect of financial years ending on or after 30 September 2013. Prior to repeal, para. 5 read as follows:

"**5(1)** If–

(a) the company (not being the wholly-owned subsidiary of a company incorporated in the United Kingdom) has in the financial year given money for charitable purposes, and
(b) the money given exceeded £2000 in amount, the directors' report for the year must contain, in the case of each of the purposes for which money has been given, a statement of the amount of money given for that purpose.

5(2) If–

(a) at the end of the financial year the company has subsidiaries which have, in that year, given money for charitable purposes, and
(b) it is not itself the wholly owned subsidiary of a company incorporated in the United Kingdom, sub-paragraph (1) does not apply to the company. But, if the amount given in that year for charitable purposes by the company and the subsidiaries between them exceeds £2000, the directors' report for the year must contain, in the case of each of the purposes for which money has been given by the company and the subsidiaries between them, a statement of the amount of money given for that purpose.

5(3) Money given for charitable purposes to a person who, when it was given, was ordinarily resident outside the United Kingdom is to be left out of account for the purposes of this paragraph.

5(4) For the purposes of this paragraph, **"charitable purposes"** means purposes which are exclusively charitable, and as respects Scotland a purpose is charitable if it is listed in section 7(2) of the Charities and Trustee Investment (Scotland) Act 2005."

Financial instruments

6(1) In relation to the use of financial instruments by a company, the directors' report must contain an indication of–

(a) the financial risk management objectives and policies of the company, including the policy for hedging each major type of forecasted transaction for which hedge accounting is used, and
(b) the exposure of the company to price risk, credit risk, liquidity risk and cash flow risk, unless such information is not material for the assessment of the assets, liabilities, financial position and profit or loss of the company.

6(2) In relation to a group directors' report sub-paragraph (1) has effect as if the references to the company were references to the company and its subsidiary undertakings included in the consolidation.

6(3) In sub-paragraph (1) the expressions **"hedge accounting"**, **"price risk"**, **"credit risk"**, **"liquidity risk"** and **"cash flow risk"** have the same meaning as they have in Council Directive 78/660/EEC on the annual accounts of certain types of companies, and in Council Directive 83/349/EEC on consolidated accounts.

Miscellaneous

7(1) The directors' report must contain–

(a) particulars of any important events affecting the company which have occurred since the end of the financial year,

(b) an indication of likely future developments in the business of the company,

(c) an indication of the activities (if any) of the company in the field of research and development, and

(d) (unless the company is an unlimited company) an indication of the existence of branches (as defined in section 1046(3) of the 2006 Act) of the company outside the United Kingdom.

7(2) In relation to a group directors' report paragraphs (a), (b) and (c) of sub-paragraph (1) have effect as if the references to the company were references to the company and its subsidiary undertakings included in the consolidation.

PART 2 – DISCLOSURE REQUIRED BY COMPANY ACQUIRING ITS OWN SHARES ETC.

8 This Part of this Schedule applies where shares in a public company–

(a) are purchased by the company or are acquired by it by forfeiture or surrender in lieu of forfeiture, or in pursuance of any of the following provisions (acquisition of own shares by company limited by shares)–

    (i) section 143(3) of the Companies Act 1985,
    (ii) Article 153(3) of the Companies (Northern Ireland) Order 1986, or
    (iii) section 659 of the 2006 Act, or

(b) are acquired by another person in circumstances where paragraph (c) or (d) of any of the following provisions applies (acquisition by company's nominee, or by another with company financial assistance, the company having a beneficial interest)–

    (i) section 146(1) of the Companies Act 1985,
    (ii) Article 156(1) of the Companies (Northern Ireland) Order 1986, or
    (iii) section 662(1) of the 2006 Act applies, or

(c) are made subject to a lien or other charge taken (whether expressly or otherwise) by the company and permitted by any of the following provisions (exceptions from general rule against a company having a lien or charge on its own shares)–

    (i) section 150(2) or (4) of the Companies Act 1985,
    (ii) Article 160(2) or (4) of the Companies (Northern Ireland) Order 1986, or
    (iii) section 670(2) or (4) of the 2006 Act.

History – In the opening words, "public" inserted by SI 2013/1970, reg. 7(1) and (3)(c), with effect from 1 October 2013 in respect of financial years ending on or after 30 September 2013.

9 The directors' report for a financial year must state–

(a) the number and nominal value of the shares so purchased, the aggregate amount of the consideration paid by the company for such shares and the reasons for their purchase;

(b) the number and nominal value of the shares so acquired by the company, acquired by another person in such circumstances and so charged respectively during the financial year;

(c) the maximum number and nominal value of shares which, having been so acquired by the company, acquired by another person in such circumstances or so charged (whether or not during that year) are held at any time by the company or that other person during that year;

(d) the number and nominal value of the shares so acquired by the company, acquired by another person in such circumstances or so charged (whether or not during that year) which are disposed of by the company or that other person or cancelled by the company during that year;

(e) where the number and nominal value of the shares of any particular description are stated in pursuance of any of the preceding sub-paragraphs, the percentage of the called-up share capital which shares of that description represent;

(f) where any of the shares have been so charged the amount of the charge in each case; and

(g) where any of the shares have been disposed of by the company or the person who acquired them in such circumstances for money or money's worth the amount or value of the consideration in each case.

PART 3 – DISCLOSURE CONCERNING EMPLOYMENT ETC. OF DISABLED PERSONS

10(1) This Part of this Schedule applies to the directors' report where the average number of persons employed by the company in each week during the financial year exceeded 250.

10(2) That average number is the quotient derived by dividing, by the number of weeks in the financial year, the number derived by ascertaining, in relation to each of those weeks, the number of persons who, under contracts of service, were employed in the week (whether throughout it or not) by the company, and adding up the numbers ascertained.

10(3) The directors' report must in that case contain a statement describing such policy as the company has applied during the financial year–

(a) for giving full and fair consideration to applications for employment by the company made by disabled persons, having regard to their particular aptitudes and abilities,

(b) for continuing the employment of, and for arranging appropriate training for, employees of the company who have become disabled persons during the period when they were employed by the company, and

(c) otherwise for the training, career development and promotion of disabled persons employed by the company.

10(4) In this Part–

(a) **"employment"** means employment other than employment to work wholly or mainly outside the United Kingdom, and "employed" and "employee" are to be construed accordingly; and

(b) **"disabled person"** means the same as in the Disability Discrimination Act 1995.

PART 4 – EMPLOYEE INVOLVEMENT

11(1) This Part of this Schedule applies to the directors' report where the average number of persons employed by the company in each week during the financial year exceeded 250.

11(2) That average number is the quotient derived by dividing, by the number of weeks in the financial year, the number derived by ascertaining, in relation to each of those weeks, the number of persons who, under contracts of service, were employed in the week (whether throughout it or not) by the company, and adding up the numbers ascertained.

11(3) The directors' report must in that case contain a statement describing the action that has been taken during the financial year to introduce, maintain or develop arrangements aimed at–

(a) providing employees systematically with information on matters of concern to them as employees,

(b) consulting employees or their representatives on a regular basis so that the views of employees can be taken into account in making decisions which are likely to affect their interests,

(c) encouraging the involvement of employees in the company's performance through an employees' share scheme or by some other means,

(d) achieving a common awareness on the part of all employees of the financial and economic factors affecting the performance of the company.

11(4) In sub-paragraph (3) **"employee"** does not include a person employed to work wholly or mainly outside the United Kingdom; and for the purposes of sub-paragraph (2) no regard is to be had to such a person.

PART 5 – POLICY AND PRACTICE ON PAYMENT OF CREDITORS

12 [Repealed.]

History – Para. 12 repealed by SI 2013/1970, reg. 7(1) and (3)(d), with effect from 1 October 2013 in respect of financial years ending on or after 30 September 2013. Prior to repeal, para. 12 read as follows:

"**12(1)** This Part of this Schedule applies to the directors' report for a financial year if–

(a) the company was at any time within the year a public company, or

(b) the company did not qualify as small or medium-sized in relation to the year by virtue of section 382 or 465 of the 2006 Act and was at any time within the year a member of a group of which the parent company was a public company.

12(2) The report must state, with respect to the next following financial year–

(a) whether in respect of some or all of its suppliers it is the company's policy to follow any code or standard on payment practice and, if so, the name of the code or standard and the place where information about, and copies of, the code or standard can be obtained,

(b) whether in respect of some or all of its suppliers it is the company's policy–

(i) to settle the terms of payment with those suppliers when agreeing the terms of each transaction,

(ii) to ensure that those suppliers are made aware of the terms of payment, and

(iii) to abide by the terms of payment,

(c) where the company's policy is not as mentioned in paragraph (a) or (b) in respect of some or all of its suppliers, what its policy is with respect to the payment of those suppliers; and if the company's policy is different for different suppliers or classes of suppliers, the report must identify the suppliers to which the different policies apply.

In this sub-paragraph references to the company's suppliers are references to persons who are or may become its suppliers.

12(3) The report must also state the number of days which bears to the number of days in the financial year the same proportion as X bears to Y where–

X = the aggregate of the amounts which were owed to trade creditors at the end of the year; and

Y = the aggregate of the amounts in which the company was invoiced by suppliers during the year.

12(4) For the purposes of sub-paragraphs (2) and (3) a person is a supplier of the company at any time if–

(a) at that time, he is owed an amount in respect of goods or services supplied, and

(b) that amount would be included under the heading corresponding to item E.4 (trade creditors) in format 1 if–

(i) the company's accounts fell to be prepared as at that time,

(ii) those accounts were prepared in accordance with Schedule 1 to these Regulations, and

(iii) that format were adopted.

12(5) For the purpose of sub-paragraph (3), the aggregate of the amounts which at the end of the financial year were owed to trade creditors is taken to be–

(a) where in the company's accounts format 1 of the balance sheet formats set out in Part 1 of Schedule 1 to these Regulations is adopted, the amount shown under the heading corresponding to item E.4 (trade creditors) in that format,

(b) where format 2 is adopted, the amount which, under the heading corresponding to item C.4 (trade creditors) in that format, is shown as falling due within one year, and

(c) where the company's accounts are prepared in accordance with Schedule 2 or 3 to these Regulations or the company's accounts are IAS accounts, the amount which would be shown under the heading corresponding to item E.4 (trade creditors) in format 1 if the company's accounts were prepared in accordance with Schedule 1 and that format were adopted."

PART 6 – DISCLOSURE REQUIRED BY CERTAIN PUBLICLY-TRADED COMPANIES

13(1) This Part of this Schedule applies to the directors' report for a financial year if the company had securities carrying
voting rights admitted to trading on a regulated market at the end of that year.

13(2) The report must contain detailed information, by reference to the end of that year, on the following matters–

  (a) the structure of the company's capital, including in particular–

   (i)   the rights and obligations attaching to the shares or, as the case may be, to each class of shares in the company, and
   (ii) where there are two or more such classes, the percentage of the total share capital represented by each class;

  (b) any restrictions on the transfer of securities in the company, including in particular–

   (i)   limitations on the holding of securities, and
   (ii) requirements to obtain the approval of the company, or of other holders of securities in the company, for a transfer of securities;

  (c) in the case of each person with a significant direct or indirect holding of securities in the company, such details as are known to the company of–

   (i)   the identity of the person,
   (ii)   the size of the holding, and
   (iii) the nature of the holding;

  (d) in the case of each person who holds securities carrying special rights with regard to control of the company–

   (i)   the identity of the person, and
   (ii) the nature of the rights;

  (e) where–

   (i)   the company has an employees' share scheme, and
   (ii) shares to which the scheme relates have rights with regard to control of the company that are not exercisable directly by the employees, how those rights are exercisable;

  (f) any restrictions on voting rights, including in particular–

   (i)   limitations on voting rights of holders of a given percentage or number of votes,
   (ii)   deadlines for exercising voting rights, and
   (iii) arrangements by which, with the company's co-operation, financial rights carried by securities are held by a person other than the holder of the securities;

  (g) any agreements between holders of securities that are known to the company and may result in restrictions on the transfer of securities or on voting rights;

  (h) any rules that the company has about–

   (i)   appointment and replacement of directors, or
   (ii) amendment of the company's articles of association;

  (i) the powers of the company's directors, including in particular any powers in relation to the issuing or buying back by the company of its shares;

  (j) any significant agreements to which the company is a party that take effect, alter or terminate upon a change of control of the company following a takeover bid, and the effects of any such agreements;

(k) any agreements between the company and its directors or employees providing for compensation for loss of office or employment (whether through resignation, purported redundancy or otherwise) that occurs because of a takeover bid.

13(3) For the purposes of sub-paragraph (2)(a) a company's capital includes any securities in the company that are not admitted to trading on a regulated market.

13(4) For the purposes of sub-paragraph (2)(c) a person has an indirect holding of securities if–

(a) they are held on his behalf, or
(b) he is able to secure that rights carried by the securities are exercised in accordance with his wishes.

13(5) Sub-paragraph (2)(j) does not apply to an agreement if–

(a) disclosure of the agreement would be seriously prejudicial to the company, and
(b) the company is not under any other obligation to disclose it.

13(6) In this paragraph–

"securities" means shares or debentures;

"takeover bid" has the same meaning as in the Takeovers Directive;

"the Takeovers Directive" means Directive 2004/25/EC of the European Parliament and of the Council;

"voting rights" means rights to vote at general meetings of the company in question, including rights that arise only in certain circumstances.

14 The directors' report must also contain any necessary explanatory material with regard to information that is required to be included in the report by this Part.

PART 7 – DISCLOSURES CONCERNING GREENHOUSE GAS EMISSIONS

15(1) This Part of this Schedule applies to the directors' report for a financial year if the company is a quoted company.

15(2) The report must state the annual quantity of emissions in tonnes of carbon dioxide equivalent from activities for which that company is responsible including–

(a) the combustion of fuel; and
(b) the operation of any facility.

15(3) The report must state the annual quantity of emissions in tonnes of carbon dioxide equivalent resulting from the purchase of electricity, heat, steam or cooling by the company for its own use.

15(4) Sub-paragraphs (2) and (3) apply only to the extent that it is practical for the company to obtain the information in question; but where it is not practical for the company to obtain some or all of that information, the report must state what information is not included and why.

16 The directors' report must state the methodologies used to calculate the information disclosed under paragraph 15(2) and (3).

17 The directors' report must state at least one ratio which expresses the quoted company's annual emissions in relation to a quantifiable factor associated with the company's activities.

18 With the exception of the first year for which the directors' report contains the information required by paragraphs 15(2) and (3) and 17, the report must state not only the information required by paragraphs 15(2) and (3) and 17, but also that information as disclosed in the report for the preceding financial year.

19 The directors' report must state if the period for which it is reporting the information required by paragraph 15(2) and (3) is different to the period in respect of which the directors' report is prepared.

20 The following definitions apply for the purposes of this Part of this Schedule–

"emissions" means emissions into the atmosphere of a greenhouse gas as defined in section 92 of the Climate Change Act 2008 which are attributable to human activity;

"tonne of carbon dioxide equivalent" has the meaning given in section 93(2) of the Climate Change Act 2008.

History – Pt. 7 inserted by SI 2013/1970, reg. 7(1) and (3)(e), with effect from 1 October 2013 in respect of financial years ending on or after 30 September 2013.

SCHEDULE 8   Regulation 11

QUOTED COMPANIES: DIRECTORS' REMUNERATION REPORT
PART 1 – INTRODUCTORY

1(1) In the directors' remuneration report for a financial year ("the relevant financial year") there must be shown, subject to sub-paragraph (2), the information specified in Parts 2, 3, and 4.

1(2) The directors' remuneration policy as specified in Part 4, may, subject to subparagraph (3), be omitted from the directors' remuneration report for a financial year, if the company does not intend, at the accounts meeting at which the report is to be laid, to move a resolution to approve the directors' remuneration policy in accordance with section 439A of the 2006 Act.

1(3) Where the directors' remuneration policy is omitted from the report in accordance with sub-paragraph (2), there must be set out in the report the following information–

(a) the date of the last general meeting of the company at which a resolution was moved by the company in respect of that directors' remuneration policy and at which that policy was approved; and
(b) where, on the company's website or at some other place, a copy of that directors' remuneration policy may be inspected by the members of the company.

2(1) Information required to be shown in the report for or in respect of a particular person must be shown in the report in a manner that links the information to that person identified by name.

2(2) Nothing in this Schedule prevents the directors setting out in the report any such additional information as they think fit, and any item required to be shown in the report may be shown in greater detail than required by the provisions of this Schedule.

2(3) Where the requirements of this Schedule make reference to a "director" those requirements may be complied with in such manner as to distinguish between directors who perform executive functions and those who do not.

2(4) Any requirement of this Schedule to provide information in respect of a director may, in respect of those directors who do not perform executive functions, be omitted or otherwise modified where that requirement is not applicable to such a director and in such a case, particulars of, and the reasons for, the omission or modification must be given in the report.

2(5) Any requirement of this Schedule to provide information in respect of performance measures or targets does not require the disclosure of information which, in the opinion of the directors, is commercially sensitive in respect of the company.

2(6) Where information that would otherwise be required to be in the report is not included in reliance on sub-paragraph (5), particulars of, and the reasons for, the omission must be given in the report and an indication given of when (if at all) the information is to be reported to the members of the company.

2(7) Where any provision of this Schedule requires a sum or figure to be given in respect of any financial year preceding the relevant financial year, in the first directors' remuneration report prepared in accordance with this Schedule, that sum or figure may, where the sum or figure is not readily available from the reports and accounts of the company prepared for those years, be given as an estimate and a note of explanation provided in the report.

PART 2 – ANNUAL STATEMENT

3 The directors' remuneration report must contain a statement by the director who fulfils the role of chair of the remuneration committee (or, where there is no such person, by a director nominated by the directors to make the statement) summarising for the relevant financial year–
- (a) the major decisions on directors' remuneration;
- (b) any substantial changes relating to directors' remuneration made during the year; and
- (c) the context in which those changes occurred and decisions have been taken.

PART 3 – ANNUAL REPORT ON REMUNERATION

Single total figure of remuneration for each director

4(1) The directors' remuneration report must, for the relevant financial year, for each person who has served as a director of the company at any time during that year, set out in a table in the form set out in paragraph 5 ("the single total figure table") the information prescribed by paragraphs 6 and 7 below.

4(2) The report may set out in separate tables the information to be supplied in respect of directors who perform executive functions and those who do not.

4(3) Unless otherwise indicated the sums set out in the table are those in respect of the relevant financial year and relate to the director's performance of, or agreement to perform, qualifying services.

5(1) The form of the table required by paragraph 4 is–

	Single	Total	Figure	Table		
	a	b	c	d	e	Total
Director 1	xxx	xxx	xxx	xxx	xxx	xxx
Director 1	xxx	xxx	xxx	xxx	xxx	xxx

5(2) The directors may choose to display the table using an alternative orientation, in which case references in this Schedule to columns are to be read as references to rows.

6(1) In addition to the columns described in paragraph 7, columns–

- (a) must be included to set out any other items in the nature of remuneration (other than items required to be disclosed under paragraph 15) which are not set out in the columns headed "(a)" to "(e)"; and
- (b) may be included if there are any sub-totals or other items which the directors consider necessary in order to assist the understanding of the table.

6(2) Any additional columns must be inserted before the column marked "Total".

7(1) Subject to paragraph 9, in the single total figure table, the sums that are required to be set out in the columns are–

    (a)   in the column headed "a", the total amount of salary and fees;

    (b)   in the column headed "b", all taxable benefits;

    (c)   in the column headed "c", money or other assets received or receivable for the relevant financial year as a result of the achievement of performance measures and targets relating to a period ending in that financial year other than–

        (i)   those which result from awards made in a previous financial year and where final vesting is determined as a result of the achievement of performance measures or targets relating to a period ending in the relevant financial year; or

        (ii) those receivable subject to the achievement of performance measures or targets in a future financial year;

    (d)   in the column headed "d", money or other assets received or receivable for periods of more than one financial year where final vesting–

        (i)   is determined as a result of the achievement of performance measures or targets relating to a period ending in the relevant financial year; and

        (ii) is not subject to the achievement of performance measures or targets in a future financial year;

    (e)   in the column headed "e", all pension related benefits including–

        (i)   payments (whether in cash or otherwise) in lieu of retirement benefits;

        (ii) all benefits in year from participating in pension schemes;

    (f)   in the column headed "Total", the total amount of the sums set out in the previous columns.

7(2) Where it is necessary to assist the understanding of the table by the creation of subtotals the columns headed "a" to "e" may be set out in an order other than the one set out in paragraph 5.

8(1) In respect of any items in paragraph 7(1)(c) or (d) where the performance measures or targets are substantially (but not fully) completed by the end of the relevant financial year–

    (a)   the sum given in the table may include sums which relate to the following financial year; but

    (b)   where such sums are included, those sums must not be included in the corresponding column of the single total figure table prepared for that following financial year; and

    (c)   a note to the table must explain the basis of the calculation.

8(2) Where any money or other assets reported in the single total figure table in the directors' remuneration report prepared in respect of any previous financial year are the subject of a recovery of sums paid or the withholding of any sum for any reason in the relevant financial year–

    (a)   the recovery or withholding so attributable must be shown in a separate column in the table as a negative value and deducted from the column headed "Total"; and

    (b)   an explanation for the recovery or withholding and the basis of the calculation must be given in a note to the table.

8(3) Where the calculations in accordance with paragraph 10 (other than in respect of a recovery or withholding) result in a negative value, the result must be expressed as zero in the relevant column in the table.

9(1) Each column in the single total figure table must contain, in such manner as to permit comparison, two sums as follows–

    (a)   the sum set out in the corresponding column in the report prepared in respect of the financial year preceding the relevant financial year; and

    (b)   the sum for the relevant financial year.

9(2) When, in the single total figure table, a sum is given in the column which relates to the preceding financial year and that sum, when set out in the report for that preceding year was given as an estimated sum, then in the relevant financial year–

(a) it must be given as an actual sum;
(b) the amount representing the difference between the estimate and the actual must not be included in the column relating to the relevant financial year; and
(c) details of the calculation of the revised sum must be given in a note to the table.

10(1) The methods to be used to calculate the sums required to be set out in the single total figure table are–

(a) for the column headed "a", cash paid to or receivable by the person in respect of the relevant financial year;
(b) for the column headed "b", the gross value before payment of tax;
(c) for column "c", the total cash equivalent including any amount deferred, other than where the deferral is subject to the achievement of further performance measures or targets in a future financial year;
(d) for column "d"–

   (i) the cash value of any monetary award;
   (ii) the value of any shares or share options awarded, calculated by–

      (aa) multiplying the original number of shares granted by the proportion that vest (or an estimate);
      (bb) multiplying the total arrived at in (aa) by the market price of shares at the date on which the shares vest; and

   (iii) the value of any additional cash or shares receivable in respect of dividends accrued (actually or notionally);

(e) for the column headed "e",–

   (i) for the item in paragraph 7(1)(e)(i), the cash value;
   (ii) for the item in paragraph 7(1)(e)(ii), what the aggregate pension input amount would be across all the pension schemes of the company or group in which the director accrues benefits, calculated using the method set out in section 229 of the Finance Act 2004 where–

      (aa) references to **"pension input period"** are to be read as references to the company's financial year, or where a person becomes a director during the financial year, the period starting on the date the person became a director and ending at the end of the financial year;
      (bb) all pension schemes of the company or group which provide relevant benefits to the director are deemed to be registered schemes;
      (cc) all pension contributions paid by the director during the pension input period are deducted from the pension input amount;
      (dd) in the application of section 234 of that Act, the figure 20 is substituted for the figure 16 each time it appears;
      (ee) subsections 229(3) and (4) do not apply; and
      (ff) section 277 of that Act is read as follows–

      277 For the purposes of this Part the valuation assumptions in relation to a person, benefits and a date are–

         (a) if the person has not left the employment to which the arrangement relates on or before the date, that the person left that employment on the date with a prospective right to benefits under the arrangement,

(b) if the person has not reached such age (if any) as must have been reached to avoid any reduction in the benefits on account of age, that on the date the person is entitled to receive the benefits without any reduction on account of age, and

(c) that the person's right to receive the benefits had not been occasioned by physical or mental impairment.

10(2) For the item in paragraph 7(1)(e)(ii) where there has not been a company contribution to the pension scheme in respect of the director, but if such a contribution had been made it would have been measured for pension input purposes under section 233(1)(b) of the Finance Act 2004, when calculating the pension input amount for the purposes of subparagraph (1)(e)(ii) it should be calculated as if the cash value of any contribution notionally allocated to the scheme in respect of the person by or on behalf of the company including any adjustment made for any notional investment return achieved during the relevant financial year were a contribution paid by the employer in respect of the individual for the purposes of section 233(1)(b) of the Finance Act 2004.

10(3) For the purposes of the calculation in sub-paragraph (1)(d)(ii)–

(a) where the market price of shares at the date on which the shares vest is not ascertainable by the date on which the remuneration report is approved by the directors, an estimate of the market price of the shares shall be calculated on the basis of an average market value over the last quarter of the relevant financial year; and

(b) where the award was an award of shares or share options, the cash amount the individual was or will be required to pay to acquire the share must be deducted from the total.

Definitions applicable to the single total figure table

11(1) In paragraph 7(1)(b) **"taxable benefits"** includes–

(a) sums paid by way of expenses allowance that are–

(i) chargeable to United Kingdom income tax (or would be if the person were an individual, or would be if the person were resident in the United Kingdom for tax purposes), and

(ii) paid to or receivable by the person in respect of qualifying services; and

(b) any benefits received by the person, other than salary, (whether or not in cash) that–

(i) are emoluments of the person, and

(ii) are received by the person in respect of qualifying services.

11(2) A payment or other benefit received in advance of a director commencing qualifying services, but in anticipation of performing qualifying services, is to be treated as if received on the first day of performance of the qualifying services.

Additional requirements in respect of the single total figure table

12(1) In respect of the sum required to be set out by paragraph 7(1)(b), there must be set out after the table a summary identifying–

(a) the types of benefits the value of which is included in the sum set out in the column headed "b"; and

(b) the value (where significant).

12(2) For every component the value of which is included in the sums required to be set out in the columns headed "c" and "d" of the table by paragraphs 7(1)(c) and (d), there must be set out after the table the relevant details.

12(3) In sub-paragraph (2) **"the relevant details"** means–

    (a) details of any performance measures and the relative weighting of each;

    (b) within each performance measure, the performance targets set at the beginning of the performance period and corresponding value of the award achievable;

    (c) for each performance measure, details of actual performance relative to the targets set and measured over the relevant reporting period, and the resulting level of award; and

    (d) where any discretion has been exercised in respect of the award, particulars must be given of how the discretion was exercised and how the resulting level of award was determined.

12(4) For each component the value of which is included in the sum set out in the column headed "c" of the table, the report must state if any amount was deferred, the percentage deferred, whether it was deferred in cash or shares, if relevant, and whether the deferral was subject to any conditions other than performance measures.

12(5) Where additional columns are included in accordance with paragraph 6(1)(a), there must be set out in a note to the table the basis on which the sums in the column were calculated, and other such details as are necessary for an understanding of the sums set out in the column, including any performance measures relating to that component of remuneration or if there are none, an explanation of why not.

Total pension entitlements

13(1) The directors' remuneration report must, for each person who has served as a director of the company at any time during the relevant financial year, and who has a prospective entitlement to defined benefits or cash balance benefits (or to benefits under a hybrid arrangement which includes such benefits) in respect of qualifying services, contain the following information in respect of pensions–

    (a) details of those rights as at the end of that year, including the person's normal retirement date;

    (b) a description of any additional benefit that will become receivable by a director in the event that that director retires early; and

    (c) where a person has rights under more than one type of pension benefit identified in column headed "e" of the single total figure table, separate details relating to each type of pension benefit.

13(2) For the purposes of this paragraph, "defined benefits", "cash balance benefits" and "hybrid arrangement" have the same meaning as in section 152 of the Finance Act 2004.

13(3) "Normal retirement date" means an age specified in the pension scheme rules (or otherwise determined) as the earliest age at which, while the individual continues to accrue benefits under the pension scheme, entitlement to a benefit arises–

    (a) without consent (whether of an employer, the trustees or managers of the scheme or otherwise), and

    (b) without an actuarial reduction,

but disregarding any special provision as to early repayment on grounds of ill health, redundancy or dismissal.

Scheme interests awarded during the financial year

14(1) The directors' remuneration report must for each person who has served as a director of the company at any time during the relevant financial year contain a table setting out–

(a) details of the scheme interests awarded to the person during the relevant financial year; and

(b) for each scheme interest–

    (i) a description of the type of interest awarded;

    (ii) a description of the basis on which the award is made;

    (iii) the face value of the award;

    (iv) the percentage of scheme interests that would be receivable if the minimum performance was achieved;

    (v) for a scheme interest that is a share option, an explanation of any difference between the exercise price per share and the price specified under paragraph 14(3);

    (vi) the end of the period over which the performance measures and targets for that interest have to be achieved (or if there are different periods for different measures and targets, the end of whichever of those periods ends last); and

    (vii) a summary of the performance measures and targets if not set out elsewhere in the report.

14(2) In respect of a scheme interest relating to shares or share options, **"face value"** means the maximum number of shares that would vest if all performance measures and targets are met multiplied by either–

(a) the share price at date of grant or

(b) the average share price used to determine the number of shares awarded.

14(3) Where the report sets out the face value of an award in respect of a scheme interest relating to shares or share options, the report must specify–

(a) whether the face value has been calculated using the share price at date of grant or the average share price;

(b) where the share price at date of grant is used, the amount of that share price and the date of grant;

(c) where the average share price is used, what that price was and the period used for calculating the average.

Payments to past directors

15 The directors' remuneration report must, for the relevant financial year, contain details of any payments of money or other assets to any person who was not a director of the company at the time the payment was made, but who had been a director of the company before that time, excluding–

(a) any payments falling within paragraph 16;

(b) any payments which are shown in the single total figure table;

(c) any payments which have been disclosed in a previous directors' remuneration report of the company;

(d) any payments which are below a *de minimis* threshold set by the company and stated in the report;

(e) payments by way of regular pension benefits commenced in a previous year or dividend payments in respect of scheme interests retained after leaving office; and

(f) payments in respect of employment with or any other contractual service performed for the company other than as a director.

Payments for loss of office

16 The directors' remuneration report must for the relevant financial year set out, for each person who has served as a director of the company at any time during that year, or any previous year, excluding payments which are below a *de minimis* threshold set by the company and stated in the report–

(a) the total amount of any payment for loss of office paid to or receivable by the person in respect of that financial year, broken down into each component comprised in that payment and the value of each component;

(b) an explanation of how each component was calculated;

(c) any other payments paid to or receivable by the person in connection with the termination of qualifying services, whether by way of compensation for loss of office or otherwise, including the treatment of outstanding incentive awards that vest on or following termination; and

(d) where any discretion was exercised in respect of the payment, an explanation of how it was exercised.

Statement of directors' shareholding and share interests

17 The directors' remuneration report for the relevant financial year must contain, for each person who has served as a director of the company at any time during that year–

(a) a statement of any requirements or guidelines for the director to own shares in the company and state whether or not those requirements or guidelines have been met;

(b) in tabular form or forms–

    (i) the total number of interests in shares in the company of the director including interests of connected persons (as defined for the purposes of section 96B(2) of the Financial Services and Markets Act 2000);

    (ii) total number of scheme interests differentiating between–

      (aa) shares and share options; and
      (bb) those with or without performance measures;

    (iii) details of those scheme interests (which may exclude any details included elsewhere in the report); and

    (iv) details of share options which are–

      (aa) vested but unexercised; and
      (bb) exercised in the relevant financial year.

Performance graph and table

18(1) The directors' remuneration report must–

(a) contain a line graph that shows for each of–

    (i) a holding of shares of that class of the company's equity share capital whose listing, or admission to dealing, has resulted in the company falling within the definition of "quoted company", and

    (ii) a hypothetical holding of shares made up of shares of the same kinds and number as those by reference to which a broad equity market index is calculated,

    (iii) a line drawn by joining up points plotted to represent, for each of the financial years in the relevant period, the total shareholder return on that holding; and

(b) state the name of the index selected for the purposes of the graph and set out the reasons for selecting that index.

18(2) The report must also set out in tabular form the following information for each of the financial years in the relevant period in respect of the director undertaking the role of chief executive officer–

(a) total remuneration as set out in the single total figure table;

(b) the sum set out in the table in column headed "c" in the single total figure table expressed as a percentage of the maximum that could have been paid in respect of that component in the financial year; and

(c)   the sum set out in column headed "d" in the single total figure table restated as a percentage of the number of shares vesting against the maximum number of shares that could have been received, or, where paid in money and other assets, as a percentage of the maximum that could have been paid in respect of that component in the financial year.

18(3) For the purposes of sub-paragraphs (1), (2) and (6), **"relevant period"** means the specified period of financial years of which the last is the relevant financial year.

18(4) Where the relevant financial year–

(a)   is the company's first financial year for which the performance graph is prepared in accordance with this paragraph, **"specified"** in sub-paragraph (3) means "five";
(b)   is the company's "second", "third", "fourth", "fifth" financial year in which the report is prepared in accordance with this Schedule, **"specified"** in sub-paragraph (3) means "six", "seven", "eight", "nine" as the case may be; and
(c)   is any financial year after the fifth financial year in which the report is prepared in accordance with this Schedule, **"specified"** means "ten".

18(5) Sub-paragraph (2) may be complied with by use of either–

(a)   a sum based on the information supplied in the directors' remuneration reports for those previous years, or,
(b)   where no such report has been compiled, a suitable corresponding sum.

18(6) For the purposes of sub-paragraph (1), the "total shareholder return" for a relevant period on a holding of shares must be calculated using a fair method that–

(a)   takes as its starting point the percentage change over the period in the market price of the holding;
(b)   involves making–

(i)   the assumptions specified in sub-paragraph (7) as to reinvestment of income, and
(ii)   the assumption specified in sub-paragraph (9) as to the funding of liabilities; and

(c)   makes provision for any replacement of shares in the holding by shares of a different description;

and the same method must be used for each of the holdings mentioned in sub-paragraph (1).

18(7) The assumptions as to reinvestment of income are–

(a)   that any benefit in the form of shares of the same kind as those in the holding is added to the holding at the time the benefit becomes receivable; and
(b)   that any benefit in cash, and an amount equal to the value of any benefit not in cash and not falling within paragraph (a), is applied at the time the benefit becomes receivable in the purchase at their market price of shares of the same kind as those in the holding and that the shares purchased are added to the holding at that time.

18(8) In sub-paragraph (7) **"benefit"** means any benefit (including, in particular, any dividend) receivable in respect of any shares in the holding by the holder from the company of whose share capital the shares form part.

18(9) The assumption as to the funding of liabilities is that, where the holder has a liability to the company of whose capital the shares in the holding form part, shares are sold from the holding–

(a)   immediately before the time by which the liability is due to be satisfied, and
(b)   in such numbers that, at the time of the sale, the market price of the shares sold equals the amount of the liability in respect of the shares in the holding that are not being sold.

18(10) In sub-paragraph (9) **"liability"** means a liability arising in respect of any shares in the holding or from the exercise of a right attached to any of those shares.

Percentage change in remuneration of director undertaking the role of chief executive officer

19(1) The directors' remuneration report must set out (in a manner which permits comparison) in relation to each of the kinds of remuneration required to be set out in each of the columns headed "a", "b" and "c" of the single total figure table the following information–

(a) the percentage change from the financial year preceding the relevant financial year in respect of the director undertaking the role of the chief executive officer; and

(b) the average percentage change from the financial year preceding the relevant financial year in respect of the employees of the company taken as a whole.

19(2) Where for the purposes of sub-paragraph (1)(b), a comparator group comprising the employees taken as a whole is considered by the company as an inappropriate comparator group of employees, the company may use such other comparator group of employees as the company identifies, provided the report contains a statement setting out why that group was chosen.

19(3) Where the company is a parent company, the statement must relate to the group and not the company, and the director reported on is the director undertaking the role of chief executive officer of the parent company, and the employees are the employees of the group.

Relative importance of spend on pay

20(1) The directors' remuneration report must set out in a graphical or tabular form that shows in respect of the relevant financial year and the immediately preceding financial year the actual expenditure of the company, and the difference in spend between those years, on–

(a) remuneration paid to or receivable by all employees of the group;

(b) distributions to shareholders by way of dividend and share buyback; and

(c) any other significant distributions and payments or other uses of profit or cashflow deemed by the directors to assist in understanding the relative importance of spend on pay.

20(2) There must be set out in a note to the report an explanation in respect of subparagraph (1)(c) why the particular matters were chosen by the directors and how the amounts were calculated.

20(3) Where the matters chosen for the report in respect of sub-paragraph (1)(c) in the relevant financial year are not the same as the other items set out in the report for previous years, an explanation for that change must be given.

Statement of implementation of remuneration policy in the following financial year

21(1) The directors' remuneration report must contain a statement describing how the company intends to implement the approved directors' remuneration policy in the financial year following the relevant financial year.

21(2) The statement must include, where applicable, the–

(a) performance measures and relative weightings for each; and

(b) performance targets determined for the performance measures and how awards will be calculated.

21(3) Where this is not the first year of the approved remuneration policy, the statement should detail any significant changes in the way that the remuneration policy will be implemented in the next financial year compared to how it was implemented in the relevant financial year.

21(4) This statement need not include information that is elsewhere in the report, including any disclosed in the directors' remuneration policy.

Consideration by the directors of matters relating to directors' remuneration

22(1) If a committee of the company's directors has considered matters relating to the directors' remuneration for the relevant financial year, the directors' remuneration report must–

    (a) name each director who was a member of the committee at any time when the committee was considering any such matter;

    (b) state whether any person provided to the committee advice, or services, that materially assisted the committee in their consideration of any such matter and name any person that has done so;

    (c) in the case of any person named under paragraph (b), who is not a director of the company (other than a person who provided legal advice on compliance with any relevant legislation), state–

        (i) the nature of any other services that that person has provided to the company during the relevant financial year;

        (ii) by whom that person was appointed, whether or not by the committee and how they were selected;

        (iii) whether and how the remuneration committee has satisfied itself that the advice received was objective and independent; and

        (iv) the amount of fee or other charge paid by the company to that person for the provision of the advice or services referred to in paragraph (b) and the basis on which it was charged.

22(2) In sub-paragraph (1)(b) **"person"** includes (in particular) any director of the company who does not fall within sub-paragraph (1)(a).

22(3) Sub-paragraph (1)(c) does not apply where the person was, at the time of the provision of the advice or service, an employee of the company.

22(4) This paragraph also applies to a committee which considers remuneration issues during the consideration of an individual's nomination as a director.

Statement of voting at general meeting

23 The directors' remuneration report must contain a statement setting out in respect of the last general meeting at which a resolution of the following kind was moved by the company–

    (a) in respect of a resolution to approve the directors' remuneration report, the percentage of votes cast for and against and the number of votes withheld;

    (b) in respect of a resolution to approve the directors' remuneration policy, the percentage of votes cast for and against and the number of votes withheld; and,

    (c) where there was a significant percentage of votes against either such resolution, a summary of the reasons for those votes, as far as known to the directors, and any actions taken by the directors in response to those concerns.

PART 4 – DIRECTORS' REMUNERATION POLICY

Introductory

24(1) The information required to be included in the directors' remuneration report by the provisions of this Part must be set out in a separate part of the report and constitutes the directors' remuneration policy of the company.

24(2) Where a company intends to move a resolution at a meeting of the company to approve a directors' remuneration policy and it is intended that some or all of the provisions of the last approved directors' remuneration policy are to continue to apply after the resolution is approved, this fact must be stated in the policy which is the subject of the resolution and it must be made clear which provisions of the last approved policy are to continue to apply and for what period of time it is intended that they shall apply.

24(3) Notwithstanding the requirements of this Part, the directors' remuneration policy part of the report must set out all those matters for which the company requires approval for the purposes of Chapter 4A of Part 10 of the 2006 Act.

24(4) Where any provision of the directors' remuneration policy provides for the exercise by the directors of a discretion on any aspect of the policy, the policy must clearly set out the extent of that discretion in respect of any such variation, change or amendment.

24(5) The directors' remuneration policy (or revised directors' remuneration policy) of a company in respect of which a company moves a resolution for approval in accordance with section 439A of the 2006 Act must, on the first occasion that such a resolution is moved after 1st October 2013 set out the date from which it is intended by the company that that policy is to take effect.

Future policy table

25(1) The directors' remuneration report must contain in tabular form a description of each of the components of the remuneration package for the directors of the company which are comprised in the directors' remuneration policy of the company.

25(2) Where the report complies with sub-paragraph (1) by reference to provisions which apply generally to all directors, the table must also include any particular arrangements which are specific to any director individually.

25(3) References in this Part to **"component parts of the remuneration package"** include, but are not limited to, all those items which are relevant for the purposes of the single total figure table.

26 In respect of each of the components described in the table there must be set out the following information–

(a) how that component supports the short and long-term strategic objectives of the company (or, where the company is a parent company, the group);
(b) an explanation of how that component of the remuneration package operates;
(c) the maximum that may be paid in respect of that component (which may be expressed in monetary terms, or otherwise);
(d) where applicable, a description of the framework used to assess performance including–

(i) a description of any performance measures which apply and, where more than one performance measure applies, an indication of the weighting of the performance measure or group of performance measures;
(ii) details of any performance period; and
(iii) the amount (which may be expressed in monetary terms or otherwise) that may be paid in respect of–

(aa) the minimum level of performance that results in any payment under the policy, and

(bb) any further levels of performance set in accordance with the policy;

(e) an explanation as to whether there are any provisions for the recovery of sums paid or the withholding of the payment of any sum.

27 There must accompany the table notes which set out–

(a) in respect of any component falling within paragraph 26(d)(i)–(iii), an explanation of why any performance measures were chosen and how any performance targets are set;

(b) in respect of any component (other than salary, fees, benefits or pension) which is not subject to performance measures, an explanation of why there are no such measures;

(c) if any component did not form part of the remuneration package in the last approved directors' remuneration policy, why that component is now contained in the remuneration package;

(d) in respect of any component which did form a part of such a package, what changes have been made to it and why; and

(e) an explanation of the differences (if any) in the company's policy on the remuneration of directors from the policy on the remuneration of employees generally (within the company, or where the company is a parent company, the group).

28 The information required by paragraph 25 may, in respect of directors not performing an executive function, be set out in a separate table and there must be set out in that table the approach of the company to the determination of–

(a) the fee payable to such directors;

(b) any additional fees payable for any other duties to the company;

(c) such other items as are to be considered in the nature of remuneration.

Approach to recruitment remuneration

29(1) The directors' remuneration policy must contain a statement of the principles which would be applied by the company when agreeing the components of a remuneration package for the appointment of directors.

29(2) The statement must set out the various components which would be considered for inclusion in that package and the approach to be adopted by the company in respect of each component.

29(3) The statement must, subject to sub-paragraph (4), set out the maximum level of variable remuneration which may be granted (which can be expressed in monetary terms or otherwise).

29(4) Remuneration which constitutes compensation for the forfeit of any award under variable remuneration arrangements entered into with a previous employer is not included within sub-paragraph (3) of this paragraph, but is subject to the requirements of subparagraphs (1) and (2).

Service contracts

30 The directors' remuneration policy must contain a description of any obligation on the company which–

(a) is contained in all directors' service contracts;

(b) is contained in the service contracts of any one or more existing directors (not being covered by paragraph (a)); or

(c) it is proposed would be contained in directors' service contracts to be entered into by the company

and which could give rise to, or impact on, remuneration payments or payments for loss of office but which is not disclosed elsewhere in this report.

31 Where the directors' service contracts are not kept available for inspection at the company's registered office, the report must give details of where the contracts are kept, and if the contracts are available on a website, a link to that website.

32 The provisions of paragraphs 30 and 31 relating to directors' service contracts apply in like manner to the terms of letters of appointment of directors.

Illustrations of application of remuneration policy

33 The directors' remuneration report must, in respect of each person who is a director (other than a director who is not performing an executive function), set out in the form of a bar chart an indication of the level of remuneration that would be received by the director in accordance with the directors' remuneration policy in the first year to which the policy applies.

34(1) The bar chart must contain separate bars representing–

(a) minimum remuneration receivable, that is to say, including, but not limited to, salary, fees, benefits and pension;
(b) the remuneration receivable if the director was, in respect of any performance measures or targets, performing in line with the company's expectation;
(c) maximum remuneration receivable (not allowing for any share price appreciation).

34(2) Each bar of the chart must contain separate parts which represent–

(a) salary, fees, benefits, pension and any other item falling within sub-paragraph 34(1)(a);
(b) remuneration where performance measures or targets relate to one financial year;
(c) remuneration where performance measures or targets relate to more than one financial year.

34(3) Each bar must show–

(a) percentage of the total comprised by each of the parts; and
(b) total value of remuneration expected for each bar.

35(1) A narrative description of the basis of calculation and assumptions used to compile the bar chart must be set out to enable an understanding of the charts presented.

35(2) In complying with sub-paragraph (1) it is not necessary for any matter to be included in the narrative description which has been set out in the future policy table required by paragraph 25.

Policy on payment for loss of office

36 The directors' remuneration policy must set out the company's policy on the setting of notice periods under directors' service contracts.

37 The directors' remuneration policy must also set out the principles on which the determination of payments for loss of office will be approached including–

(a) an indication of how each component of the payment will be calculated;
(b) whether, and if so how, the circumstances of the director's loss of office and performance during the period of qualifying service are relevant to any exercise of discretion; and
(c) any contractual provision agreed prior to 27th June 2012 that could impact on the quantum of the payment.

Statement of consideration of employment conditions elsewhere in company

38 The directors' remuneration policy must contain a statement of how pay and employment conditions of employees (other than directors) of the company and, where the company is a parent company, of the group of other undertakings within the same group as the company, were taken into account when setting the policy for directors' remuneration.

39 The statement must also set out–

(a) whether, and if so, how, the company consulted with employees when drawing up the directors' remuneration policy set out in this part of the report;
(b) whether any remuneration comparison measurements were used and if so, what they were, and how that information was taken into account.

Statement of consideration of shareholder views

40 The directors' remuneration policy must contain a statement of whether, and if so how, any views in respect of directors' remuneration expressed to the company by shareholders (whether at a general meeting or otherwise) have been taken into account in the formulation of the directors' remuneration policy.

PART 5 – PROVISIONS OF THE DIRECTORS' REMUNERATION REPORT WHICH ARE SUBJECT TO AUDIT

41 The information contained in the directors' remuneration report which is subject to audit is the information required by paragraphs 4 to 17 (inclusive) of Part 3 of this Schedule.

PART 6 – REVISED DIRECTORS' REMUNERATION POLICY

42 A revised directors' remuneration policy prepared in accordance with section 422A of the 2006 Act must contain all those matters required by Part 4 of this Schedule to be in the directors' remuneration policy.

43 A revised directors' remuneration policy must be set out in the same manner as required by Part 4 of this Schedule in respect of that part of the directors' remuneration report.

PART 7 – INTERPRETATION AND SUPPLEMENTARY

44(1) In this Schedule–

"amount", in relation to a gain made on the exercise of a share option, means the difference between–

(a) the market price of the shares on the day on which the option was exercised; and
(b) the price actually paid for the shares;

"company contributions", in relation to a pension scheme and a person, means any payments (including insurance premiums) made, or treated as made, to the scheme in respect of the person by anyone other than the person;

"emoluments" of a person–

(a) include salary, fees and bonuses, sums paid by way of expenses allowance (so far as they are chargeable to United Kingdom income tax or would be if the person were an individual or would be if the person were resident in the United Kingdom for tax purposes), but
(b) do not include any of the following, namely–

    (i) the value of any share options granted to him or the amount of any gains made on the exercise of any such options;
    (ii) any company contributions paid, or treated as paid, in respect of him under any pension scheme or any benefits to which he is entitled under any such scheme; or
    (iii) any money or other assets paid to or received or receivable by him under any scheme;

"pension scheme" means a retirement benefits scheme within the meaning given by section 150(1) of the Finance Act 2004 which is–

(a) one in which the company participates or
(b) one to which the company paid a contribution during the financial year;

"performance measure" is the measure by which performance is to be assessed, but does not include any condition relating to service:

"performance target" is the specific level of performance to be attained in respect of that performance measure;

"qualifying services", in relation to any person, means his services as a director of the company, and his services at any time while he is a director of the company–

(a) as a director of an undertaking that is a subsidiary undertaking of the company at that time;
(b) as a director of any other undertaking of which he is a director by virtue of the company's nomination (direct or indirect); or
(c) otherwise in connection with the management of the affairs of the company or any such subsidiary undertaking or any such other undertaking;

"remuneration committee" means a committee of directors of the company having responsibility for considering matters related to the remuneration of directors;

"retirement benefits" means relevant benefits within the meaning given by section 393B of the Income Tax (Earnings and Pensions) Act 2003 read as if subsection (2) were omitted;

"scheme" (other than a pension scheme) means any agreement or arrangement under which money or other assets may become receivable by a person and which includes one or more qualifying conditions with respect to service or performance that cannot be fulfilled within a single financial year, and for this purpose the following must be disregarded, namely–

(a) any payment the amount of which falls to be determined by reference to service or performance within a single financial year;
(b) compensation in respect of loss of office, payments for breach of contract and other termination payments; and
(c) retirement benefits;

"scheme interest" means an interest under a scheme;

"shares" means shares (whether allotted or not) in the company, or any undertaking which is a group undertaking in relation to the company, and includes a share warrant as defined by section 779(1) of the 2006 Act;

"share option" means a right to acquire shares;

"value" in relation to shares received or receivable on any day by a person who is or has been a director of a company, means the market price of the shares on that day.

44(2) In this Schedule **"compensation in respect of loss of office"** includes compensation received or receivable by a person for–

(a) loss of office as director of the company, or
(b) loss, while director of the company or on or in connection with his ceasing to be a director of it, of–

   (i)   any other office in connection with the management of the company' affairs; or
   (ii) any office as director or otherwise in connection with the management of the affairs of any undertaking that, immediately before the loss, is a subsidiary undertaking of the company or an undertaking of which he is a director by virtue of the company's nomination (direct or indirect);

(c) compensation in consideration for, or in connection with, a person's retirement from office; and

(d)   where such a retirement is occasioned by a breach of the person's contract with the company or with an undertaking that, immediately before the breach, is a subsidiary undertaking of the company or an undertaking of which he is a director by virtue of the company's nomination (direct or indirect)–

(i)   payments made by way of damages for the breach; or
(ii) payments made by way of settlement or compromise of any claim in respect of the breach.

44(3) References in this Schedule to compensation include benefits otherwise than in cash; and in relation to such compensation references in this Schedule to its amounts are to the estimated money value of the benefit.

44(4) References in this Schedule to a person being **"connected"** with a director, and to a director **"controlling"** a body corporate, are to be construed in accordance with sections 252 to 255 of the 2006 Act.

45 For the purposes of this Schedule emoluments paid or receivable or share options granted in respect of a person's accepting office as a director are to be treated as emoluments paid or receivable or share options granted in respect of his services as a director.

46(1) The following applies with respect to the amounts to be shown under this Schedule.

46(2) The amount in each case includes all relevant sums paid by or receivable from–

(a)   the company; and
(b)   the company's subsidiary undertakings; and
(c)   any other person,

except sums to be accounted for to the company or any of its subsidiary undertakings or any other undertaking of which any person has been a director while director of the company, by virtue of section 219 of the 2006 Act (payment in connection with share transfer: requirement of members' approval), to past or present members of the company or any of its subsidiaries or any class of those members.

46(3) Reference to amounts paid to or receivable by a person include amounts paid to or receivable by a person connected with the person or a body corporate controlled by the person (but not so as to require an amount to be counted twice).

47(1) The amounts to be shown for any financial year under Part 3 of this Schedule are the sums receivable in respect of that year (whenever paid) or, in the case of sums not receivable in respect of a period, the sums paid during that year.

47(2) But where–

(a)   any sums are not shown in the directors' remuneration report for the relevant financial year on the ground that the person receiving them is liable to account for them as mentioned in paragraph 46(2), but the liability is thereafter wholly or partly released or is not enforced within a period of 2 years; or
(b)   any sums paid by way of expenses allowance are charged to United Kingdom income tax after the end of the relevant financial year or, in the case of any such sums paid otherwise than to an individual, it does not become clear until the end of the relevant financial year that those sums would be charged to such tax were the person an individual,

those sums must, to the extent to which the liability is released or not enforced or they are charged as mentioned above (as the case may be), be shown in the first directors' remuneration report in which it is practicable to show them and must be distinguished from the amounts to be shown apart from this provision.

48 Where it is necessary to do so for the purpose of making any distinction required by the preceding paragraphs in an amount to be shown in compliance with this Schedule, the directors may apportion any payments between the matters in respect of which these have been paid or are receivable in such manner as they think appropriate.

49 The Schedule requires information to be given only so far as it is contained in the company's books and papers, available to members of the public or the company has the right to obtain it.

History – Sch. 8 substituted by SI 2013/1981, reg. 3 and Sch., with with effect from 1 October 2013. The following transitional provision is made by SI 2013/1981, reg. 4:

4(1) The amendments made by these Regulations to the 2008 Regulations do not apply to a company in respect of a financial year ending before 30th September 2013.

4(2) The provisions of the 2008 Regulations as they stood immediately before 1st October 2013 continue to apply in respect of a financial year ending before 30th September 2013.

4(3) The provisions of Part 6 of Schedule 8 apply to a revised directors' remuneration policy set out in a document in accordance with section 422A (3) of the Companies Act 2006 on or after 1st October 2013.

Prior to substitution, Sch. 8 read as follows:

"SCHEDULE 8   Regulation 11

QUOTED COMPANIES: DIRECTORS' REMUNERATION REPORT

PART 1 – INTRODUCTORY

1(1) In the directors' remuneration report for a financial year ("the relevant financial year") there must be shown the information specified in Parts 2 and 3.

1(2) Information required to be shown in the report for or in respect of a particular person must be shown in the report in a manner that links the information to that person identified by name.

PART 2 – INFORMATION NOT SUBJECT TO AUDIT

Consideration by the directors of matters relating to directors' remuneration

2(1) If a committee of the company's directors has considered matters relating to the directors' remuneration for the relevant financial year, the directors' remuneration report must–

(a) name each director who was a member of the committee at any time when the committee was considering any such matter;

(b) name any person who provided to the committee advice, or services, that materially assisted the committee in their consideration of any such matter;

(c) in the case of any person named under paragraph (b), who is not a director of the company, state–

    (i) the nature of any other services that that person has provided to the company during the relevant financial year; and

    (ii) whether that person was appointed by the committee.

2(2) In sub-paragraph (1)(b) **"person"** includes (in particular) any director of the company who does not fall within sub-paragraph (1)(a).

Statement of company's policy on directors' remuneration

3(1) The directors' remuneration report must contain a statement of the company's policy on directors' remuneration for the following financial year and for financial years subsequent to that.

3(2) The policy statement must include–

(a) for each director, a detailed summary of any performance conditions to which any entitlement of the director–

    (i) to share options, or

    (ii) under a long term incentive scheme, is subject;

(b) an explanation as to why any such performance conditions were chosen;

(c) a summary of the methods to be used in assessing whether any such performance conditions are met and an explanation as to why those methods were chosen;

(d) if any such performance condition involves any comparison with factors external to the company–

    (i) a summary of the factors to be used in making each such comparison, and

    (ii) if any of the factors relates to the performance of another company, of two or more other companies or of an index on which the securities of a company or companies are listed, the identity of that company, of each of those companies or of the index;

(e)   a description of, and an explanation for, any significant amendment proposed to be made to the terms and conditions of any entitlement of a director to share options or under a long term incentive scheme; and

(f)   if any entitlement of a director to share options, or under a long term incentive scheme, is not subject to performance conditions, an explanation as to why that is the case.

3(3) The policy statement must, in respect of each director's terms and conditions relating to remuneration, explain the relative importance of those elements which are, and those which are not, related to performance.

3(4) The policy statement must summarise, and explain, the company's policy on–

(a)   the duration of contracts with directors, and

(b)   notice periods, and termination payments, under such contracts.

3(5) In sub-paragraphs (2) and (3), references to a director are to any person who serves as a director of the company at any time in the period beginning with the end of the relevant financial year and ending with the date on which the directors' remuneration report is laid before the company in general meeting.

Statement of consideration of conditions elsewhere in company and group

4 The directors' remuneration report must contain a statement of how pay and employment conditions of employees of the company and of other undertakings within the same group as the company were taken into account when determining directors' remuneration for the relevant financial year.

Performance graph

5(1) The directors' remuneration report must–

(a)   contain a line graph that shows for each of–

(i)   a holding of shares of that class of the company's equity share capital whose listing, or admission to dealing, has resulted in the company falling within the definition of **"quoted company"**, and

(ii)   a hypothetical holding of shares made up of shares of the same kinds and number as those by reference to which a broad equity market index is calculated, a line drawn by joining up points plotted to represent, for each of the financial years in the relevant period, the total shareholder return on that holding; and

(b)   state the name of the index selected for the purposes of the graph and set out the reasons for selecting that index.

5(2) For the purposes of sub-paragraphs (1) and (4), **"relevant period"** means the five financial years of which the last is the relevant financial year.

5(3) Where the relevant financial year–

(a)   is the company's second, third or fourth financial year, sub-paragraph (2) has effect with the substitution of "two", "three" or "four" (as the case may be) for "five"; and

(b)   is the company's first financial year, **"relevant period"**, for the purposes of subparagraphs (1) and (4), means the relevant financial year.

5(4) For the purposes of sub-paragraph (1), the **"total shareholder return"** for a relevant period on a holding of shares must be calculated using a fair method that–

(a)   takes as its starting point the percentage change over the period in the market price of the holding;

(b)   involves making–

(i)   the assumptions specified in sub-paragraph (5) as to reinvestment of income, and

(ii)   the assumption specified in sub-paragraph (7) as to the funding of liabilities, and

(c)   makes provision for any replacement of shares in the holding by shares of a different description; and the same method must be used for each of the holdings mentioned in sub-paragraph (1).

5(5) The assumptions as to reinvestment of income are–

(a)   that any benefit in the form of shares of the same kind as those in the holding is added to the holding at the time the benefit becomes receivable; and

(b)   that any benefit in cash, and an amount equal to the value of any benefit not in cash and not falling within paragraph (a), is applied at the time the benefit becomes receivable in the purchase at their market price of shares of the same kind as those in the holding and that the shares purchased are added to the holding at that time.

5(6) In sub-paragraph (5) **"benefit"** means any benefit (including, in particular, any dividend) receivable in respect of any shares in the holding by the holder from the company of whose share capital the shares form part.

5(7) The assumption as to the funding of liabilities is that, where the holder has a liability to the company of whose capital the shares in the holding form part, shares are sold from the holding–

(a)   immediately before the time by which the liability is due to be satisfied, and

(b)   in such numbers that, at the time of the sale, the market price of the shares sold equals the amount of the liability in respect of the shares in the holding that are not being sold.

5(8) In sub-paragraph (7) **"liability"** means a liability arising in respect of any shares in the holding or from the exercise of a right attached to any of those shares.

Service contracts

6(1) The directors' remuneration report must contain, in respect of the contract of service or contract for services of each person who has served as a director of the company at any time during the relevant financial year, the following information–

(a)   the date of the contract, the unexpired term and the details of any notice periods;

(b)   any provision for compensation payable upon early termination of the contract; and

(c)   such details of other provisions in the contract as are necessary to enable members of the company to estimate the liability of the company in the event of early termination of the contract.

6(2) The directors' remuneration report must contain an explanation for any significant award made to a person in the circumstances described in paragraph 15.

PART 3 – INFORMATION SUBJECT TO AUDIT

Amount of each director's emoluments and compensation in the relevant financial year

7(1) The directors' remuneration report must for the relevant financial year show, for each person who has served as a director of the company at any time during that year, each of the following–

(a)   the total amount of salary and fees paid to or receivable by the person in respect of qualifying services;

(b)   the total amount of bonuses so paid or receivable;

(c)   the total amount of sums paid by way of expenses allowance that are–

(i)   chargeable to United Kingdom income tax (or would be if the person were an individual), and

(ii)   paid to or receivable by the person in respect of qualifying services;

(d)   the total amount of–

(i)   any compensation for loss of office paid to or receivable by the person, and

(ii)   any other payments paid to or receivable by the person in connection with the termination of qualifying services;

(e)   the total estimated value of any benefits received by the person otherwise than in cash that–

(i)   do not fall within any of paragraphs (a) to (d) or paragraphs 8 to 12,

(ii)   are emoluments of the person, and

(iii) are received by the person in respect of qualifying services; and

(f)   the amount that is the total of the sums mentioned in paragraphs (a) to (e).

7(2) The directors' remuneration report must show, for each person who has served as a director of the company at any time during the relevant financial year, the amount that for the financial year preceding the relevant financial year is the total of the sums mentioned in paragraphs (a) to (e) of sub-paragraph (1).

7(3) The directors' remuneration report must also state the nature of any element of a remuneration package which is not cash.

7(4) The information required by sub-paragraphs (1) and (2) must be presented in tabular form.

Share options

8(1) The directors' remuneration report must contain, in respect of each person who has served as a director of the company at any time in the relevant financial year, the information specified in paragraph 9.

8(2) Sub-paragraph (1) is subject to paragraph 10 (aggregation of information to avoid excessively lengthy reports).

8(3) The information specified in sub-paragraphs (a) to (c) of paragraph 9 must be presented in tabular form in the report.

8(4) In paragraph 9 **"share option"**, in relation to a person, means a share option granted in respect of qualifying services of the person.

9 The information required by sub-paragraph (1) of paragraph 8 in respect of such a person as is mentioned in that sub-paragraph is–

(a)   the number of shares that are subject to a share option–

(i)   at the beginning of the relevant financial year or, if later, on the date of the appointment of the person as a director of the company, and

(ii)   at the end of the relevant financial year or, if earlier, on the cessation of the person's appointment as a director of the company, in each case differentiating between share options having different terms and conditions;

(b)   information identifying those share options that have been awarded in the relevant financial year, those that have been exercised in that year, those that in that year have expired unexercised and those whose terms and conditions have been varied in that year;

(c)   for each share option that is unexpired at any time in the relevant financial year–

(i)   the price paid, if any, for its award,

(ii)   the exercise price,

(iii) the date from which the option may be exercised, and

(iv)   the date on which the option expires;

(d)   a description of any variation made in the relevant financial year in the terms and conditions of a share option;

(e)   a summary of any performance criteria upon which the award or exercise of a share option is conditional, including a description of any variation made in such performance criteria during the relevant financial year;

(f)   for each share option that has been exercised during the relevant financial year, the market price of the shares, in relation to which it is exercised, at the time of exercise; and

(g)   for each share option that is unexpired at the end of the relevant financial year–

   (i)   the market price at the end of that year, and

   (ii)   the highest and lowest market prices during that year, of each share that is subject to the option.

10(1) If, in the opinion of the directors of the company, disclosure in accordance with paragraphs 8 and 9 would result in a disclosure of excessive length then, (subject to subparagraphs (2) and (3))–

(a)   information disclosed for a person under paragraph 9(a) need not differentiate between share options having different terms and conditions;

(b)   for the purposes of disclosure in respect of a person under paragraph 9(c)(i) and (ii) and (g), share options may be aggregated and (instead of disclosing prices for each share option) disclosure may be made of weighted average prices of aggregations of share options;

(c)   for the purposes of disclosure in respect of a person under paragraph 9(c)(iii) and (iv), share options may be aggregated and (instead of disclosing dates for each share option) disclosure may be made of ranges of dates for aggregation of share options.

10(2) Sub-paragraph (1)(b) and (c) does not permit the aggregation of–

(a)   share options in respect of shares whose market price at the end of the relevant financial year is below the option exercise price, with

(b)   share options in respect of shares whose market price at the end of the relevant financial year is equal to, or exceeds, the option exercise price.

10(3) Sub-paragraph (1) does not apply (and accordingly, full disclosure must be made in accordance with paragraphs 8 and 9) in respect of share options that during the relevant financial year have been awarded or exercised or had their terms and conditions varied.

Long term incentive schemes

11(1) The directors' remuneration report must contain, in respect of each person who has served as a director of the company at any time in the relevant financial year, the information specified in paragraph 12.

11(2) Sub-paragraph (1) does not require the report to contain share option details that are contained in the report in compliance with paragraphs 8 to 10.

11(3) The information specified in paragraph 12 must be presented in tabular form in the report.

11(4) For the purposes of paragraph 12–

(a)   **"scheme interest"**, in relation to a person, means an interest under a long term incentive scheme that is an interest in respect of which assets may become receivable under the scheme in respect of qualifying services of the person; and

(b)   such an interest **"vests"** at the earliest time when–

   (i)   it has been ascertained that the qualifying conditions have been fulfilled, and

   (ii)   the nature and quantity of the assets receivable under the scheme in respect of the interest have been ascertained.

11(5) In this Schedule **"long term incentive scheme"** means any agreement or arrangement under which money or other assets may become receivable by a person and which includes one or more qualifying conditions with respect to service or performance that cannot be fulfilled within a single financial year, and for this purpose the following must be disregarded, namely–

(a)   any bonus the amount of which falls to be determined by reference to service or performance within a single financial year;

(b)   compensation in respect of loss of office, payments for breach of contract and other termination payments; and

(c)   retirement benefits.

12(1) The information required by sub-paragraph (1) of paragraph 11 in respect of such a person as is mentioned in that sub-paragraph is–

(a)   details of the scheme interests that the person has at the beginning of the relevant financial year or if later on the date of the appointment of the person as a director of the company;

(b)   details of the scheme interests awarded to the person during the relevant financial year;

(c)   details of the scheme interests that the person has at the end of the relevant financial year or if earlier on the cessation of the person's appointment as a director of the company;

(d)   for each scheme interest within paragraphs (a) to (c)–

> (i)   the end of the period over which the qualifying conditions for that interest have to be fulfilled (or if there are different periods for different conditions, the end of whichever of those periods ends last); and
>
> (ii)   a description of any variation made in the terms and conditions of the scheme interests during the relevant financial year; and

(e)   for each scheme interest that has vested in the relevant financial year–

> (i)   the relevant details (see sub-paragraph (3)) of any shares,
>
> (ii)   the amount of any money, and
>
> (iii)   the value of any other assets, that have become receivable in respect of the interest.

12(2) The details that sub-paragraph (1)(b) requires of a scheme interest awarded during the relevant financial year include, if shares may become receivable in respect of the interest, the following–

(a)   the number of those shares;

(b)   the market price of each of those shares when the scheme interest was awarded; and

(c)   details of qualifying conditions that are conditions with respect to performance.

12(3) In sub-paragraph (1)(e)(i) **"the relevant details"**, in relation to any shares that have become receivable in respect of a scheme interest, means–

(a)   the number of those shares;

(b)   the date on which the scheme interest was awarded;

(c)   the market price of each of those shares when the scheme interest was awarded;

(d)   the market price of each of those shares when the scheme interest vested; and

(e)   details of qualifying conditions that were conditions with respect to performance.

Pensions

13(1) The directors' remuneration report must, for each person who has served as a director of the company at any time during the relevant financial year, contain the information in respect of pensions that is specified in sub-paragraphs (2) and (3).

13(2) Where the person has rights under a pension scheme that is a defined benefit scheme in relation to the person and any of those rights are rights to which he has become entitled in respect of qualifying services of his–

(a)   details–

> (i)   of any changes during the relevant financial year in the person's accrued benefits under the scheme, and
>
> (ii)   of the person's accrued benefits under the scheme as at the end of that year;
>
> *[version of sub-paragraph (b) applying in relation to financial years beginning on or after 6 April 2008 and ending before 26 June 2009]*

(b)   the transfer value, calculated in a manner consistent with "Retirement Benefit Schemes – Transfer Values (GN 11)" published by the Institute of Actuaries and the Faculty of Actuaries and dated 6th April 2001, of the person's accrued benefits under the scheme at the end of the relevant financial year;

> *[version of sub-paragraph (b) applying in relation to financial years beginning on or after 6 April 2008 and not ending before 26 June 2009]*

(b)   the transfer value, calculated in accordance with regulations 7 to 7E of the Occupational Pension Schemes (Transfer Values) Regulations 1996, of the person's accrued benefits under the scheme at the end of the relevant financial year;

(c)   the transfer value of the person's accrued benefits under the scheme that in compliance with paragraph (b) was contained in the directors' remuneration report for the previous financial year or, if there was no such report or no such value was contained in that report, the transfer value, calculated in such a manner as is mentioned in paragraph (b), of the person's accrued benefits under the scheme at the beginning of the relevant financial year;

(d)   the amount obtained by subtracting–

> (i)   the transfer value of the person's accrued benefits under the scheme that is required to be contained in the report by paragraph (c), from
>
> (ii)   the transfer value of those benefits that is required to be contained in the report by paragraph (b), and then subtracting from the result of that calculation the amount of any contributions made to the scheme by the person in the relevant financial year.

13(3) Where–

(a)   the person has rights under a pension scheme that is a money purchase scheme in relation to the person, and

(b)   any of those rights are rights to which he has become entitled in respect of qualifying services of his, details of any contribution to the scheme in respect of the person that is paid or payable by the company for the relevant financial year or paid by the company in that year for another financial year.

Notes – Para. (2)(b) substituted by SI 2009/1581 reg 12(1) and (3): 27 June 2009 applying in relation to financial years beginning on or after 6 April 2008 which have not ended before 27 June 2009

Excess retirement benefits of directors and past directors

14(1) Subject to sub-paragraph (3), the directors' remuneration report must show in respect of each person who has served as a director of the company–

(a) at any time during the relevant financial year, or

(b) at any time before the beginning of that year, the amount of so much of retirement benefits paid to or receivable by the person under pension schemes as is in excess of the retirement benefits to which he was entitled on the date on which the benefits first became payable or 31st March 1997, whichever is the later.

14(2) In subsection (1) **"retirement benefits"** means retirement benefits to which the person became entitled in respect of qualifying services of his.

14(3) Amounts paid or receivable under a pension scheme need not be included in an amount required to be shown under sub-paragraph (1) if–

(a) the funding of the scheme was such that the amounts were or, as the case may be, could have been paid without recourse to additional contributions; and

(b) amounts were paid to or receivable by all pensioner members of the scheme on the same basis; and in this sub-paragraph **"pensioner member"**, in relation to a pension scheme, means any person who is entitled to the present payment of retirement benefits under the scheme.

14(4) In this paragraph–

(a) references to retirement benefits include benefits otherwise than in cash; and

(b) in relation to so much of retirement benefits as consists of a benefit otherwise than in cash, references to their amount are to the estimated money value of the benefit, and the nature of any such benefit must also be shown in the report.

Compensation for past directors

15 The directors' remuneration report must contain details of any significant award made in the relevant financial year to any person who was not a director of the company at the time the award was made but had previously been a director of the company, including (in particular) compensation in respect of loss of office and pensions but excluding any sums which have already been shown in the report under paragraph 7(1)(d).

Sums paid to third parties in respect of a director's services

16(1) The directors' remuneration report must show, in respect of each person who served as a director of the company at any time during the relevant financial year, the aggregate amount of any consideration paid to or receivable by third parties for making available the services of the person–

(a) as a director of the company, or

(b) while director of the company–

    (i) as director of any of its subsidiary undertakings, or

    (ii) as director of any other undertaking of which he was (while director of the company) a director by virtue of the company's nomination (direct or indirect), or

    (iii) otherwise in connection with the management of the affairs of the company or any such other undertaking.

16(2) The reference to consideration includes benefits otherwise than in cash; and in relation to such consideration the reference to its amount is to the estimated money value of the benefit.

The nature of any such consideration must be shown in the report.

16(3) The reference to third parties is to persons other than–

(a) the person himself or a person connected with him or a body corporate controlled by him, and

(b) the company or any such other undertaking as is mentioned in sub-paragraph (1)(b)(ii).

PART 4 – INTERPRETATION AND SUPPLEMENTARY

17(1) In this Schedule–

"amount", in relation to a gain made on the exercise of a share option, means the difference between–

(a) the market price of the shares on the day on which the option was exercised; and

(b) the price actually paid for the shares;

"company contributions", in relation to a pension scheme and a person, means any payments (including insurance premiums) made, or treated as made, to the scheme in respect of the person by anyone other than the person;

"defined benefit scheme", in relation to a person, means a pension scheme which is not a money purchase scheme in relation to the person;

"emoluments" of a person–

(a) includes salary, fees and bonuses, sums paid by way of expenses allowance (so far as they are chargeable to United Kingdom income tax or would be if the person were an individual), but

(b) does not include any of the following, namely–

    (i) the value of any share options granted to him or the amount of any gains made on the exercise of any such options;

    (ii) any company contributions paid, or treated as paid, in respect of him under any pension scheme or any benefits to which he is entitled under any such scheme; or

    (iii) any money or other assets paid to or received or receivable by him under any long term incentive scheme;

"long term incentive scheme" has the meaning given by paragraph 11(5); **"money purchase benefits"**, in relation to a person, means retirement benefits the rate or amount of which is calculated by reference to payments made, or treated as made, by the person or by any other person in respect of that person and which are not average salary benefits;

"money purchase scheme", in relation to a person, means a pension scheme under which all of the benefits that may become payable to or in respect of the person are money purchase benefits in relation to the person;

"pension scheme" means a retirement benefits scheme within the meaning given by section 611 of the Income and Corporation Taxes Act 1988;

"qualifying services", in relation to any person, means his services as a director of the company, and his services at any time while he is a director of the company–

(a) as a director of an undertaking that is a subsidiary undertaking of the company at that time;

(b) as a director of any other undertaking of which he is a director by virtue of the company's nomination (direct or indirect); or

(c) otherwise in connection with the management of the affairs of the company or any such subsidiary undertaking or any such other undertaking;

"retirement benefits" means relevant benefits within the meaning given by section 612(1) of the Income and Corporation Taxes Act 1988;

"shares" means shares (whether allotted or not) in the company, or any undertaking which is a group undertaking in relation to the company, and includes a share warrant as defined by section 779(1) of the 2006 Act;

"share option" means a right to acquire shares;

"value", in relation to shares received or receivable on any day by a person who is or has been a director of the company, means the market price of the shares on that day.

17(2) In this Schedule **"compensation in respect of loss of office"** includes compensation received or receivable by a person for–

(a) loss of office as director of the company, or

(b) loss, while director of the company or on or in connection with his ceasing to be a director of it, of–

(i) any other office in connection with the management of the company's affairs, or

(ii) any office as director or otherwise in connection with the management of the affairs of any undertaking that, immediately before the loss, is a subsidiary undertaking of the company or an undertaking of which he is a director by virtue of the company's nomination (direct or indirect);

(c) compensation in consideration for, or in connection with, a person's retirement from office; and

(d) where such a retirement is occasioned by a breach of the person's contract with the company or with an undertaking that, immediately before the breach, is a subsidiary undertaking of the company or an undertaking of which he is a director by virtue of the company's nomination (direct or indirect)–

(i) payments made by way of damages for the breach; or

(ii) payments made by way of settlement or compromise of any claim in respect of the breach.

17(3) References in this Schedule to compensation include benefits otherwise than in cash; and in relation to such compensation references in this Schedule to its amounts are to the estimated money value of the benefit.

17(4) References in this Schedule to a person being "connected" with a director, and to a director "controlling" a body corporate, are to be construed in accordance with sections 252 to 255 of the 2006 Act.

18(1) For the purposes of this Schedule emoluments paid or receivable or share options granted in respect of a person's accepting office as a director are to be treated as emoluments paid or receivable or share options granted in respect of his services as a director.

18(2) Where a pension scheme provides for any benefits that may become payable to or in respect of a person to be whichever are the greater of–

(a) such benefits determined by or under the scheme as are money purchase benefits in relation to the person; and

(b) such retirement benefits determined by or under the scheme to be payable to or in respect of the person as are not money purchase benefits in relation to the person, the company may assume for the purposes of this Schedule that those benefits will be money purchase benefits in relation to the person, or not, according to whichever appears more likely at the end of the relevant financial year.

18(3) In determining for the purposes of this Schedule whether a pension scheme is a money purchase scheme in relation to a person or a defined benefit scheme in relation to a person, any death in service benefits provided for by the scheme are to be disregarded.

19(1) The following applies with respect to the amounts to be shown under this Schedule.

19(2) The amount in each case includes all relevant sums paid by or receivable from–

(a) the company; and

(b) the company's subsidiary undertakings; and

(c) any other person, except sums to be accounted for to the company or any of its subsidiary undertakings or any other undertaking of which any person has been a director while director of the company, by virtue of section 219 of the 2006 Act (payment in connection with share transfer: requirement of members' approval), to past or present members of the company or any of its subsidiaries or any class of those members.

19(3) Reference to amounts paid to or receivable by a person include amounts paid to or receivable by a person connected with him or a body corporate controlled by him (but not so as to require an amount to be counted twice).

20(1) The amounts to be shown for any financial year under Part 3 of this Schedule are the sums receivable in respect of that year (whenever paid) or, in the case of sums not receivable in respect of a period, the sums paid during that year.

20(2) But where–

(a) any sums are not shown in the directors' remuneration report for the relevant financial year on the ground that the person receiving them is liable to account for them as mentioned in paragraph 19(2), but the liability is thereafter wholly or partly released or is not enforced within a period of 2 years; or

(b) any sums paid by way of expenses allowance are charged to United Kingdom income tax after the end of the relevant financial year or, in the case of any such sums paid otherwise than to an individual, it does not become clear until the end of the relevant financial year that those sums would be charged to such tax were the person an individual, those sums must, to the extent to which the liability is released or not enforced or they are charged as mentioned above (as the case may be), be shown in the first directors' remuneration report in which it is practicable to show them and must be distinguished from the amounts to be shown apart from this provision.

21 Where it is necessary to do so for the purpose of making any distinction required by the preceding paragraphs in an amount to be shown in compliance with this Part of this Schedule, the directors may apportion any payments between the matters in respect of which these have been paid or are receivable in such manner as they think appropriate.

22 The Schedule requires information to be given only so far as it is contained in the company's books and papers, available to members of the public or the company has the right to obtain it."

SCHEDULE 9   Regulation 12

INTERPRETATION OF TERM "PROVISIONS"
PART 1 – MEANING FOR PURPOSES OF THESE REGULATIONS

Definition of "provisions"

1(1) In these Regulations, references to provisions for depreciation or diminution in value of assets are to any amount written off by way of providing for depreciation or diminution in value of assets.

1(2) Any reference in the profit and loss account formats or the notes to them set out in Schedule 1, 2 or 3 to these Regulations to the depreciation of, or amounts written off, assets of any description is to any provision for depreciation or diminution in value of assets of that description.

2 References in these Regulations to provisions for liabilities or, in the case of insurance companies, to provisions for other risks are to any amount retained as reasonably necessary for the purpose of providing for any liability the nature of which is clearly defined and which is either likely to be incurred, or certain to be incurred but uncertain as to amount or as to the date on which it will arise.

2A At the balance sheet date, a provision must represent the best estimate of the expenses likely to be incurred or, in the case of a liability, of the amount required to meet that liability.

History – Para. 2A inserted by SI 2015/980, reg. 40, with effect in relation to–

(a) financial years beginning on or after 1 January 2016, and
(b) a financial year of a company beginning on or after 1 January 2015, but before 1 January 2016, if the directors of the company so decide.

2B Provisions must not be used to adjust the value of assets.

History – Para. 2B inserted by SI 2015/980, reg. 40, with effect in relation to–

(a) financial years beginning on or after 1 January 2016, and
(b) a financial year of a company beginning on or after 1 January 2015, but before 1 January 2016, if the directors of the company so decide.

PART 2 – MEANING FOR PURPOSES OF PARTS 18 AND 23 OF THE 2006 ACT

Financial assistance for purchase of own shares

3 The specified provisions for the purposes of section 677(3)(a) of the 2006 Act (Companies Act accounts: relevant provisions for purposes of financial assistance) are provisions within paragraph 2 of this Schedule.

Redemption or purchase by private company out of capital

4 The specified provisions for the purposes of section 712(2)(b)(i) of the 2006 Act (Companies Act accounts: relevant provisions to determine available profits for redemption or purchase out of capital) are provisions of any of the kinds mentioned in paragraphs 1 and 2 of this Schedule.

Net asset restriction on public companies distributions

5 The specified provisions for the purposes of section 831(3)(a) of the 2006 Act (Companies Act accounts: net asset restriction on public company distributions) are–

(a) provisions within paragraph 2 of this Schedule, and
(b) in the case of an insurance company, any amount included under liabilities items Ba (fund for future appropriations), C (technical provisions) and D (technical provisions for linked liabilities) in a balance sheet drawn up in accordance with Schedule 3 to these Regulations.

Distributions by investment companies

6 The specified provisions for the purposes of section 832(4)(a) of the 2006 Act (Companies Act accounts: investment companies distributions) are provisions within paragraph 2 of this Schedule.

Justification of distribution by references to accounts

7 The specified provisions for the purposes of section 836(1)(b)(i) of the 2006 Act (Companies Act accounts: relevant provisions for distribution purposes)–

(a) are provisions of any of the kinds mentioned in paragraphs 1 and 2 of this Schedule, and
(b) in the case of an insurance company, any amount included under liabilities items Ba (fund for future appropriations), C (technical provisions) and D (technical provisions for linked liabilities) in a balance sheet drawn up in accordance with Schedule 3 to these Regulations.

Realised losses

8 The specified provisions for the purposes of section 841(2)(a) of the 2006 Act (Companies Act accounts: treatment of provisions as realised losses) are provisions of any of the kinds mentioned in paragraphs 1 and 2 of this Schedule.

History – Para. 8 inserted by SI 2009/1581, reg 12(1) and (4): 27 June 2009 applying in relation to financial years beginning on or after 6 April 2008 which have not ended before 27 June 2009.

SCHEDULE 10

Regulation 13

GENERAL INTERPRETATION

Capitalisation

1 "Capitalisation", in relation to work or costs, means treating that work or those costs as a fixed asset.

Financial instruments

2 Save in Schedule 2 to these Regulations, references to **"derivatives"** include commodity-based contracts that give either contracting party the right to settle in cash or in some other financial instrument, except where such contracts–
- (a) were entered into for the purpose of, and continue to meet, the company's expected purchase, sale or usage requirements,
- (b) were designated for such purpose at their inception, and
- (c) are expected to be settled by delivery of the commodity (for banking companies, see the definition in paragraph 94 of Schedule 2 to these Regulations).

3(1) Save in Schedule 2 to these Regulations, the expressions listed in sub-paragraph (2) have the same meaning as they have in Directive 2013/34/EC of the European Parliament and of the Council of 26 June 2013 on the annual financial statements etc of certain types of undertakings and Council Directive 91/674/EEC of 19 December 1991 on the annual accounts and consolidated accounts of insurance undertakings (for banking companies, see the definition in paragraph 96 of Schedule 2 to these Regulations).

3(2) Those expressions are "available for sale financial asset", "business combination", "commodity-based contracts", "derivative", "equity instrument", "exchange difference", "fair value hedge accounting system", "financial fixed asset", "financial instrument", "foreign entity", "hedge accounting", "hedge accounting system", "hedged items", "hedging instrument", "held for trading purposes", "held to maturity", "monetary item", "receivables", "reliable market" and "trading portfolio".

History – Para. 3(1) substituted by SI 2015/980, reg. 41, with effect in relation to–
- (a) financial years beginning on or after 1 January 2016, and
- (b) a financial year of a company beginning on or after 1 January 2015, but before 1 January 2016, if the directors of the company so decide.

Former para. 3(1) read as follows:

"**3(1)** Save in Schedule 2 to these Regulations, the expressions listed in sub-paragraph (2) have the same meaning as they have in Council Directive 78/660/EEC on the annual accounts of certain types of companies(a) and 91/674/EEC on the annual accounts and consolidated accounts of insurance undertakings(b) (for banking companies, see the definition in paragraph 96 of Schedule 2 to these Regulations)."

Fixed and current assets

4 "Fixed assets" means assets of a company which are intended for use on a continuing basis in the company's activities, and **"current assets"** means assets not intended for such use.

Fungible assets

5 "Fungible assets" means assets of any description which are substantially indistinguishable one from another.

Historical cost accounting rules

6 References to the historical cost accounting rules are to be read in accordance with paragraph 30 of Schedule 1, paragraph 38 of Schedule 2 and paragraph 36(1) of Schedule 3 to these Regulations.

Leases

7(1) "Long lease" means a lease in the case of which the portion of the term for which it was granted remaining unexpired at the end of the financial year is not less than 50 years.

7(2) "Short lease" means a lease which is not a long lease.

7(3) "Lease" includes an agreement for a lease.

Listed investments

8(1) "Listed investment" means an investment as respects which there has been granted a listing on–

(a) a recognised investment exchange other than an overseas investment exchange, or
(b) a stock exchange of repute outside the United Kingdom.

8(2) "Recognised investment exchange" and **"overseas investment exchange"** have the meaning given in Part 18 of the Financial Services and Markets Act 2000.

Loans

9 A loan or advance (including a liability comprising a loan or advance) is treated as falling due for repayment, and an instalment of a loan or advance is treated as falling due for payment, on the earliest date on which the lender could require repayment or (as the case may be) payment, if he exercised all options and rights available to him.

Materiality

10 Amounts which in the particular context of any provision of Schedules 1, 2 or 3 to these Regulations are not material may be disregarded for the purposes of that provision.

Participating interests

11(1) A **"participating interest"** means an interest held by an undertaking in the shares of another undertaking which it holds on a long-term basis for the purpose of securing a contribution to its activities by the exercise of control or influence arising from or related to that interest.

11(2) A holding of 20% or more of the shares of the undertaking is to be presumed to be a participating interest unless the contrary is shown.

11(3) The reference in sub-paragraph (1) to an interest in shares includes–

(a) an interest which is convertible into an interest in shares, and
(b) an option to acquire shares or any such interest, and an interest or option falls within paragraph (a) or (b) notwithstanding that the shares to which it relates are, until the conversion or the exercise of the option, unissued.

11(4) For the purposes of this regulation an interest held on behalf of an undertaking is to be treated as held by it.

11(5) In the balance sheet and profit and loss formats set out in Schedules 1, 2 and 3 to these Regulations, "participating interest" does not include an interest in a group undertaking.

11(6) For the purpose of this regulation as it applies in relation to the expression "participating interest"–

   (a) in those formats as they apply in relation to group accounts, and

   (b) in paragraph 19 of Schedule 6 (group accounts: undertakings to be accounted for as associated undertakings),

the references in sub-paragraphs (1) to (4) to the interest held by, and the purposes and activities of, the undertaking concerned are to be construed as references to the interest held by, and the purposes and activities of, the group (within the meaning of paragraph 1 of that Schedule).

Purchase price

12 **"Purchase price"**, in relation to an asset of a company or any raw materials or consumables used in the production of such an asset, includes any consideration (whether in cash or otherwise) given by the company in respect of that asset or those materials or consumables, as the case may be.

Realised profits and realised losses

13 **"Realised profits"** and **"realised losses"** have the same meaning as in section 853(4) and (5) of the 2006 Act.

Staff costs

14(1) **"Social security costs"** means any contributions by the company to any state social security or pension scheme, fund or arrangement.

14(2) **"Pension costs"** includes–

   (a) any costs incurred by the company in respect of any pension scheme established for the purpose of providing pensions for persons currently or formerly employed by the company,

   (b) any sums set aside for the future payment of pensions directly by the company to current or former employees, and

   (c) any pensions paid directly to such persons without having first been set aside.

14(3) Any amount stated in respect of the item **"social security costs"** or in respect of the item **"wages and salaries"** in the company's profit and loss account must be determined by reference to payments made or costs incurred in respect of all persons employed by the company during the financial year under contracts of service.

Scots land tenure

15 In the application of these Regulations to Scotland, **"land of freehold tenure"** means land in respect of which the company is the owner; **"land of leasehold tenure"** means land of which the company is the tenant under a lease.

Index

Accounting adjustments
FRS 101 accounts, 4.2
Accounting for transactions and
year end balances using IFRS, 7.1
EU endorsement process, 7.1.2
IFRIC Interpretations, 7.1.2
overview, 7.1.1
standards that are EU endorsed
but not yet effective, 7.1.2
Accounting policies
borrowing costs, Appendix 1
construction contracts, Appendix 1
foreign currencies, Appendix 1
government grants, Appendix 1
property, plant and equipment, Appendix 1
retirement benefit costs, Appendix 1
revenue recognition, Appendix 1
Accounting principles, Appendix 2
Accounting standards – see
Financial reporting framework in UK
Accounts formats
FRS 101 accounts, 4.3
Accumulated profits, Appendix 1
Annual report on remuneration
single total figure of remuneration
for each director, Appendix 2
Annual statement, Appendix 2
Application guidance to FRS 100
equivalent disclosures in financial
statements of the group, 3.3
parent's accounts using an
equivalent GAAP, 3.3
Auditor's report, 13.3
requirements of auditing standards, 13.3.2
requirements of the law
audited accounts, 13.3.1
contents of an audit report, 13.3.1
Available-for-sale financial assets, Appendix 1
Bank overdrafts and loans, Appendix 1
Banking groups
foreign currency translation, Appendix 2
information as to undertaking in which
shares held as a result of financial
assistance operation, Appendix 2
non-controlling interests and associated
undertakings, Appendix 2
related party transactions, Appendix 2
Borrowing costs, 10.3, Appendix 1
accounting amendments arising
from law, 10.3.4
exemptions given by FRS 101, 10.3.3
overview of accounting differences
between IFRS-based FRS 101
and old UK GAAP, 10.3.2
relevant standards under IFRS, 10.3.1
resulting disclosure requirements, 10.3.4

Capital commitments, Appendix 1
Capital reserves, Appendix 1
Capitalisation, Appendix 2
Cash and cash equivalents, Appendix 1
Companies Act group accounts
acquisition and merger accounting, Appendix 2
associated undertakings, Appendix 2
deferred tax balances, Appendix 2
elimination of group transactions, Appendix 2
general rules, Appendix 2
joint ventures, Appendix 2
minority interests, Appendix 2
non-controlling interests, Appendix 2
related party transactions, Appendix 2
total amount of directors'
remuneration, Appendix 2
Companies Act individual accounts
requirements in UK law, 4.1
Companies not required to prepare
group accounts
construction of references to shares
held by company, Appendix 2
exemption from giving information on
significant holdings in non-subsidiary
undertakings, Appendix 2
financial years of subsidiary
undertakings, Appendix 2
holdings in subsidiary undertakings, Appendix 2
Companies required to prepare
group accounts
associated undertakings, Appendix 2
construction of references to shares
held by parent company or group, Appendix 2
group's membership of certain
undertakings, Appendix 2
holdings in subsidiary undertakings, Appendix 2
joint ventures, Appendix 2
requirement to give information on other
significant holdings of parent
company or group, Appendix 2
subsidiary undertakings, Appendix 2
Company accounts
accounting adjustments – see
Accounting adjustments
legal status of FRS 101 accounts
Companies Act accounts, 4.1
IAS accounts, 4.1
requirements in UK law, 4.1
Construction contracts, Appendix 1
Contingent liabilities, Appendix 1
Convertible loan notes, Appendix 1
Critical accounting estimates and
judgments, Appendix 1
Current value accounting rules
alternative valuation of fixed-income
securities, Appendix 2

application of the depreciation rules, Appendix 2
revaluation reserve, Appendix 2
valuation of assets, Appendix 2
Definitions and meanings
amount, Appendix 2
company contributions, Appendix 2
current value, Appendix 2
defined benefit scheme, Appendix 2
emoluments, Appendix 2
highest paid director, Appendix 2
long term investment scheme, Appendix 2
money purchase benefits, Appendix 2
money purchase scheme, Appendix 2
pension scheme, Appendix 2
provisions, Appendix 2
qualifying services, Appendix 2
remuneration committee, Appendix 2
remuneration, Appendix 2
retirement benefits, Appendix 2
scheme interest, Appendix 2
scheme, Appendix 2
securities, Appendix 2
share option, Appendix 2
shares, Appendix 2
takeover bid, Appendix 2
taxable benefits, Appendix 2
value, Appendix 2
voting rights, Appendix 2
Derivative financial instruments, Appendix 1
Directors' remuneration policy
approach to recruitment
remuneration, Appendix 2
future policy table, Appendix 2
illustrations of application of
remuneration policy, Appendix 2
policy on payment for loss of office, Appendix 2
service contracts, Appendix 2
statement of consideration of employment
conditions elsewhere in
company, Appendix 2
statement of consideration of
shareholder views, Appendix 2
Directors' remuneration report, Appendix 2
Directors' report, Appendix 2
asset values, Appendix 2
basic information requirements, 13.2
charitable donations, Appendix 2
financial instruments, Appendix 2
political donations and expenditure, Appendix 2
statement about disclosure of information to
auditors, 13.2
statement of directors' responsibilities, 13.2
Disclosure exemptions, Appendix 1
Disclosure on employment etc.
of disabled persons, Appendix 2
Disclosure required by company acquiring
its own shares, Appendix 2
Disclosure required by publicly-traded
companies, Appendix 2
Disclosures
overlaying FRS 101 exemptions, 7.2
Disclosures for banking companies
and groups, Appendix 2

Disclosures on Greenhouse gas
emissions, Appendix 2
Discontinued operations
generally, 9.2
Discontinued operations, Appendix 1
Disposal groups
generally 9.2, Appendix 1
Distribution by investment
companies, Appendix 2
Dividends, Appendix 1
Employee benefits, 11.4, Appendix 1
accounting amendments arising
from law, 11.4.4
exemptions given by FRS 101, 11.4.3
overview of accounting differences
between IFRS-based FRS 101
and old UK GAAP, 11.4.2
relevant standards under IFRS, 11.4.1
resulting disclosures
defined benefit plans, 11.4.5
defined contribution plan, 11.4.5
share-based payments, 11.4.5
summary of disclosure requirements, 11.4.1
Employee involvement, Appendix 2
Equity instruments, Appendix 1
Fair value accounting
accounting for changes in value, Appendix 2
determination of fair value, Appendix 2
fair value reserve, Appendix 2
hedged items, Appendix 2
inclusion of financial instruments at
fair value, Appendix 2
other assets that may be included at
fair value, Appendix 2
Finance costs, Appendix 1
Finance income, Appendix 1
Financial assets at fair value through
profit or loss, Appendix 1
Financial assistance for purchase
of own shares, Appendix 2
Financial institution
definition, 8.1
special provisions
disclosure exemptions exceptions, 8.2
Financial instruments, 10.6, Appendix 1,
Appendix 2
disclosures, 4.4, 6.4
accounting amendments arising
from law, 10.6.4
exemptions given by FRS 101, 10.6.3
overview of accounting differences
between IFRS-based FRS 101
and old UK GAAP, 10.6.2
relevant standards under IFRS, 10.6.1
resulting disclosure requirements, 10.6.5
Financial reporting framework in UK
accounting standards
application of financial reporting
requirements (FRS 100), 2.2
financial reporting standard applicable in the
UK and Republic of Ireland (FRS 102), 2.2
financial reporting standard applicable
to micro-entities regime (FRS 105), 2.2
insurance contracts (FRS 103), 2.2
interim financial reporting (FRS 104), 2.2

reduced disclosure framework (FRS 101), 2.2
entity types and standards used, 2.3
generally, 2.1
Financial statements
basis of preparation, Appendix 1
standards and interpretations – see
Standards and interpretations
Fixed and current assets, Appendix 2
Foreign currency issues, 11.3, Appendix 1
accounting amendments arising from law, 11.3.4
exemptions given by FRS 101, 11.3.3
overview of accounting differences
between IFRS-based FRS 101
and old UK GAAP, 11.3.2
relevant standards under IFRS, 11.3.1
resulting disclosures
foreign exchange, 11.3.5
hyperinflation, 11.3.5
summary of disclosure requirements, 11.3.1
FRS 101
concept of equivalence
application guidance to FRS 100, 3.3
background, 3.3
equivalence in FRS 101, 3.3
equivalence in FRS 102, 3.3
eligibility for FRS 101
scope, 3.1
limited, Appendix 1
note on disclosures, 3.4
reasons to choose FRS 101
subsidiaries of listed parents, 3.5
shareholder approval, 3.2
Fungible assets, Appendix 2
Goodwill, Appendix 1
Government grants, Appendix 1
Groups and business combinations, 10.1
accounting amendments arising from law, 10.1.4
exemptions given by FRS 101, 10.1.3
overview of accounting differences
between IFRS-based FRS 101
and old UK GAAP, 10.1.2
relevant standards under IFRS, 10.1.1
resulting disclosures
business combinations, 10.1.5
interests in other entities (IFRS 12,
with the only relevant parts for
investment entities), 10.1.5
separate financial statements, 10.1.5
Hedging reserve, Appendix 1
Held-to-maturity financial assets, Appendix 1
Historical cost accounting rules
assets included at a fixed amount, Appendix 2
determination of cost, Appendix 2
development costs, Appendix 2
excess of money owed over value received
as an asset item, Appendix 2
goodwill, Appendix 2
substitution of original amount where price or
cost unknown, Appendix 2
valuation of assets, Appendix 2
Historical cost accounting rules, Appendix 2
Impairment, 10.2, Appendix 1
Income tax expense, Appendix 1
Income taxes, 11.2

accounting amendments arising from law, 11.2.4
exemptions given by FRS 101, 11.2.3
overview of accounting differences
between IFRS-based FRS 101
and old UK GAAP, 11.2.2
relevant standards under IFRS, 11.2.1
resulting disclosures, 11.2.5
summary of disclosure requirements, 11.2.1
Information about benefits of directors
provisions applying only to unquoted
companies
compensation to directors for loss
of office, Appendix 2
excess retirement benefits of directors
and past directors, Appendix 2
highest paid director's emoluments, Appendix 2
sums paid to third parties in respect of
directors' services, Appendix 2
provisions applying to quoted and
unquoted companies
total amount of directors' remuneration,
Appendix 2
Information not subject to audit
consideration by the directors of matters relating
to directors' remuneration, Appendix 2
performance graph, Appendix 2
service contracts, Appendix 2
statement of company's policy on directors'
remuneration, Appendix 2
statement of consideration of conditions
elsewhere in company and
group, Appendix 2
**Information on related undertakings
required in preparing Companies
Act or IAS accounts**
financial information on subsidiary
undertakings, Appendix 2
identification of ultimate parent
company, Appendix 2
membership of certain undertakings, Appendix 2
parent undertaking drawing up accounts for
larger group, Appendix 2
shares and debentures of company held by
subsidiary undertakings, Appendix 2
significant holdings in undertakings other than
subsidiary undertakings, Appendix 2
subsidiary undertakings, Appendix 2
Information subject to audit
amount of each director's emoluments
and compensation in the relevant
financial year, Appendix 2
compensation of past directors, Appendix 2
excess retirement benefits of directors
and past directors, Appendix 2
long term incentive schemes, Appendix 2
pensions, Appendix 2
share options, Appendix 2
sums paid to third parties in respect of a
director's services, Appendix 2
**Information supplementing profit
and loss account**
appropriations, Appendix 2
commissions, Appendix 2
particulars of business, Appendix 2

particulars of tax, Appendix 2
post balance sheet events, Appendix 2
separate statement of certain items
of income and expenditure, Appendix 2
**Insurance companies: Companies Act
individual accounts**
general rules and formats, Appendix 2
Intangible assets – see Tangible assets
**Interpretation of references
to beneficial interest**
employer's charges and other rights
of recovery, Appendix 2
residual interests under pension and employees'
share schemes, Appendix 2
trustee's right to expenses, remuneration,
indemnity etc. Appendix 2
Inventories, 10.5, Appendix 1
accounting amendments arising from law, 10.5.4
exemptions given by FRS 101, 10.5.3
overview of accounting differences
between IFRS-based FRS 101
and old UK GAAP, 10.5.2
relevant standards under IFRS, 10.5.1
resulting disclosure requirements, 10.5.5
Investment entity
definition, 8.3
special provisions, 8.4
Investment property, 10.4, Appendix 1
accounting amendments arising from law, 10.4.4
exemptions given by FRS 101, 10.4.3
overview of accounting differences
between IFRS-based FRS 101
and old UK GAAP, 10.4.2
relevant standards under IFRS 10.4.1
resulting disclosure requirements
cost model, 10.4.5
fair value model, 10.4.5
**Justification of distribution by references to
accounts, Appendix 2**
Keeping up with change 7.3
**Large and Medium-sized Companies and
Groups (Accounts and Reports)
Regulations 2008**
citation and interpretation
commencement and application, Appendix 2
form and content of accounts
banking companies, Appendix 2
Companies Act group accounts, Appendix 2
Companies Act individual accounts (companies
other than banking and insurance
companies), Appendix 2
information about related undertakings,
Appendix 2
insurance companies, Appendix 2
medium-sized companies: exemptions
for Companies Act individual accounts,
Appendix 2
Leases, Appendix 2
Leasing, 10.7, Appendix 1
accounting amendments arising from law, 10.7.4
exemptions given by FRS 101, 10.7.3
overview of accounting differences
between IFRS-based FRS 101
and old UK GAAP, 10.7.2

relevant standards under IFRS, 10.7.1
resulting disclosure requirements
lessees – finance leases, 10.7.5
lessees – operating leases, 10.7.5
lessors – finance leases, 10.7.5
lessors – operating leases, 10.7.5
Limited Liability Partnerships
eligibility to apply FRS 101
accounting requirements, 5.1
LLP Regulations, 5.1
statutory instruments, 5.1
note on challenging areas
group reconstructions, 5.3
members' capital and loans, 5.3
members' remuneration, 5.3
merger accounting, 5.3
pension promises, 5.3
specifics within the standard
accounts formats, 5.2
disclosures, 5.2
FRS 101 requirement, 5.2
Listed investments, Appendix 2
Loans and receivables, Appendix 1, Appendix 2
Materiality, Appendix 2
**Net asset restriction on public companies
distributions, Appendix 2**
Non-derivative financial assets, Appendix 1
Non-derivative financial liabilities, Appendix 1
Notes to the accounts
assets, Appendix 2
debt and other fixed-income
securities, Appendix 2
details of assets charged, Appendix 2
details of indebtedness, Appendix 2
disclosure of accounting policies, Appendix 2
fixed cumulative dividends, Appendix 2
guarantees and other financial commitments,
Appendix 2
important: group undertakings, Appendix 2
information on fair value of assets and liabilities,
Appendix 2
information where investment property
and living animals and plants included
at fair value, Appendix 2
investments, Appendix 2
leasing transactions, Appendix 2
maturity analysis, Appendix 2
memorandum items: group undertakings,
Appendix 2
provision for taxation, Appendix 2
reserves and dividends, Appendix 2
reserves and provisions, Appendix 2
share capital and debentures, Appendix 2
subordinated liabilities, Appendix 2
sums denominated in foreign currencies,
Appendix 2
sundry assets and liabilities, Appendix 2
transferable securities, Appendix 2
unmatured forward transactions, Appendix 2
Obligations under finance leases, Appendix 1
Operating lease commitments, Appendix 1
Other disclosures, 12.3
accounting amendments arising from law, 12.3.4
exemptions given by FRS 101, 12.3.3

overview of accounting differences
between IFRS-based FRS 101
and old UK GAAP, 12.3.2
relevant standards under IFRS, 12.3.1
resulting disclosures
additional disclosures for biological
assets where fair value cannot
be measured reliably, 12.3.5
agriculture, 12.3.5
exploration for and evaluation of mineral
resources, 12.3.5
government grants, 12.3.5
insurance contracts, explanation
of recognised amounts, 12.3.5
nature and extent of risks arising from
insurance contracts, 12.3.5
summary of disclosure requirements, 12.3.1
Other financial liabilities, Appendix 1
Participating interests, Appendix 2
Patents and trademarks, Appendix 1
**Policy and practice on payment
of creditors, Appendix 2**
Post balance sheet events, 12.1
accounting amendments arising from law, 12.1.4
exemptions given by FRS 101, 12.1.3
overview of accounting differences
between IFRS-based FRS 101
and old UK GAAP, 12.1.2
relevant standards under IFRS, 12.1.1
resulting disclosures
date of authorisation for issue, 12.1.5
non-adjusting events after the
reporting period, 12.1.5
updating disclosure about conditions
at the end of the reporting period, 12.1.5
Primary statements
IAS 1 formats – minimum line items
allocation of profit or loss and other
comprehensive income
(IAS 1 para. 81B), 9.1
other comprehensive income items
(IAS 1 para. 81A and 82), 9.1
profit or loss items (IAS 1 para. 82), 9.1
statement of changes in equity
(IAS 1 para. 106, 106A, 107), 9.1
statement of financial position items
(IAS 1 para. 54), 9.1
IFRS financial statements components, 9.1
Property, plant and equipment, Appendix 1
Provisions and contingencies, Appendix 1
accounting amendments arising from law, 10.8.4
exemptions given by FRS 101, 10.8.3
overview of accounting differences
between IFRS-based FRS 101
and old UK GAAP, 10.8.2
relevant standards under IFRS, 10.8.1
resulting disclosure requirements, 10.8.5
Purchase price, Appendix 2
Quoted companies, Appendix 2
Realised losses, Appendix 2
Realised profits, 4.5, Appendix 2
**Redemption or purchase by private company
out of capital, Appendix 2**
**Reduced Disclosure Framework – Disclosure
exemptions from EU-adopted IFRS for
qualifying entities (FRS 101), Appendix 1**

Related parties, 12.2
accounting amendments arising
from law, 12.2.4
exemptions given by FRS 101, 12.2.3
overview of accounting differences
between IFRS-based FRS 101
and old UK GAAP, 12.2.2
relevant standards under IFRS, 12.2.1
resulting disclosures
all entities, 12.2.5
government-related entities, 12.2.5
summary of disclosure requirements, 12.2.1
Related party transactions
trading transactions, Appendix 1
Republic of Ireland, FRS 101 law
financial instruments, 6.4
Irish legislation
Companies Act 2006, 6.2
Large and Medium-sized Companies
and Groups (Accounts and Reports)
Regulations 2008, 6.2
small companies, 6.3
Required formats, Appendix 2
**Research and development expenditure,
Appendix 1**
Results from operating activity, Appendix 1
Retirement benefit costs, Appendix 1
Revaluation reserves, Appendix 1, Appendix 2
Revenue including grant income, 11.1
accounting amendments arising from law, 11.1.4
exemptions given by FRS 101, 11.1.3
overview of accounting differences
between IFRS-based FRS 101
and old UK GAAP
construction contracts, 11.1.2
government grants, 11.1.2
revenue, 11.1.2
service concession arrangements, 11.1.2
relevant standards under IFRS, 11.1.1
resulting disclosures
construction contracts, 11.1.5
government grants, 11.1.5
revenue, 11.1.5
service concession arrangements, 11.1.5
summary of disclosure requirements, 11.1.1
**Revised directors' remuneration policy,
Appendix 2**
Rules for determining provisions
long-term business provision, Appendix 2
provision for unearned premiums, Appendix 2
provision for unexpired risks, Appendix 2
provisions for claims outstanding
accounting on a non-annual basis, Appendix 2
equalisation reserves, Appendix 2
general business, Appendix 2
technical provisions, Appendix 2
Scots land tenure, Appendix 2
Share capital, Appendix 1
Share-based payments – see Employee benefits
Staff costs, Appendix 2
Standards and interpretations
basis of measurement, Appendix 1
first-time adoption of FRS 101, Appendix 1
going concern, Appendix 1

summary of significant accounting
policies, Appendix 1
Strategic report
generally, 13.1
Subsequent events, Appendix 1
Tangible assets, 10.2
accounting amendments arising from law, 10.2.4
exemptions given by FRS 101, 10.2.3
overview of accounting differences
between IFRS-based FRS 101
and old UK GAAP, 10.2.2
relevant standards under IFRS, 10.2.1
resulting disclosure requirements
estimates used to measure recoverable
amounts of cash-generating units
containing goodwill or intangible
assets with indefinite useful lives, 10.2.5
impairment, 10.2.5
intangible assets, 10.2.5
intangible assets measured after recognition
using the revaluation model, 10.2.5
other information, 10.2.5
property, plant and equipment, 10.2.5

research and development expenditure, 10.2.5
Taxation
deferred tax, Appendix 1
Transition to FRS 101
designation of financial assets or financial
liabilities, 9.3
IFRS 1 requirement, 7.4, 9.3
reconciliations, 9.3
use of deemed cost
after severe hyperinflation, 9.3
fair value, 9.3
investments in subsidiaries, jointly controlled
entities and associates, 9.3
oil and gas assets, 9.3
Valuation at fair value
accounting for changes in value, Appendix 2
determination of fair value, Appendix 2
fair value reserve, Appendix 2
hedged items, Appendix 2
inclusion of financial instruments
at fair value, Appendix 2
other assets that may be included
at fair value, Appendix 2